MW00778436

Cultural Memory and Western Civilization
Functions, Media, Archives

Cultures invest great efforts into creating a long-term memory on the basis of oral transmission, media technology, and institutional frameworks. This book provides an introduction to the concept of cultural memory, focusing on the "arts" of its construction, particularly various media such as writing, images, bodily practices, places, and monuments. Examining the period from the European Renaissance to the present, Aleida Assmann reveals the close association between cultural memory and the arts, arguing that the artists who have supplemented, criticized, transformed, and opposed it are its most lucid theorists and acute observers. Her analysis also addresses the interaction of cultural memory with individual memory and the ways in which cultural memory supports or subverts social and political identity constructions. Ultimately, this book offers a comprehensive overview of the history, forms, and functions of cultural memory, which has become a central analytical tool for scholars across disciplines.

Aleida Assmann is a professor of English literature and literary theory in the department of literature, art, and media at the University of Konstanz in Germany. She has also been a guest lecturer at universities, including Rice, Princeton, Yale, and the University of Chicago. She is the author of several German-language books and has received international recognition for her scholarship, including the Max Planck Research Prize for History and Memory in 2009 and an Honorary Doctorate from the Theological Faculty at the University of Oslo in 2008.

Cultural Memory and Western Civilization

Functions, Media, Archives

ALEIDA ASSMANN

University of Konstanz, Germany

CAMBRIDGE
UNIVERSITY PRESS

CAMBRIDGE
UNIVERSITY PRESS

32 Avenue of the Americas, New York NY 10013-2473, USA

Cambridge University Press is part of the University of Cambridge.

It furthers the University's mission by disseminating knowledge in the pursuit of education, learning, and research at the highest international levels of excellence.

www.cambridge.org
Information on this title: www.cambridge.org/9780521165877

First published in Germany for Verlag as Erinnerungsräume: Formen und Wandlungen des kulturellen Gedächtnisses
First English edition 2011
Reprinted 2013

A catalog record for this publication is available from the British Library.

Library of Congress Cataloging in Publication data
Assmann, Aleida.
  [Erinnerungsräume. English]
  Cultural memory and Western civilization : Functions, media, archives / Aleida Assmann. – 1st English ed.
    p. cm.
Includes bibliographical references and index.
ISBN 978-0-521-76437-7 (hardback) – ISBN 978-0-521-16587-7 (paperback)
1. European literature – History and criticism.   2. Memory in literature.
3. Memory (Philosophy)   4. Technology and civilization.   I. Title.
PN704.A8713   2011
901 – dc23   2011029541

ISBN 978-0-521-76437-7 Hardback
ISBN 978-0-521-16587-7 Paperback

Cover image: David de Heem, Vanitas. With kind permission of Graf von Schönborn Kunstsammlungen, Pommersfelden.

Contents

List of Illustrations

Preface

To republish a book after twelve years is a great challenge, especially when it is a contribution to a field that has grown rapidly and changed beyond recognition. How individual and collective memory interact, how the past is tied to the present and the future, how it is continuously reconstructed, how it is reduced to what we want to live with, and how it continues to rupture and unsettle our identities – these and other mysteries have stimulated the interest and energy of researchers all over the world and the results now fill whole libraries. The quality of this worldwide cumulative and ongoing interest in the topic of memory goes far beyond the allegiance to a specific academic discourse or theoretical paradigm. It is, rather, an answer to global changes and challenges in our cultural moorings and a way to cope with two phenomena that became ever more pressing after 1989: a growing interest in questions of (collective) identity and transmission on the one hand and the new experience of traumatic or "hot" pasts that will not fade away on the other.

The book starts from the Roman "art of memory" that was designed to enhance the memory of the individual and moves to the arts of memory in general, that, in their plurality and interaction, are responsible for constructing, transforming, observing, and critiquing the cultural memory of a society. The following chapters document how deeply literature and the arts are rooted in and engaged with issues of personal, political, and cultural memory. The basic thesis is that to a large extent, the artists shape our memory because it is they who give to the transitory and ephemeral "a local habitation and a name" (Wordsworth), thus creating what "the world will not willingly let die" (Milton). The arts, however, are not only engaged in immortalizing persons, events, experiences, and values through their compelling narratives and images. The arts also provide a continuous discourse on the potentials and problems of cultural memory. This book argues that in literary texts and artistic works we can discover the most lucid theory and criticism of memory, long before modern theorists such as Freud, Warburg, and Benjamin entered the scene.

Over the last decade, my own engagement with the topic has moved in other directions as well. In two books and various essays that have appeared since this book's German publication, I have explored the social and political dimensions of cultural memory, focusing on constructions of collective identity from social generations to whole nations within their respective historical contexts. Another book is in preparation that will more generally deal with the institutions of cultural memory. In the process of revising and translating the present book, I have refrained from making substantial changes in order to preserve a text that has attained its own historical place in the evolution of the memory discourse. Working together on the manuscript with David Henry Wilson was a continuous joy and challenge; he helped me to translate my often somewhat austere prose fraught with terminology into fluent, accessible, conversational English. Andreas Kraft assisted me in the irksome bibliographical task of finding English translations for many of the quotes and references used. The whole project was made possible through the generous funding of the humanities' "cluster of excellence" of the University of Konstanz. However, long before these pragmatic problems were tackled and overcome, it was Werner Kelber from Rice University, Texas, who pushed the project of an English translation. He pursued this project over the years with an unfaltering energy, promoting it with the weight of his professional authority and personal commitment. I am also deeply grateful to Beatrice Rehl of Cambridge University Press, Brigitte Coulton of Aptara, and Valerie Neumann who have so competently assisted me in taking the book over its last hurdles on its long way to an English-speaking readership.

Konstanz, August 2011, Aleida Assmann

Introduction

"People talk so much about memory only because there's none left."[1]
Pierre Nora's much quoted remark from his *Realms of Memory* confirms
the well-known paradox that you need to lose something before you
can become fully conscious of it. Consciousness generally develops in
terms of what has passed, and this process fits in logically with the
retrospective nature of memory, since the latter only begins when the
experience to which it refers has run its complete course. Let us first
look at the second part of Nora's dictum – the claim that there is no
memory left. Is it true, and if it is, what sort of memory is not left?

Anyone who, for instance, equates real knowledge with learning by
rote will have to accept that nowadays the latter is of little relevance.
Learning a dozen verses or the five-times multiplication table by heart
no longer figures in the way children are taught. It is true, of course,
that the World Memory Championships still take place every year, with
virtuosos competing for their place in the *Guinness Book of Records*,[2]
but there can be no denying that the "golden age" of this particular

[1] Pierre Nora, *Realms of Memory: Rethinking the French Past.* Volume 1: Conflicts and Divisions, trans. Arthur Goldhammer, Columbia University Press: New York, Chichester, West Surrey 1996, 1.
[2] Ulrich Ernst has meticulously compiled a list of memory virtuosos from Antiquity through to the present, in fiction and in real life. "Die Bibliothek im Kopf: Gedächtniskünstler in der europäischen und amerikanischen Literatur," *Zeitschrift für Literaturwissenschaft und Linguistik 105* (1997), 86–123.

art has long since faded. In the days of Antiquity, the phenomenon of outstanding mnemonic capacity was attributed to generals, statesmen, and kings, whereas now it is associated with the entertainment industry or even the sphere of the pathological: the gap between the memory artist and the memory freak seems to have become very small.

After all, why should one learn things by heart when they are so easy to pick up from a book or a computer? Indeed, the decline of rote learning may be said to have coincided with the astonishingly swift advance of electronic data storage, although even before the computer relieved memory of its active function, the value of rote learning had already come into question. In early Greece, Plato had argued that it did not represent true knowledge. In his dialogue *Phaidros*, he not only criticized writing, but he also mocked the new technique of the Sophists, which was meant to help memorize the written word verbatim.

The history of the art of memory was, from the very beginning, accompanied in Western culture by radical criticism because deep-seated memories rarely conformed to accepted standards of reason and empiricism. "I'll knock those fairy tales out of your head," cries a character in a satire by Persius;[3] and in the middle of the 17th century the doctor and theologian Sir Thomas Browne dissolved the alliance between tradition, knowledge, and memory when he wrote: "Knowledge is made by oblivion, and to purchase a clear and warrantable body of Truth, we must forget and part with much we know."[4]

The Renaissance brought a revival of the art of memory, but again this was accompanied by criticism. Harald Weinrich has drawn attention to this tradition, which among others includes Montaigne and Cervantes. Cervantes' *Don Quixote* can even be read as a manifesto for "the basic dissociation of mind and memory," and Montaigne's essays amount to a fundamental "rejection of the pedagogics of high-performance memory."[5] With the rise of modernity, authors have

---

[3] "...ueteres auias tibi de pulmone reuello." A. Persi Flacci and D. Ivni Ivvenalis, *Satirae*. Eddidit Breviqve Adnotatione Critica Denvo Instrvxit W.V. Clausen, Oxford University Press 1992 Satvra V, 92/21.

[4] Sir Thomas Browne, *Selected Writings*, ed. Sir G. Keynes, London 1968, 227.

[5] a) Translated from Harald Weinrich, "Gedächtniskultur – Kulturgedächtnis," in Merkur, 45, Heft 508 (1991), 569–582. See also Harald Weinrich, *Lethe: The Art and*

constantly devalued all forms of memory in the name of reason, nature, life, originality, individuality, innovation, progress, and whatever other gods they may worship. Weinrich puts it this way:

In any case, it is clear that the "hostility" first noted by Huarte between reason and memory, and evident throughout Europe ever since the Enlightenment, led to a general war against memory, with enlightened reason finally emerging as the victor. Since then, without being ashamed, we freely admit to having a poor memory, whereas one seldom hears anyone complaining that they have poor reason.[6]

By "memory," Nora probably does not mean the learning capacity of mnemotechnics so much as the general cultural tradition of educational memory, which binds the individual to a particular region or nation.[7] The feature sections of our newspapers often complain about the disappearance of cultural memory. Joachim Fest, for example, argued that "enthusiasm for destruction" is not a new phenomenon. In 19th- and 20th-century Germany, "again and again, out of aversion or confusion," political and cultural coherence has been ripped apart, and finally, in addition to "many traditions, authorities and taboos," the student revolts of the later 1960s willfully destroyed traditions together with lines of descent.[8] The Germanist and Goethe specialist Albrecht Schöne believes that even now a creeping cultural revolution is taking place, another "epochal shift" in which there is a whole "spiritual and intellectual continent" being set adrift:

What is breaking away here from our cultural foundations, and is fading away from the collective basis and capacity for understanding that has encompassed the generations, is by no means confined to the great works of the Western canon. It applies just as much to the diaries of our grandfathers and to the letters of our grandmothers.[9]

Critique of Forgetting, trans. Steven Rendall. Ithaca, NY, London: Cornell University Press 2004.

[6] Translated from Harald Weinreich, "Gedächtniskultur – Kulturgedächtnis," in Merkur 508 (1991), 569–582.

[7] Both learning and educational memory have been combined by memory psychologists under the category of "semantic memory."

[8] Joachim Fest, "Das Zerreissen der Kette. Goethe und die Tradition," *FAZ*, June 21, 1997, No. 141. The phrase "enthusiasm for destruction" stems from Goethe.

[9] Albrecht Schöne's acceptance speech on being awarded the Reuchlin Prize on 17 January 1995 in Pforzheim, in *Die Zeit* August 18, 1995, No. 34, p. 36.

Communication between eras and generations is broken when a particular store of common knowledge disappears. Just as the great works, like Goethe's *Faust*, can only be read against the indispensable background of greater, older works like the Bible – which William Blake called "the great Code of Art"[10] – the records of our great-grandparents can only be read against the background of orally transmitted family histories. Schöne sees a parallel between the *cultural* memory that transcends eras and is supported by normative texts, and the *communicative* memory, which generally links three generations through memories passed on by word of mouth. On both levels, cultural and communicative, Schöne discerns a decline in memory.

Along similar lines, Nora describes the current memory crisis as the present being uncoupled from the past. He speaks of an "increasingly rapid slippage of the present into a historical past that is gone for good," a process in which experiences "still lived in the warmth of tradition, in the silence of custom, in the repetition of the ancestral" are being ripped out. He also identifies the destructive power that is at work here: the "conquest and eradication of memory by history." Whatever we now regard as memory is in "its final consumption in the flames of history."[11] With this diagnosis, Nora echoes Nietzsche's assessment of historical scholarship as a catastrophic force that erodes the sources of living memory and collective identity. His comments might also be related to the current crisis of testimony based on the *experiential memory* of a rapidly dwindling number of witnesses who survived the greatest of all 20th-century catastrophes, the Holocaust. On this subject, the historian Reinhart Koselleck writes:

With the shift of generations the object of historical research will undergo a decisive change. The embodied experience of the survivor's *present past* gives way to a *pure past* which is disconnected from sensuous experience. [. . .] With fading memory the temporal distance to the historical event not only becomes greater but also takes on a different quality. Soon the only remaining source of information will come from the written records, augmented by pictures, films, memoirs.[12]

[10] See Northrop Frye, *The Great Code. The Bible and Literature*, London 1982.

[11] Pierre Nora, "Between Memory and History: Les Lieux de Mémoire," *Representations* 26, Spring 1989, 7–24; here, 7 f and 13.

[12] Reinhart Koselleck, Epilogue to Charlotte Beradt, *Das Dritte Reich des Traums*, Frankfurt a.M. 1994, st 2321, 117–132; here 117.

Koselleck describes the change from the still present to the pure past as the irreversible replacement of living historical experience by scholarly historical research. What exactly does that mean?

> The criteria for research become more factual, but they are also perhaps less *colourful*, less experiential, even if they give promise of greater insight and greater objectivity. The moral involvement, the hidden protective mechanisms, the accusations and the attributions of guilt – all these techniques of mastering the past *lose* their political and existential relevance, they fade out and cede to detailed historical scholarship and to theoretically orientated analysis.[13]

Less colorful, loss, fading out – these are terms describing an unstoppable process of forgetting, which Koselleck sees as leading directly from the living, personal reality of memory to the scholarly abstraction of historical research. History according to this model must first "die" in the heads, hearts, and bodies of those who have lived through it before it can rise phoenix-like from the ashes of experience to take on new life as scholarship. So long as there are survivors, bringing with them their emotions, claims, and objections, academic perspective runs the risk of distortion. And, therefore, objectivity is not simply a matter of method and scholarly criteria but is also based on *mortification*, as the involvement and the suffering must first fade and die.

I would like to argue that in the present day what is happening is the exact opposite of the process described by Koselleck. We are very far from an automatic process in which the experiential reality of the Holocaust is silently passing into the custody of professional historians. The temporal distance from the historic event has not made this memory less colorful, but if anything it is now closer and more immediate than ever. Statements like the following are not uncommon: "The more distant Auschwitz becomes, the closer this event and the memory of this crime comes to us."[14] Instead of being delegated to professional historians into whose sole competence Koselleck expects and wishes to see it placed, it has been reclaimed by society. We have witnessed that far from automatically fading and ceding to historical scholarship, memory has been sharpened and reshaped in

---

[13] Ibid. (my italics, A.A.).

[14] Linda Reisch, Preface to Hanno Loewy (ed.), *Holocaust: Die Grenzen des Verstehens. Eine Debatte über die Besetzung der Geschichte*, Reinbek 1992, 7.

historically new ways. We are currently facing, reconstructing, and discussing new forms of memory that open up an access to the past that is distinct from and complementary to that which is provided by historical scholarship. Living memory thus gives way to a cultural memory that is underpinned by media – by material carriers such as memorials, monuments, museums, and archives. While individual recollections spontaneously fade and die with their former owners, new forms of memory are reconstructed within a transgenerational framework, and on an institutional level, within a deliberate policy of remembering or forgetting. There is no self-organization and self-regulation of cultural memory – it always depends on personal decisions and selections, on institutions and media. The transposition of individual living to artificial cultural memory and thus from short-term to long-term memory is a highly complex process fraught with problems: it brings together temporal extension with the threat of distortion, reduction, and manipulation that can only be averted through continuous public criticism, reflection, and discussion.

Nora's comment on the disappearance of memory in our present is contradicted by essays written by a group of American doctors, psychologists, and cultural historians. They refer to the growing role of memory in public life and stress its new and, indeed, unprecedented importance for our culture:

We live in a time when memory has entered public discourse to an unprecedented degree. Memory is invoked to heal, to blame, to legitimate. It has become a major idiom in the construction of identity, both individual and collective, and a site of struggle as well as identification.[15]

While certain types of memory – such as rote learning, classical education, and personal experience of the *Shoah* (Holocaust) – have declined or are fading, other forms like those of politics and the media are evidently gaining in importance. The past, which becomes farther and farther removed from us, obviously does not pass automatically and exclusively into the hands of the professional historian; it continues to make its impact on the present in the form of competing claims and obligations. The general discourse of historiography

---

[15] Paul Antze and Michael Lambek, eds., *Tense Past: Cultural Essays in Trauma and Memory*, New York and London 1997, VII.

now finds itself in collocation with a great variety of often contradictory memories, which demand the right to social recognition. No one today would deny that these memories, based on individual experiences and transformed into collective claims, have become a vital and controversial element of modern culture.

The first part of Nora's dictum – that people talk so much about memory – is therefore much easier to confirm. Over the last twenty years there has been a continual surge in the quantity of literature on the subject. Interest in memory evidently goes far beyond being just one more academic fashion of the moment. This enduring fascination suggests that a wide variety of questions and interests – cultural, scientific, social, and informational – are stimulated and consolidated at this particular point of intersection. The computer as a simulated mode of recollection offers an important background for cultural study, as does modern neurology with its new insights into the buildup and breakdown of neuronal networks. The range of approaches alone makes it clear that memory is a phenomenon that no single discipline can call its own.

The subject not only transcends the borders of individual disciplines, in the sense that there is no one profession that can provide an all-embracing concept of it; it also shows itself to be highly controversial within the individual disciplines themselves. Virginia Woolf has warned us: "Memory is inexplicable."[16] Literature, indeed, has always taught us that there are different and even contradictory approaches toward memory. "I would enshrine the spirit of the past / For future restoration," wrote William Wordsworth. T. S. Eliot, by contrast, bemoaned the fact that "there's no memory you can wrap in camphor / But the moths will get in."[17] And we might introduce another pair of authors who took contrary positions with regard to the workings of memory. Italo Svevo, at the beginning of the 20th century, adopted what we today would call a *constructivist view.*

The past is always new; as life proceeds it changes, because parts of it that may have once seemed to have sunk into oblivion rise to the surface and others vanish without a trace because they have come to have such slight importance.

[16] Virginia Woolf, *Orlando: A Biography* (1928), Harmondsworth 1975, 56.
[17] William Wordsworth, *The Prelude* 1805, XI, v. 342–343; T. S. Eliot, *The Cocktail Party*, London 1969, 49.

The present conducts the past in the way a conductor conducts an orchestra. It wants these particular sounds, or those – and no others. That explains why the past may at times seem very long and at times very short. It thunders forth or murmurs *pianissimo*. The only part of it that is highlighted is the part that has been summoned up to illumine, and to distract us from, the present; and it is then that one recalls pleasant memories and regrets more vividly than recent happenings.[18]

At roughly the same time, Marcel Proust emphasized the authenticity of memory and highlighted its involuntary character: "This book, the most difficult of all to decipher, is also the only one dictated to us by reality, the only one 'impressed' into us by reality itself."[19] Svevo's comments anticipate the approach of the systems theory of memory, according to which the past is a construction freely built according to the demands of the respective present. Proust's concept, on the other hand, is of a present that is influenced by a particular past that eludes the scope of intentional construction. Proust compares the presence of the past in human consciousness to a photographic negative, of which it is not possible to say in advance whether it will or will not one day be developed.

Many explanations have been offered for the new predominance and enduring fascination of the memory paradigm. They include the decline of modernization theory, with its emphasis on progress and grand expectations for the future; the end of a philosophy of the subject, which focuses on the rational, self-contained individual; the end of one-track disciplines in the humanities, with their ever narrowing range of specialization. Against this background, the subject of memory emerges both as a new field of interdisciplinary approaches and as a problem that impinges directly on many different areas of society in a rapidly changing world.

None of these factors, however, quite suffice to explain why there is now such an obsessive preoccupation with the study of memory – this book being just one example. Unlike the ceaselessly effective continuity of tradition, the workings of memory are sporadic, fractured, and

---

[18] Italo Svevo, "Death," in *Short Sentimental Journey and Other Stories*, trans. Beryl de Zoete, L. Collinson Morely, and Ben Johnson (Berkeley 1967), 302.

[19] "Le livre aux caractères figurés, non tracés par nous, est notre seul livre": Marcel Proust, *A la recherche du temps perdu vol. III, Le temps retrouvé*, Bibliothèque de la Pléiade, Gallimard, Paris 1954, 880.

enervated under the impact of trauma. Memory always needs a stimulus, and, according to Heiner Müller, begins with a shock. Nothing could have provided a greater shock than the catastrophic destruction and oblivion that marked the middle of the 20th century. It is therefore only logical that, from a European and especially a German perspective, in the aftermath of this unprecedented violence and destruction advocates of memory stepped forward – as did Simonides in the Roman legend – to view the settings of such catastrophes. When we accept this connection between excessive violence in the past and the memory boom of the present, Nora's statement loses much of its paradoxical quality and can testify to the ways in which later generations process the traumatic heritage of the mid-20th century.

In this book I address the complex phenomenon of memory from many angles and trace lines of development as well as problems and their contexts. For this reason I switch among *traditions* (mnemotechnics and forms of identity), *perspectives* (individual, collective, and cultural memory), *media* (texts, images, places), and *discourses* (literature, history, art, psychology, and so on). The text is divided into three parts: the first deals with functions, the second with media, and the third with means of storing cultural memory. The presentation of the different functions and discourses of memory will be shaped by a number of conceptual distinctions. That between "storing" and "remembering," for instance, goes together with the distinction between memory as art and memory as power; and this entails two largely independent traditions of discourse: the familiar one of rhetorical mnemotechnics and the less known psychological one that identifies memory as one of three mental faculties also known as internal senses. The former tradition aims to give an orderly Gestalt to knowledge, while the latter is concerned with interaction between memory, imagination, and common sense. The distinction between memory as *ars* and memory as *vis* is also more generally related, respectively, to the storage and the identity functions of memory.

Remembrance of the dead, posthumous fame, and historical memory are three forms of reference to the past that are differentiated in early modernity and develop into independent and possibly competing functions of cultural memory. The third chapter of this book illustrates by way of a literary example cases of "memory politics" in the broadest sense. Both deal with the importance of memory for the formation of identity. Shakespeare's *Histories* construct a national identity by way of historical memories, whereas Wordsworth's *The Prelude* fashions an individual identity through biographical memories. This chapter focuses on a creative reconstruction of memory – a process that inevitably also deploys the power of forgetting. The following chapter on memory boxes discusses the selection and vital importance of memory contents in terms of literary examples from different historical periods. What is important or unimportant, and how can the important be preserved? The first example is a medieval ark constructed in spiritual space to contain and safeguard important Christian knowledge; a second example is a chest described and constructed by the German poet Heinrich Heine that enshrines reading matter essential to his life (and death); and the last example is a heavy chest of books whose plunge into an abyss shatters the burden of a life-threatening cultural memory. The last chapter addresses more generally the seminal question of selection, forgetting, and storage capacity. It introduces the distinction between "storage" and "functional" memory, which connects back to memory *ars* and *vis*.

If one studies memory from a medical or psychological standpoint, it is fair enough to concentrate solely on the organic field of neurological structures and processes. However, as soon as one shifts the focus to social life as embedded in culture, one is forced to consider the technical *media* by which memory is formed and communicated. When the Russian Tartu-School semioticians and culturologists Yuri Lotman and Boris Uspenski defined culture as the "non-hereditary memory of a collective," they were emphasizing the dependence of cultural memory on particular practices and media.[20] This type of memory does not come into existence or persist of its own accord; it has to be created, established, communicated, continued, reconstructed, and appropriated. Individuals and cultures construct their memories interactively through communication by speech, images, and rituals. Without such representations, it is impossible to build a memory that can transcend generations and historical epochs, but this also means that with the changing nature and development of the various media, the constitution

---

[20] Yuri M. Lotman and Boris A. Uspenski, *The Semiotics of Russian Culture*, Ann Arbor 1984, 3.

of the memory will also be continually changing. The technical media incorporate recording systems of all kinds, and since the 19th century these are no longer confined to language but have expanded to images and, since the 20th century, to voices and sounds as well.

The second part of the book is, therefore, devoted to the media that provide the material support underlying cultural memory, framing it and interacting with individual human memories. A plethora of technical devices now blur the boundaries between the interior and the exterior of the mind. The fact that such boundaries are difficult to define is made especially clear by the metaphorical language used by philosophers, artists, and scholars to describe the mechanisms of memory. Even the oldest descriptions use metaphors of technical systems of recording, and these in turn reflect the changes that have taken place in the history of media – from tablets and parchments to photography, film, and computers. The latter confront us with an epoch-making turning point, as writing – the dominant metaphor of memory for the last twenty-five hundred years – gives way to the megatrope of the electronic net or Web. Writing is developing more and more in the direction of linkages. In what direction, then, are the basic premises of memory theory heading? From the very beginnings of writing in Egypt during the second millennium BCE right through to the end of the 20th century, we have testimonies that favored writing above all other media, regarding it as providing the most reliable and the most durable record. The cultural aim of conquering time seems to be closely linked to this phase of western metaphysics; it made the "spirit" into an immaterial power transcending history and the "letter" into the medium most suited to preserve and communicate it. After the extended dominance of the print age, the governing principle in the era of electronic writing is now the permanent overwriting and reconstruction of memory. Through information technology and new research into the structure of the brain, we are now experiencing a change of paradigm, by which the concept of a lasting written record is being replaced by the principle of continuous rewritings.

Every medium opens up its own access to cultural memory. Writing, which follows and records speech, stores different things – and stores them differently – from images, which register impressions and experiences that are independent of language. Ever since Roman mnemotechnics, a special power has been attributed to the so-called *imagines agentes* – a power also discovered in symbols and archetypes that reach deep into the individual dreamworld and the cultural unconscious. But the body too can be regarded as a personal medium, insofar as the psychic and mental processes of remembering are not only neurological but also somatic. The body stabilizes memories through habituation, and reinforces them through the power of affect. The latter as an integral component of memory has an ambivalent quality: it can be regarded as a sign of authenticity, but also as a driver for distortion. If the violence of an experience is so overwhelming that its memory is disconnected from consciousness and inaccessibly stored within the body, we speak of a trauma. This physically stored memory expresses itself through symptoms and blocks the way to conscious recall. After writing, images, and the body, a fourth medium of memory is that of particular geographical sites, which through important religious, historical, or biographical events may turn into places of memory. Places may also confirm and preserve memories across phases of cultural forgetting. For instance, a particular tradition may have died out, but after a while pilgrims or historically oriented tourists may return to the places that are important to them and discover a landscape, a monument, or a ruin. This leads to "reanimations" in which the place reactivates the memory, but also memory reactivates the place, because biographical and cultural memory can never arise solely out of places; these can only trigger and support the memory process in conjunction with other media. Whenever a tradition has disappeared, "ghost towns" arise that give free rein to the imagination or bring back what has been suppressed.

The third part of the book deals with a very different place of memory: the *archive*. In contrast to the sensually concrete memory linked to bodies and places, the archive exists independently of both, and so remains abstract and general. A precondition for its existence as a collective store of knowledge is a material data-carrier that must function as a support, above all, for the written word. Archives, therefore, depend on technical media. The recordability of data has now been vastly expanded by such new technologies as photography, film, various mobile electronic information devices, and videos, and all of these now confront the archivist with an array of new problems relating to storage.

The archive is not just a place in which documents from the past are preserved; it is also a place where the past is constructed and produced. The latter process depends partly on social, political, and cultural interests, but it is determined as well by the prevailing media and technologies. The archive first came into being through the material, fixed form of writing that codified information for later usage and thus laid the foundations for extended bureaucracies of power. With the modern switch to a dynamic, electronic form of registration, the basic structure of the archive is also changing. In addition to shelf after shelf of boxes and files that have gathered the dust of centuries, the archives have been invaded by "hi-tech" machines with an ever expanding capacity for storage and ever faster ways of processing, transferring, and accessing information. The digital age, as some futurists tell us, is already inventing totally new forms of archiving; and it will not be long before the archive will archive itself as an interesting but obsolete monument.

However, the current crisis facing cultural memory is not confined to the problems caused by the new media. This is evident from the work of artists born after World War II who work in the aftermath of a shattered cultural memory. The self-reflexive art of these artists highlights the processes of remembering and forgetting. They explore and expose the storage systems of books and archives that they use as new artistic formats for their work. It is striking that such art has started to focus so intently on memory at the very moment when society is in danger of losing it or trying to brush it aside. Artistic memory in this instance does not function as storage, but as an index, a reference to a human "depot of suffering" that is retranslated into communication. Thus, the artists' work becomes a mirror or, as Heiner Müller puts it, a "gauge" to measure the current amount of oblivion and suppression within the collective consciousness. Today, the arts have developed new and emphatic ways of focusing on the memory crisis as their theme, and they are finding new forms to express the dynamic movement of cultural remembering and forgetting.

Outside the archive, *waste* accumulates. This is made up of all the remnants of civilization that have not been collected and yet form a collection that can be defined as the converse image of the archive. Waste as a "negative store," however, does not stand only for disposal, destruction, and oblivion; it is also stands for latent memory, which takes its place between functional and storage memory and lives on from one generation to the next in a no-man's land between presence and absence. The border between archive and refuse is a very flexible one. Krzysztof Pomian has pointed out that waste need not be the last phase in an object's "use life" after losing its function and dropping out of practical circulation, the object is neutralized, can take on new significance, and can acquire the new status of a meaningful sign. In this sense, the seemingly insignificant discards become what he calls a *semiophor* – a visible sign of something invisible and ungraspable, like the past, or a person's identity.[21]

Even if the historical or artistic view can turn the prose of some of these remnants into the poetry of memory, there is still an endless amount of debris left over, which we do not want to restore and which indeed cannot be restored. Whatever is left over may refer either to the archive or to the waste, but in any case, the remnants can never be definitively eliminated. Structurally, the waste is as important to the archive as forgetting is to memory. Indeed, it is these negative elements that art installations and fantasy tales bring back to our awareness, as they conduct their experimental archiving of whatever the current culture has rejected.

---

[21] Krzysztof Pomian, *Der Ursprung des Museums. Vom Sammeln*, Berlin 1986, 92.

PART ONE

FUNCTIONS

1

Memory as *Ars* and *Vis*

As many roads lead to memory as to Rome – theology, philosophy, medicine, psychology, history, sociology, literature, art, and the media. The literary road branches off in two directions, and the signpost indicates *ars* one way and *vis* the other. Let us deal first with memory as an art. The tradition that has been revived in recent years is the discourse of classical Roman mnemotechnics, in which the term "art" is used in its old sense of technique. Mnemotechnics not only have a long tradition, but also go back to an unforgettable foundational legend: the story of the Greek poet Simonides, who invented the art of memory under spectacular circumstances, which we will look at in detail in the next chapter. This mnemotechnical method, which Simonides created spontaneously, was later developed by Cicero and Quintilian into a systematic mode of learning. It combined *loci* and *imagines* (places and images) and used them as the elements of a system of mental writing with which important information could be coded and engraved on the memory. The Roman method transferred memory from verbal to visual forms of encoding, and thus from the ear to the (inner) eye, its aim being to write signs directly into the "table" of the mind. It was conceived as a process that could be learned and used for a large variety of purposes, and aimed to provide safe storage and identical reproduction of the relevant information. Mnemotechnics focused on space and filtered out the dimension of time.

This technique can indeed be used in all kinds of situations. One can memorize a speech to be made in court, where it will be much more effective than a reading, one can quote the relevant salutary passage from the Bible, or learn by heart all the information necessary to pass a factual test. The learning and rote learning in our culture and our educational institutions entail corresponding physical and mental mnemotechnics that, unlike the Roman, do not depend solely on the eye and imaginary visualization, but also involve the ear (e.g., through the repetition of sounds) and the body (through movements, rhythms, counting on the fingers, and so on).

Interest in memory was kindled in literary studies with the rediscovery of ancient mnemotechnics. *The Art of Memory* is the title of a groundbreaking book by Dame Frances Yates, an eminent Renaissance scholar who specialized in occult movements during the early modern age and whose work in the 1960s brought to light a long-lost tradition.[1] It was Yates who paved the way for literary scholars like Renate Lachmann and Anselm Haverkamp, who some twenty-five years later were able to take up the paradox of the "forgotten art of memory" and link mnemotechnics with advanced theories such as intertextuality, psychoanalysis, and deconstruction. Thus the ancient tradition of rhetorical *memoria* became surprisingly current and, as a new starting point for literary research, it proved to be impressively productive.[2] There can be no doubting the importance of this tradition, and we see it confirmed again and again throughout this book. We must not forget, however, that there is a different access to memory that cannot be grasped in terms of a topological organization of knowledge. In particular, this concerns the link between memory and identity – a connection that entails cultural acts of remembrance, commemoration, eternalization, past and future references and projections, and, last but by no means least, forgetting, which is integral to all of these actions.

The road to memory that I have signposted as *ars* may be called *storage*, by which I mean every mechanical process that aims at an identity between recording and retrieving. Whenever the process has

---

[1] Frances Amelia Yates, *The Art of Memory*, Chicago 1966.
[2] Renate Lachmann, *Gedächtnis und Literatur. Intertextualität in der russischen Moderne*, Frankfurt a.M. 1990; Engl. *Memory and literature: Intertextuality in Russian Modernism*, trans. R. Sellars and A. Wall, Minneapolis 1997; Anselm Haverkamp and Renate Lachmann (eds.), *Gedächtniskunst: Raum – Bild – Schrift. Studien zur Mnemotechnik*, Frankfurt a.M. 1991; Anselm Haverkamp and Renate Lachmann (eds.), *Memoria. Vergessen und Erinnern, Poetik und Hermeneutik XV*, Munich 1993.

recourse to material aids, this goal appears self-evident – for instance, if we write a letter to someone, we can assume that when it arrives, all the words we wrote, and not just a percentage of them, will reach the addressee. The same applies to a book we buy or the data we call up on our computer: we expect that after an interval all the bytes will come back to us just as they were when we filed them. As the art of mnemotechnics proves, however, storage is possible even without technical apparatus. Indeed, it is a special function of human memory evinced by the recitation of such things as liturgical texts, poems, mathematical formulae, or historical facts.

All of this changes radically when we follow the sign marked *vis*. If Cicero was the patron of mnemotechnics, Nietzsche (to whom we will return quite a few times) was the patron of memory as a bestower of identity. Whereas storage is designed to rule out the problem of time, transience, and change, in this form of memory it becomes acute. Mnemotechnics operate on the hypothesis that there can be an exact correspondence between input and output; the *vis* memory, however, brings out the difference. We must therefore distinguish between the "process of storage" and the "process of remembering." Unlike memorizing and rote learning, very often remembering is not a deliberate act. One simply remembers something or one does not. It might be more accurate to say: something internalizes itself in us, and only afterward do we become conscious of it. In German, there are two words for memory, *Gedächtnis* and *Erinnerung,* and F. G. Jünger tried to distinguish between them: *Gedächtnis* is derived from the verb *denken,* to think, and is linked to knowledge; whereas, *Erinnerung* literally means internalization, and may be associated with personal experience. Jünger writes that we can (re-)produce the contents of *Gedächtnis* to the extent that we have learned and absorbed them. "The contents of *Erinnerungen,* however, are never consciously learned and reproduced."[3]

Remembering is basically a reconstructive process; it always starts in the present, and so inevitably at the time when the memory is recalled, there will be shifting, distortion, revaluation, reshaping. In the period between present action and future recall, memory does not wait patiently in its safe house; it has its own energy and is exposed to a process of transformation. The term *vis* reminds us that in this

---

[3] Friedrich Georg Jünger, *Gedächtnis und Erinnerung,* Frankfurt a.M. 1957, 48.

case memory is not a protective container but an immanent power, a driving force that follows its own rules. This force can hinder recall, as in forgetting, or it can block it completely, as in suppression, but it can also be steered by an insight, a desire, or a new set of requirements, any one of which may lead to memories taking on a new form. The act of storage counters time and oblivion, the effects of which are nullified by the use of particular techniques. The act of remembering occurs within time, which plays an active role in the process. In particular, part of the psychological dynamism of memory consists in the fact that remembering and forgetting are always inextricably bound together. The one makes the other possible. We might also say that forgetting is the enemy of storage and the ally of memory. This unavoidable interplay between remembering and forgetting underlies the anthropological power that is unknown to machines. They are able to store, and can do so infinitely better than humans can with the help of mnemotechnics, but they have so far proved utterly incapable of the psychic act of remembering.

The difference between memory as *ars* and as *vis* can be traced back to two different traditions of discourse in Antiquity. In the context of Roman rhetoric, *memoria* was presented as one of five phases in the process of producing and retrieving information: *inventio* referred to the finding of a subject matter, *dispositio* to the mental organization of the material, *elocutio* to the embellishment of speech, *memoria* to its memorization, and finally *actio* to the oral performance. In addition to this tradition of rhetoric, there was the ancient psychological discourse in which memory was regarded as a *vis*, or *ingenita virtus* of central anthropological importance, and was classified as one of three mental faculties, alongside imagination and common sense. From Antiquity through the Middle Ages and into the modern era, views of how the brain was constructed were determined by the doctrine of these three internal senses. Beginning with Aristotle and Galen, this doctrine was systematically elaborated upon and taken over by Christian, Jewish, and Arab philosophers of the Middle Ages; and handed down in the same form to those of modern times.[4]

---

[4] Aristotle, *On Memory and Recollection. Text, Translation, Interpretation and Reception in Western Scholasticism*, ed. by David Bloch, Leiden, Boston 2007, 24–51; Harry Austryn Wolfson, "The Internal Senses in Latin, Arabic, and Hebrew Philosophical Texts," *Harvard Theological Review* 28 (April 1935), 69–133.

The three internal senses were contrasted with the five external, and were localized in three lobes of the brain. Unlike the external senses, they function without any direct contact with the external world; they are cognitive or "spiritual" faculties, which are used to process the information provided by the external senses. For centuries this concept remained surprisingly constant, both in regard to the location and the individual functions of the internal senses. The forebrain was the site of *imagination,* which translated sensory data into mental images but could also produce images independently, for example, in dreams. The midbrain housed *common sense* ("ingenium"), which processed the sensory data, tested opinions, distinguished between utterances, and formed judgments. The hindbrain was the home of memory, which stored everything and kept it ready for retrieval. This model of the brain, which we come across again in the architectural metaphor of a tower with three rooms and three occupants, does not separate the different lobes but has them interacting and shows us how their functions determine and control one another. Separation leads to problems. If, for instance, the images provided by the imagination are not regulated by common sense, they can lead to symptoms of madness.

In the 18th century, the spatial paradigm of mnemotechnics gave way to a temporal focus. For this historic switch from *ars* to *vis*, we may take as an example Vico, who released memory from its rhetorical context and transposed it into an anthropological one. He was able to do this by linking it to the other, psychological discourse and viewing memory as one of the three human mental faculties, along with imagination and common sense. As he found this force to be especially well developed in children, he concluded that it must also have been particularly predominant in the early history of mankind. Thus, he shifted rhetorical memory not only into a psychological but also into an historical and genetic context. The new science of anthropology came into being in the 18th century precisely through the construction of this historical and genetic perspective.[5]

In rhetoric, the greatest emphasis was laid on the first phase of the process, the art of the *inventio,* whereas *memoria* only followed at a later

---

[5] Hans Robert Jauss, in *Studien zum Epochenwandel der ästhetischen Moderne,* Frankfurt a.M. 1989, 23, says that the original factor leading to the birth of the science of anthropology was the new mythology characteristic of the Enlightenment, with its nostalgic longing for beginnings. On Vico, see ibid., 33 f.

stage when the finished text had to be learned by heart so that it could be presented with maximum effect. Vico reversed this sequence. He placed memory, which he no longer construed as a reproductive but as a genuinely productive faculty, at the beginning of the history of the human mind. He saw memory as the civilizing force in the times before the advent of writing. Jürgen Trabant, building on Vico's momentous transposal, wrote that the topic "is quite obviously not only seen as the first phase in rhetoric, but also as the beginning of human thought and of human culture in general."[6]

Vico's return to the beginning does not take place through myth but through an historical labor of memory that step by step makes its way from later phases to earlier. This process has to move from the word back to the image, then back to myth, or – to use his own words – "from the academies" of written culture to the "great forest" of prehistory. The poetic images and universal symbols of that prehistory open up before the archaeological and historical gaze that penetrates through the varnish of abstract reasoning. Looking down from the heights of rational thought, one can see the wild roots that led to it. The thoughts of philosophy, which we had taken to be timeless, are not – and the word should be taken quite literally – "thinkable" without the foundations of language that grew up through the long course of time. Vico called the new science, which focused on tracing the phases of this long history, "philology," which he contrasted with the timeless rationality of "philosophy." Philology is thus the disciplined art of remembering that, by following the thread of language through etymologies, finds its way back to the long buried visual substance of poetic, sensual, primeval imagery. According to Jacob Grimm, a similar journey backward through time can also be effected through the art of etymology "which acts as a beacon where no written history can lead us."[7]

---

[6] Jürgen Trabant, "Memoria – Fantasia – Ingegno," in *Memoria, Vergessen und Erinnern*, 412 (see n. 1).

[7] Jacob Grimm, *Kleinere Schriften I*, Berlin 1864, 302.

2

The Secularization of Memory

Memoria, Fama, Historia

THE ART OF MEMORY AND REMEMBRANCE OF THE DEAD

The anthropological heart of cultural memory is *remembrance* of the dead. It was the duty of the relatives to keep the names of their dead folk alive, and to pass them on to their descendants. This remembrance had both a religious and a secular significance, which can be summed up by the contrasting terms *pietas* and *fama*. The former refers to the family's obligation to preserve honorable memories of the deceased, whereas for *fama*, or fame and glory, one can to a certain extent prepare and accomplish much during one's own lifetime. Fame is a secular form of self-immortalization, and it has a great deal to do with the image that a person creates of himself. The Greek and Roman preoccupation with glory in posterity was superseded by medieval Christianity, through which people were more concerned with the salvation of the soul and eternal afterlife.

Even religious remembrance depends not only on the Book of God, the Bible, but also on the rites and practices of the living, and the cult that links them with the dead can be considered the earliest and most widespread form of social memory. This immortalization of individuals was at the center of Ancient Egyptian culture, and was celebrated every year at the Festival of the Desert Valley where the families went to the graves of their loved ones (as they still do today in Arabic Egypt) and shared a meal with them. Eating and drinking are basic modes of community building, and at the graveside they become a ritual way of reintegrating the deceased ancestors into the family.

Eating with the dead was still a widespread custom in Roman and Early Christian times, until the Church under Bishop Ambrosius in the late 4th century repressed such family rituals and replaced them with a more centralized version.[1] Instead of the family's commemoration of individual members, there was now a collective commemoration of martyrs, whose remains were transported to the churches; and instead of the private meal within the family circle, there was now a new social gathering in the form of the Communion.

The medieval practice of commemoration consisted of two elements: care of the dead and care of the poor.[2] Both elements were connected by a third: the institution of purgatory. The clearer the features of this mythical landscape became, the greater was the uncertainty over salvation, and so the stronger became the efforts of the Christians to find ways of softening the potential torments awaiting them. Purgatory represented an intermediate stage of suffering between the death of the individual and God's Last Judgment, and according to Pope Gregory the Great, the fate of the dead during this phase of transition could be favorably influenced by the actions of the living. By paying for special masses and sponsoring the feeding of the poor, one could assist the souls in purgatory on their way to salvation and also invest into one's own afterlife. This was encouraged by the churches and monasteries, and some like Cluny, which specialized in such programs, transformed them into a mass industry of salvation.

Care of the dead meant immortalizing their names, and so on anniversaries and feast days a mass would be held and the name would be written in the proverbial "Book of Life." Divine bookkeeping was a

---

[1] For details see Otto Gerhard Oexle, "Die Gegenwart der Lebenden und der Toten," in Karl Schmid (ed.), *Gedächtnis, das Gemeinschaft stiftet*, Freiburger Akademie Schriften, Freiburg 1985, 79 ff. In view of the endless efforts by the Church to ban it, one may assume that the practice of the funeral repast continued to flourish. With regard to "memorial pictures" as an expression of the presence of the dead, see Otto Gerhard Oexle, "Memoria als Kultur," in Otto Gerhard Oexle (ed.), *Memoria als Kultur*, Veröffentlichungen des Max-Planck-Instituts für Geschichte 121, Göttingen 1995, 9–78; here 43 ff.

[2] See Joachim Wollasch, "Toten und Armensorge," in Schmid (ed.), *Gedächtnis*, (see n. 1) 9–38 (quote p. 23). He explains in detail how memorial services for the dead led to a well-developed system of welfare for the poor that spread throughout Europe, but he also explains how the liturgical and economic demands of this cult grew out of all proportion (e.g., in Cluny), until the dead were virtually taking over the lives of the living.

task that was taken more and more out of the hands of the Almighty and transferred to the pens of the monks. When religious communities formed alliances, they would exchange their lists of names (which could go up to about thirty thousand), each promising the other a reciprocal memorial. Care of the poor consisted in gifts and donations of money that could be used to provide food – charitable deeds designed to make up for the sins of the donors. It was, then, essential to remain in the memory of the community, because masses and alms for the poor might have a favorable impact on the career of the soul in purgatory.

This institutional remembrance of the dead lasted well into the 18th century when it was abolished through cultural changes both in the legal system and in the concept of the subject. Historians see the clearest indication of this change as being the abolition of the legal rights of the dead person.

"The concept of the presence of the dead, i.e. of their legal and social status in the memory of the living, faded out in the course of the 18th century, and around 1800, with the beginning of the modern age, disappeared completely. [...] Indeed in the modern age, by contrast to preceding eras, the dead no longer hold legal rights. They are no longer subjects of the law. According to modern law, their legal status is expunged by death."[3]

The importance of remembering the dead as a paradigm of cultural memory can be illustrated by two legends connected with a Greek poet. Simonides of Keos (ca. 557–467 BCE) is the hero of a story that Cicero made into the foundational legend of mnemotechnics.[4] He is said to have been the first poet paid to sing not only of gods and heroes but also of mortal men. The story goes that he was commissioned by the boxer Skopas to create a poem in his honor, to be performed at a feast in his house. The poem that Simonides performed to the assembled company was not, however, altogether to the liking of his patron. As was quite normal in the tradition of this genre, in addition to praising the person to whom it was dedicated, the poem contained a long passage about the gods – in this case the heavenly twins Castor and

[3] Ibid.
[4] Cicero, *De oratore II*, 86, 352–354. Engl. trans. *On the Ideal Orator* (with Introduction, Notes, Appendixes, Glossary, and Indexes), James M. May and Jakob Wisse, Oxford 2001, 219.

Pollux. Skopas'reaction was sarcastic: Simonides should only expect half of his agreed fee, and he should go and get the rest from the gods whom he had praised so eloquently. The poet was then summoned outside because there were two strangers at the door asking to see him. Simonides went out, but there was no trace of the two strangers. At precisely this moment, disaster struck: Skopas' banquet hall collapsed, burying the host and all his guests in the ruins. Simonides' reward from the gods, we learn, was his miraculous escape. But this is not yet the end of the story as told by Cicero. The poet's services were needed once more, this time not for the purpose of bestowing fame and glory, but for that of remembering the dead. A proper burial was not possible without prior identification of the victims. As Simonides had memorized the exact order in which they had all been sitting, he was able to give the respective name back to each of the mutilated bodies. Thanks to his intervention, the families were able to honor and remember their dead by giving them a worthy burial. From the perspective of ancient mnemotechnics, this somewhat gruesome story has a happy ending. Simonides invents a new system that demonstrates the power of the human memory over death and destruction. This system, moreover, could be applied to other cases and could easily be taught and learned in the future.

Paradoxically, when we look at the actual history of this foundational legend of Roman mnemotechnics, we are immediately confronted with questions about the reliability of memory. Quintilian was swift to cast substantial doubts on its credibility. He expressed uncertainty as to where the banquet hall in question was supposed to have stood – in Pharsalos, or in Kranon. Such scruples over the historical authenticity of the tale carry less weight today. Stefan Goldmann has studied its history, which he regards as a "process of transformation and fusion of past and present experiences through social imagination." And he goes further: he assumes that Cicero's existing text was the result of "many generations writing and weaving together historical and mythical events." He even speaks of a "historical screen memory."[5] Thus, the actual origin of the art of memory need not

---

[5] Stefan Goldmann, "Statt Totenklage Gedächtnis. Zur Erfindung der Mnemotechnik durch Simonides von Kreos," *Poetica* 2 (1989), 43–98; here 46.

itself constitute an authentic memory, but instead demonstrates the flexibility of memory.

There is another traditional story concerning Simonides. On his wanderings through foreign lands he is said to have come upon a corpse that lay unburied by the wayside. He broke off his journey in order to ensure that the dead stranger was given a worthy burial. The following night, the ghost of the dead man visited him in a dream and warned him against a sea voyage that he was planning to make. The ship that Simonides had intended to sail on – but, of course, did not – was in fact wrecked, and sank, killing everyone on board. William Wordsworth penned a late memorial to Simonides in the form of a sonnet:

> I find it written of Simonides
> That travelling in strange countries once he found
> A corpse that lay expos'd upon the ground,
> For which, with pains, he caused due obsequies
> To be performed, and paid all holy fees.
> Soon after, this man's Ghost unto him came
> And told him not to sail as was his aim,
> On board a ship then ready for the seas.
> Simonides, admonished by the ghost,
> Remained behind; the ship the following day
> Set sail, was wrecked, and all on board were lost.
> Thus was the tenderest Poet that could be,
> Who sang in ancient Greece his moving lay,
> Saved out of many by his piety.[6]

This second legend does not focus on the mnemonic power but on the piety of Simonides, illustrated by his kindness in paying for the burial of a stranger in a foreign land. Wordsworth called him the "tenderest Poet" and ends his sonnet with the word "piety," because this act shows that humanity should not be confined to one's in-group but

[6] William Wordsworth, *The Poetical Works*, ed. Ernest de Selincourt, Oxford 1954, vol. 3, 408. In his essay, Goldmann mentions and authenticates this second tale, and draws a picture of Simonides as a "Psychopompos" or shaman, inspired by the heavenly twins and taking the souls of the dead across the threshold to the Underworld.

extends to the whole of mankind. Just like his respect for the gods in the first legend, his respect for the dead earns him the reward of miraculous protection from a disaster that kills all except himself. The ghost of the dead man appears here as a guardian angel and benefactor – the exact opposite of the frightening avenger that most people expect a ghost to be. Thus, piety has another important function: it placates the dead and ameliorates any danger associated with their return.

In both legends, the name of Simonides shines forth against a background of death, destruction, and oblivion. It is his name and his story that have found their way into cultural memory, thanks not least to Cicero's narrative and Wordsworth's poem: "Saved out of many." And both legends very clearly reflect the original connection between the different forms of memory: piety, remembrance of the dead, fame, and mnemotechnics. Remembrance of the dead is common to both legends, but while it remains in the background of the first story, it is in the foreground of the second. Piety and memory, as it turns out, are the cultural response to a universal taboo. The dead must be laid to rest, because otherwise they will disturb the peace of the living and endanger the well-being of society.

FAMA

Dignum laude virum Musa vetat mori[7]

In Cicero's story, the boxer Skopas did not employ Simonides as a mnemotechnician but as a publicity agent. His function was to help reinforce the reputation of one man among his contemporaries, so that his name would go down forever in posterity. "Fame is the most certain form of immortality, and to live long means to survive in the memory of man. The longest life is one whose great and wonderful deeds of glory have been recorded in the eternal annals of historiography," wrote the humanist Gerolamo Cardano in his book on wisdom.[8]

---

[7] The Muse does not allow the praiseworthy man to die (Horace, *Carminum* IV, 8).

[8] Gerolamo Cardano, *De Sapienta*, 506, col. 1, quoted from E. F. Rice, Jr., *The Renaissance Idea of Wisdom*, Cambridge, Mass. 1958, 172.

These comments lay emphasis on three interconnected conditions for *fama*: great deeds, a record of them, and remembrance by posterity. Immortality of the name is the secular variation on immortality of the soul. It does not require family members, priests, monasteries, or acts of charity, but singers, poets, and historians. Religious *memoria* concerns personal memory and the salvation of the soul, whereas worldly fame entails social remembrance by posterity. In Ancient Egypt, religious *memoria* and worldly fame were still closely connected, but in Greece they were quite separate. The cult of fame involved new social institutions that were independent of the cult of the dead. Poets were recognized as professional immortalizers, and they were highly respected as the lords of (a second) life and death. They were the officials who inscribed the name of the hero directly into the memory of generations to come. Originally fame had been the privilege of rulers, but in Greece, thanks to the stimulus of competition, it became democratized. Nevertheless, this revolutionary expansion of cultural memory categorically excluded women. In order to enable their citizens to qualify for immortality, the city-states set up contests in which sportsmen could do battle and artists could vie with one another for inspiration. But even outstanding deeds were only a precondition and never a guarantee of fame. The guarantee could only come from the bard, who would immortalize the deeds in his poem. He alone could promise the hero the privilege of overcoming the mortal fate of man by creating a perpetual memory of his deeds. The poet's function was that of a gatekeeper to eternal glory. Physical death could be overcome by immortalizing the name and deeds of the individual, and in such a culture the poet was held to possess a special gift (or magic power) of long-distance communication, thanks to which he could address even the unborn generations of the future.

Alexander's Tears at the Grave of Achilles

In the 34th and 35th cantos of his epic poem *Orlando Furioso*, Ariosto created an image for the process whose result we call "fame." He talks of an old man who helps the Fates by collecting the nameplates from the empty reels of life and carrying them to a river in his cloak. From the riverbank he throws his load into the waters, which carry the names away till they sink into the mud. A flock of birds flies over the river, and now and then they snap up a name, but they cannot fly very far with their burden:

> When they would raise themselves in upward flight,
> They have not strength the burden to sustain;
> So that perforce in Lethe's water light
> The worthy names which lasting praise should gain.
> Two swans there are amid those birds, as white,
> My lord, as is your banner's snowy grain;
> Who catch what names they can, and evermore
> With those return securely to the shore.[9]

Only the swans are able to carry the names safely to another shore, and pass them over to a nymph, who in turn consecrates them in the Temple of Immortality.

> To Immortality 'tis sacred; there
> A lovely nymph, that from the hill descends,
> To the Lethean river makes repair;
> Takes from those swans their burden, and suspends
> The names about an image, raised in air
> Upon a shaft, which in mid fane ascends;
> There consecrates and fixes them so fast,
> That all throughout eternity shall last.
>
> (35/16)

The meaning of this image is explained in the following stanza:

> Rare as those gentle swans are poets too,
> That well the poet's name have merited,
> As well because it is Heaven's will, that few
> Great rulers should the paths of glory tread,
> As through foul fault of sordid lordlings, who
> Let sacred Genius beg his daily bread;
> Who putting down the Virtues, raise the tribe
> Of Vices, and the liberal arts proscribe.
>
> (35/23)

---

[9] Ariosto, *Orlando Furioso*, Vol. II, 35 / 14, trans. by William Stewart Rose (1775–1843), Online Medieval and Classical Library.

Ariosto combines the image of the rare immortality of names with a lesson about princes and those in power. If they are concerned about their own fame, they should pay more respect to poets, and take better care of them. Ariosto and other Renaissance poets thus reconstructed the western myth of immortality, which they were then able to use as a means of ensuring their own social importance.

The complicity between hero and bard and the positive self-image of the poet were highlighted in the Renaissance by a popular anecdote.[10] This is the tale of Alexander, who shed bitter tears at the grave of Achilles. In Castiglione's conversations about the virtues of the courtier, which he published in 1528 one year before he died, Pietro Bembo recalls the story that he uses to demonstrate the superiority of the fine arts over the sword.

> The great Macedo, when he proched neer
> Fiers Achilss famous Toumb, thus said and sight:
> 'O happy Prince that found a Tromp so cleer,
> And happy he that prayed so worthy a wight.'

"And if Alexander envied Achilles not for his deedes but for his fortune that gave him so great luck to have his actes renowned by Homer, a man may gather he estemed more the letters of Homer than the armes of Achilles."[11]

Edmund Spenser also used this tale to illustrate the *fama* function of poetry. Following the example of Virgil's pastoral verse, his *Shepheardes Calender* is divided up according to the months of the year. Poetry as the subject of poetry is typical of the eclogue, and in *October* two shepherds discuss society's attitude toward literature. The question they raise concerns the manner in which society bestows recognition on the poet: is it through "price," "prayse," "gayne," or "glory"? The unpaid, and therefore unhappy, poet complains that one cannot live on praise alone, and he looks back to a golden age when poets enjoyed not only the esteem of their contemporaries but also substantial remuneration.

---

[10] See *Christen in der Wüste: Drei Hieronymus-Legenden*, with German translation and commentary by Manfred Fuhrmann, Zürich, Munich 1983, 37.

[11] Baldessar Castiglione, *The Book of the Courtier*, I, XLV, Vol. 1, trans. by Sir Thomas Hoby (1561) and ed. Walter Raleigh for David Nutt, Publisher, London 1900.

A Maecenas or Augustus, however, is no longer to be found anywhere
in the English court:

> But ah Mecoenas is yclad in claye,
> And great Augustus long ygoe is dead.[12]

Spenser published the eclogues himself in 1579, and was thus one of
the very first modern English authors to combine literary and commercial production. Here, however, he is mourning for the old tradition
of royal patronage, which guaranteed the poet the two things he must
now fight for himself: recognition and material security.

Under the old system of patronage, these were offered to him in
exchange for a clearly defined quid pro quo: he must guarantee the
immortal fame of his patron. The *October* eclogue focuses on just the
one side of this exchange – namely, the money the poet expects to
receive from the prince – but the other side is mentioned in a footnote,
and consists precisely in the prince's immortality. The key expression
"for ever," which is scarcely in need of further annotation, becomes
the pretext for a detailed "gloss" explaining the relationship between
the poet and the hero. The poem itself makes it very clear that the
poet is nothing without the support of his powerful patron, but the
footnote is equally emphatic that the powerful patron will get nowhere
without the support of his poet. "The deed requires a singer of tales"[13]
was commonplace in Antiquity, but it was a self-evident truth that had
obviously got lost, and needed to be recalled to mind in a footnote to
Spenser's poem:

For ever. He [the poet] showeth the cause why Poets were wont to be had in such
honour of noblemen, that is, that by them their worthiness and valour should
through their famous poesis be commended to all posterities. Wherefore it
is said, that Achilles had never been so famous, as he is, but for Homer's
immortal verses, which is the only advantage which he had of Hector. And
also that Alexander the great, coming to his tomb in Sigaeum, with natural
tears blessed him, that ever it was his hap to be honoured with so excellent a
poet's work, as so renowned and ennobled only by his means.[14]

---

[12] *The Shepheardes Calender, October*, verse 6162, *The Poetical Works of Edmund Spenser*,
ed. J. C. Smith and P. Selincourt, London, New York 1965, 457.
[13] I have adopted this expression from Jochen Martin.
[14] Spenser, *Works*, 459 (see n.12).

It is clear that Alexander's tears are shed out of self-pity, because he does not have a Homer to record his own great deeds. His high esteem of the poet's gift is illustrated in the same gloss by an anecdote that fits perfectly with the Renaissance self-image of the poet:

So favoured he the only name of a poet, which praise otherwise was in the same man no less famous, that when he came to ransacking of king Darius' coffers, whom he lately had overthrown, he found in a little coffer of silver the two books of Homer's works, as laid up there for special jewels and riches, which he taking thence, put one of them daily in his bosom, and the other every night laid under his pillow. Such honour have Poets always found in the sight of Princes and noble men . . . [15]

We will return to this part of the story (which Heinrich Heine picked up almost 300 years later). In the Greco-Roman culture of *fama*, greatness, glory, and immortality through the memory of posterity were the priceless and exclusive gifts that only a poet could bestow on the hero. Alexander the Great wept in his admiration for Homer, because he had no Homer of his own to record his mighty works for posterity. Spenser evokes this ancient culture at a time in history when authors needed the backing of Antiquity in their efforts to build a new image for their vocation.

Temples and Monuments to Fame

In the Greek polis, or city-states, it was not only through great artistic or sporting achievements that one could achieve glory, but also and especially through military feats and death in battle. This democratization of fame, which sanctified the death of every fallen soldier, was an invention of the Ancient Greeks. At the center of the rhetoric of *fama* is the concept of fame as the best monument. A grave gives support to the private memories of the family, but a monument reaches out to a far wider community – a polis, or even a nation. "I shall not have a grave, but a monument!" cries the eponymous heroine of Euripides' *Iphigenie in Aulis* at the vital moment when she realizes the importance of her sacrificial death to the whole community. The promise of glory means exchanging the narrow, temporary memory of the family for

[15] Ibid.

the great and eternal memory of the collective. In his famous funeral oration for the fallen Athenians, Pericles puts this promise into words that firmly anchor the exchange of the mortal body for immortal reputation in the western cult of *fama*:

Together they gave their lives, and individually they took as their reward the praise which does not grow old and the most glorious of tombs – not where their bodies lie, but where their fame lives on in every occasion for speech and ceremony, an everlasting memory. Famous men have the whole earth as their tomb. Their record is not only the inscription on gravestones in their own land, but in foreign countries too the unwritten memorial which lives in individual hearts, the remembrance of their spirit rather than their achievement.[16]

Such words of promise have drawn soldiers into battle, from the Peloponnesian Wars to World War II and beyond, and this promise of national and extraterritorial immortality finds its concrete form in a vast range of monuments. The bombastic and sometimes inept politics of national memory finds expression in forms that range from the Tomb of the Unknown Warrior to vast military cemeteries.[17] According to Benedict Anderson, the most impressive emblem of modern nationalism is the Cenotaph and the empty tombs of unknown soldiers. He writes: "Yet void as these tombs are of identifiable mortal remains or immortal souls, they are nonetheless saturated with ghostly *national* imaginings."[18]

From its very beginnings, however, the idea of the glorious monument has always aroused scepticism in view of its symbolic material form, which is confined to a single space and whose evocative power will eventually fade to nothing. Often built into the monument is a striking contradiction between the claim to immortality and the actual fate of the monument. Percy Bysshe's Shelley's *Ozymandias* is the

---

[16] Thucydides, *The Peloponnesian War*, translated by Martin Hammond, Oxford 2009, 94–95 (2.43).

[17] See George L. Mosse, *Fallen Soldiers. Reshaping the Memory of the World Wars*, New York, Oxford 1990, and Reinhard Koselleck, "Kriegerdenkmale als Identitätsstiftungen der Überlebenden," in Odo Marquard and Karlheinz Stierle (eds.), *Identität. Poetik und Hermeneutik VIII*, Munich 1979.

[18] Anderson supports his thesis that nationalism and the cult of the dead are interconnected with the following intellectual experiment: the tomb of an unknown Marxist or Liberal is unimaginable. Benedict Anderson, *Imagined Communities. Reflections on the Origin and Spread of Nationalism*, London, New York 1990, 9.

perfect example. On the pedestal of the shattered statue a despotic oriental ruler had engraved the words:

> My name is Ozymandias, king of kings:
> Look on my works, ye Mighty, and despair!'
> Nothing beside remains. Round the decay
> Of that colossal wreck, boundless and bare
> The lone and level sands stretch far away.[19]

This recurrent experience has moved humans of all periods to abandon temples and monuments and look for a more spiritual form of memory that exists within living people.

In the Middle Ages, when divine memory represented the extreme heights of human aspiration, worldly fame had little cultural worth. The allegorical *fama*, which was such a dominant concept in classical Antiquity and the Renaissance period, was viewed in the Middle Ages as a dubious figure. Chaucer's tale *The House of Fame* (1383) tells of the temple of the goddess Fama, whose palace stands

> Right even in middle of the weye
> Betwixen hevene, erthe, and see[20]

The central position is important, because this is where news from all over the world is collected. No matter what is said, whispered, written, or sung, a special law of gravity carries it here. This vast collective information center, with an ear-splitting hubbub like that of a stock exchange, is ruled over by Fama, who is no less fickle than her sister Fortuna. She is not bound by any code of truth or ethics, but again like Fortuna is in league with Time. And so her palace is not built on granite but on a massive block of ice. On the south side, the carved reports of fame have already weathered very badly, whereas those on the shaded north side are still well preserved.

The contents of this temple of memory consist of the great deeds performed by the heroic forebears. Here too, however, the deeds have not gained their place in the temple because they happened,

---

[19] Percy Bysshe Shelley, "Ozymandias," in Kelvin Everest and Geoffrey Matthews (eds.), *The Poems of Shelley*, London et al. 2000 (2nd edition), Vol. 2, 310–311; here 311.

[20] G. Chaucer, *House of Fame*, II, in *Complete Works*, ed. W. W. Skeat, London 1969, 713 ff.

but because they were transformed into narrative and song. When it comes to the bookkeepers of memory, Chaucer does not distinguish between poets and historians. They are all the "mediators" (Krzysztof Pomian) of fame, whether they are called Josephus, Statius, Homer, Virgil, Ovid, Lucan, or Claudian. In pre-writing cultures, it was not books but bards who were the mediators. One might even call them "data carriers," for that was how they were visualized – as columns bearing the objects of fame. But just as the heroes were dependent on the bards, so too were the bards dependent on the fickle Fama. Which delegation would be granted a place of honor and which would not had nothing to do with merit, and certainly nothing to do with the poetic power of perfect verse like that of Horace or Shakespeare. It was only the unpredictable will of Fama, the capricious patroness of social memory, that decided what would survive and what would disappear.

The Renaissance diverged from the Middle Ages by restoring the classical veneration of Fama. In the eyes of the humanists, she was no longer a dubious figure but represented man's noblest aspirations. This is made very clear by Pietro Aretino's reinterpretation of the story of the Tower of Babel. He identified totally with the project of the Babylonians, who with this building hoped to achieve everlasting glory. While life is short, fame is long, provided one takes the time and trouble to achieve it. With this interpretation Aretino did away with the guilt complex underlying the biblical myth, and also removed from the story the presence of a jealous God who destroyed the hybrid construction. As an enlightened atheist, Aretino attributed its destruction to purely meteorological factors: the top of the tower caused a build-up of clouds, and this in turn gave rise to a thunderstorm that scattered all the builders in a panic.[21]

The revaluation of fame was linked to the secularization of time and memory. During the Renaissance, memory of the dead and mindfulness of one's own death receded and gave way to the hope of immortality through cultural achievements. Life after death was no longer exclusively at the discretion of God, but found its earthly

[21] Arno Borst, *Der Turmbau von Babel. Geschichte der Meinungen über Ursprung und Vielvalt der Sprachen und Völker*, Munich 1957–63; 1995, Vol. 3, Part 1, 1111–1112.

counterpart in posterity – "a life beyond life" as Milton expressed it. The concept of God's eternal judgment and record that directed man's actions and reckonings to this final "account" now had to compete with the books of men who created their own system of memory and recognition.

The most important instrument in the construction of this new time-and-memory dimension was, according to the humanists of the Renaissance, writing. In the age of the printing press, authorship took on a new meaning. The traditional attribution of fame to the hero of the poem now shifted to the maker of the poem. Writing was a means of immortalization not just for the celebrated hero but also for the writer. George Pettie, who was one of England's first commercially successful authors, wrote: "The only way to win immortalitie is either to doo thinges worth the writing, or to write thynges worthy the readyng."[22] This new concept of authorship, it should be noted, preceded the invention of the printing press. In 1408 the poet John Gower was laid to rest in a church in Southwark. The memorial sculpture on his tomb shows the reclining poet with his head resting on the three works that constituted his claim to fame.[23] In this statue the traditional memory of the dead has already entered into an alliance with the new cult of fame.

Unlike Chaucer's Temple of Fama, such edifices were later built by human hand, no longer dependent on unpredictable whim.[24] Society itself created institutions to preserve memories, and it acted both as patron and as guarantor of its own memory, setting itself up as the judge of which names should live and which should die. Quite often the posthumous bestowal of fame has had a compensatory element: what may have been scorned by a person's contemporaries is honored by subsequent generations. "Poor Lafontaine," wrote Heine – himself the object of a problematic reception history that has still not

---

[22] George Pettie, in Karl J. Holzknecht (ed.), *Sixteenth-Century English Prose*, New York 1954, 297.

[23] Jan Bialostocki, "Books of Wisdom and Books of Vanity," in *In Memoriam J.G. van Gelder 1903–1980*, Utrecht 1982, 37–67; here 39 f.

[24] On the subject of the Temple of Fame and Voltaire's "temple du goût" as a canonic metaphor for "bon sens," see H. U. Gumbrecht, in Aleida and Jan Assmann (eds.), *Kanon und Zensur*, Munich 1987, 286 ff.

straightened itself out – "in his lifetime asked only for a piece of bread, and after his death was given 40,000 francs' worth of marble."[25]

The 19th century created new settings for memory. A particular role was played by the museum, which took over the pseudo-sacral components of the temple or pantheon. The exhibition halls and historical pageants presented and still present a vivid and comprehensive visual display of the normative past.[26] The juxtaposition or sequence of items in a spatial setting enables the observer to travel through history, offering a panorama of all the different eras at a single viewing. Time is thus transformed into space or, to be more precise, into the space of memory, in which it is constructed, represented, and perpetuated. Along with the boom in museums that presented *national* history, and historical dramas that staged it,[27] there was a sudden surge in the number of monuments erected to commemorate *local* history. The reason for this lay in a certain tension between the ruler's desire for representation and the similar aspirations of the middle classes. Karl Scheffler noted this phenomenon in 1907:

> The current mania for monuments is a consequence of political constitutionalism; it expresses itself all the more forcibly as the division of power between the crown and the people is contested. The public monument as an end in itself only existed [. . .] since the princes defiantly thrust the pictures of their ancestors before the eyes of the citizens, and the citizens responded to this provocation by honouring of their own political and spiritual leaders with statues. In this competition, not an inch of public space is left vacant.[28]

By the end of the 20th century, as the public debate over the Berlin Holocaust Memorial has shown, nothing much had changed. In the

---

[25] Dietrich Schubert, in Aleida Assmann and Dietrich Harth (eds.), *Mnemosyne. Formen und Funktionen kultureller Erinnerung*, Frankfurt a.M. 1991, 101.

[26] On all-embracing places of memory see Günter Hess, "Bildersaal des Mittelalters. Zur Typologie illustrierter Literaturgeschichte im 19. Jahrhundert," in Christophe Cormeau (ed.), *Deutsche Literatur im Mittelalter. Kontakte und Perspektiven. Hugo Khan zum Gedenken*, Stuttgart 1979, 501–546; Nikolaus Gussone, "Deutscher Bildersaal. Ein Versuch über Bildprägungen im kulturellen Gedächtnis des Deutschen" in Wilhelm Gössmann and Klaus-Heinrich Roth (eds.), *Poetisierung – Politisierung. Deutschlandbilder in der Literatur bis 1848*, Paderborn 1994, 243–269.

[27] Wolfgang Struck, *Konfigurationen der Vergangenheit. Deutsche Geschichtsdramen im Zeitalter der Restauration*, Studien zur deutschen Literatur, 143, Tübingen 1997.

[28] Karl Scheffler, *Moderne Baukunst*, Berlin 1907, 128, quoted from H. E. Mittig, in Mittig and Plagemann (eds.), *Denkmäler im 19. Jahrhundert. Deutung und Kritik*, Munich 1972, 287 f.

history of monuments, there has been no letup in the clash between the central and the regional, between unity and diversity, or between the different historical perspectives. The multiplication of political agents – nations, small states, cities, monarchs, aristocrats, and political parties – has created a contested domain of political aspirations that again find their expression in monuments. In this time of crisis, the growing insecurity of the political groups is manifest in the production of monuments that have become increasingly numerous and theatrical; they are no longer directed toward posterity so much as they constitute a means of influencing contemporary society. Some seek to stabilize and perpetuate the present by negating the course of history, while others are revolutionary, looking toward the future and appealing to those forces of history that are still in the making.[29] The Holocaust Memorial, by contrast, is exclusively historical, marks the end of the principle of *fama*, and returns to the original form of cultural memory – remembrance of the dead.

HISTORIA

Origins and Memory

While *fama* looks forward to future generations who will preserve forever an event deemed to be unforgettable, memory looks backward through the veil of oblivion into the past; it follows long faded, long forgotten tracks, and reconstructs those elements that are considered important for the present. This interest in history as a source of information about one's own origins and identity came about long before the 19th century and the rise of the nation-state. The Renaissance had already witnessed a veritable boom in court and dynastic historiography. Between the 15th and 17th centuries, the "Time of the Church" with its emphasis on salvation; and the pragmatic "Time of the Merchant" with its emphasis on business, the weighing up of risks, the calculation of interest rates; were joined by a third category: "The Time of the Archivist, Chronicler and Historian," who dug down into the past in order to find the roots of the present. Their

[29] Ibid., 290 f.

research was in demand when the privileges of genealogical legiti-mation and self-determination passed from the king to princes, the nobility, the cities, and to successful members of the middle class. The research concerned the origin of a particular family or group, and it was a sign of the new pressure of competition. Once the dual authority of Emperor and Pope had been shattered, a wide variety of potential history makers came to the fore. Aristocrats, patricians, and cities could all take on an identity of their own and underpin their legitimacy through the reconstructive narrative of history.[30] This use of the past was conditioned by the "need for legitimation, repre-sentation, and identity in the competitive situation of early modern social and political movements of differentiation."[31] Jan-Dirk Müller describes this development in the context of the court,[32] while Horst Wenzel discusses it on the municipal and patrician level. Histories of origin were traced in accordance with the degree to which the his-tory makers were distinguished from one another and the monopoly of power was transferred from "the hand of God and His represen-tative on Earth, the ruler," to the feudal lords and the patricians. These secular histories deviated from the overall history of "God's grace," with the effect that the Renaissance witnessed a pluraliza-tion of histories – a process in contrast to the "unification of his-tory," a new concept that Reinhart Koselleck dates back to the late 18th century.

The pluralization of history was also linked to the expanding scope of the media. In the age of the printing press, writing opened up new areas of memory because print broke the monopoly of the Church and the court over memory, thus facilitating new modes of access to the past. This in turn unleashed new battles over what constituted

[30] Oexle, "Die Gegenwart der Lebenden und der Toten," 75 (see n. 1) includes, as par-ticipants in the construction of "group memories," families, groups of relations, the "houses" and generations of aristocrats and the bourgeoisie, monastic communities, guilds, fraternities, universities, and communes. Group memory has a dual function: first, it binds all living members to the group, and second, historical memory is a vital and constitutive element in the origin and survival of such groups.

[31] Siegfried Wiedenhofer, "Das Alte und das Neue. Tradition zwischen Humanismus and Reformation," in Stefan Rhein (ed.), *Essays for the First Award of the Melanchthon-preis*, Sigmaringen 1988, 35.

[32] Jan-Dirk Müller, *Gedechtnus. Literatur und Hofgesellschaft um Maximilian I*. Forschun-gen zur Geschichte der älteren deutschen Literatur 2, Munich 1982.

true and false memories.[33] Professional chroniclers were given the task of using the new technique of writing to authenticate the claims of the ruler. Such a function was fulfilled, for instance, by the Bavarian Chronicle, which blurred the distinction between religious memory and historical memory: "since writing is a treasure chamber, it should preserve the treasure of all honours, memories of the almightiness of God and also of our own holiness, which is the holy Christian faith, the commandments of God which He gives to all men, the effects of good and evil deeds, preserving the past and all present actions for those to come."[34]

The Historical Sense

There is a world of difference between bemoaning the mutability of the world and observing the historical changes that take place in it. An important area in which these may be experienced empirically is language change. It is therefore not unusual for historical consciousness to begin with consciousness of language. Dante referred to an image from Horace's Odes when he compared the changeability of linguistic sounds to the leaves on the trees.[35] Chaucer also emphasized this phenomenon: "Ye knowe eek, that in forme of speche is change / Withinne a thousand yeer."[36] However, as no single life span can encompass a thousand years, it is necessary to find a medium through which to record such changes. While texts written in the dead language of Latin could keep their historical forms intact, those written in the so-called vulgar languages revealed no such stability. In early modern times, the more that was written in these unfixed and unfixable languages, the more evident became the feature that escaped contemporary perception – namely, the silent process of language change. The rhythms of such changes, however, became noticeably

---

33 See Horst Wenzel, "Alls in ain summ zu pringen. Füertrers 'Bayrische Chronik' und sein 'Buch der Abenteuer' am Hof Albrechts IV.," Mittelalter-Rezeption, in Peter Wapnewski (ed.), *Ein Symposion*, Stuttgart 1986, 10–31, which deals with the wide range of historical claims and the conflict between "true and false traditions."

34 Wenzel, "Füertrers 'Bayrische Chronik,'" II.

35 Dante, *Divina Commedia, Paradiso III*, 26, verse 124 ff.

36 G. Chaucer, *Troilus and Criseyde*, Book II, verse 22 f., in *Complete Works*, ed. W. W. Skeat, London 1969, 221.

faster, and they could even be recorded during one's own lifetime. And so it was writing, which had been conceived of as a guarantee of durability, that also became a medium for the manifestation of change.

While language change happens of its own accord without any intrusive effect, changes in the domain of the law are more easily perceived and may even introduce more doubts about the stability of cultural values. At the end of the 16th century (1592), the Puritan church historian Richard Hooker had a powerful dig at the validity of Old Testament law when he stated: "That which hath been once most sufficient may wax otherwise by alteration of time and place."[37] Along with Thomas Aquinas, Hooker distinguished between three types of law: moral, ceremonial, and judicial. Of these three, only the moral – the Ten Commandments – remained valid independently of time, whereas the other two systems were considered to be subject to temporal change: ceremonial law had been superseded through Jesus Christ, and judicial law through changes in the social structure. Hooker's approach established a concept of history that separated the new from the old, the current from the obsolete, and the temporal from the eternal.

In England the Reformation shed doubt on traditions and so made people more and more aware of a distinction between the present and the past. The introduction by force of a new and binding system of values led to this distinction being radicalized, and after such a violent break it was no longer possible to look back on a normative past, which provided the roots for present-day codes. The historian Keith Thomas writes: "The dramatic rupture with the medieval past occasioned by the Reformation created a sense of separateness and of an unbridgeable divide. This made it possible to perceive the recent past, not just as a collection of founding myths and precedents, but as the embodiment of an alternative way of life and set of values."[38]

The critical light shed by Renaissance historiographers on ancient texts and sources did not instantly engender a fully fledged scientific approach to history. At this time there was neither the interest nor the

---

[37] Richard Hooker, *Laws of Ecclesiastical Policy* (1592), Book III, Sec. X, quoted from Peter Burke, "Law and the Sense of the Past," in *The Renaissance Sense of the Past*, London 1969, 32–39.
[38] Keith Thomas, *The Perception of the Past in Early Modern England*, London 1983, 9.

institutional backing for such an approach. Criticism or affirmation did not take place in any neutral setting of scientific research, but was carried out in the context of a political contest over the validity of contradictory memories. The nation-state that was emerging by writing its own history had to snatch that history from its opponents and refashion it according to its own purposes. By applying new critical standards to the evaluation of sources, the past could be recaptured from the hands of the monks and the Church. Historical scrutiny and philology thus became crucial weapons in the struggle against rival constructions of tradition. In one of his texts, to which we will return in a moment, Spenser rhymed "memory" with "forgery."[39]

At the beginning of the 17th century, the ancient historian Edmund Bolton wrote a clear outline of the ethos of critical historiography, but at the same time he also showed clearly that this was an ideal rather than an established practice:

Indifferency and even dealing are the Glory of Historians. [...] This admirable Justice and Integrity of Historians, as necessary as it is, yet is nothing in these Days farther off from Hope. For all late Authors that ever yet I could read among us convey with them, to Narrations of things done fifteen or sixteen hundred years past, the Jealousies, Passions, and Affections of their own Time. Our Historians must therefore avoid this dangerous Syren, alluring us to follow our own Prejudices, unless he mean only to serve a Side and not to serve Truth and Honesty.[40]

A sense of history developed during the Renaissance, when people became conscious of the fact that direct access to the past was blocked by forgetfulness and dislocation. This did not, however, by any means, break the normative power of the past. Sixteenth-century historiography was still largely "monumental" (to use Nietzsche's term): it examined and preserved whatever was considered worthy of remembrance, or decisive for identity, or relevant to the future. But the link to the past had to be newly created – new origins had to be found and new genealogies reconstructed to counter the effects of forgetting. Where there were no surviving documents, relics became paramount. Historical interest in these arose from the need to authenticate traditions

---

[39] Burke, *The Renaissance Sense of the Past*, 5off. (see n. 37).
[40] Edmund Bolton, "Hypercritica," 1618, in Joel Springarn (ed.), *Critical Essays of the Seventeenth Century*, Bloomington 1957, Vol. 1, 91, 93.

that helped forge identity, and the critical study of sources likewise had its roots in the effort to (de-)stabilize identity through memory. Krzysztof Pomian, in his research into the history of the cultural heritage, shows that there was a shift in the activity of collecting – from the treasure chambers of medieval churches and monasteries to the private collections of princes, which flourished between the 14th and 18th centuries, and later became part of state and national collections. This activity is closely bound to the sense of history and to the experience of change and rupture. He writes:

The history of the formation of the cultural heritage is conditioned by a series of breaks: changes in collective beliefs, ways of living, technological revolutions, advocacy of new lifestyles to replace the old. Every break deactivates the function of particular classes of artifacts and causes their relegation to the ranks of waste products, to what is abandoned and forgotten. This is what happened after the Christianization of the Roman Empire, the invasion of the barbarians, and every industrial and practically every political revolution.[41]

The Grave of Oblivion

In Chaucer's Palace of Fama, no distinction is made between poets and historians. Both groups are joined together by the task of preserving the memory of great deeds. Although Herodotus in the introduction to his history shifted the focus from what was worth remembering to what was worth knowing, he still maintained the traditional link between historiography and memory.[42]

In Elizabethan England history was a subject that poets felt was just as much their province as that of the court historians. Thomas Nashe, one of the very first professional authors, praised those poets

---

[41] Krzysztof Pomian, "Museum und kulturelles Erbe," in Gottfried Korff, Martin Roth (eds.), *Das historische Museum. Labor – Schaubühne – Identitätsfabrik*, Frankfurt a.M. 1990, 41–64; here 62.

[42] "This is the showing forth of the Inquiry of Herodotus of Halikarnassos so that neither the deeds of men may be forgotten by lapse of time, nor the works great and marvellous, which have been produced some by Hellenes and some by Barbarians, may lose their renown; and especially that the causes may be remembered for which these waged with one another." (Herodotus, *The Histories*, translated by G. C. Macaulay and revised throughout by Donald Lateiner, New York 2004, 1st Book, 3.) Cicero described historiography as a weapon against oblivion, and thus played a fundamental role in the orientation of Renaissance historiographers.

whose historical dramas successfully planted the national past in the consciousness of their contemporaries: "Our forefathers valiant acts (that haue line long buried in rustie brasse, and wormeeaten bookes) are reuiued, and they themselues raised from the Graue of Obliuion, and brought to pleade their aged Honours to open presence."[43]

The national, historical memory rises like a ghost out of this "Graue of Obliuion." The discovery of the gulf between present and past marked the invention of a national history and the construction of a collective memory, which took place in the form of a search for the past that had been lost in this gulf. Consciousness of forgetting and reconstruction of the past led to awareness, awakening, remembering, revival. The dialectics of rejection and acceptance, forgetting and remembering is at the heart of what we understand by "Renaissance."

Another example of this new interest in national memory can be gleaned once again from Edmund Spenser. There is a scene in his allegorical epic *The Faerie Queene* (1596), which he dedicated to Elizabeth I and wrote far away from the court, when the Queen had sent him to Ireland to assist in her brutal colonial campaign against the Catholic population. In the second book he relates how two knights visit a castle, which turns out to be an allegorical figure for the human body. The knights are introduced into the various parts of this architecture, and are provided with a basic course in anthropology. Their last stop is at the library, which is housed in the tower and represents human memory. There they find dust-covered folios, manuscripts, and scrolls that show the ravages of time, though in this case their worm-eaten condition authenticates their documentary value.

The two knights are deeply impressed with this site and desire to sit and read in this wonderful library. As they spend the rest of the day studying a folio, the story itself is interrupted to follow them through their reading. The two volumes are called *Briton moniments* and *Antiquitie of Fairie land*. These titles were invented by Spenser

---

[43] The printer William Caxton wrote in a similar vein: "The fruytes of virtue ben immortal, specially whanne they ben wrapped in the benefice of hystoryes." Holzknecht (ed.), *Sixteenth-Century English Prose*, New York 1954, 42. On the subject of Shakespeare's view of history, between the official Tudor version and a critical, progressive concept, see Th. Metscher, in Klaus Garber (ed.), *Nation und Literatur im Europa der frühen Neuzeit*, Tübingen 1989, 469–515.

himself; they refer to historical sagas, which are the new genre of national historiography. In the introductory proem to Book II, Spenser expressly apologizes for this act of poetic license:

Monuments, Relics and Graves

> Right well I wote most mighty Souveraine,
> That all this famous antique history,
> Of some th'aboundance of an idle braine
> Will judged be, and painted forgery,
> Rather then matter of iust memory.

"Matter of iust memory," however, is precisely what concerns Spenser – memory of a common past and common origins that will bestow an identity and underpin the state. The problem with this heroic past is only that it is hidden from view, inaccessible, and extremely questionable. The events and deeds of a great but obscure past therefore need to find confirmation through places and objects. Relics that fulfill the function of confirmation take on the status of "monuments," and so the *Briton moniments* are constantly invoked as such silent witnesses of history: "... yet of his victories / Braue moniments remaine, which yet that land enuies" (II, X, 21). These relic-monuments have the task of linking the events of a wonderful past to the real present. They are bridges across the gulf of oblivion, but they are also indicators of that gulf. One of the two readers is none other than Prince Arthur himself, who breaks off his reading with a spontaneous song of praise – not to God, but to the Motherland. It is to the Motherland that this new "patriot" owes not only his living space ("common breath") and his nourishment ("nouriture"), but also his history[44]:

> Deare country. O how dearely deare
> Ought thy remembraunce, and perpetuall band
> Be to thy foster Childe, that from thy hand

---

[44] See Edwin Greenlaw, *Studies in Spenser's Historical Allegory*, Baltimore 1932, and Hans Ulrich Seeber, "Edmund Spenser und die nationale Monarchie," in Garber (ed.), *Nation*, 453–461, 466 (see Chapt. 2, n. 43): "The separation of a national monarchy, released from universal ties, demands an originating myth of its own. [...] The typological schema of salvational history, which places Elizabeth in line with Arthur, Brutus, and the Trojans, lends to the ruling royal house the gloss of classical and divine origin."

> Did common breath and nouriture receaue?
> How brutish is it not to understand,
> How much to her we owe, that all vs gaue,
> That gaue vnto vs all, what euer good we haue.
> (II, X, 69)

Both Nashe and Spenser talk of "worme-eaten books". This is an indication that people now focus their attention on something that is not only old but also has not been used or cared for over a long period – something that was present but had been forgotten. One would scarcely add the epithet "worm-eaten" to the Bible, for example, or to the works of the Church Fathers, which were continually used in worship, interpreted in commentaries, and carefully copied in the scriptoria. Spenser's interest in memory and old libraries was connected to a new historicism that resulted from acts of secularization. Two generations earlier, Henry VIII had dissolved the monasteries and had closed most of their libraries. He had sent around a special commission whose task it was to examine the precious contents and keep those that they considered worth keeping. In 1534, John Leland was ordered "to peruse and diligently to serche al the libraries of monasteries and collegies of this yowre noble reaulme, to the intente that the monumentes of auncient writers as welle of other nations, as of this yowr owne province mighte be brought owte of deadely darkenes to lyvely lighte."[45]

The prescribed task of the antiquarian shows clearly the close connection between the break with tradition and the discovery of the past. In this case, both activities stem from one source: those who destroy the monasteries are also those who will use the broken fragments of the past to construct a new history of origins, which will emerge "oute of deadely darkenes to lyvely light." With the dissolution of the monasteries and their libraries, and the erection of new libraries, Tudor England underwent a radical restructuring of its cultural memory. The memory of the Church was replaced by new memories: those of the nation and the archive of humanist scholarship.

---

45 Leland's New-Year's Gift, in *The itinerary of John Leyland in or about the Years 1535–1543*, ed. Lucy Toulmin Smith, London 1964, Vol. I, xxxvii. See Aleida Assmann, "This blessed plot, this earth, this realm, this England. Zur Entstehung des englischen Nationalbewusstseins in der Tudorzeit," in Garber (ed.), *Nation*, 446 f. (see n. 44).

Interest in the national identity gave impetus to an archival movement that collected the remains of a forgotten past.[46] At the center of this interest was everything that could provide information about the heroic deeds of that past and the established national traditions inherited from it. Suddenly people began to discover monuments all around them.[47] The farmer plowing his field would come across the remains of a Roman water pipe, or would unearth a Bronze Age helmet. The concrete confirmation of this topographical memory became the principal preoccupation of the archivists and antiquarians. One of those who adopted this new genre that combined history, the documentation of monuments, and topographical stocktaking was a friend of Spenser's named William Camden, who wrote a book called *Britannia* (1586). Like Leland before him, Camden was an ethnographer in his own country. In his atlas of memories and customs, he compiled a kind of Baedecker, the information for which he had gleaned personally from his travels, interviews, and studies of ancient documents. He achieved for England what Flavio Biondo had earlier done for Italy.[48]

Relics that had come down into the present from a dim and distant past were accompanied by oral legends that wound around them like ivy. It was the work of the archivists to identify these relics and conscientiously record every detail. Thus there developed a kind of home-grown historical tourism, as people came to gaze at the relics of their own national history. This was where Caesar set up camp; William the Conqueror stuck his flag in there; here is the sword that cut off the head of Thomas Becket; Robin Hood drank from this stream; and King Arthur and his knights sat at this round table. The dimensions of time and space, national history and topography, were all gathered into a single landscape of national memory.

Let us now take a leap from the 16th to the 19th century and look at the renewed interest in ruins and monuments of the dead. In Goethe's *Elective Affinities*, Ottilie notes in her diary that the second life, which one enters through memory media such as stones, pictures,

---

[46] Burke, *The Renaissance*, 21 ff. (see n. 37).

[47] Thomas, *The Perception of the Past*, 4f. (see n. 38).

[48] Flavio Biondo, *Roma ristorata (1440–46)*, see Burke, *The Renaissance*, 25 f. (see n. 37).

and writings, generally lasts much longer than the first, but it is far from being unlimited:

When we see the many sunken tombstones, worn by the footsteps of church-goers, and the churches, collapsed over their own memorial-tablets for the dead – life after death seems to us, indeed, a second life which man enters in the form of the portrait and the inscription, in which he exists longer than in his life-span. But this memorial, this second existence, will also be effaced – sooner or later. Time does not relinquish its rights, either over human beings or over monuments.[49]

While the remains of past cultures and eras are to be found in ruins, those of past generations are to be found in graves. The nocturnal thoughts that moved an 18th-century English poet in a country churchyard centered on fame and forgetting. For Thomas Gray, the life of the dead people buried there had passed forever. The visitor might try to use the meager remnants in order to conjure up individual scenes from these past lives, but they can only remain anonymous general images conjured up by the imagination and not by the memory. To this he adds a reflection on the leveling power of death:

> The boast of heraldry, the pomp of pow'r,
> And all that beauty, all that wealth e'er gave,
> Awaits alike th'inevitable hour.
> The paths of glory lead but to the grave.[50]

While Death is the great democrat bestowing the same fate on everyone, fame – as we saw in Ariosto's image of the swans – is the great selector, the filter that immortalizes the names of some and extinguishes those of others. Of the dead that are buried in Gray's churchyard, posterity has kept no memory, but they are still included in the communal church service:

> Not you, ye Proud, impute to These the fault,
> If Mem'ry o'er their Tomb no trophies raise,

---

[49] Johann Wolfgang Goethe, *Elective Affinites*, translated by Elisabeth Mayer and Louise Bogan, Chicago 1963, 159.

[50] Thomas Gray, "Elegy Written in a Country Churchyard," in Arthur Johnston (ed.), *Selected Poems of Thomas Gray and William Collins*, London 1967, 40–50.

> Where thro' the long-drawn isle and fretted vault
> The pealing anthem swells the note of praise.
>
> (37–40)

Where *fama* has no rights, the Christian cult of the dead remains steadfast. For the "short and simple annals of the poor" no literary Muse is needed; name, dates, and a few pious words at the graveside replace the urge for earthly self-immortalization.

> Their name, their years, spelt by th'unletter'd muse,
> The place of fame and elegy supply:
> And many a holy text around she strews,
> That teach the rustic moralist to die.
>
> (81–84)

Particularly revealing are the thoughts concerning the conditions of fame that fill the second part of the poem. The visitor reflects on the fact that extraordinary deeds and qualities obviously exist independently of fame, and he wonders how many unsung heroes might lie buried in this churchyard:

> Full many a gem of purest ray serene,
> The dark unfathom'd caves of ocean bear;
> Full many a flower is born to blush unseen,
> And waste its sweetness on the desert air.
> Some village-Hampden, that with dauntless breast
> The little Tyrant of his fields withstood;
> Some mute inglorious Milton here may rest,
> Some Cromwell guiltless of his country's blood.
>
> (53–60)

In the first version of his poem, Gray chose Cato, Cicero, and Caesar as the archetypes of fame, which in the second version he replaced with native names. The march of fame across the borders of culture, from the timeless classics to contemporary national history, comes to a halt before the ordinary folk in the country churchyard. The heroes that are buried here remained virtual, not because they lacked the qualities of greatness, but because the constraints of their environment did not allow them to develop and fulfill their greatness. Their insignificance is due to the circumstances of their lives, but fate, which prevented these peasants' sons from reading "their hist'ry in a nation's eye," is not criticized, because the visitor is convinced that the price of greatness is too high. Fame only follows those who aspire to greatness, and more often than not greatness comes with single-mindedness, ruthlessness, cruelty, and blindness. Greatness is the cause of much suffering, both for those who consider themselves to be heroes, and for those who are ruled by them.

With this evaluation of greatness as something ambivalent, and even socially dangerous, *fama* has undergone a radical change. Gray's "Elegy," the third and final section of which anticipates the death of the visitor himself, ends with an epitaph for the unknown poet: "A Youth to Fortune and to Fame unknown." The poem is a double monument: it establishes and confirms the fame of the canonical poet Thomas Gray, and it anticipates a paradox that is central to the modern age: the fame of an unknown. It commemorates the many nameless and forgotten people, reminding us of the general course of oblivion.

The degree to which the fame of the few feeds off the anonymity of the many has been demonstrated in an essay by Thomas Laqueur.[51] In Shakespeare's plays of war, battles are usually concluded with a kind of balance sheet, listing the dead. On such occasions, it is generally just a few names that are announced and mourned for, and they are always characters from the old aristocracy, who are deemed worthy of remembrance as bearers of a collective name. The vast majority of fallen soldiers are not mentioned and remain anonymous. They have no place in political remembrance of the dead. "None else of name" is the harsh formula that ends public commemoration of the fallen heroes after Shakespeare's battles.

The fact that cultural memory of proper names is an exclusive privilege has also been borne out by feminist research, for instance, in relation to authorship. Barbara Hahn has shown "that an author's name is definitely not something natural, but is the effect of writing within a specific system of text production."[52] The question of whether a work will be confined to the short-term memory of the book market or accepted in the long-term memory of canonized texts depends on

[51] Thomas Laqueur, "Von Agincourt bis Flandern: Nation, Name und Gedächtnis," in Uli Bielefeld and Gisela Engel (eds.), *Bilder der Nation. Kulturelle Konstruktionen der Nationalen am Beginn der europäischen Moderne*, Hamburg 1998.

[52] Barbara Hahn, *Unter falschem Namen. Von der schwierigen Autorschaft der Frauen*, Frankfurt a.M. 1991, 8.

social institutions of conservation and desecration, honor and rejection. Feminist research has penetrated into the general consciousness, and has come up with the insight that "greatness" is a predicate made by men for men. In the late 18th century, Gray observed that the light of *fama* never shone upon the poor or the marginalized members of society; we now observe that it never or rarely falls on women either. No matter what the names may be – Cato, Cicero, and Caesar; or Hampden, Milton and Cromwell – in the annals of history, fame and women are rarely found together. At every social level, women form the anonymous background against which male glory shines all the more brightly. As long as entry into the cultural memory is conditioned by heroism or canonization, women systematically disappear into cultural oblivion. It is a classic case of structural amnesia.

3

The Battle of Memories in Shakespeare's Histories

The connection between memory and identity has taken on new relevance since the 1980s. This is due to the abolition and reconstruction of political and cultural borders all over the world. In Europe, the lifting of the barriers between East and West brought to an end an era of memories frozen under the ice of two rigidly opposed doctrines. In the East, ethnic identities made a comeback, along with "their languages, cultures, histories, and gods." This unexpected development was described as the "return" or the "awakening" of history.[1] In this context, the term "history" did not refer to the academic study of the past, but was seen as a live, or newly inspired collective consciousness, a "remembered past." In this form it became almost overnight a primary force for political mobilization. Instead of "emancipation," which linked the promise of future self-determination with a break from the past and from origins, the key word became "identity." "Who am I?" was the leading question, and even more significantly, "Who are we?" Self-definition meant establishing one's sexual, ethnic, and political position. In this context, Teresa de Lauretis, a feminist literary theorist, defined identity as "an active construction and a discursively mediated political interpretation of one's history."[2] In other words, we define

---

[1] Frank Schirrmacher (ed.), *Im Osten erwacht die Geschichte: Essays zur Revolution in Mittel- und Osteuropa*, Stuttgart 1990; Krzysztof Michalski (ed.), *Rückkehr der Geschichte, Transit – Europäische Revue* 2, Frankfurt a.M. 1991.

[2] Teresa de Lauretis, "The Essence of the Triangle or, Taking the Rise of Essentialism Seriously: Feminist Theory in Italy, the U.S. and Britain," *Differences* I, 1991, 12.

ourselves through that which collectively we remember and forget.[3]
A reconstruction of identity always entails a reconstruction of memory, which applies as much to communities as it does to individuals.
It takes place through the rewriting of history books, the demolition
of monuments, and the renaming of official buildings, streets, and
squares. The reunited Germany of the 1990s thus found itself newly
confronted by a problem of identity and memory. Which unified German memories were to be retained, and which discarded?

The awakening of history and the return of memories were greeted
euphorically in 1989 as a "new complexity, a new wealth of differences, nuances, interconnections and tensions."[4] We now know that
the end of the bipolarity of the Cold War did not immediately "bring to
light the infrastructure of civilized Europe," but instead brought out
the bloodstained maps of older battlefields. The return of obsolete
borders and new enemy stereotypes also depends on the release and
political manipulation of memories. This tangle of virulent memories
has no difficulty mixing recent ones of unpaid scores from the two
world wars with epic traditions reaching back over centuries. The Battle of Amselfeld, a national myth and political landmark for the Serbs,
preceded the Battle of Agincourt by twenty-six years, but one can
hardly imagine the French turning this defeat into a landmark of
foundational memory and national identity the way the Serbs did.
Today it would seem that the Cold War barriers between East and
West have given way to a new, invisible dividing line that separates the
industrialized nations with their ethos of "continuous obsolescence,
dumping and erasure" from those societies where the forces of tradition have remained as effective as ever.[5] Perhaps we can even speak of

---

[3] Ernest Renan defines the nation as a collection of individuals who have a great deal
in common and have also forgotten a great deal in common: "Or l'essence d'une
nation est que tous les individus aient beaucoup de choses en commun, et aussi que
tous aient oublié bien des choses." Quoted by Anderson, *Imagined Communities*, 15
(see Chapt. 2, n. 18).

[4] Karl Schlögel, "Der dramatische Übergang zu einer neuen Normalität – Europa am
Ende der Nachkriegszeit," in Schirrmacher (ed.), *Im Osten erwacht die Geschichte*, 37
(see n.1).

[5] See Botho Strauss, "Anschwellender Bockgesang," *Der Spiegel*, 8.2, 1993, 6/47, 202–
207; here 203. Also Dubravka Oraic Tolic, *FAZ*, 17.5,1993, No. 113, 13: "With its
project for a limitlessly technologized focus on the present, the West cannot see
the people of Bosnia-Herzegovina as subjects defined by fate, who have the right to

a new polarity between societies that prefer to forget and those that like to remember.

In this chapter, I try to show that Shakespeare's Histories deal with problems that are not so very far removed from those of the present. My main thesis is that the real actors in these dramas are memories. They come into play whenever actions are motivated, legitimized, or interpreted, and whenever there is a meaning to be attributed to the world. We will see that memory is the secret agent at the very heart of history and power, just as it is the defining element of personal and collective identity. We will look at the dynamics of memory in Shakespeare's history plays from three perspectives:

1) the link between memory and personal identity demonstrating its notorious instability and malleability, as well as the factors that condition its basic availability or unavailability;

2) the link between memory and history, focusing on the political exploitation of historical memories and on the possibility or impossibility of putting an end to malignant memories;

3) the link between memory and nationhood, showing the important contribution made by Shakespeare's plays to a new construction of history, and examining the circumstances under which a new nation needs a history.

MEMORY AND IDENTITY

This study of memory in Shakespeare's Histories begins with its most obvious manifestation – for example, in individual characters. Memory is among the most unreliable of all human faculties. Present affects and goals shape human remembering and forgetting, for they are the gatekeepers that determine what will or will not be accessible at any given moment. "As he who acts," according to Nietzsche, is "without a conscience" in the sense of "without knowledge."[6] By this he means that at the moment of action, the person who acts has only a small part of his knowledge and of his memories at his disposal, and never

---

remember their past and to defend that past as a guarantee of their present and their future."

[6] Friedrich Nietzsche, "On the Uses and Disadvantages of History for Life," *Untimely Meditations*. Part Two, trans. R. J. Hollingdale, Cambridge 1983, 57–123; here 64.

the full complement. It is precisely this selectivity of memories that makes man fundamentally limited and biased, but at the same time it also makes him capable of action. "He forgets most things so as to do one thing, he is unjust towards what lies behind him, and recognizes the rights only of that which is now to come into being and no other rights whatever."[7] This unjust forgetting is countered by the morality of conscience, but that is not very reliable either.

Nietzsche famously praised the power of forgetting as people's ability to protect themselves against their own damaging or distracting memories – a faculty that he showed to be strikingly lacking in Hamlet. But what Nietzsche saw as a positive force was regarded by Shakespeare as a fault. This is made clear in the final scene of *Richard III* in which we listen to the unhappy Edward IV. In this scene forgetting and remembering come together in a startling clash: Edward is painfully aware that he has forgotten most things to do one thing, that he has been unjust toward what is behind him, and has recognized only one law – the law of that which had to be done. His fears and the need to protect himself have made him susceptible to intrigue: he had been quite prepared to see his brother in the dark light that Gloucester had thrown on him, and he had forgotten the many debts of gratitude he owed to Clarence: the latter's defection from Warwick's camp, saving his life at the Battle of Tewksbury, and all the tokens of brotherly love:

> All this from my remembrance brutish wrath
> Sinfully pluck'd, and not a man of you
> Had so much grace to put it in my mind.[8]
> (R. III, II,1, 119–121)

His counselors share the guilt of this forgetfulness, for they should have reminded him of the faded memories. It is clear that Shakespeare does not idealize the partiality of memory but, on the contrary, shows that the maturity and wisdom of a man will appear in the degree to which he gives access to his own inopportune memories and is able to integrate them.

---

[7] Ibid.

[8] William Shakespeare, *King Richard III*, ed. Antony Hammond, Arden Edition of the Works of William Shakespeare, London, New York 1981.

Anger and fear make people forget, as is evident from the example of Edward; hatred and revenge, however, sharpen the memory. Gratitude does not remain as deeply imprinted on the memory as do injustice and dishonor.[9] The latter do not fade; and therefore the problem arises as to how one can free oneself from them. Under certain circumstances, for the personal process of maturing, forgetting the past can be just as important as remembering it.[10]

A vivid example of such circumstances is provided by the scene in which Henry V makes his first appearance at court as king. The closest friends and advisers of the dead king look on this change of rule with considerable apprehension – most of all the Lord Chief Justice, who as the great upholder of the law had strongly criticized the prince for his shiftless, not to say lawless, lifestyle. He is resigned to a catastrophic revolution: "O God! I fear all will be overturn'd!" His fears are plain to see, and when challenged by Henry, he goes on the attack, to the effect that if the law is to remain in force, the new king will have "no just cause to hate me." At first Henry is shocked, and makes it clear that a whole series of humiliating memories stand between them:

> How might a prince of my great hopes forget
> So great indignities you laid upon me?
> What! Rate, rebuke, and roughly send to prison
> Th'immediate heir of England! Was this easy?
> May this be wash'd in Lethe and forgotten?[11]
>
> (2 H IV, V,2, 68–72)

But again the Lord Chief Justice responds to the challenge with one of his own: "Your Highness pleased to forget my place, / The majesty and power of law and justice." What takes place in this scene is a radical reconstruction of identity acted out through the medium of remembering and forgetting. The process takes place in three stages, each of which entails a metaphorical switch in the relationship between father and son. Initially, the new king offers himself to those who are

---

9 "Most necessary 'tis that we forget / To pay ourselves what to ourselves is debt," says the Player King in *Hamlet* III, 2, 187–188, ed. Harold Jenkins, Arden Edition, London, New York 1982, 299.

10 Harald Weinrich has written a cogent and penetrating book on this subject: *Lethe, Kunst und Kritik des Vergessens*, Munich 1997; Engl. trans. Steven Rendall: *Lethe: The Art and Critique of Forgetting* (see Introduction, n. 5).

11 *The Second Part of Henry IV*, ed. A. R. Humphreys, Arden Edition, London 1966.

mourning the death of his father as a comforting father figure on his own account: "I'll be your father and your brother too; / Let me but bear your love, I'll bear your cares." In the course of this encounter, though, the Lord Chief Justice tells him to imagine himself as a father with a son who scorns the dignity of his royal rank: "Be now the father and propose a son [. . .] / Behold yourself so by a son disdain'd." And finally Henry reaches out his hand to his adversary, with the words: "There is my hand. / You shall be as a father to my youth."

It is not enough that the *legality* of the succession is established; the new ruler must also prove his *legitimacy* in terms of his own personal worth. This proof is provided by the change of identity that is drama- tized here as a battle of memories. Those of the prince, which consist of his humiliating experiences at the hands of the Lord Chief Justice, must be refashioned into those of the new king, whose duty it is to uphold the law that had previously condemned him. The seal is set on his legitimacy only when he spontaneously debases himself from his position as symbolic father to that of humble son, from all-powerful sovereign to willing recipient of wise counsel. With the handshake – an astonishing gesture by a king who wields absolute power – might gives way to right. So far, so good. But there is a high price to pay for this identity change, which is the subsequent harsh and uncompromis- ing rejection of his former companions. Once Prince Hal has become King Henry, he brusquely turns his back on his old friend Falstaff, and early memories are banished like a bad dream:

> I know thee not, old man. Fall to thy prayers.
> How ill white hairs become a fool and jester!
> I have long dreamt of such a kind of man,
> So surfeit-swell'd, so old, and so prophane;
> But, being awak'd I do despise my dream.
> (2 H IV; V,5, 47–51)

Such reshaping of memory in the service of "identity work" is very different from the opportunistic manipulation of memory carried out by Richard III. He is as masterly at twisting memories as he is at staging emotions. A particularly striking example of this is the scene in which he asks Queen Elizabeth, the grieving widow whose sons he has murdered, for her daughter's hand in marriage. He declares this shameless effrontery to be an act of reparation for (alleged) past wrongs, and piously recommends the healing powers of forgetfulness:

> So in the Lethe of thy angry soul
> Thou drown the sad remembrance of those wrongs
> Which thou supposest I have done to thee.
>
> (R III; IV, 4, 251–253)

However, she does the precise opposite. She reminds him of all his bloody deeds, eliciting from him the dismissive response: "Harp not on that string, madam; that is past." As the guilty party, he has the strongest possible motive to get rid of the past and exchange it for the future: "Plead what I will be, not what I have been; / Not my deserts, but what I will deserve." For Elizabeth, however, forgetting would be a destruction of her own identity: "Shall I forget to be myself?" This is exactly what he is aiming at, and as soon as her resisting memories give way to his forceful temptations he can ridicule her as a "shallow, changing woman." However, later, even Richard III cannot rid himself so easily of his memories. The ghosts that visit him during the night before the last battle may be interpreted as the resurfacing of suppressed memories, and the Elizabethans would have seen them as the instances of guilt with which conscience confronts the sinner in order to give him one last chance to repent his sins.[12] But Richard resists even this final onslaught of memory by simply amputating his conscience: "Conscience is but a word that cowards use" (V, 3, 310).

At this point, it might be useful to say a few words about the memories of women in Shakespeare.[13] As the objects of men's love, they are as fickle as the widow Elizabeth; as the survivors of husbands and sons who have generally met a violent death, however, they are the personification of obstinate memories of suffering and the desire for

---

[12] On the subject of conscience as the last instance of resistant memories, Polydor Vergil wrote: "a conscyence ... which, thowght at none other time, yeat in the last day of owr life ys woont to represent to us the memory of our sinnes commyttid, and withall to shew unto us the paynes immynent for the same, that, being uppon good cause penytent at that instant for our evell led lyfe, we may be compellyd to go hence to heavynes of hart." Quoted from Lily B. Campbell, *Shakespeare's Histories: Mirrors of Elizabethan Policy*, San Marino 1947, 60 f.

[13] A detailed analysis of this subject is to be found in Nicole Loraux, "Mothers in Mourning," Ithaca, London 1998 (Series: *Myth and Poetics*, ed. by Gregory Nagy), which also covers Shakespeare's history plays.

revenge. Apart from Joan of Arc, virtually no female characters in the Histories are killed either on or off stage.[14] In the new historical present, they are the bearers of grief and hate carried over from a former time that will not fade away. They are the "remembrancers" (a medieval euphemism for debt-collectors).[15] They are also "Furies of remembrance," who carry around with them traumatic images of guilt and terror – a role that is particularly striking in the first and last plays of the two tetralogies. In *Richard II* it is the widow of the murdered Thomas Gloucester who brings past horrors into the present and demands revenge. In *Richard III* the role is taken over by Queen Margaret, though she plays no active part but instead simply commentates, rather like a Greek chorus. She is an allegory of the accumulated burden of guilt, and her presence in the first and fourth acts shows clearly that the overwhelming force of these virulent memories can no longer be contained. They express themselves through prophecies of doom, and Margaret herself – who boasts before the other women about the duration and degree of her suffering – acts as their bookkeeper; she not only describes them but also counts them and sets them off against those of others. She is the personification of Nemesis, the avenging, living memory of the civil war. Her hour of triumph comes with the general downfall that signals the end of the civil war.

MEMORY AND HISTORY

The memories of the women cast a dark shadow over the present, as do the vengeful memories of the men. They are the fuel for the fatal engine of civil war, because the enmity is nourished by characters who cannot forget.[16] One prominent bearer of vengeful memories is old Mortimer, who on his deathbed passes them on to his nephew, Richard Plantagenet of York (I H V1; II, 5). It is this genealogy of hate

---

[14] The one exception is perhaps Anne Neville, widow of the young Edward and later married to Richard III.

[15] Peter Burke, "History as Social Memory," in Thomas Butler (ed.), *Memory, History, Culture and the Mind*, Oxford 1989, 97–113; here 110.

[16] Machiavelli warns the conqueror of a city to beware the memory of its inhabitants, which cannot be conquered quite so easily: "Whatever a conqueror may do or try to prevent: the inhabitants will never forget – unless torn apart and dispersed – their freedom and their old memories and will invoke them at every opportunity." Niccolò Machiavelli, *The Prince*, Oxford 1984, 19.

memories that maintains the impetus for the various rebellions and later the Wars of the Roses.

Shakespeare begins his cycle of plays with a scene in which the ruler is unable to keep memories under control. Richard II's efforts to settle the quarrel between Bolingbroke and Mowbray and broker a peace are unsuccessful, because the battle of memories has now gone too far. Other rulers after him will also fail. Richard's solution for an end to the feud is as simple as it is impractical: "Forget, forgive, conclude and be agreed" (R II; I, 1; 156). If people could forget according to the command of a king, there would be no more plots, misunderstandings, or disasters, and everyone would live happily and unhistorically ever after. However, it transpires that the feudal commandment to remember dishonor outweighs the monarch's instruction to forget it, and so there will have to be a duel, and God will decide who is the winner. The king dismisses his cousin Bolingbroke with the words: "Lament we may, but not revenge thee dead" (R II; I, 3, 58). If Bolingbroke loses, only one form of memory will be allowed, and that will be mourning – remembrance of the dead; the other kind of memory as the spur to revenge is strictly forbidden. Remembrance and resentment are two forms of memory that provide very different stimuli. When history perpetuates a violent combination of guilt and revenge, the only solution is to find a way to limit and calm the virulent recollections that keep the fatal process going. Settling disputes and establishing peace can therefore only be done by taming, containing, and eventually transforming collective memories.

Richard's futile command to "forgive, forget, conclude, and be agreed" is basically the privilege of the king, who in his high office plays the role of the Almighty as history's accountant. He is God's representative on Earth, and as such he incorporates the divine qualities of wrath and clemency. By ordering the two parties to forget, he can break the self-perpetuating chain of violence. The power to erase political guilt comes under the heading of "amnesty," but this *clementia* or "lenity" has nothing to do with individual emotions – it is a public, legal act. Relations that have been poisoned by guilt and revenge are purged by royal forgetting, which will lead to the offer of a new beginning. It is as if the slate of history is wiped clean. Amnesty, however, is not to be confused with amnesia, which is an amorphous, unconscious, and aimless forgetting, whereas amnesty is deliberate and

purposeful – a form of self-assertion and even censorship, because
it bans the public circulation of devisive memories within society.[17]
Amnesty breaks the destructive link between guilt and revenge, and it
is a vital precondition for a new age of peace.[18]

However, the problem still remains as to how the order to forget can
possibly be implemented. Usually rebels will not even trust a royal offer
of amnesty, because they are afraid that from then on the poisoned
atmosphere will preclude any kind of trust, and doubt and suspicion
will undermine all protestations of loyalty. Worcester is unwilling even
to pass on the king's offer of amnesty:

> It is not possible, it cannot be,
> The king should keep his word in loving us;
> He will suspect us still.[19]
>
> (1 H IV; V, 2, 407)

In 2 Henry IV, the Archbishop of York is more trusting, and explains
the principles of amnesty in some detail, not realizing that in this case
they are being used as a fatal strategy against the enemy:

> No, no, my lord, note this: the King is weary
> Of dainty and such picking grievances;
> For he hath found to end one doubt by death
> Revives two greater in the heirs of life:

---

[17] There is a revealing extract from Johannes Gross's notebook, N.F. 87, continued
in the magazine of *Die Zeit*: "'Nie davon sprechen, immer daran denken!' [Never
speak about it, always think about it!] This was a well-known and much quoted
aphorism said to stem from French revanchism after the annexation of Alsace-
Lothringen in 1871. It was a German version of the French 'Pensons-y toujours,
n'en parlons jamais,' which Gambetta included in his Chambéry speech in 1872,
laying emphasis on the second part of the exhortation: 'n'en parlons jamais.' This
diplomatic formulation led Clemenceau in the late 1870s to criticize Gambetta for
preparing the way for reconciliation between France and Germany through a subtle
acceptance of relinquishment. The expression became proverbial only in Germany;
it is rarely to be found in French compilations of quotes."

[18] Nicole Loreaux, "L'oubli dans la cité," in *Le Temps de la Réflexion* I (1980), discusses
law in Athenian polis, which punished anyone who raised the subject again after a
legally binding settlement. See also: "De l'amnestie et de son contraire," in *Usages de
l'oubli*, Paris 1988, 24–26; Lucian Hölscher, "Geschichte und Vergessen," *Historische
Zeitschrift*, No, 249 (1989), 1–17.

[19] William Shakespeare, *The First Part of King Henry IV*, ed. A. R. Humphreys, Arden
Edition, London 1960.

> And therefore will he wipe his tables clean.
> And keep no tell-tale to his memory
> That may repeat and history his loss
> To new remembrance.
>
> (2 H IV; IV,1, 197–204)

Shakespeare also draws attention to another complication in the principle of amnesty. The ruler can only show leniency and grant amnesty if there is no personal guilt involved. If he himself has done wrong, then he can only appeal to a higher power to forget and forgive. This is Richard II's situation, and his appeal founders because of his guilt. He refuses to read out the list of his crimes in an act of self-incrimination because this would legalize his dethronement, and instead of carrying out the ritual of public confession, he indulges in a spontaneous interpretation of his own reflection in the mirror with a theatrical, self-conscious cleverness that evades any true confrontation with himself and the problem of conscience. His successor, the usurper Bolingbroke, is also riddled with guilt, and as a king has to live under the dark cloud of his memories.[20] The basis of his kingship is the burden of a guilty conscience that he hopes to alleviate by an act of penance. This is to take the form of a crusade to Jerusalem, through which he hopes that the two factions in the civil war will unite to fight against an external enemy, the heathen. Thus the crusade is not a religious mission so much as a political strategy to divert attention away from internal disputes and onto a common cause.[21] Henry

---

[20] A characteristic feature of his bad conscience is insomnia. His inability to sleep is also his inability to forget:

> O sleep! O gentle sleep!
> Nature's soft nurse, how have I frighted thee,
> That thou no more will weigh my eyelids down
> And steep my senses in forgetfulness.
>
> (2 H IV; III, 1, 5 ff.)

Thomas More describes Richard III as a king haunted by sleeplessness and "stormy remembrance," see *The English Works*, ed. W. E. Campbell, London, New York 1927–1931, I, 433.

[21] The doctrine of the aggressive foreign policy has been repeated at many different times. In the 19th century, Carlyle diverted internal conflicts outward by neutralizing the problem of class conflict through an emphasis on race. According to him, the Teutonic race (Saxondom) was destined to rule the world.

IV sums up this political lesson in his deathbed instructions to his son:

> Therefore, my Harry,
> Be it thy course to busy giddy minds
> With foreign quarrels, that action hence borne out
> May waste the memory of the former days.
>
> (1 H IV; IV, 5, 212–215)

Henry IV hopes the crown that had lain uneasy on his head will be passed unsullied to his son, who will receive it as his legitimate successor and not as a usurper. His greatest desire is that the guilt attached to it will go with him to his grave.

In Shakespeare's historical cosmos, however, guilt is not confined to the individual; it sets in motion a chain of cause and effect that reaches far beyond the fate of one man. The son must therefore expect the father's guilt to rebound on him, and so he is forced to remember history, bear the guilt of others, and perform the requisite rituals of atonement. In his prayer before the all-important Battle of Agincourt, Henry V appeals to God to forget the sins of his father:

> Not to-day, O Lord!
> O not to-day, think not upon the fault
> My father made in compassing the crown![22]
>
> (H V; IV, 1, 298–300)

He goes on to list the rites that he has performed in order to elicit God's merciful forgetfulness: he has reburied Richard II's body with all due ceremony and contrite tears, built two chantries for him, and in his memory given lots of money to the poor.

There is one more way in which *Henry V* is highly relevant to our search for connections between memory and history. We look in more detail later at the memories engraved on the bodies of soldiers, but for the moment we take just one example of this medium of memory: it is a scene right at the beginning of the play, which shows very clearly how history is made out of memories. The Archbishop of Canterbury and the Bishop of Ely express their fear that the crown, whose finances

---

[22] William Shakespeare, *King Henry V*, ed. T. W. Craik, Arden Edition, London 1995.

are notoriously weak, might confiscate the treasures of the Church. In order to avert such a disaster, they call on the ambitious king to remember Salic Law. They embody the functions of legal advisers, archivists, and philologists, and act as authoritative guardians of the historical heritage. It is their interpretation of the legal documents that will give legitimacy to political claims, and because the consequences of their readings can be so grave, these must be beyond all suspicion of falsehood. The truthfulness of historical research is, of course, not yet subject to methodological testing, as in the age of source criticism, but is still entirely dependent on the conscience of the interpreter. The Archbishop delivers a scholarly history lesson to the king about genealogies, territorial divisions, and the laws of succession going back over the last 500 years. The king takes his political decisions in accordance with this history lesson. His motive for attacking France and expanding his territory is justified by memories of events that go back over 500 years. This is a vivid illustration of Nietzsche's dictum "[T]hat life is in need of the services of history"[23] and of Hans Blumenberg's observation that tradition consists not of relics but of legacies and testaments. The scene puts into practice the principle of "historical fundamentalism."[24]

A similar method of acquiring present legitimacy by way of the past is to invoke mythical paradigms. In this context, Nietzsche spoke of a monumental past that is indistinguishable from mythical fiction. "Monumental history," he wrote, "deceives through analogy; it uses seductive similarities to entice the brave to rashness, and the enthusiast to fanaticism."[25] Henry is reminded of his glorious ancestors, who fought and won great battles on French soil. He is duty bound to emulate the deeds of Edward III, and his son Edward the Black Prince: "Awake remembrance of these valiant dead, / And with your puissant arm renew their feats" (H V; I,2, 115–116). *Historia magistra vitae* or, to be more precise, *historia magistra regis* – history is the textbook from which the king learns his lessons. These lessons are applied on the bloody battlefield of power politics.

---

[23] Nietzsche, "On the Uses and Disadvantages of History," 67 (see n. 6).
[24] Hans Blumenberg, *Die Lesbarkeit der Welt*, Frankfurt a.M. 1981, 375.
[25] Nietzsche, "On the Uses and Disadvantages of History," 67 (see n. 6).

MEMORY AND NATIONHOOD

The old concept of history consisted mainly in preserving memory. Elizabethan historiographers took this definition over from Herodotus and Cicero and described their work as a battle against the arch enemy oblivion.[26] The connection was made by the classical goddess of Fama, whose task it was to record historic deeds through oral tradition, poetry, or history books. Julius Caesar is the embodiment of the historical hero who ensured that his actions would not be forgotten by writing his own personal record of them. "Fame" and "valour" were the terms used by Shakespeare's contemporaries in their emphasis on the patriotic function of the Histories as an epic account of the nation's history.[27] As befitted their time, they stressed the exemplary, educational function of poetry, which presented larger-than-life models that were to be either imitated or shunned. Subsequently, the didactic element mingled with the propagandist, and it is scarcely surprising that these aspects of the plays are of little interest to us today. Historians such as Eric Hobsbawm and sociologists like Benedict Anderson have shed new light on the connection between nation-building and historical memory, using terms like "invented traditions" and "imagined communities," and so the old questions can now be addressed in new ways.[28] With this approach, cultural fictions appear not as falsehoods needing to be unmasked but as myths that underpin history. In this context, one can distinguish five factors that mark the new concept of history in Shakespeare's plays.

1) *The end of historical fundamentalism* – There is a wide gap separating Shakespeare's time from the historical periods that the plays

---

[26] Edward Halle, court chronicler of the Tudor dynasty (*The Union of the two noble houses . . .* , Fols. ccli f.) called oblivion "the ancard enemie," "the suckyng serpent," "the deadly darte," "the defacer."

[27] See Thomas Nashe, *Pierce Penilesse his Supplication to the Diuell*, in *Works*, ed. R. B. McKerrow, I, 212 f. Thomas Heywood, *An Apology for Actors*, London 1612, Scholars' Facsimiles & Reprints, New York 1941. Patriotic memories could easily be integrated with political propaganda in order to lay emphasis on English superiority. This is why during the Anglo-French wars the tetralogies were once again immensely popular, and indeed one of Richard III's tirades (V, 3, 328 ff.) actually drew a round of applause as it articulated the xenophobia of the time. See A. C. Sprague, *Shakespeare's Histories – Plays for the Stage*, London 1964, 3.

[28] Eric Hobsbawm and Terence Ranger (eds.), *The Invention of Tradition*, Cambridge 1983; Anderson, *Imagined Communities*, (see Chapt. 2, n. 18).

recall. The reconciliation between enemies that Richard II was unable to effect did not take place until a hundred years later, through Henry VII. The Tudors broke the historical chain of disasters arising out of those memories, and their "posthistory" staged the monarchy as a kind of mythical golden age that was independent of the past. They represented a new dawn, and developed a new relationship with the past that entailed unlearning previous usages of historical memory. Now it was no longer possible to use worm-eaten documents as an historical justification for power politics, because the monarchy had become part of a new order – that of the nation-state, in which ancient pieces of parchment had become obsolete or "historical." Once the past had receded into history, it could no longer be used as a basis for political aspirations or as a blueprint for future action.[29]

2) *From feudal to national memory* – The new nation needed to separate itself from old memories. These related primarily to Nemesis and Fama – vengeance and glory, as the dominant forces of the old feudal system of memory. In the feudal order, people were not viewed as individuals but as bearers of a name and links in a chain. A person took on his identity in relation to the whole, of which he was just a part, because individuals were transient, whereas the genealogical line and the family name were immortal. Within this set of values, the name was all important, and it must be shielded from shame, its honor and glory safeguarded at all times. Other values, including the integrity of the body, were subordinate to this code; it was a basic tenet of feudal ethics that the individual must be prepared to die in order to protect the good name of his family.

With this obligation to remember, the feudal ethic was quite literally a dead end for the vast majority, because it offered as little to the individual as to the general community. All it did was guarantee the identity of the powerful aristocratic families, thus protecting a social hierarchy that had to be dismantled to make way for the absolutist, territorial state of early modern times. In England the concept of the

---

[29] Macaulay compares France, which freed itself from its history through its Revolution, to England, where there was no corresponding break between the old and the new. "But where history is regarded as a repository of titledeeds, on which the rights of governments and nations depend, the motive to falsification becomes almost irresistible." Thomas Babington Macaulay, *The History of England from the Accession of James II*, Vol. I, London, New York 1907, 27.

nation evolved simultaneously with that of the absolutist state, and the new guiding principle that bypassed (but did not abolish) social rank was patriotism. In this context, national history became a common point of reference; the conflicting feudal memories were replaced with history as the collective, national genealogy of the English people.

Separating oneself from old memories does not necessarily mean forgetting them. "Forgive, forget, conclude, and be agreed" may have been the motto with which the Histories began, but ultimately it was not the forgiving and forgetting that united former foes but the shared memory of the nation, which was recorded in the Tudor history books. In these works, old memories were inherited, but they were also transformed. The chronicler Halle wrote in the dedication to his history of the civil war: "What nobleman of the most ancient origin, whose family history would not have been contaminated by this separation!"[30] Shakespeare transformed the history books of his time into works of art, in which feudal memory is transformed into national memory, the feudal code into a national code. In the light of this history, the individual sees himself as part of an all-embracing identity, whereas sanctification through bloodshed and legitimation through origins are replaced by identification with a common history. The feudal worship of a name gives way to the patriotic worship of one's country, and family pride is superseded by national pride.[31]

3) *Historical memory and the formation of national identity* – All of this completely changed the use that was made of history. Until then, as we have seen, works of history were commissioned by kings and written for the benefit of kings, because they alone were its "makers." Now, it was the nation as well as the king that became the subject of history, and it was written both for and about the nation. With the people being the addressees of history, the memory of it underwent a radical structural change. It no longer served principally to instruct

---

[30] Edward Halle, *Dedication to the King, The Union of the Two Noble and Illustre Families*, quoted from Lily B. Campbell, *Shakespeare's Histories: Mirrors of Elizabethan Policy*, London 1964, 69.

[31] This is also the view of Zdenek Stribrny, "Henry V and History," in Arnold Kettle (ed.), *Shakespeare in a Changing World: 12 Essays for the 400th Anniversary of his Birth*, London 1964. He writes: "[...] the whole conflict between France and England is presented as an encounter between the surviving feudal order and the English nation-state as it developed in Shakespeare's own time."

or legitimize the ruler, but instead it helped to fashion a collective identity. Nietzsche described this function as "antiquarian," by which he meant the piety of whoever "looks back to whence he has come, where he came into being, with love and loyalty [...]. The history of his city becomes for him the history of himself; he reads its walls, its towered gate, its rules and regulations, its holydays, like an illuminated diary of his youth and in all this he finds again himself, his force, his industry, his joy, his judgment, his folly and vices."[32] Nation-building and (antiquarian) historical memories are interconnected, and the process is carried out just as much by poets and dramatists as by historians and antiquarians. It should not be forgotten that Shakespeare's Histories were not seen initially as a contribution to world literature so much as to the historical formation of a nation. "Historical" is not, however, the same as "historicized": unlike later stagings, Shakespeare's plays concentrate on history not as something past but as something present. This had been the case since the Middle Ages, but what was new was the shift from a moral to a patriotic approach. Samuel Taylor Coleridge picked up on precisely this point when he laid emphasis on the "spirit of patriotic reminiscence"[33] that permeates the dramas. Once again, Shakespeare's presentation of history has a new addressee. It is no longer a basic lesson in how to educate princes, or a fable about rising and falling, and it is not directed at kings in particular or Christians in general; the target is the English people, and it is they who will become bearers of their own history. National unity, which welded together the English, Welsh, Irish, and Scottish on the battlefield of Agincourt, takes place in the theater as a process of integration between all social classes and all ways of life. This does mean that ethnic, regional, or social differences are leveled out, let alone eliminated, by the national framework; it only offers the inclusive myth of a new, shared identity. A national army and a national stage are both organs of this collective identity, but in the new context historical memory no longer directly guides historical action.[34] Staged resentment and staged revenge lose their potential

---

[32] Nietzsche, "On the Uses and Disadvantages of History," 72 f. (see n. 6).
[33] Samuel Taylor Coleridge, *Shakespearean Criticism*, London 1967, ed. Raynor, II, 143.
[34] This made public communications all the more important, though it was still difficult to control them through censorship.

destructiveness, and so although they are not forgotten, the communal act of remembering actually replaces action, and to a certain degree constitutes the bolt that closes the door on the past. What one has learned to remember does not require repetition, and so the theatrical repetition of history replaces the malignant pressure for history to repeat itself, as most potently symbolized by Queen Margaret and her burning desire for eternal revenge.

4) *The memorableness of history* – The plays are educational on at least three different levels: they provide us with a history lesson, they interpret history, and they monumentalize it. All three levels are linked to memory. The history lesson consists in providing the audience with some basic facts, such as genealogies, successions, and battles, in a manner that will genuinely bring them to life.[35] Interpretation emerges from the comprehensive pattern that Shakespeare has woven into his plays. The individual dramas coalesce into a memorable whole, with all the qualities of an Aristotelian fable, with a clear beginning, middle, and end. The beginning is the seed from which grows the whole sequence of civil wars: this root of all the evil consists in Bolingbroke's overthrow of the rightful yet incompetent heir to the throne, Richard II. The middle is the Battle of Agincourt, the glorious high point in a saga of guilt, intrigue, and disaster. The end is the cessation of all hostilities, as civil war gives way to the harmonious rule of the Tudors, who lead the nation out of the darkness of its history and into a golden age of peace. It is this end that endows the whole past history with meaning and with direction. As for monumentalizing history, this takes place through the vivid presentation on stage of striking characters and scenes. The dramatic, emotional impact is unforgettable, and the aesthetic structure and intensity of the action provide images that take on a monumental presence in the spectator's memory.

Literary critics tend to equate aestheticization with disinterest and detachment, but here it is used to give life to the abstractness of historical facts. By endowing them with aesthetic form, Shakespeare also endows them with meaning that helps both to shape and to perpetuate

---

[35] Before Shakespeare this function was fulfilled by the Chronicle Plays, which covered English history from the time of the Norman Conquest through to the present, drumming in all the most important facts and figures. For the nation-state in early modern times, history was a crucial factor in creating and cementing identity.

memories. Thus history, poetry, and memory enter into a symbiotic relationship, which entails two terms that I deal with later in more detail: *imagines agentes* and *pathos formulae*. These are integral to the manner in which history is imprinted on national memory.

5) *The creation of a national myth* – With his Histories, Shakespeare contributed to the creation of a new national myth. He helped to draw the contours of a national identity, which naturally gains in distinctness when it is set against a foreign background. The borders that had previously divided the feudal classes internally were now transferred to external territory in the interests of national integration. In other words, internal conflicts gave way to external – a change that may be illustrated by a highly significant detail. The problem here was national *fama*, which was the future element contained within national memory. Just as the monumental and mythical paradigms of the past were invoked in order to endow the present with "power, diligence, desire, judgement" (Nietzsche), the patriotic deeds of the present had to appear worthy of being inscribed in the memory of posterity. The feudal ethos, which had placed the value of the name above that of the body, therefore changed into a patriotic ethos that placed the good of the community above the value of the individual human life.[36] The reward for self-sacrifice was immortality, as the dead would live on forever in the nation's collective memory. Willingness to die and the promise of immortality went hand in hand, and this was the connection that lay at the heart of the nation's political theology. Nationalism as a kind of religion was by no means an invention of the 18th and 19th centuries. As already seen, Euripides invoked it in *Iphigenie in Aulis*, where the heroine adopts the ideal attitude toward patriotic

---

[36] I am distinguishing here between two different forms of nationalism, one secular and one religious. I would define secular nationalism mainly in terms of the protection and rights that citizens may enjoy as individuals; religious nationalism consists principally in the duties the state imposes on its citizens as members of a community. These duties should not, however, appear to be some kind of chore imposed from outside – they must feel like an inner compulsion. With religious nationalism, the main duty of the citizen is to be prepared to die for his country. In order to get him to this level of commitment, the state must subject him to a deeply symbolic form of training whereby he will learn to exchange the security of society and the welfare of his own body for the "higher" cause of a glorious, patriotic death. He can only become a true member of the religious nation-state when he has fully accepted this set of values.

self-sacrifice. Initially, in the first phase of the learning process, she is confronted with the bitter senselessness of such a demand, but the instinct for personal survival is overcome during the second phase, in which her own death is put in perspective against the collective good of the nation. Iphigenie learns the lesson that she can now teach to every soldier: "I shall not have a grave, but a monument!"

In *Henry V* there is a pivotal scene that focuses on this close connection between sacrificial death and national memory. Before the king goes into battle, for example, before anyone knows the outcome, he speaks of the undying fame associated with this day by projecting himself into a distant future and looking back at the actual present. He prophesies that the nation will be united by this one glorious memory, and the heroic soldiers who return to their homes will celebrate the anniversary of the battle till the end of their days, showing their scars, talking of their brave deeds, and extolling the fame of their fallen comrades. Tales of their exploits will be passed down from father to son, and the day, which is named after St. Crispin, will be fixed forever in the memory of the nation. Thus the calendar of the holy saints will serve to help commemorate the soldier saints who brought glory to the nation:

> And Crispin Crispian shall ne'er go by,
> From this day to the ending of the world,
> But we in it shall be remembered.
> (H V; IV,3, 57–59)

In Shakespeare, the English style of memory is clearly distinguished from the French, and to a certain extent even this small detail gives us some insight into the formation of cultural identity and national distinctness in its early stages.[37] The English style expresses itself through spontaneous informality and intimacy of family celebrations, in which soldiers themselves share rituals of commemoration. The French style is very different. Although they too replace a saint of the Church (St. Denis) with the name of a national saint (Joan of Arc), those who sing her praises are not the people in the front line, but dignitaries from the Church – priests and monks, who ostentatiously parade

---

[37] Henry V is conceived not only as the ideal ruler, but also as the archetype of Englishness. Courage, a sense of responsibility, and piety are among the traditional virtues of the ruler, and they are joined by straightforwardness, dislike of rhetoric, and deep loyalty to the community as features of the new national character.

through the streets. After Joan's death, a pyramid is to be erected to her, and her ashes will be carried around in a precious urn at "high festivals."[38] The Roman Catholic pomp and circumstance lavished on the French saints is in sharp contrast to the embodied memorial rites of the English, who will show their scars to their children and proudly recount their experiences. It is made clear that to be English is to detest idolatry and to build one's pyramids in the patriotic hearts of one's fellow countrymen.

We have seen that memory plays a major role on various levels in Shakespeare's history plays, and it is evidently far from being a single unified force. Evaluation of it is also problematical, because whatever it may achieve can only emerge from each individual context. Clearest of all is the potential for conflict arising out of the one-sidedness of all recollections. The battle of memories is fought over different interpretations of reality, and just as it splits the individual, it also splits both parties in the various civil wars.

The "remembered past" is therefore not to be equated with the objectively detached study of the past that we like to call "history." It is always mixed with projected identities, interpretations of the present, and the need for validation. That is why our study of memory has taken us into the depths of political motivation and the formation of national identity, for what we have here is all the raw material that goes to the making of identities, histories, and communities. The study of national memory is quite distinct from that of mnemotechnics and the art and capacity of memory; it deals with memory as a dynamic force that drives both action and self-interpretation. This force is part of what the French call *imaginaire*. We should not underestimate this a form of imagination as a mere fiction. Such fictions or inventions underpin all cultural constructions.[39]

Memory in Shakespeare's Histories can be seen operating at different levels, and we can distinguish between them in terms of intratextual, contextual and textual. The *intratextual* concerns the

---

[38] See I H IV, I,6, 19–29.

[39] Anderson, *Imagined Communities*, 15 (see Chapt. 2, n. 18), disagrees with Ernest Gellner, "who is so anxious to show that nationalism masquerades under false pretences that he assimilates 'invention' to 'fabrication', 'falsity', rather than to 'imagining' and 'creating'. In this way he implies that 'true' communities exist that can be advantageously juxtaposed to nations. In fact, all communities larger than primordial villages of face-to-face contact (and perhaps even these) are imagined."

characters – the motives and intentions that drive them, and the limitations of their human vision. The *contextual* level involves the spectators of the drama, who witness the transformation of history into a national myth. This is the level at which the conflict between memories is settled by the construction of a collective memory that becomes a national possession. It no longer tells its addressees what they should do, but it does tell them who they are. They learn to recognize themselves as a unique group with a unique history.

This view of Shakespeare's Histories as national myth opens up a broader perspective – namely, that of the impact literature has on social life. Their reception down through the ages shows that they lend themselves to political exploitation. The nationalistic element lost its currency for the next generation, which was once again divided by civil war, but in the 19th century the plays were used as propaganda to justify the expansion of the empire. This does not explain, however, why they have been able to survive even this kind of exploitation and are still read and performed all over the world. They are clearly not simply national literature, but – and here the third, *textual* level comes in – world literature. Shakespeare did not handle the material of history as a historian, but as a dramatist, and his prime concern was to put it on stage as effectively as possible. And so he focused on sharp contrasts, tense situations, rapid changes of tempo, scandal, pathos, and also elements of comic relief. Added to this gripping verbal and visual presentation of history was one more level: that of reflection. The plays are filled with social and anthropological insights, and imbued with a basic skepticism that helps to keep them fresh. Even if the political effect of the memories is no longer applicable to us today, and so cannot be reactivated, nevertheless the dramatic and human power remain as effective as ever on the textual level. Today these plays no longer tell us what to do, or who we are, but they continue to give us a vivid depiction of how identities are fashioned and dismantled, and how high a price must sometimes be paid for them.

EPILOGUE AT THE THEATER

An actor named Peter Roggisch, who had played various kings in the "Wars of the Roses," wrote a book in 1993 (dedicated to the director

Peter Palitzsch) looking back over his experiences. It begins with a cryptic verse:

> "It takes a while for us to recognize,
> That we are nought but memory... when was't"?[40]

He is reminiscing about a fragment of memory, such as may linger on in an actor's mind. He adds:

"This – or something like it – is the beginning of King Henry VI's last monologue. *The Wars of the Roses*. When was that? I think it was 1967/68. The scene takes place in the Tower. The crown is brought back to the King. He waves it aside. It was a thin bangle, I think, which I held out before me – gilded bronze. The King philosophizes, meditates... about power and weakness.... Just how did the text go? 'Shadow splinters': that was a phrase. And the word 'politics.' The last word, I think. An abdication scene – end of the role. The deposed King."

This is how the actor remembered a part he had played long ago. In order to reconstruct what he called his "Suchmonolog" (search monologue), Roggisch hunted through Shakespeare and various translations of the plays, but without success. He looked at every single monologue spoken by every single king, but the fragment he remembered did not fit in anywhere. He asked Peter Palitzsch about it, but the latter had no precise recollection either; when he had moved to Berlin, he had thrown away many of his papers. Nevertheless, Roggisch continued on his quest, and at long last he found the text that had been used for the Stuttgart production: *The Wars of the Roses, Part Two*. On page 52 he found his long-lost monologue.

> *London. The Tower. Henry is sitting on a bed, the crown in his hands.*
> "It takes a while for us to recognize,
> And at some time it seems to us a mercy,
> That we are nought but memory, 'when was't?'
> The name of King and disappearing with it
> The memory of him and it: 'who was't?'
> (*Carefully he puts the crown on his head.*)
> I feel it once again, the gentle pressure
> One soon forgets, all custom, nearly all...

---

[40] Peter Roggisch, "Der Suchmonolog. Arbeit mit Peter Palitzsch," in Rainer Mennicken (ed.), *Peter Palitzsch, Regie im Theater*, Frankfurt a.M. 1993, 67–77; here 67.

> And yet one can't escape, it carves the brow
> And draws a circle into the thin skin
> And marks the thought, at first but barely felt,
> Then sharp, then comes the feeling, hope and action,
> And shadow splinters shade the mind and soul . . .
> – Leave me to live in peace, far far away
> From blood-soak'd history – from politics."[41]

This monologue is remarkable for a number of reasons. One of them is that it shows the dynamics of remembering and forgetting from an actor's perspective. Most verses of his role have been lost after this long interval, but some are unforgettable enough to haunt him and keep him searching. The main point, however, is that Roggisch could never have found this monologue in the works of Shakespeare. The text can tell us much about Shakespeare's view on memory *ex negativo*. The tone of the monologue, the gradual fading of life into memory, and memory into oblivion, or present into past, is very close to our own hearts, but is not an emotion that we find in Shakespeare's plays. This nostalgic memory was an invention of the Romantics and Victorians. In Shakespeare's monologues, kings do not come to recognize that soon they will be "nought but memory," because memory (in the sense of fame) is precisely what they crave. "We shall be remembered," Henry V promises his men on the eve of Agincourt, and he is not thinking of the past but of the future. The memory of Shakespeare's kings is another name for fame and glory. It has no tinge of melancholy, because it is associated with survival in the minds of those who are to come – a secular immortality. "When was't," / The name of King and disappearing with it / The memory of him and it: "who was't?" The name is all important, because it is the emblematic focal point of future remembrance and undying fame.

Although you will not find melancholic or nostalgic approaches to memory in Shakespeare, there is certainly pessimism, to be seen when the hope of fame is thrown into doubt. In the graveyard scene, Hamlet seems pessimistic about the prospects of lasting glory when he talks with the gravediggers and muses on the fact that nothing is left of Alexander the Great or Julius Caesar except a lump of clay. At the end, he himself is deeply concerned that he will leave a "wounded name,"

---

[41] Ibid., 76–77.

and so he asks his friend Horatio to "report me and my cause aright/
To the unsatisfied." Prospero's view is just as radical, as he muses on
his enchanted island in *The Tempest*. After he has entertained Miranda
and Ferdinand with a show much like a masque at court, he closes the
proceedings with the following famous words:

> Our revels now are ended. These our actors,
> As I foretold you, were all spirits, and
> Are melted into air, into thin air:
> And, like the baseless fabric of this vision,
> The cloud-capp'd towers, the gorgeous palaces,
> The solemn temples, the great globe itself,
> Yea, all which it inherit, shall dissolve,
> And, like this insubstantial pageant faded,
> Leave not a rack behind. We are such stuff
> As dreams are made on, and our little life
> Is rounded with a sleep.
>
> (*The Tempest*, IV, 1, 148–158)

Here, it is true, Prospero talks of fading, but this is not the fading
of human memory – it is the fading first of a fiction and then, by
extension, of life and all earthly reality. In this vision, everything will
disappear, and one day the whole world will have passed into oblivion.

Along with prospective future memory and radical forgetting,
Shakespeare's plays contain another form of retrospective memory
that is communicated through narratives. Plays like *The Tempest* and
The Winter's Tale end, after the endurance of much suffering, with the
comforting prospect of the different parties telling each other about
their adventures and ordeals. Narration is a way of overcoming and
at the same time of sharing past conflicts, estrangements, and separations. But only someone who has survived such ordeals can remember
and recount. Richard II is a king for whom this comfortable retrospection is not possible: after being deposed, he is imprisoned in the
Tower and then murdered. And yet he of all people had longed for
such moments of peace, and he would have loved nothing more than
to remember and narrate instead of having to act. His desire to "tell
sad stories" corresponds to a flight from the present. As he cannot
control the here and now, he fantasizes about escaping in a future
that will take away the reality of his fears and torments – a time when
he will have survived them and they will be nothing but memories. By

setting his own history into a future within a future, he anticipates a perspective that he himself will never be granted.

> For God's sake let us sit upon the ground
> And tell sad stories of the death of kings:
> How some have been depos'd, some slain in war,
> Some haunted by the ghosts they have deposed,
> Some poisoned by their wives, some sleeping kill'd;
> All murdered . . .
>
> (R II,l, II,2, 155–160; see also V, 1, 37–50)

All of these tales end, like his own life, in disaster, but there is a fundamental difference between the experience and the story. By moving onto the level of remembrance and narration, Richard is able to withdraw from the direct pressures of reality and to fictionalize his own life. He is, so to speak, out of synch with himself, and splits himself into the man living the life and the man observing it. In this way, he can go on ahead of events, and then look back over them like a detached stranger.

From the Shakespearean perspective, we must wait two hundred years – from the early 17th to the early 19th century – before we come upon the mood that underlies Peter Roggisch's "search monologue." Of William Wordsworth, who will be the subject of the next chapter, it can truly be said that the poet is preoccupied with the thought of people and living experiences one day becoming "nought but memory." The transformation or indeed transubstantiation of life into memory is his overriding theme, as it was to be later for Proust, and again just like Proust, Wordsworth endows poetic memory with a completely new meaning in terms of the stabilization, renewal, and justification of life.

4

Wordsworth and the Wound of Time

Each man is a memory to himself.

Wordsworth, *The Prelude*

MEMORY AND RECOLLECTION

The transition from memory as art to memory as power is one that we will now look at through the work of William Wordsworth. Classical mnemotechnics went out of favor in the 17th and 18th centuries, and this led to the discovery of memory in the sense of recollection. Already by the end of the 16th century, Shakespeare had ridiculed its scholarly patterns of thought and expression. In *As You Like It*, memory is compared to old biscuits: the more dried-up the mind, the more bizarre the memory. This is how Jaques describes Touchstone:

> A fool, a fool! I met a fool i' th' forest
> [...] in his brain,
> Which is as dry as the remainder biscuit
> After a voyage, he hath strange places cramm'd
> With observation, the which he vents
> In mangled forms.
>
> (II, 7, 12–42)[1]

---

[1] William Shakespeare, *As You Like It*, ed. Agnes Latham, Arden Edition London 1975, 48–50. Another example of Shakespearean memory criticism is the grotesque figure of the Latin tutor Holofernes (inspired by Rabelais) in *Love's Labour's Lost* (IV,2). H. Weinrich, "Gedächtniskultur – Kulturgedächtnis," 567–582, and also in *Lethe,*

Indeed, the transformation of memory was already in full swing during the 16th century. Erasmus proposed a new form of teaching that moved away from the rigidity of "rote recall" and instead brought into operation principles such as reactivation, reformulation, and reinterpretation.[2] *Memoria verborum* (memory of words) was replaced by *memoria rerum* (memory of things) before it finally lost its central position, as writing and print culture took over. In the print age, criticism of memory was directed against senseless overloading; thus a new economy and order were imposed on knowledge with a wholesale clear-out of whatever was deemed irrelevant. Once more, Sir Thomas Browne's statement has to be recalled: "Knowledge is made by oblivion, and to purchase a clear and warrantable body of Truth, we must forget and part with much we know."[3]

John Bender and David Wellbery, in a pioneering essay, have traced the development of what is generally termed the decline of rhetoric in literature.[4] They distinguish five elements that they regard as contributing to this decline[5]:

1) The ideal of objective truth that leads to reason becoming scientific and universal.

2) The complementary revaluation of subjectivity in the legal context of authorship and the literary context of originality.

3) The politics and economics of Liberalism, with its emphasis on unseen, abstract, and internalized communication.

39–49 (see Introduction, n. 5) traces the loss of "memory's cultural relevance," but also points out that in the context of medicine and the "humours," the mind is associated with dryness and the memory with damp. Under these conditions, a dried-up memory would be particularly bad.

[2] See Thomas M. Greene, *The Light in Troy. Imitation and Discovery in Renaissance Poetry*, New Haven 1982, 31. The next major shift in memory criticism came in 1775, in the context of Herder's educational reforms.

[3] Browne, *Selected Writings* (see Introduction, n. 4).

[4] See Jünger, *Gedächtnis und Erinnerung*, 141 (see Chapt. 1, n. 2), who would like to strip memory of its philosophical dignity and is hostile to the "equally monstrous and barren writings that are devoted to the *ars memoriae*." Officially, rhetoric was withdrawn from the syllabus at French universities in 1885. On its lengthy, latent posthistory see Klaus Dockhorn, *Macht und Wirkung der Rhetorik. Vier Aufsätze zur Ideengeschichte der Vormoderne*, Respublica literaria 2, Bad Homburg, Berlin, Zurich 1968, who convincingly corrects the impression that rhetoric came to an abrupt end.

[5] John Bender and David E. Wellbery (eds.), *The Ends of Rhetoric. History, Theory, Practice*, Stanford 1990, 3–39; here, especially 22f.

4) Literacy and the print culture, with the concomitant changes in the structure of the general public.

5) The consolidation of the nation-state as the basis of a distinct cultural identity.[6]

In retrospect, it turns out that rhetoric had been the string that had bound a variety of things together. Once the knots had loosened, differentiation became the order of the day, and this provided the roots of the modern age. Rhetoric had guaranteed the unity of truth, affect, and style, and the one was impossible without the others. The contrary ideal of a nonpersonal, linguistically neutral truth made it possible to seek a universalized rationality, which expressed itself in new disciplines such as science, jurisprudence, and philosophy. Rhetoric had guaranteed the unity of objectivity and subjectivity, which since the Enlightenment had been split into different discourses. In the light of modern distinctions, rhetoric was now condemned as an annoying hybridization – it was far too subjective when it needed to be objective, and remained distant and objective when it was subjectivity that was required. And finally, rhetoric had guaranteed unity between Antiquity and the modern age through the continuity of tradition. With the split between the past and the present, time could now be seen as an ever-widening gulf, reflected by a new historical consciousness and temporal alienation.

Complex changes in the structure of memory, and in the values and practices associated with it, also took place within the framework of lexical distinctions.[7] The term "memory" was linked with other

---

[6] Manfred Fuhrmann, *Rhetorik und öffentliche Rede. Über die Ursachen des Verfalls der Rhetorik im ausgehenden 18. Jahrhundert* (Konstanzer Universitätsreden 147), Konstanz 1983, considers this final point to be the only relevant one: "Only the nationalization of all European intellectual life provides an adequate explanation for the disappearance of courses in rhetoric, i.e., for the most radical change that classical European education had undergone since heathen Antiquity had given way to the Christian Middle Ages." (18)

[7] Concerning this structural change in memory, see O. G. Oexle, in Schmid (ed.), *Gedächtnis*, 99 (see Chapt. 2, n.1). At the end of the 18th century, memory was "relieved of its links to metaphysics, and was assigned without metaphysical status to the individual and to history. Memory still has the task of basing the unity of the individual and the unity of history on reflection, but it no longer has at its disposal any kind of link to ontic reality." Of especial note is J. G. Droysen's definition of history as no longer being the "sum of events" and the "course of all things," but as "knowledge of things that have happened" (i.e., memory).

terms like "tradition" and "rhetoric," whereas "recollection" was associated increasingly with "subjectivity" and "writing." Wordsworth also
pinpointed this distinction in a short poem entitled

> *Memory:* A pen – to register; a key –
> That winds through secret wards;
> Are well assigned to Memory
> By allegoric bards.
>
> As aptly also might be given
> A pencil to her hand;
> That, softening objects, sometimes even
> Outstrips the heart's demand.
>
> That smooths foregone distress, the lines
> Of lingering care subdues,
> Long-vanished happiness refines,
> And clothes in brighter hues.
>
> Yet, like a tool of Fancy, works
> Those spectres to dilate
> That startle Conscience, as she lurks
> Within her lonely seat.
>
> O! that our lives, which flee so fast,
> In purity were such,
> That not an image of the past
> Should fear that pencil's touch!
>
> Retirement then might hourly look
> Upon a soothing scene,
> Age steal to his allotted nook
> Contented and serene;
>
> With heart as calm as lakes that sleep,
> In frosty moonlight glistening;
> Or mountain rivers, where they creep
> Along a channel smooth and deep,
> To their own far-off murmurs listening.[8]

The poem is divided into three sections, each of which deals with a
different form of memory.

Memoria (Stanza 1): the pen and the key are named as traditional emblems of memory. The pen captures words, and is used as

---

[8] William Wordsworth, *The Poetical Works*, Vol. 4, 101f. (see Chapt. 2, n. 6).

a metonym for the technique of writing, which gives lasting material form to the sound of the words. The key stands for rooms and stores in which objects are kept safely locked away. Fixing the past through writing, and collecting and preserving it in closed spaces, corresponds to traditional metaphors of rhetorical *memoria* with its writing tablets and copious storerooms.

A characteristic element of this form of memory is the straightforward concept of recording and storing. Once something has been fixed in a certain order, the passing of time makes no difference, and it can be reproduced without loss or distortion. *Memoria* as *ars* is modeled on the durability of writing and the security of safe storage – it arranges, trains, and processes human memory in such a way that it becomes a spacious and reliable repository for words, thoughts, images, and ideas. In this form of memory, time is shut out, and it is believed that whatever has been kept in storage will remain intact and unchangeable.

Recollection (stanzas 2,3,4): A big step is taken from traditional *memoria* to Romantic recollection through the seemingly minor distinction between pen and pencil. "Pen," derived from the Latin *penna* (feather), is a neutral word for a writing instrument. "Pencil" (which is not used here in the modern sense of a lead rod inside a wooden shaft) refers to a fine brush. With the addition of a single syllable, we move out of the sphere of writing and into that of painting. The brush is used to color scenes, and to introduce light and shade. Samuel Johnson's dictionary emphasizes the power of illusion that the brush can create.[9] Instead of recording the contours of the scenes, it conveys their atmosphere.

In place of *memoria* as the art of recording and accumulating memories, the power of recollection works on existing material with a great degree of latitude. In Wordsworth, its broad function is cosmetic and therapeutic: what has faded with time is given new color, what was lost is restored, and what gave pain is palliated. Recollection does not heal the wounds, but softens them. This formative power is, of course, accompanied by the danger that it will take on a life of its own. The

---

9 Samuel Johnson, *Dictionary of the English Language*, Boston 1806, uses a verse of Dryden's as an illustration: "Pencils can by one slight touch restore / Smiles to that changed face, that wept before."

fourth verse names conscience as an uncontrollable agent and as the dynamic force that lurks behind all the romanticizing and soothing magic of recollection. At its center, recollection harbors pain and irredeemable guilt. It is from this hidden source that specters of the past emerge at their own bidding, which cannot be controlled by rational consciousness.

Anamnesis (stanzas 5,6,7): In spite of the will to control and soften the workings of recollection, the brush of memory is wielded in the last instance by the unseen hand of guilt and conscience. With the exclamatory "O!" that begins the fifth stanza, the speaker turns away from the reality of memory, which tells him that there is no "retirement" for memory and conscience, no backward glance without regret, no rest and relaxation at the end of one's life. In his counterfactual vision, the poet imagines an ideal vision of memory that is not disturbed by guilt but is pure and direct. His metaphors for the uncompromised memory are calm lakes and the music of channels "communicating" with the mountain rivers from which they have descended. Peace, contentment, serenity, purity – these would be the qualities of an ideal anamnesis, a recollection that does not need to be touched up because it is free from feelings of shame, guilt, and remorse.

Memoria, recollection, anamnesis – these are the three conflicting zones of memory through which we will, in due course, be following Wordsworth. The decline of *memoria* forms the background against which subjective memory began to take over during the Enlightenment (Locke). The problem of *recollection* became more complex with the advent of Romanticism, because it was split into the two vectors of affirmative subjectivity (through manipulative recollection) and loss of subjectivity (through mystic anamnesis). Recollection is linked to subjective memory, creativity, poetic imagination, and self-construction. Anamnesis is a form of counter-memory that transcends the patterns of self-construction.

MEMORY AND IDENTITY

John Locke and David Hume

As the culture of memory faded, personal recollection took on greater and greater cultural relevance. With the waning of tradition, continuity in time could no longer be taken for granted; it became a task that had to be accomplished within the framework of the individual's life history. It was Locke who brought about a turning point in the relationship between memory and identity. Previously, it had long been customary to build identity through genealogy, and the present only assumed substance and meaning in the light of an extensive prehistory. As a philosopher in the era of the modern middle class, Locke replaced the genealogical identities of family, institution, dynasty, or nation with individual identity drawn exclusively from the life of the person concerned. This was actually in keeping with the Puritan autobiography, for which the most important instruments were memory, self-observation, and writing – the same tools that built the foundations of the bourgeois subject.

An important tool for the construction of the modern self was observation.[10] Just as the natural sciences objectify the material world, self-observation objectifies autobiography. Descartes' *cogito* is characterized by timelessness, because the observer takes himself out of the flow of time – indeed obliviousness to time is one of the traditional qualities of the philosopher. Outside the range of time, memory has no chance to become the object of focus.[11] Locke distanced himself from these philosophical premises when he defined the subject basically through the act of recollection. His insights into the temporality of human existence and the synthesizing power of memory are to be found in Chapters 10 and 27 of the second book of his *Essay Concerning Human Understanding*. We need to consider these in some

---

[10] "We must consider what a person stands for; which, I think, is a thinking intelligent being that has reason and reflection and can consider itself as itself, the same thinking thing in different times and places; which it does only by that consciousness which is inseparable from thinking and, as it seems to me, essential to it: it being impossible for anyone to perceive without perceiving that he does perceive." John Locke, *An Essay Concerning Human Understanding*, ed. John W. Yolton, London 1964, Vol. 2, XXVII, §9. See Charles Taylor, *Sources of the Self. The Making of the Modern Identity*, Cambridge 1989, 143–176.

[11] This strange obliviousness to time and memory still characterizes philosophical descriptions. Charles Taylor (see previous note), who has written a comprehensive description of how the self emerged on the threshold of the modern age, uses terms like "mind," "consciousness," "hegemony of reason," and "radical reflexivity," but "memory" does not figure in his terminology. The significant role played by memory in modern reflections on the self is simply not recognized. Taylor does briefly mention the memory problem in a footnote, but only in order to emphasize the absurdity of Locke's position, See C. Taylor, ibid., 543, note 17.

detail, because they form the background to the Romantic concept of identity through recollection.[12]

Locke was one of the memory theorists who abandoned the tradition of *memoria*. Like Augustine, he did not regard memory and oblivion as opposites, because what was remembered was marked by the forgotten – indeed the latter represented an indispensable aspect of memory because it always left its traces on what was remembered.[13]

"There seems to be a constant decay of all our ideas, even those which are struck deepest and in minds the most retentive [. . .] Thus the ideas as well as children of our youth often die before us; and our minds represent to us those tombs to which we are approaching: where, though the brass and marble remain, yet the inscriptions are effaced by time and the imagery moulders away."[14]

Memory for Locke is no airtight container that can protect its contents from decay. Remembering and forgetting intermingle in the gradual disintegration and permanent disappearance of experiences and ideas in time. Memory is therefore not a bulwark against time; it is our most delicate sensor in registering time – or, as Locke says, it is "the tomb" we carry around inside us.

As the wound of time cries out to be healed, memory, continuity, and identity become urgent issues. How can a rational being's individuality be preserved across the gulfs of time and forgetfulness? "That which seems to make the difficulty is this: that this consciousness being interrupted always by forgetfulness, there being no moment of our lives wherein we have the whole train of all our past actions before our eyes in one view. [. . .] I say, in all these cases, our consciousness being interrupted, and we losing sight of our past selves, doubts are raised whether we are the same thinking being, i.e. the same substance, or no."[15]

[12] On the problem of personal identity in general and Locke in particular, see Amélie Oksenberg Rorty (ed.), *The Identities of Persons*, Berkeley, Los Angeles, London 1976, especially 4, 11, 67ff., 139ff., with further references.

[13] After Hobbes, a certain whiff of decomposition was associated with memories and imaginings – in this context, he spoke of a "decaying sense." Concerning the history of the imaginary from the English Enlightenment through to Romanticism, see Wolfgang Iser, *The Fictive and the Imaginary. Charting Literary Anthropology*, Baltimore and London 1993, 171ff.

[14] Locke, *Essay*, Vol. 2, X, §5 (see Chapt. 4, 10).

[15] Ibid., Vol. 2, XXVII, §10.

The Cartesian subject thinks; therefore she/he is; the Lockean subject is, in so far as she/he remembers. The self has no objective extension and no unquestionable continuity, but from a given point in time it can extend itself as retrospective or prospective consciousness. With the aid of consciousness, past episodes can be integrated into the present and hence into the self. What Locke calls "consciousness" is therefore an achievement of remembering – a means of integrating the past and hence of guiding, organizing, and constructing the self:

[...] [C]onsciousness, as far as ever it can be extended, should it be to ages past, unites existences and actions very remote in time into the same person [...] That with which the consciousness of this present thinking thing can join itself makes the same person and is one self with it, and with nothing else, and so attributes to itself and owns all the actions of that thing as its own, as far as that consciousness reaches, and no further.[16]

Locke formulated a new concept of the individual that fitted in neatly with the demands of middle-class society. The claim to unconditional equal rights by law required a new sense of social and ethical responsibility and accountability. Parallel to Locke's political writings, in which he linked the emergence of individuality to reason, labor, and property, his philosophical writings associated individuality with consciousness, self-observation, and the connecting function of memory. Coleridge later also stressed this connecting function: "There does not exist a more important rule nor one more fruitful in its consequences, moral as well as logical, than the rule of connecting our present mind with our past – from the breach of it result almost all the pernicious errors in our education of children and indeed of our general treatment of our fellow creatures."[17] Locke's concept of the modern subject incorporates time and memory: the construction of

---

[16] Ibid., Vol. 2, XXVII, §§16 and 17.

[17] Alice D. Snyder, *Coleridge on Logic and Learning. With Selections from the Unpublished Manuscripts*, New Haven 1929, 60. G. W. Leibniz, who was a contemporary of Locke's, also drew attention to the bridging function of memory. See O. G. Oexle, in Schmid (ed.), *Gedächtnis*, 99 (see Chapt. 2, n. 1): "In his *Nouveaux essais sur l'entendement humain*, G.W. Leibniz [...] defined memory as the force that links every individually existing thing with the whole universe, makes every present pregnant with the future and loaded with the past, and also constructs the individual as an identity in itself."

the self is based on continuous, productive acts of appropriating past experiences and future possibilities.[18]

Locke's connecting function of memory did not go unchallenged. For Hume it was nothing but pure mystification. What Locke calls "identities," Hume calls "fictions," which are devised to conceal the changeability of circumstances. "In order to justify to ourselves this absurdity, we often feign some new and unintelligible principle, that connects the objects together, and prevents their interruption and variation. Thus we feign continu'd existence of the perceptions of our senses, to remove the interruption, and run into the notion of a soul, and self, and substance, to disguise the variation."[19] As soon as one looks more closely, what may appear to be an identity becomes diffuse. The various aspects "are nothing but a bundle or collection of different perceptions, which succeed each other with an inconceivable rapidity and are in a perpetual flux and movement."[20]

The term that fits this situation far more aptly than "identity" is "diversity." For the skeptic Hume, the individual is nothing more than the stage for rapidly changing impressions, feelings, and thoughts: "The mind is a kind of theatre, where several perceptions successively make their appearance; pass, re-pass, glide away, and mingle in an infinite variety of postures and situations."[21]

Hume had his reasons for this extreme position in the debate over memory and identity. He saw himself as the Newton of philosophy, and claimed to have discovered the units and laws of gravity governing the mind. These units were called "impressions" and "ideas," and their combination and sequence followed the principles of similarity, proximity, and causality. There is no room in his model for an additional organizational principle under the heading of identity. The exclusive

---

[18] Locke distinguishes between three types of identity:

> *material identity of the substance* depending on a mass of the same particles;
> *organic identity of the soul* depending on a continued organization that preserves identity in the change of the material substance;
> *personal identity of the self* depending on a personal consciousness that preserves identity in the change of immaterial substance.

[19] David Hume, *A Treatise of Human Nature* (Book I, IV, 6: "Of personal identity"), Ernest C. Moosner (ed.), Harmondsworth 1969, 302.

[20] Ibid., 252.

[21] Ibid., 253.

validity of the laws of association postulated by Hume is thrown into doubt by the connecting function of memory put forward by Locke.[22] Anyone who seriously linked personal identity to authentication by memory would not, according to Hume, bring about a unification of the personality but, on the contrary, a fragmentation: "For how few of our past actions are there, of which we have any memory? Who can tell me, for instance, what were his thoughts and actions on the first of January 1715, the 11th of March 1719, and the 3rd of August 1733? Or will he affirm, because he has entirely forgot the incidents of these days, that the present self is not the same person with the self of that time?"[23] Hume deconstructed Locke's concept of personal identity. For the Romantics, both the constructive and the deconstructive approach to the problem of identity played a crucial role.

William Wordsworth

As observed in the chapter on *fama*, it was poets and historians who provided the media for cultural memory in societies with and without writing. The task, from Homer through Pindar and Virgil to Chrétien de Troyes and Spenser, was to immortalize first public and then private names and deeds by rescuing them from the dark depths of oblivion and giving them a permanent home in memory. In Wordsworth's time, the functions of poetry and history were already quite distinct. From now on, poets had their own part to play in carrying out the tasks of cultural memory by tackling those memorable events that did not find their way into the history books. For Wordsworth these comprised, for instance, names and incidents of everyday country life that he himself deemed worthy of recording:

> No little band of yet remembered names
> Whom I, in perfect confidence, might hope
> To summon back from lonesome banishment,
> And make them inmates in the hearts of men
> Now living, or to live in times to come.[24]

[22] For Hume, memory has no particular function and is subsumed under the basic laws of the mind. The law of associations in the chain of cause and effect, for instance, works just as reliably outside as inside the boundaries of personal memory.

[23] Hume, ibid., 262.

[24] William Wordsworth, *The Prelude*, 1805, I, 172–176.

Wordsworth hoped to set "time, place and manners" in men's minds, but above all he wanted to record his own life. Autobiographies and memoirs had long been written for religious or other personal reasons, but they never aspired to the wider, representative value implied by Wordsworth's deliberate choice of the epic as his genre. Instead of stories of general import, like those in the Bible, or national sagas, he wove together a narrative of individual memories. This innovation, unprecedented in the genre, is already to be observed in the fact that initially the work had no title. *The Prelude* was added posthumously; Wordsworth's own heading was *Poem Title not yet fixed upon by William Wordsworth Addressed to S.T. Coleridge.* Of the subject matter, he wrote that it was "a long poem upon the formation of my own mind." In this epic, the source of inspiration, the content, and the narrative voice are all one, and the epic element is that of heroism. What is heroic in this undertaking is the desire for autonomous, poetic self-construction – or radical autogenesis.

Wordsworth makes the formation of his personal identity into an epic project, and for this his most important medium is memory. Initially, this means self-observation within the flow of time, looking back on himself, splitting, and doubling himself. As had already been the case with Puritan autobiographies, the self is divided into the rememberer and the remembered. They are separated qualitatively, not through moral conversion but through time, for one cannot bring back the past without at the same time perceiving a gap within oneself:

> [...] so wide appears
> The vacancy between me and those days
> Which yet have such self-presence in my mind,
> That, sometimes, when I think of it, I seem
> Two consciousnesses, conscious of myself
> And of some other Being.[25]

Otherness in one's own self is experienced as something painful – a wound of time. The philosophy of the senses makes memory appear as a faded, decayed form of the original experience. What was once

---

[25] Ibid., II, 28–33.

vividly present diminishes with time and, as in Peter Palitzsch's "Shakespearean" monologue, becomes "nought but memory."

> I am sad
> At thought of raptures now for ever flown;
> Even unto tears I sometimes could be sad
> To think of, to read over, many a page,
> Poems withal of name, which at that time
> Did never fail to entrance me, and are now
> Dead in my eyes, dead as a theatre
> Fresh emptied of spectators.[26]

We are not far removed from Hume's theater of the mind: the permanent succession of images and ideas does not allow for any resuscitation, and there are no mnemotechnical remedies to cure this sickness of lost realities. Memory takes on a very different quality, for in the age of print its focus is less on the recall of knowledge than on the reproducibility of feelings. A page in a book can be opened and read, and a place can be revisited, but the emotions that were once linked to these will not automatically be rekindled. Memory is only a dull reflection of the original experience, and there can be no way back.

Romantic memory, then, is not a reproduction but a replacement. It is an evocative embellishment devised to cover an obvious gap – a supplement created by the poetic imagination. Wordsworth rejects the illusion that memories can provide reliable reproductions, and he does not even trust himself to distinguish between memory and retrospective projection:

> Of these and other kindred notices
> I cannot say what portion is in truth
> The naked recollection of that time,
> And what may rather have been called to life
> By after-meditation.[27]

What memory loses in terms of authenticity, however, it gains in terms of creativity, as we will soon see. Experience and identity, which in life are radically different, are now to be welded together through poetry.

[26] Ibid., V, 568–575.
[27] Ibid., III, 645–648.

Wordsworth's images for this process are the chain and the rainbow. His vision of the continuity, integrity, and identity of the self through the different stages of aging and consciousness finds its expression in a wish:

> And I could wish my days to be
> Bound each to each by natural piety.[28]

RECOLLECTION: MEMORY AND IMAGINATION

In Wordsworth's Romantic epic, memory plays the role of a Muse. What separates him from Proust is his desire for control in the act of poetic remembering: his Muse allows virtually no access to the forces of contingency, involuntary impulses, or erratic associations. The epic reflects a disciplined poetic process in which memory and imagination become inseparably entwined.

Wordsworth's recollections are quite distinct from the current, three-phase model of artificial data storage systems – a model that, despite the spread of other systems, still plays a relevant role in memory psychology:[29]

Phase 1 (take in): this is perception through the senses, which gains entry to memory on condition that it is either violent and intense or repeated and familiar.

Phase 2 (storage): the perception is stored in the memory over time.

Phase 3 (retrieval): the sensual perception is recalled into the present as a re-sensualized memory.

In Wordsworth's three-phase model, the first one is also perception, in the form of "the spontaneous overflow of powerful feelings."[30] Here we find ourselves in the exclusive present that Hölderlin called "selige Selbstvergessenheit" [blessed self-forgetting] and that Wordsworth associates with speechlessness. He finds this state especially prevalent

---

[28] Wordsworth, *The Poetical Works*, Vol. 1, 226 (see Chapt. 2, n. 6): "*My heart leaps up when I behold.*"

[29] See Alan Baddeley, "The Psychology of Remembering and Forgetting," in Thomas Butler (ed.), *Memory, History, Culture and the Mind*, Oxford 1989, 51.

[30] Wordsworth, Preface to the Second Edition of the "Lyrical Ballads," in *The Poetical Works*, Vol. 2, 383–404; here 400 (see Chapt. 2, n. 6).

in children. This phase precedes the dynamics of memory, and the latter are fundamentally incapable of ever recapturing it.

The second phase involves time and language. The creative process begins with retrospection: "It takes its origin from emotion recollected in tranquillity."[31] Nothing is simply recalled – it has to be newly created, and a new emotion emerges from the amalgamation of the original emotion with the supplementary memory. And just as the former emotion gives rise to new feelings, so these feelings now give rise to the poem. There is no direct route from life to poetry, because poetry is made not from the original emotions but from memories of memories.

In the third phase, new emotions are generated out of memory: "The emotion is contemplated until, by a species of re-action, the tranquillity gradually disappears, and an emotion, kindred to that which was before the subject of contemplation, is gradually produced, and does itself actually exist in the mind."[32] The first, lost present is thus replaced by a newly created "secondary present," for life itself – as in Phase 1 – eludes the grasp of the poet. His material is memories that must inevitably lose the vitality and freshness of the original feelings, but that in the process of poetic contemplation can be deliberately worked on and invested with new emotions.[33]

Wordsworth's three-phase model rejects the concept of storage. Instead of recording, preserving, and retrieving, his model proceeds from irretrievable loss to supplementary new creation, and it is this "supplementation" that underpins his model. Freud used the term "belatedness" to describe the process in which perceptions take on their meaning only through the act of retrospective remembrance, which may occur years or even decades later. According to this view,

---

[31] Ibid.

[32] Ibid., 400f.

[33] In the preface to the "Lyrical Ballads" (1798), which he published jointly with Coleridge, the poet is characterized as having the ability to provide his own stimuli. As far as external stimuli are concerned, he is "habitually impelled to create them where he does not find them." He also has "a disposition to be affected more than other men by absent things as if they were present; an ability of conjuring up in himself passions." (Wordsworth, Preface, 393). K. Dockhorn points out that there is a parallel here to Schiller's recommendation: "He may write out of gentle and distancing memory, but never under the present dominance of emotions that he is to convey to us with beauty." (101)

remembering is not a passive reflection but the productive act of a new perception and a kind of rewriting. Remembering and understanding both have supplementation in common. For Freud, the inaccessibility of the "original" entailed rewriting, whereas for Wordsworth it led to imaginary powers of recollection.[34] The poetic imagination supplements what life constantly subtracts – namely, presence.

Discontinuity, loss, and posteriority are integral to Wordsworth's view of the human condition. Although Nature is divine and everlasting, culture is under constant threat of decay and irretrievable loss. At the beginning of Book 5 of *The Prelude*, he puts forward the idea that after a catastrophe Nature is able to reconstruct itself as if by magic, whereas for humans there is no comparable hope of automatic renewal. Humans rely on tradition, and whatever they create, invent, or compose is in danger of being forgotten. Wordsworth's vision is that of the melancholic who has lost both memory and culture and is damned to survive himself. Into his modern melancholy he incorporates an older form of melancholy drawn from Shakespeare's Sonnet 64:

> [...] man
> As long as he shall be the child of earth,
> Might almost "weep to have" what he may lose,
> Nor be himself extinguished, but survive
> Abject, depressed, forlorn, disconsolate.[35]

ANAMNESIS: MYSTIC REFLECTIONS

Romantic memory is ambivalent: it is both the weapon that inflicts the wound of time and the medicine that is applied to the wound. With the aid of recollection, as supplementary memory, the pain is softened though never healed. The power of healing comes in a different form that is cleansed of the effects of time as well as the active, subjective workings of the imagination. This form of memory, which I have called

---

[34] See Jacques Derrida, *Writing and Difference*, London, New York, reprinted 2009, 266: the non-present text consists "of archives which are always already transcriptions. [...] Everything begins with reproduction [...]: repositories of a meaning which was never present, whose signified presence is always reconstituted by deferral, *nachträglich*, belatedly, *supplementarily*."

[35] Wordsworth, *The Prelude*, V, 24–28 (see Chapter 8, n. 43).

anamnesis, is the opposite of recollection. It is the passive, receptive, mystic, and one might even say "feminine" counter to the "masculine" power of imagination.

Anamnesis is not actively attainable; its "eternal moments" are as uncontrollable as they are unexpected, and they tear holes in the deliberately woven web of memories that make up identity. The intrusion of such experiences breaks the continuity of poetic self-construction. Such a mystic moment of transition is described in *Tintern Abbey*:

> [...] that serene and blessed mood,
> In which the affections gently lead us on,
> Until, the breath of this corporeal frame
> And even the motion of our human blood
> Almost suspended, we are laid asleep
> In body, and become a living soul:
> While with an eye made quiet by the power
> Of harmony, and the deep power of joy,
> We see into the life of things.
>
> (41–49)

As the gaze is suspended, the eye becomes the gateway to something that cannot be seen so much as sensed. Such an eye, like the calm lakes in the poem *Memory*, is an image for the mystic state of the soul – a state that arises in a sequence of phases:

1. Suspension of gravity, loss of wakeful consciousness, transition into an in-between state
2. Relaxation, expansion of the soul to its limits
3. Motionlessness, brooding silence, complete stillness
4. Contact between man and Nature, the divine sinks deep into the soul

Here are two more examples from *The Prelude*:

> [...] oh, then, the calm
> And dead still water lay upon my mind
> Even with a weight of pleasure, and the sky.
> Never before so beautiful, sank down
> Into my heart, and held me like a dream.[36]

---

[36] Ibid., II, 176–180. Paul de Man, who also quotes some of these passages, sees them as indicating the dilemma of consciousness "to be in an endlessly precarious state of

The second example commemorates a boy who grew up in Nature but died at the age of twelve. He could imitate the voices of owls so perfectly that they would play a game of echoes with him. When there were pauses that extended into silences,

> Then sometimes, in that silence while he hung
> Listening, a gentle shock of mild surprise
> Has carried far into his heart the voice
> Of mountain torrents; or the visible scene
> Would enter unawares into his mind,
> With all its solemn imagery, its rocks,
> Its woods, and that uncertain heaven, received
> Into the bosom of the steady lake.[37]

Such are the moments of *Shechinah*, when the divine enters the soul of man. They are moments of pure presence, in which the wound of time is healed, and the impressions they make are deeper and more direct than all those experiences that are condemned to pass into the posteriority of memory. Wordsworth associates the absolute presence of *Shechinah* with children, who have, as it were, the civil rights to Nature. He sees his other self in them – the long-lost, original form of anamnesis that unexpectedly removes the bonds of subjectivity. They have that for which his poetic technique is only a substitute, because it cannot write directly into the soul but only on paper.

The wound of time is the Romantic equivalent of a fall in status – it is the leftovers from a form of duration that is peculiar to Nature. Disappearing into time entails alienation, but every theory of alienation contains a salvational vision of unity. Gnosis mythologized this theory into a drama of forgetting and remembering, with two contradictory

---

suspension" – a state that at any time might lapse into unconsciousness; he speaks of "the fall into death" (de Man, *The Rhetoric of Romanticism*, New York 1984, 54).

37 *The Prelude*, V, 406–413. One cannot help wondering how such experiences can be conveyed in the third person. How does the poet know all this? In fact there is an earlier version of these lines – which were among the earliest to be written – and it is in the first person. It is significant that the experience is transposed to a child, of whom nothing else is known other than the fact that he died before consciousness could develop an individual identity. Radical anamnesis is the prerogative of the child; it can be neither developed nor preserved. Of course the poet himself survives the death of this "boy of Winander," but for him anamnesis is only indirect, and accessible only through retrospection and the contemplation of the boy's gravestone. See Geoffrey Hartman, *Wordsworth's Poetry 1787–1814*, New Haven, London 1971, 19–22.

forms of memory battling against each other: one removed individuality, and so participated in the divine; the other enhanced individuality,
and obliged man to bear it on his earthly journey through life. The
second memory is the forgetting of the first; divine memory is dark-
ened and suppressed into unrecognizability by that which is acquired
here on Earth. "Gnosis" is nothing less than the restoration of the first
memory – the rediscovery of its faded tracks.

On the threshold of the modern age, Gnostic ideas had become
irrelevant. They stood in the way of modernity, and Locke made
every effort to disprove doctrines like anamnesis and rebirth, because
they were obstacles to the consolidation of social identity. Individuality, distinctiveness, sound common sense – these were the essential
social and political requirements. Any weakening of the self through
a loss of individuality meant a weakening of the modern concept of
identity.

Two or three generations later, Locke's principles had become a
social reality. In the meantime, however, they had also revealed the
negative side of property-owning individualism. The society Locke had
envisaged had proved to be one of egotists. Such conditions therefore
gave rise to new problems – how to curb self-interest, how to create
social bonds, how to find a metaphysical counter to alienation and
loneliness.[38] Wordsworth tried to overcome the social isolation with
his theory of "habits,"[39] and the metaphysical isolation with his theory
of anamnesis.

The Enlightenment image of man as a subjective self was partly
rejected by the Romantics. While the modern concept of common
sense led to the emergence of the "self," the Romantics revived the

---

[38] One example is love – a term that Locke mentions under "desires," and subordinates
to individual experiences of pleasure and pain, whereas for the Romantics it became
a magic formula as well as being a central concept especially in *The Prelude*. It stands
for the Utopian and one might even say the religious counter image to everything
that is so confused and confusing in human society.

[39] The theory of "habits," like that of anamnesia, aims to shut out memory and establish
continuity and simultaneity. Nature, which was constantly before Wordsworth's eyes
during his childhood ("The scenes [...] /Remained in their substantial lineaments / Depicted on the brain, and to the eye / Were visible, a daily sight"), does
not become a memory but a permanent and substantial part of himself ([...] did
at length / Become habitually dear, and all /Their hues and forms were by invisible
links / Allied to the affections," *The Prelude* I, 637–640).

concept of the soul,[40] which led to a divine center of being that transcended individuality – a "non-self." Locke's empirical view aimed to place man as a social self within a rapidly modernizing world, whereas Wordsworth's spiritual vision of man as a soul tried to link him with his divine, self-transcending origins. Locke saw himself as the modern founder of knowledge; Wordsworth saw himself as the prophet of lost wisdom. The path to this was anamnesis, which as we have seen is the reverse side of recollection. It went in exactly the opposite direction to Locke's path from the soul to the *tabula rasa.* In opposition to the impartiality of sensual empiricism, which had built knowledge on the firm foundations of experience, Wordsworth advanced a theory of anamnesis, whose poetic monument is his famous ode *Intimations of Immortality from Recollections of Early Childhood.*[41] This ode stages the Gnostic drama of remembering and forgetting. It runs through the lifespan of the individual, in which the child is wise, close to Nature, and godlike, whereas the adult is knowing, socialized, and "fallen." The delicate bond that binds him to the divine is irrevocably broken in adulthood, and this endows the lost condition with the aura of wholeness and holiness.

What applies to people also applies to language. In the third book of his essays, Locke shows that the basic foundation of knowledge is language. Wordsworth and his fellow Romantics look from the language of humans to the language of Nature, and they elucidate social conditions in terms of metaphysical conditions. The epiphanies in which man witnesses the divine are called "sublime," and what Nature reveals to man at such special moments has far more to do with theology than with natural history. Nature becomes a form of writing, of

---

[40] This concept of the soul is Hellenistic and pagan, and stems from the Gnostic, hermetic, neo-Platonic tradition. It enjoyed a renaissance through the neo-Platonism of the Florentine Academy, and also made its way to England (Cambridge Platonism), where Wordsworth may have fastened onto this tradition. See Aleida Assmann, "'Werden was wir waren' Anmerkungen zur Geschichte der Kindheitsidee," in *Antike und Abendland* 29 (1978).

[41] As a negative counterpart to Wordsworth's myth of childhood, see Locke, Essay II, I, 6: "He that attentively considers the state of a child, at his first coming into the world, will have little reason to think him stored with plenty of ideas, that are to be the matter of his future knowledge."

holy writ, that tells of first and last things. The Alps, for instance, are for Wordsworth's generation

> Characters of the great Apocalypse,
> The types and symbols of Eternity,
> Of first, and last, and midst, and without end.[42]

The concepts of anamnesis and the sublime have one thing in common: they denote a crossing of borders between this world and another. Both concepts entail experiences of transcendence, in which the "yoke of the Earth" is shaken off, the subject moves beyond consciousness, and the contours of the social self disappear. In moments of anamnesis, the curtain is drawn back, revealing a view of the foundations of human existence:

> Our destiny, our nature, and our home
> Is with infinitude, and only there . . . [43]

I have suggested that as *memoria* and rhetoric faded, new forms made their way to the fore. With Locke, there was a general upgrading of individual recollection as a means of constructing personal identity. The Romantics went much farther along this path. At a time when history was moving at an alarming speed, they experienced the temporality and transience of human life with a new urgency. As in Shakespeare's Histories, memory plays a major part in Wordsworth's poetry, either as a means of eternalizing important moments, or as an aid to the construction of the self. He drew poetic consequences from his view that the individual created himself by using the power of the imagination to work on the materials of memory. "Each man is a memory to himself" (*The Prelude*, III, 189) is the basic principle behind his art, which he applied of course to himself: "A Traveller I am, / And all my tale is of myself" (*The Prelude*, III, 196 f.). *The Prelude* is the heroic project of autobiography as autogenesis, and the driving force behind it is not the Puritan's scrutiny of his own conscience, but the poetic power of imagination (although it must be acknowledged that

---

[42] Wordsworth, *The Prelude*, VI, 570–572.
[43] Ibid., VI, 538–539.

the poem *Memory* does provide a reminder that the hidden residues of guilt set the wheels of the poetic memory in motion).

Recollections, which are the form of memory aided by the imagination, stand under the influence of time. They are characterized by their indistinctness, their faded tracks, and the permanent danger that they will be lost forever. There are no mnemotechnical devices that can counter this erosion by time, but imagination can help to do so. Emotions, which can be neither preserved nor reproduced, can nevertheless be created anew under the conditions of belatedness, and can take on a second, supplementary life of their own.

Ecstatic anamnesis brings out the passive reverse side of active, masculine imagination. It marks the point at which the (heroic / hybrid) project of autogenesis turns into selflessness and the surrender of the self. The enclosing walls of subjective consciousness are broken open, to offer a view of another world and another self. The Romantic self gives way to this greater form of being, which is none other than what we might call the de-individualized soul. Wordsworth shows us that recollection and anamnesis, self and soul, are by no means mutually exclusive, but in fact condition one another. And indeed it is even possible to detect in this Romantic dialectic the beginnings of a different dialectic to which we will return in due course: that of voluntary and involuntary memory.

5

Memory Boxes

> As in life, so in reading a man of heart has only a few trusted friends.
>
> Herder, Letters for the Advancement of Humanity

Exploring places of memory is not limited to temporal horizons of the past that prove to have meaning for the future. Each of the three sections of this study contains at least one chapter that deals with spatial concretizations of memory. This chapter deals with objects in which important documents are preserved. There are both mobile and immobile places of memory. Unlike the archive, which I return to later, the box is mobile and strictly confined. In the Middle Ages, people used chests with iron fittings to store their parchments, and they spoke of them as "treasure chests." The Latin word for box or chest is *arca*, from which is derived "ark," as in Noah's Ark. The latter provided safe refuge, but Noah had to impose strict conditions of selection for entry: only two animals from each species were allowed on board. In this respect, Noah's Ark is a microcosm of the world at large, for the tighter the space, the more limited and hence the more valuable is the content. When the Israelites were wandering in the desert, they took with them a chest containing the commandments that God had given to Moses: the Ark of the Covenant. When Aeneas left the burning city of Troy, he carried on his shoulders not only his aged father but also the souls of his ancestors, the sacred Penates.[1]

---

[1] See Virgil, *Aeneid*, Book 2, 717. It is significant that Aeneas is not allowed to touch the Penates until his warrior's hands have been ritualistically washed. The image has

Such portable containers may be seen as images for the contrac-
tion of cultural memory. I will consider three such images, taken from
different historical periods: Noah's ark, as interpreted by Hugh of
St. Victor from the 12th century, Darius's coffer, as described by Heinrich Heine in the 19th century, and the box of books from a short
story by E. M. Forster around 1900. Looking at these containers of
memory will give us insights into the selection processes that govern
the construction of cultural memory.

MEMORY AS AN ARK — HUGH OF ST. VICTOR'S CHRISTIAN MNEMOTECHNICS

For the medieval world, reading was of the utmost importance as an
activity of collecting, learning, and healing. It lay at the very heart of the
monastic life and was practiced as the art of methodically guided meditation. Its importance, however, depended on its being underpinned
by memory. The Scriptures demanded a very special art of reading,
which Hugh compared to a gigantic hall in which every sound draws its
significance from the harmony of the whole. In order that each individual passage should truly be heard to convey the complete harmony
including the overtones of the fourfold meaning of the Scriptures (literal, allegorical, moral, anagogical), one needed to practice special
exercises, which Hugh took over from classical mnemotechnics.

The ancient art of memory had its setting in the public spaces of the
city. The importance of public speaking was linked to the importance
of this art, and in Rome, for instance, its range extended from politics
to the law. Quintilian (35–100 AD) addressed his textbook on the art of
memory principally to jurists. In its early days, Christianity had no need
of classical mnemotechnics, and the Church Fathers neglected the art
because they were not interested in rhetoric and the political culture
of public speaking. Their focus lay not on writing and presenting their
own texts, but on the liturgical performance and interpretation of the
Scriptures, and for these purposes classical mnemotechnics offered
little assistance.

to be visualized on three levels: Aeneas carries Anchises, and Anchises carries the
Penates.

The revival of mnemotechnics in the 12th century coincided, among other factors, with the encyclopedic projects of the time. There was a desire to collect all available knowledge, arrange it, and harmonize it. Hugh played his part in the medieval revival of the art of memory with two writings on mnemotechnics: *De tribus maximis circumstantiis gestorum* and *De arca Noe morali.* These were not written for politicians or jurists but for monks, and his aim was to instruct them in the art not of public speaking but of "memorial reading." By adapting classical mnemotechnics for Christian purposes, Hugh built up a memory that laid the foundations for a cultural identity.

In the first of these writings, Hugh begins with spatial models of order and their orientation toward an inner vision. In the following passage, in which he addresses his young pupil, he sets out the basic principles of classical mnemotechnics applied to the reading process:

> My child. Wisdom is a treasure and thy heart is the place to store it. When you learn wisdom, you gather valuable treasures; they are immortal treasures that do not fade nor lose their lustre. The treasures of wisdom are manyfold, and there are many hiding places in your heart: here for gold, there for silver, elsewhere again for precious stones...You must learn to distinguish these spots, to know which is where, in order to remember where you have placed this thing or that...Just observe the money-changer in the market and do like him. See how his hand darts into the appropriate satchel... and instantly draws out the right coin.[2]

The spatial order contained in this image is given a precise and succinct formula: "*Confusio* is the mother of ignorance and forgetfulness, *discretio* brings intelligence to light and strengthens the memory."[3] What this amounts to is that an imaginary space is to be so structured that it should contain as many memorized entries as possible, each with its own clearly marked position, and these can be brought out again when required. This, then, is memory architecture, a kind of mental topography not unlike the structure of digital networks, where

---

[2] Hugh of St. Victor, *De tribus maximis circumstantiis gestorum*, ed. William M. Green, *Speculum* 18 (1943), 483–493; quoted from Ivan Illich, *In the Vineyard of the Text. A Commentary to Hugh's Didascalicon*, Chicago, London 1993, 36.

[3] Hugh of St. Victor, quoted from Ivan Illich, "Von der Prägung des Er-Innerns durch das Schriftbild. Überlegungen zur Arche Noah des Hugo von St. Victor," in A. Assmann and D. Harth (eds.), *Mnemosyne*, 48–56; here 49 (see Chapt. 2, n. 25).

the pupil can feel at home and can find his way around as effortlessly as the money-changer selecting from his bags. Mary Carruthers, whose book on the medieval art of memory contains detailed descriptions of memory metaphors, also highlights the money-changer's bags among the various sacred and profane containers.[4]

The word "thesaurus" has two meanings, as it refers either to the treasure or to the chest that contains it. In the case of a moneybag, there is a clear difference between the value of the container and that of the content, but if the content is holy, then the material container will also tend to be more elaborate. This is particularly so with the costly shrine (*scrinum*), in which valuable liturgical instruments, holy scriptures, books, and relics are preserved. The concept of concern, though, is Hugh's *arca*, which means a wooden chest or box in which valuable objects are transported. As they usually contained books, one might say that they were a kind of portable library that preceded the permanent libraries that were later set up in the monasteries. Because of the close link between book and box, the *arca* became a recognized metaphor for memory. Hugh, whose art of memory was applied to monastic reading, saw memory as a container for knowledge that was to be collected and preserved. This knowledge – accumulated, combined, and memorized – was called wisdom, and the heart as the seat of memory was the *arca* of wisdom. Oscillating between the material and the immaterial dimensions of wisdom, John of Salisbury described memory as "a sort of mental bookcase, a sure and faithful custodian of perceptions."[5]

If the heart is the *arca sapientiae*, this treasure chest of wisdom must be very carefully constructed. Lifelong schooling of the memory is the equivalent of building the ark. The Christian mnemotechnician Hugh of St. Victor, however, endowed the word *arca* with an extra dimension when he linked it both to the ark that God instructed Noah to build when he sent down the Flood, and also to the Ark of the Covenant in which the Mosaic Laws were kept. Within this

---

4 Mary Carruthers, *The Book of Memory. A Study of Memory in Medieval Culture*, Cambridge 1990, 39. Until the 1960s, Hugh's moneybags had a parallel in the sort of container-boxes in which train conductors kept their money in cylinders sorted according to the sizes of the coins.
5 Ibid., 43.

metaphorical chest Hugh combined Bible reading, moral instruction, and memory training: "I give you [...] the ark of Noah as a model of spiritual building, which your eye may see outwardly so that your soul may be carved inwardly in its likeness."[6]

Hugh's ark is a three-story structure, following the three stages of exegesis: Noah's historic ark stands beneath the arch of Christ's church, and this in turn is encompassed by the arch that the Christian reader builds in his heart. The ark is a complex mnemotechnical construct that provides access to relevant names, times, places, and numbers mentioned in the Bible. This mnemonic structure transforms the Bible into what nowadays might be called a three-dimensional hypertext, whose entries are not only sorted into connected columns, but are also filled with all the knowledge that is relevant to salvation, so that whatever element is focused on will evoke other important elements in a controlled sequence. Illich speaks of an "advanced three-dimensional multi-coloured monster memory scheme." It has been calculated that one would need about 220 square meters of paper in order to compile a legible plan of Hugh's mnemotechnical ark.[7] He himself compared it to a pharmacy – a shop full of valuable things:

In it, you will find whatever you are searching for, and when you have found something, you will think of many more things. Here the richness of our story of salvation is told from the beginning to the end of the world, and here is the constitution of our universal church; here the compact tale of historic events, and here the secrets of the sacraments, and here the step-by-step sequence of answers, judgements, meditations, observations, good deeds, virtues and rewards.[8]

Hugh's ark is both container and content. The wisdom that has taken on memorable form inside of it is not of this world; whoever enters

---

[6] Hugh, *De arca Noe morali*, I, 2; *Patrologiae cursus completus* [...] *omnium sanctorum patrum*. Series Latina, Vol. 176, 622 B, Paris 1844–1864; see Carruthers, *The Book of Memory*, 44 (see n. 4).

[7] Illich, *In the Vineyard of the Text*, 37 f. (see Chapt. 5, n. 2). Pater Patrice Sicard in fact succeeded in creating this artwork in considerably less space. In a comprehensive 13-volume edition of Hugh of St. Victor's collected works, under the overall editorship of Pater Rainer Berndt, S. J., Pater Sicard was entrusted with the volume on Noah's ark, and he supplemented the text with a construction of the memory plan in the format of a folding plate. (I am indebted to Claudia Sticher for this information.)

[8] Hugh of St. Victor, *De arca Noe morali*, IV, 9; PL 680B.

into contemplation here exits the world. As a place of memory, the ark is a sanctum – an inner refuge granting exile from the world with God's blessing.

But in every person, so long as life continues in this fallen world . . . there is the Flood. The good are like those who are safely carried over the waters in a boat; the bad are like those who suffer shipwreck and must drown. Only the ship of faith steers safely across the ocean, only the ark bears us over this flood, and if we wish to be saved, then it is not enough to carry the ark in our hearts, we must also dwell within it.[9]

Hugh's ingenious ark soon became obsolete. His great unifying construct of text, knowledge, and morality fell apart with succeeding generations, who turned away from monastic reading and gave preference to scholarship. The new form of mental training abandoned the all-embracing vision that sought to encompass the whole world in memory. Around the middle of the 12th century, there was a sea change in Christian mnemotechnics: the function of memory shifted from that of an all-embracing container to that of an instrument of knowledge. Three hundred years before movable type came into use, a revolution occurred in reading habits and experiences, the consequences of which can scarcely be overestimated. Ivan Illich considers this turning point in the history of European writing to have been even more significant than the Gutenberg revolution. The movement away from monastic and toward scholarly reading was accompanied by a whole series of innovations. The most brilliant of these was the new layout of the *pagina*. The text, which had hitherto been a kind of score for liturgical or contemplative reading, was now given a clear visual format that made it much easier for the eye to process its content. The change of function and the accompanying invention of the *pagina* resulted in a new technological framework: the content of the text was no longer structured mnemonically, but instead was given an optical design through abstract signs such as titles, chapter headings, different-sized letters, colored highlights, and paragraphs. These reading aids, which also included alphabetical indexes, made it possible to organize knowledge from a variety of new perspectives. The sheer

---

[9] Ibid, 6; PL 675 B-C; Illich, *In the Vineyard of the Text*, (see n. 2).

volume of memory, vastly increased by the advent of a new writing technology, wrecked the ark.

DARIUS'S COFFER — HEINRICH HEINE

My second example of a memory box is that of Darius's coffer. This too was an ark, but the treasure was neither jewels nor animals. It contained the two volumes of Homer's works. The precious container already denotes the value of the content that must at all costs be protected against loss or destruction. Earlier, when discussing the role of poetry as the medium of fame, I looked at the October Eclogue in Spenser's cycle *The Shepheardes Calender* that made reference to Darius's coffer. The gloss to this text states:

So favoured he [Alexander the Great] the only name of a poet [. . .] that when he came to ransacking of king Darius' coffers, whom he lately had overthrown, he found in a little coffer of silver the two books of Homer's works, as laid up there for special jewels and riches, which he taking thence, put one of them daily in his bosom, and the other every night laid under his pillow. Such honour have Poets always found in the sight of Princes and noble men.[10]

Heinrich Heine excavated the same coffer from the buried treasure of historical motifs, and once more shone a literary spotlight on it. His version is to be found in the "Hebräische Melodien" that form part of the late cycle of the *Romanzero* (1851). This poem, which is dedicated to the memory of the Hispanic-Jewish poet and mystic Judah Halevi, begins with a quotation. It is a paraphrase of Psalm 137, which depicts the age-old Jewish theme of disastrous "forgetting":

> Dry with thirst, oh let my tongue cleave
> To my palate – let my right hand
> Wither off, if I forget thee
> Ever, O Jerusalem[11]

In the psalm, the memory of Jerusalem is sealed with an oath and a self-curse; it is a liturgically sacrosanct memory for the pious. In

---

[10] *The Poetical Works of Edmund Spenser*, ed. J. C. Smith and E. de Selincourt, London, Oxford, New York, Toronto 1965, 459.

[11] Heinrich Heine, "Jehuda ben Halevy," from R*omanzero*, in *The Complete Poems of Heinrich Heine. A Modern English Version by Hal Draper*, Boston 1982, 655–677, 655.

Heine's poem, however, the speaker does not belong to this group, as becomes manifest through a significant change of tone from the first to the second stanza. In the latter, the stern commandment gives way to a reminiscence by someone who has only vague memories of the canonical voices of tradition. Remembrance of Jerusalem leads to remembrance of services in the synagogue:

> Words and melody keep buzzing
> In my head today, unceasing,
> And I seem to make out voices
> Singing psalms, I hear men's voices –
>
> (655)

The verses that follow are bathed in the "twilight of remembrance" (661), like some long forgotten piece of information slowly and hesitantly making its way back into the conscious mind. Very gradually the figures emerging from the mists of forgetfulness begin to take on a shape:

> Phantom figures, which of you
> Is Jehuda ben Halevy?
> But they scurry by me quickly –
> Ghosts will shun with fear the clumsy
> Consolations of the living –
> Yet I recognized him there –
>
> (655)

After emergence and recognition come memories of the great poet, which take up the first part of the poem. The second part once again begins with a quotation from a psalm, and once again clear recollections make their way through the dreamlike webs of memory before they swiftly give way to more reverie. This time the dreamer is plunged into subjective misery, but memory rescues him by putting him back on the tracks of the great Halevi and his Jerusalem poem.

This mixture of quotations from the Bible, visions, world-weariness, legends, and historical memories is followed in the third section by something new and apparently quite unrelated: the story of Darius's coffer. The speaker's meditations on Halevi are interrupted – perhaps forgotten – when his attention focuses on a costly object. It is a precious casket that Alexander the Great plundered from Darius. This is filled with jewels, and Heine devotes no less than seventeen stanzas to Alexander's emptying it, before he finally refills it with something quite different – a papyrus scroll containing the epic poems of Homer.

Coffers and jewelry have an emblematic link to memory. The coffer is associated with collecting, containing, and preserving, whereas jewelry indicates the precious content that needs to be protected. Thus the treasure chest is something one is anxious not to lose and so places under lock and key – a favorite image for the desire to eliminate the transience of certain memories and save them from decay and oblivion.[12] Heine introduces yet another meaning: in addition to preciousness and protection, his treasure chest stands for personal selection, emotional attachment, and commitment to a particular tradition. It is this combination of meanings that turns the chest into an image for cultural memory as a whole.

The coffer episode may have seemed initially like a digression, but in fact it leads straight back to the earnestness of the first verse and to the catastrophe of forgetting. The Jews arm themselves against such a disaster through material and ritually embodied forms of memory. These include the tefillin and the mezuzah – miniature containers for unforgettable texts that are written on parchment in calligraphic handwriting, as an immunization against the sickness of forgetting. The ceremonial Jewish forms of memory shine through Heine's verses on the Persian coffer. He comes close to them, but he replaces them with as worldly a symbol as possible (the coffer) that he fills not with liturgical texts from Deuteronomy, but with Jewish poetry – namely that of Jehudah Halevi.

Heine's coffer episode provides variations on different aspects of the problem of cultural memory. First of all, there is "the parody on tradition." As already mentioned, the emptying of the casket takes up seventeen stanzas, in which Heine pinpoints with great precision a negative genealogy of loss. He inverts such basic forms of tradition as inheritance, *depositum*, and *translatio*.[13] In his tale, the "deposit" is

---

[12] Shakespeare also liked this image, and associated it with memory. He did not, however, establish any clear connection between memory and the treasure chest, but tended to play almost subliminally with the theme, using surprising turns of phrase. Sonnet 48: "Thee I have not locked up in any chest"; Sonnet 52: "So is the time that keeps you as my chest"; Sonnet 65: "Shall Time's best jewel from Time's chest lie hid?"

[13] See A. Assmann, *Zeit und Tradition. Kulturelle Strategien der Dauer*, Vienna 1998.

misappropriated, squandered, given away, and sold – exactly the sort of treatment it was supposed to be protected against. Ironically, though, this story of loss is told in the style of a genealogical table, with a continuous chain that begins in Persia, passes through Greece, Babylon, and Egypt; involves the Turks and the Christians; and ends up with Baroness Salomon Rothschild and bourgeois Paris. The genealogy, the myth of *translatio*, and the chain of tradition form the normative backdrop against which this paradoxical "tradition of loss" unfolds.

Next comes the dualism of *Athens versus Jerusalem*. The story of the coffer is one of double replacement. Alexander exchanges pearls for Homer – that is, material for cultural values – and Heine exchanges Homer for Halevi, which entails a shift from Athens to Jerusalem. The polarization and rivalry between these two pillars of western culture have too long and too changeable a history for us to sum it up in a few sentences here,[14] but it is characterized by alternating periods in which each influenced the other, or each radically departed from the other. Within the domain of literature and aesthetics, different cultural traditions can easily be blended together, and within the context of religious identity these traditions are mutually exclusive. Toward the end of his life, Heine switched from one pole to the other – a change of direction that, in typically ironic fashion, he set out in the epilogue to his *Romanzero*. He tells us that he has had an encounter with the God of the Pantheists, "but I had no use for him. This poor visionary being is intertwined and interwoven with the world, imprisoned in it as it were, and yawns in your face, will-less and powerless. To have a will of one's own one must be a person, and in order to manifest it, one must have the elbowroom."[15]

Things are not much better with the Greek gods, for whom he once had such respect. However he insists that his "return to God," which his friends call a "relapse into the old superstition," has nothing to do with any sort of conversion, which would of course imply sharp criticism of his preceding position. He confesses that on his journey from "Athens" to "Jerusalem," he may have turned away from his

---

[14] See A. Assmann, "Jordan und Helikon – der Kampf der zwei Kulturen in der abendländischen Tradition," in Jürgen Ebach and Richard Faber (eds.), *Bibel und Literatur*, Munich 1995, 97–111.

[15] Heine, *Romanzero*, 695 (see n. 11).

"old heathen gods," but he has not renounced them. He dramatizes his departure from them ("in love and friendship") in an unforgettable scene:

It was in May 1848, on the day when I went out for the last time, that I said goodbye to the gracious idols I worshipped in more fortunate times. I dragged myself to the Louvre only with great effort, and I almost broke down altogether when I entered the lofty hall where the blessed goddess of beauty, Our Lady of Milo, stands on her pedestal. I lay at her feet for a long time, and I wept so hard that I must have moved a stone to pity. The goddess also gazed down on me with compassion, but at the same time so disconsolately as if to say: Don't you see that I have no arms and so cannot help?[16]

In personal as in cultural memory there is a dire shortage of space. The more limited the capacity, the more important the selection and therefore the more valuable the content. Darius's coffer may be seen as an emblem of this narrowing down of memory. In view of the drastically reduced space, liberal freedom of choice gives way to an existential demand for a decision: Athens *or* Jerusalem. The text that the poet of the *Romanzero* would like to enclose in the coffer is an existential one with which one not only sleeps and wakes (like Alexander), but also lives and dies. However, despite all his protestations, Heine's allegiance to the great Jewish poet is cast in the subjunctive:

> In my own mind I was thinking:
> If I ever owned that casket
> And were not compelled to sell it
> Right away for ready money,
> I would keep enclosed within it
> All the poems of our rabbi –
>
> (p 667)

A third theme of this text concerns "'*Bildung*' versus tradition." The tale of Darius's coffer has an epilogue that in Section 4 begins with the words:

> My good wife's dissatisfaction
> With the chapter just concluded
> Bears especially upon the
> Precious casket of Darius.

[16] Ibid., 696.

> Almost bitterly she comments
> That a husband who was truly
> So religious would have cashed in
> That old casket on the instant,
> And would certainly have purchased
> For his lawful wedded wife
> That fine cashmere shawl she needed
> With such monumental urgence.
>
> (670)

She can think of much more sensible things to do with this valuable piece than keeping in it the writings of some obscure poet that she has never even heard of. A cardboard box would do just as well for him,

> With some very swanky Chinese
> Arabesques to decorate it,
> Like a bonbon box from Marquis
> In the Passage Panorama.
>
> (670–671)

The wife, who is familiar with pictures from the most exotic parts of the world, has remained completely ignorant of the Jewish poets of medieval Spain. These "defects / Of the French-type education" (671) present the poet with the opportunity to further accentuate the importance of Jehudah Halevi. Heine caricatures "Bildung" as a feminine domain. Because men generally had far more important things to worry about, culture was left to women in the 19th century.[17] This brand of culture in the big cities reflected their pampered aspirations and shallow demands for consumer goods. It was a time of historicism and colonialism that, according to thinkers such as Heine and Nietzsche, engendered an effeminate fascination with foreign, exotic, nonessential frippery that stuffed the living rooms of the middle classes.

> On old mummies, or the pharaohs
> Who were stuffed in ancient Egypt,
> Merovingian shadow-monarchs,
> Or unpowdered wigs on ladies,
> Or the pigtailed lords of China,

---

[17] See Ute Frevert, "Kulturfrauen und Geschäftsmänner," in Frevert, *Mann und Weib, und Weib und Mann. Geschlechter-Differenzen in der Moderne*, Munich 1995, 133–165.

> Porcelain-pagoda princes –
> All of this is crammed into them,
> Clever girls! [...]
>
> (671x)

With the spoils from ancient times, the middle classes gilded their trivial and shallow world with exotic highlights, and the splendors that emerged from historical memory were lifeless plunder – the window dressing of culture. To counter this pretentious façade that masked a culture of materialism, Heine evoked the forgotten, suppressed tradition of Halevi, and in particular he called upon Halevi's legends of the martyrs. Emphatic tradition was his answer to the pomp and circumstance of cultural "Bildung." The exiled poet's *Song of Pearl Tears* and *Minnelied to Jerusalem* were a landmark not just in medieval mystic poetry, but also in the virtuosity of Jewish memory. Halevi's *Zionide* (Ode to Zion) turned longing into the most passionate form of memory. It devotedly reconstructed the sacred topography of a city that had long since fallen into ruin and now lay in the hands of enemy crusaders. Independently of the vagaries of history, Jerusalem – both earthly and heavenly – becomes in these verses a place of survival; one might even call it Halevi's treasure chest.

What Heine seeks to lock up in Darius's coffer has the quality of a cultural text.[18] This differs from elements of "Bildung" because it entails

1) an emphatic act of selection and decision: a personal, existential commitment to a poet and his work is set against the wide and colorful range of what is considered fashionable and interesting;

2) the ethos of unalterable preservation: by means of a text from a past and now alien era, a solid foundation is maintained despite all of the radical changes of time;

3) the normative power of such texts, which transcends their aesthetic qualities: the normative connection with identity makes them into a continuous source of self-interpretation and personal guidance for life.

---

[18] See A. Assmann, "Was sind kulturelle Texte?," in Andreas Poltermann (ed.), *Literaturkanon – Medienereignis – kultureller Text. Formen interkultureller Kommunikation und Übersetzung.* (Göttinger Beiträge zur Internationalen Übersetzungsforschung, Vol. 10), Berlin 1995, 232–244.

When, with his *Romanzero,* Heine gave literary form to this critical period in his life, he raised the basic problem of the relevance and scope of culture in a modern urban society dominated by material values and consumer goods. With the rapid increase of historicist knowledge expanding as far as Egypt and China, the binding forces of tradition lost their grip. Contemporary society abandoned tradition and exchanged it for the new institutions of "Bildung," including the museums, the opera, and the theater. With his poetic version of the choice and casket, Heine pointed out a way that led from education, not back to tradition but to a personal, literary canon. The fact that for Heine this was by no means a slide back into established traditions is made especially clear by the final part of his unfinished poem. Here he speaks explicitly about tradition, not just by recalling the names of exemplary and normative ancient poets, but also in order to establish his own place among them. Between the trinity of the Spanish-Jewish poets on the one hand and Heine wasting away in his "mattress vault" on the other, a genealogical connection is established through an interpolated anecdote. His family tree of poets goes back to a certain Schemiel in the Bible who was accidentally hit by a spear that had been aimed at another target. The tradition into which Heine here incorporates himself is one that he has invented himself. It binds Judaism to art within a genealogy of the unlucky and stigmatized.

THE CRUEL BOX — E. M. FORSTER

The third of our boxes is also an *arca* that contains books. It comes from an early short story by E. M. Forster that he wrote at the beginning of the twentieth century. The first words are: "It's a cruel box." They are spoken on the platform of a small provincial railway station by a porter, who looks at it suspiciously and concludes: "The weight's cruel. That'll need a barrow."[19] The chest that he cannot possibly put on his shoulders is full of books. The narrator has been invited to spend some time in the country, and hopes to finish his dissertation on the Greek optative while he is here. He has therefore brought all the notes, materials, and books with him in the box.

With some difficulty the box is loaded onto a one-horse carriage that has been sent to fetch the narrator from the station. In the driver's

---

[19] E. M. Forster "Ansell," in *The Life to Come and Other Stories,* Harmondsworth 1975.

seat sits Ansell, who is the eponymous hero of the story. He is one of the servants at the country house that the narrator used to visit in his youth and to which, after a gap of a few years, he is now returning as a 23-year-old student at Oxford. Relations with the rustic Ansell are not exactly straightforward: as teenagers they had enjoyed a close and boisterous friendship, but with the passing years they had grown increasingly apart from one another. Ansell's career had progressed from stable boy to gardener to hunt assistant, whereas the narrator had gone to public school, won a scholarship, and is now writing his doctorate with the prospect of a post at an Oxford college. During the ride it becomes clear that the two former childhood friends no longer have anything in common.

Ansell and the first-person narrator have developed in different directions: the former has expanded his chest, and the latter has expanded his brain. The servant Ansell, who is as muscular as he is monosyllabic, is the exact opposite of the weedy intellectual narrator, and the difference between them is articulated by the latter in a number of nuanced reflections that the former sums up in a single phrase: "Them books." The narrator's preoccupation with books has left its mark on his body: his shoulders sag, his back is bent, his chest has sunk in. "All good work must wear out some muscles, and though the Greek optative wears out more than most it is none the less good work."[20]

The climax of the story takes place on a steep stretch where the road narrows and runs alongside a gorge at the bottom of which is a river. At this point, the horse shies, as it cannot balance the load on the carriage, which is now listing to one side. The rails on the side of the road nearest the gorge break, and the carriage and its occupants are all but plunged into the abyss. However, with great skill and some good fortune, Ansell manages to bring it under control again, but the box falls off and crashes down into the depths of the gorge. The narrator watches the last phase of this fall as if in slow motion:

About halfway down it hit a projecting rock, opened like a water-lily, and rained its sweetness upon the deep. Most of the books were heavy and plunged like meteors through the trees into the river. One or two of the smaller ones roosted coyly for a minute on the branches before they too slipped through and disappeared. (32)

[20] Ibid., 30.

What is described here is less a fall than a metamorphosis.[21] The books change into Nature – they become water lilies, meteors, or roosting birds. The narrator, as he describes all this, is in a state of shock and is somehow detached from his consciousness, which is no position to process the implications of the disaster; what he perceives is a different world with a beauty of its own. It is quite different with his companion, who swiftly takes command of the situation: "Those books saved us. They went at the very moment I felt 'em tugging us over the edge." (32) This comment tells us a great deal: books save people when the latter break free from them. The ballast, or overloaded consciousness, is discarded at such a turning point, and changes into self-contained Nature.

With the fall of the "cruel box" the tables are turned: the narrator, when he realizes what has happened, is thunderstruck: "I knew that my career was closed" (35), but Ansell now becomes talkative and chatters away about his daily work. The next day, after a rainy night, a few remnants are rescued from the gorge, but the pages of the dissertation are already irretrievably on their way to the sea. As consciousness ebbs and oblivion sets in, the narrator comes closer to Ansell, who like a satyr brings him back into his rustic world. The end of the story builds up an image that illustrates this sinking into forgetfulness and natural unawareness:

Liddell and Scott's Greek Lexicon remains open on the ledge where the box split. In dry weather an invisible person rapidly turns over the leaves, hurrying from one word to another. But in the damp his ardour flags. There is something rather poetical in the idea of this unembodied searcher after knowledge, and I would write a Greek epigram on him, but I am forgetting the words. (35)

Only the wind can read now, and it can do so more fluently on dry days than on wet. The Greek epigram that would have found a cosmic reader cannot be written because the dictionary is no longer

---

[21] The motif of falling books has a history of its own and occurs in other texts of Forster's. There is a close parallel in "The Story of the Siren," again connected with the writing of a dissertation: a student's notebook with entries concerning "The Deist Controversy" falls to the bottom of the Mediterranean and also undergoes a fantastic, dream-like transformation. In *Howards End* falling books actually cost one character his life.

available, and this is where the circle of forgetfulness closes. Forster's tale (1902/1903) about the burden of knowledge and the blessings of forgetfulness reads like a narrative staging of the second of Nietzsche's *Untimely Meditations*. The problem of historicism, which was raised by Heine under the heading of "Bildung," was examined by Nietzsche under the title "The Uses and Disadvantages of History for Life" (1874), a text that we will return to in the next chapter. This theme is taken up by Forster through the contrasting pair of friends. Within the narrow framework of a short story, he conjures up a therapy of forgetfulness for an over-conscious, over-intellectual age. But he is not setting two independent characters against one another here: the rustic Ansell is the creation and homoerotic projection of the Oxford scholar's own desires. Ansell is the separated doppelgänger who embodies the fantasy of another, forgotten life. And the man who formulated the vision did so in the dusty confines of his library.

The three boxes inspected in this chapter are like a prism that captures different epochs in the history of western cultural memory. Hugh's ark forms both the climax and the closure of medieval Christian mnemotechnics; with extreme dedication, virtuosity, and attention to detail it collects the complete sum of salvational knowledge in one gigantic configuration that it internalizes through memory. The meaningful book that is to be protected in this box still exists in the singular; the total sum of wisdom is congruent with the holy text of Scriptures, the interpretation of which stretches endlessly into time. With Darius's box, we move from the religious to the literary canon. But in Heine's poem, the contents are switched, with Homer's worldly epic making way for the religious poetry of a medieval Jew. By leaving Paris and Athens for Jerusalem, Heine turns his back on secular culture without, however, undergoing conversion to orthodoxy. His focus is still on poetry. Space in Darius's box is limited, and so this image of memory stands on the one hand for evaluation, and on the other for the restriction of choice within cultural memory. The urgent need for selection and existential commitment was not triggered only by Heine's personal crisis – it was a general problem of the 19th century, and evidently increased as knowledge became ever more expansive, more complex, and more rootless. In terms of time and subject matter, it is only one small step from Heine to Forster, whose short story crams all this specialized, stultifying knowledge into one tightly packed box of books. There is no longer any hope of salvation *through* books and memory; the only hope now is salvation *from* books through forgetting. The focus of Forster's tale is not the training of memory, but the training of forgetfulness. Thus the theme of the memory box has come full circle, from books and memory as a united force for salvation, through increased value by way of selection and restriction, and finally to the crisis of cultural memory as dramatized in the "cruel box," the weight of which is a crushing burden on life.

6

Function and Storage

Two Modes of Memory

The last chapter surveyed the content and fate of three memory boxes in texts that are strikingly different in terms of historical period and style of writing. This historical and literary excursion may help to prepare the ground for the theoretical chapter that follows. Its general theme is the relationship between memory and identity. Because of the intricate link between both concepts, memory is limited in scope and is geared to external purposes, such as providing a personal or collective self-image and a normative orientation in time. From the supply of available knowledge, human memory selects only the amount that is necessary to help steer a clear course through daily contingencies, radical changes, and a bewildering abundance of information. In this sense, the memory boxes discussed earlier provide an analogy for the functioning of cultural memory in general, which is constructed through acts of (more or less) rigid selection that involve modes of evaluation, social inclusion and exclusion, and technical means of preservation.

HISTORY AND MEMORY

It is not only poets and philosophers who have explored the connection between memory and identity, but also sociologists and historians. In this chapter I examine the views of collective memory theorists, for whom the distinction between history and memory has become a central issue. Each of these tends to be defined in terms of difference – that is, the one is always what the other is not. Thus the emergence of critical historiography has been described as emancipation from patterns of official memory, but it can also be seen as a vindication of the rights of human memory to oppose the magisterial authority of historiography.

I begin once more with Friedrich Nietzsche, whose essay on "The Uses and Disadvantages of History for Life" drew a polemic contrast between the usefulness of memory and the irrelevance of history "for life." He starts out from the fact that "every man and every nation [. . .] requires, in accordance with its goals, energies, and needs, a certain kind of knowledge of the past."[1] In the 19th century, with the emergence of historical scholarship, this "certain kind of knowledge" had expanded beyond all boundaries. Nietzsche regarded this as an alarming and critical situation, because he was afraid that memory was in the process of losing its ability to restrict itself and to focus on the essentials necessary to preserve a community and culture. His term for such a coherent memory profile was "horizon." As an uncontrolled mass of historical knowledge spilled out over the edges of memory, however, the border between the necessary and the worthwhile on the one hand and the trivial and random on the other was becoming blurred. For Nietzsche, knowledge of the past had become increasingly functionless in relation to future orientation. It was turning into a dead weight, and had forfeited its character as a piece of equipment suited to the demands and conditions of an ever advancing present. Through the excess baggage of history, cultural memory had lost its two central functions: those of affect and identity, that is, as a motivating force and a formative self-image. It could no longer offer any definitive answer to questions such as, "Who are we?" or "What can we use as guidelines?" Basically, Nietzsche was setting two models of culture against one another that may be summed up as "history" and "memory." In the former, which he regarded as a threat, the dead weight of the past pressed on the present, whereas in the latter – which he yearned for – the past supported and nourished the present.

Maurice Halbwachs took a very different route to establish a difference between history and memory. As an empirical sociologist, he had no culture-critical axes to grind, and his sole interest lay in what

---

[1] Nietzsche, "On the Uses and Disadvantages of History," 77 (see Chapt. 3 , n. 6).

kept people together in groups. In this context, he discovered the importance of shared memories as a mode of cohesion. From this insight he extrapolated the concept of "group memory," emphasizing the circular effect of memories stabilizing groups, just as groups also stabilize memories. Halbwachs's studies of "collective memory" showed that its stability was directly connected to the composition and nature of the group. If the latter disbanded, its individual members lost those memories that had connected them to others. A political change of framework could have the same result, because – according to Halbwachs – the memories had no sticking power of their own, but depended essentially on social interaction and confirmation. In his constructivist, functionalist theory of memory there was no room for erratic or nonfunctional memories.

Halbwachs also drew a sharp distinction between "collective memory" and "historiography." He laid particular emphasis on the following differences:

- Collective memory ensures the uniqueness and continuity of a group, whereas historical memory tries to neutralize the dimensions of affect and identity.
- Collective memories, just like the groups with which they are linked, always exist in the plural, whereas historical memory, which provides a universal framework for many histories, exists in the singular.
- Collective memory tries to preclude change, whereas historical memory actually specializes in change.

He summed all this up as follows:

The historical world is like an ocean fed by the many partial histories.[...] History can be represented as the universal memory of the human species. But there is no universal memory. Every collective memory requires the support of a group delimited in space and time. The totality of the past events can be put together in a single record only by separating them from the memory of the groups who preserved them and by serving the bonds that held them close to the psychological life of the social milieus where they occurred, while retaining only the group's chronological and spatial outline of them.[2]

---

[2] Maurice Halbwachs, *The Collective Memory. Introduced by Mary Douglas*, New York, Cambridge 1980, 84.

No one would dispute that there is such a thing as "memory *in* the group," but can there also be such a thing as "memory *of* the group"? Group memory has no organic basis, and so taken literally it is unimaginable. On the other hand, it is more than a metaphor.

The French historian Pierre Nora has shown that what steers the memory of the group is neither a "collective soul" nor an "objective mind," but a society with its signs and symbols. Through these shared symbols, the individual participates in a common memory and a common identity. Nora took the theoretical step from the interactive group bound in a co-presence in time and space, as analyzed by Halbwachs, to the abstract community that transcends time and space by defining itself through symbols. The bearers of this kind of collective memory do not need to know one another in order to share a common identity. The nation is just such a community that stabilizes its abstract unity through the media and rites of political symbolism. Nora clearly distinguishes these national symbols from the scholarly discourse of historiography. He sees live (group) memory and analytical historiography as being locked in a battle that is driven by the forces of modernization:

Memory, and history, far from being synonymous, appear now to be in fundamental opposition. [...] Memory is a perpetually actual phenomenon, a bond tying us to the eternal present; history is a presentation of the past. [...] Memory installs remembrance within the sacred; history, always prosaic, releases it again. Memory is blind to all but the group it binds [...] History, on the other hand, belongs to everyone and to no one, whence its claim to universal authority.[3]

The memory theories of Nietzsche, Halbwachs, and Nora all emphasize the constructivist, identity-forming character of memory, and affirm its rights over a neutral historiography. The basic opposition in all three theories is between embodied and disembodied, or inhabited and uninhabited: memory belongs to living beings with prejudicial perspectives, whereas history, because it "belongs to everyone and no-one," is considered to be objective and so without identity. The criteria underlying this contrast might be summed up as follows:

---

[3] Pierre Nora, "Between Memory and History: Les Lieux de Mémoire," 8f. (see Introduction, n. 10).

Inhabited Memory	*Uninhabited Memory*
• is connected with a carrier that may be a group, an institution, or an individual	• is free from a specific carrier
• builds a bridge between past, present, and future	• splits past from present and future
• proceeds selectively by remembering and forgetting	• is interested in everything, and everything is equally important
• provides values that can support identity and norms	• seeks to establish truth and suspends behavioral norms and values

FUNCTIONAL MEMORY AND STORAGE MEMORY

Having made these contrasts as explicit as possible, I must now point out that the apparently clear opposition between memory and history as outlined by the three theorists is becoming less and less tenable. Today the general consensus is that there is no such thing as historiography without some form of memory work; whether overtly or not, it cannot wholly avoid interpretation, partiality, and identity. Indeed, the pendulum has now swung to the other extreme, for there are theorists who actually equate history and memory. The journal *History and Memory*, which was founded in 1989, is indicative of this development; in many of its essays the dividing line is blurred.

The neat polarization of history and memory seems to me just as unsatisfactory as the equation of the two. I would therefore like to suggest that history and memory should be grasped as two complementary modes of cultural memory. Presenting them, like Nietzsche, as compulsory alternatives panders to the demystifying purpose of culture-critical rhetoric. We may escape these alternatives by reconstructing the problem in a different analytical context.

The fundamental step that will take us beyond the confines of either polarization or equation of memory and history is the idea that inhabited memory and uninhabited memory are complementary and not contradictory. We can call the former "functional," and we can identify its main features as being group related, selective, normative, and future-oriented. By comparison, historical scholarship is, as it were, secondhand; it feeds on past memories and in new ways reconstructs that which has lost its living relevance to the present. This "memory of past memories" is what I would like to call "storage memory." We are all familiar with the continuous process of disposal by forgetting, the irretrievable loss from generation to generation of valued knowledge and live experiences. But not all is lost forever; a small segment is assembled and preserved in cultural archives, and it is possible for historical knowledge to reclaim some of these disembodied relics and abandoned materials and perhaps even reconnect them with the functional dimension of cultural memory.

This interweaving of functional and storage memory can be illustrated by a little digression into the realm of psychotherapy. The latter proceeds theoretically from the fact that the individual's memory is constructed on different levels. One is conscious remembrance. On this level, memories and experiences are made available by being brought into a particular configuration of meaning. The production of this is very much along the lines suggested by Locke, that is, through the self-interpretation and self-definition of the individual. It reflects how much the individual knows about himself, what value he attaches to himself and others, and how he interprets his own experiences. On this configuration of memory depend which opportunities are open to the individual and which are closed. Psychotherapy can help by reconfiguring and restructuring these memories – it can make them more conscious and more integrative, and it can reflect on boundaries and so reduce the pressure of repression and help to dismantle paralyzing, self-destructive barriers. This therapeutic approach is channeled through the concept of the "story." The life story that one "inhabits" ties together memories and experiences in a narrative construction of the self that determines one's life and provides guidance for future actions.[4]

Another level in the economy of memory consists of extremely heterogeneous elements: partly inert and unproductive, partly latent and so beyond the range of focused illumination, partly too amorphous for any orderly retrieval, partly painful or shameful, and therefore deeply buried. These elements of storage memory also belong to the

---

[4] The theologian and psychotherapist Dietrich Ritschl summed up this idea in a neat aphorism: "We are the stories that we can tell about ourselves"; see Ritschl, "Das 'story'-Konzept in der medizinischen Ethik," in *Ritschl, Konzepte: Ökomene, Medizin, Ethik; Gesammelte Aufsätze*, Munich 1986, 201–212.

individual, but they form a store to which, for various reasons, he is denied direct access. In order for memory to act as a guiding force, its elements must be suited to the purpose, that is, they must be endowed with relevance and be configured to provide meaning. If in such stories "persons organize and give meaning to their experience [...] then it follows that these stories are constitutive – shaping lives and relationships."[5]

This model of the individual functional memory draws a flexible and hence productive boundary between, on the one side, chosen, interpreted, and appropriated elements – that is, those that are attached to the configuration of the story – and, on the other side, the amorphous mass of unattached elements. Functional memory is highly selective, and only gives presence to a fraction of memory's contents. "Thus, over time and of necessity, much of our stock of lived experience goes unstoried and is never 'told' or expressed. It remains amorphous; without organization and without shape."[6]

Halbwachs also distinguished between meaningful and unprocessed elements in memory. For him translation into meaning was the precondition for an individual memory to enter into the collective memory. "Every personality and every historical fact, when it enters into this memory, is transposed into a lesson, a concept, a symbol; it takes on a meaning, and becomes an element in society's system of ideas."[7] Memories that enter the magnetic field of a particular structured meaning distinguish themselves from preceding meanings and experiences. Memory produces meaning, and meaning stabilizes memory. This always entails a retrospective construction of meaning.

Storage memory, on the other hand, is the "amorphous mass" of unused and unincorporated memories that surround the functional memory like a halo. The fact that they do not fit into a story or any other configuration of meaning does not mean that they are altogether forgotten. These partly unknown and partly unconscious layers of memory form the background and unacknowledged side of functional memory. We need not necessarily conceive of these two dimensions in

5 Michael White and David Epston, *Narrative Means to Therapeutic Ends*, Adelaide 1990, 12. For drawing my attention to this text and for other suggestions, I am grateful to Helm Stierlin, Arno Retzer, and Jörg Schweitzer.
6 Ibid.
7 Maurice Halbwachs, *Das Gedächtnis und seine sozialen Bedingungen*, Frankfurt a.M. 1985, 389f.

terms of a binary opposition of conscious versus repressed memories, but may look at them in terms of creating a perspective, separating a visible foreground from an invisible background. This structure of foreground / background can account for the dynamics of change in personal and cultural memory: as soon as the dominant configurations break up, current elements may lose their unquestioned relevance and give place to latent and formerly excluded elements that may resurface and enter into new connections and narratives. The deep structure of memory, with its internal traffic between actualized and nonactualized elements, is what makes it possible for changes and innovations to take place in the structure of consciousness, which would ossify without the amorphous reserves stored in the background.

An example of the interaction between functional and storage memory is the learning process, as described from a cybernetic perspective by the political scientist Karl Deutsch: "Since all learning including changes in goals or values consists in physical internal rearrangements, it depends significantly on material resources. The learning capacity of any system or organization, that is, the range of its effective internal rearrangements, can thus be measured to some extent by the number and kinds of its uncommitted resources."[8]

The term "uncommitted resources" (*ungebundene Hilfsmittel*) shows the manner in which it can be useful to store knowledge that is no longer, not yet, or temporarily not part of the functional framework. This supplementary knowledge can give rise to a self-reflexive memory of memories that remains detached from the functional memory, allowing for it to be critically reflected, changed, and renewed. Although it does not itself construct meaning or underpin values, it can form a stabilizing or corrective framework for these functional operations.

This dual structure of a functional and a storing memory also operates on the level of culture, provided that it uses writing. In an oral culture that is based on embodied and performed modes of rote learning and memorizing techniques such as quipus, painting, rhythm, dance, music etc., a distinction between functional and storage memory is unthinkable. The space for oral memory is so confined and

---

[8] Karl W. Deutsch, *The Nerves of Government. Models of Political Communication and Control*, second printing, New York, London 1967, 96.

the techniques of memorizing are so demanding that nothing can be retained unless it has the function of establishing the group's identity and ensuring its survival. In an oral culture, there is a homeostasis between knowledge and memory; or, to quote the nostalgic words of an 18th-century scholar, it was "a time, when all man could know, was all he could remember."[9] With the introduction of writing, however, a potential external medium of storage was created that irreversibly destroyed this natural balance. Because writing allows much more to be recorded and preserved than any individual can possibly remember, the effect is a growing surplus or mass of storage. Under these circumstances, the ties between memory and identity have to be redefined, and this is done by drawing dividing lines between the purposes of storage and identity formation. The *potential* inherent in writing consists in the codification and preservation of information independently of any living bearers and of any actualization through collective stagings. The *problem* inherent in writing consists in the tendency to accumulate unlimited amounts of information. Through external aids that are independent of human memory, the confines of embodied, living memory are shattered, and conditions are created for cultural archives, abstract knowledge, radical innovations, and the forgetting of traditions.

On the cultural level, storage memory contains what is unusable, obsolete, or dated; it has no vital ties to the present and no bearing on identity formation. We may also say that it holds in store a repertoire of missed opportunities, alternative options, and unused material. Functional memory, on the other hand, consists of vital recollections that emerge from a process of selection, connection, and meaningful configuration; they are – in Halbwachs's terms – culturally framed. In functional memory, unstructured, unconnected fragments are invested with perspective and relevance; they enter into connections, configurations, compositions of *meaning* – a quality that is totally absent from storage memory.

Cultural functional memory is connected with individual persons who re-embody it as its bearers and addressees. Collective agents such as states or nations create for themselves a functional identity memory

---

[9] Robert Wood, *An Essay on the Original Genius of Homer* (1769 and 1775), reprint Anglistica & Americana 174, Hildesheim, New York 1975, 260.

through which they adapt a certain version of the past and define their goals for the future. Storage memory provides no such foundation for identity; its specific and no less important use lies in preserving more and other memories than are considered relevant by the present frames of functional memory. After the French Revolution, the archive, incorporating the abrupt devalued past, turned into a cultural institution that reinforced new forms of historical curiosity and consciousness.

The Tasks of Functional Memory

Functional memory has a variety of tasks to perform, and we now look in detail at three of them: legitimization, delegitimization, and distinction. "Legitimization" is the immediate concern of official or political memory. The typical alliance between power and memory finds expression in the elaboration of detailed historical knowledge, preferably in the form of genealogy, because power needs origins. Precisely this need is fulfilled by genealogical memory, which has both a retrospective and a prospective side. Rulers usurp not only the past, but the future as well, because they want to be remembered and so they try to ensure that their deeds will be commemorated; for example, talked and sung about, immortalized in monuments, and recorded in archives. Power desires to legitimize itself retrospectively, and to immortalize itself prospectively. Almost all the extant historical sources of the Ancient East testify to this form of memorial politics.

The problem with this official memory lies in the fact that it depends on censorship and coerced rites of commemoration. It lasts as long as the power that it supports. It drives out any unofficial remembrance that might present itself as a critically subversive functional memory. This brings us to our second category: "delegitimization."

Peter Burke writes: "It is often said that history is written by the victors. It might also be said that history is forgotten by the victors. They can afford to forget, whereas the losers are unable to accept what happened and are condemned to brood over it, relive it, and reflect how different it might have been."[10] A fairly recent example of delegitimizing memory is the commemoration in 1989 of Imre Nagy,

---

[10] Peter Burke, "History as Social Memory," in Thomas Butler (ed), *Memory, History, Culture and the Mind*, 106 (see Chapt. 3, n. 15).

who was Prime Minister of Hungary in 1956 when the Soviet troops moved in to crush the uprising, and who was subsequently executed. His memory had been erased from the history books by the Communist regime and carefully kept out of the public eye. But it could not be extinguished, and indeed its exclusion only made it all the more solid. In 1989 a group of dissidents staged a symbolic funeral, initially at a cemetery in Paris; but in the same year they reburied their hero with full ceremonial honors and mass media coverage at the cemetery in Budapest. Imre Nagy, the embodiment of an officially erased memory, now became the symbolic figure of counter-memory and a decisive influence on the process of de-Stalinization in Hungary.[11] The motif underlying counter-memory, whose bearers are the conquered and the oppressed, is the delegitimization of power that is experienced as tyrannical. It is as political as the official memory, because in both instances it is linked with a claim to power. The counter-memory serves as a foundation not of the present but of the future, anticipating the time that will follow the fall of those currently in power.

A third task of the functional cultural memory is that of "distinction." This includes all symbolic forms of expression that help to create the profile of a collective identity. Religious communities are formed through shared memories that are perpetuated and renewed by rituals and festivals. These memories consolidate references to a common foundational history, such as Pesach for the Jews in commemoration of their exodus from Egypt, or Hanukkah, in celebration of the rededication of the Temple in Jerusalem. Other examples of festivals that restage identity-forming events are to be found in Athenian democracy and the French Revolution. In the secular domain, one might refer to 19th-century national movements that reconstructed or "invented" common traditions in order to create an identity for the new political subject called "the people." With the emergence of national movements, remembering one's own history and observing one's own traditions became a patriotic duty. National memory helped to transform territories into nation-states; it also introduced a new variety of memorial politics to Europe based on museums, commemorative practices, and new forms of democratic participation.

---

[11] Lecture given by Mate Szabo at a conference on Collective Memory organized by Harry Pross in Weiler im Allgäu, summer 1991.

The Tasks of Storage Memory

Functional memory makes a political statement and it profiles a distinct identity. Storage memory forms the counterpart to the different tasks and perspectives outlined earlier. What it is capable of achieving can best be gauged from where it is kept under complete control or has been eliminated, as in totalitarian states. In Stalinist Russia, cultural storage memory was the target of meticulous destruction; nothing was permitted that did not pass through the eye of the official doctrinal needle. Orwell depicted such conditions graphically in *1984*, and as we now know all too well, the scenario was not exaggerated.

Storage memory may be seen as an important reservoir for future functional memories. This is not only a precondition for the cultural phenomenon called the "Renaissance," but it is more generally a fundamental resource for all cultural renewal and change. It is equally important as a corrective to current functional memories in any society. If the borders between functional memory and storage memory remain permeable, elements can be exchanged, patterns of meaning can be altered, and even the general framework can be restructured. Without this border traffic between the different realms of cultural memory, drawing upon a reservoir of unused possibilities, alternatives, contradictions, criticisms, and unremembered incidents, change would be excluded and memory would be fixed and made absolute.

Orwell appears to have taken it for granted that storage memory will automatically form itself if the authorities cease to manipulate or erase it, but this is far from the case. Storage memory itself is no more natural or spontaneous than functional memory; it needs to be supported by institutions that preserve, conserve, organize, open up, and circulate cultural knowledge. Archives, museums, libraries, and memorial sites all play their part in this task, as do research institutes and universities, by resisting the automatic expulsion of the past from everyday memory just as they resist its deliberate exclusion from the functional memory. These institutions have a special license to relieve memory of its direct social usages. A culture that does not value the "otherness" of the past for its own sake does not create those open spaces in which the arts, the sciences, and the imagination can flourish. Built into these domains is a detachment from the immediate purposes and needs of the present, and this allows for exploration and innovation. It is precisely because of this detachment that storage memory is so vital for society – it creates a context in which different functional memories are embedded, and so to a certain degree it represents their external background, from where the restricted view of the past may be relativized, criticized, and ultimately even changed. Both functional and storage memory interact in a dialectical relationship that is to be found in liberal, literate cultures; and their future is to a large extent dependent on this ongoing intercourse.

There is an important distinction in historiographic terminology that can throw an additional light on the relationship between functional and storage memory. Lutz Niethammer has highlighted two terms that are used in the context of the study of historical sources (*Quellenkunde*).[12] These terms are "tradition" and "remnants." (They are closely related to a similar distinction made by Jacob Burckhardt, who referred to them as "texts" and "traces"; this distinction is discussed in the chapter on traces). Whereas tradition (or texts) refers to the conscious, deliberate articulations that construct meaning and convey messages across time, the remnants (or traces) correspond to contingent fragments and relicts that have fallen out of their contexts and carry no inscribed meaning of their own. Whereas the traditions have to be read within historical cultural frames, the remnants are opaque, indeterminate signs that must be deciphered within a framework that is to be created by the respective historian. The remnants constitute evidence for another kind of history and must be read very much in the way that a detective reads a crime scene. We may perhaps compare Niethammer's remnants to the *mémoire involontaire* that is no longer or not yet accessible to consciousness. Whereas Orwell imagines a dystopian world in which all traces of the past that might yield an alternative view of the world are erased and forgotten, other important memory theorists from De Quincey to Proust and Freud proceed from the assumption "that nothing is completely forgotten, but that all perceptions find in the traces of memory some kind of faded, suppressed, or overwritten imprint which in principle can be retrieved."[13] As an eminent scholar of oral history, Niethammer is particularly

---

[12] Lutz Niethammer, "Die postmoderne Herausforderung. Geschichte als Gedächtnis im Zeitalter der Wissenschaft," in Wolfgang Küttler, Jörn Rüsen, and Ernst Schulin (eds.), *Geschichtsdiskurs, Vol. 1: Grundlagen und Methoden der Historiographiegeschichte*, Frankfurt a.M. 1993, 31–49; here 46.

[13] Ibid., 44.

intrigued by the remnant aspect of sources, in which he sees the material expression of a collective unconscious that has neither been incorporated into the past production of meaning nor entirely fallen victim
to suppression. The remnants are what has *not* been handed down,
or has been handed down subliminally, "settling in the intermediate
area between social consciousness and loss."[14] Niethammer's distinction between tradition and remnants can help to further illuminate the
relation between functional memory and storage memory. His critical
historiography, following that of Halbwachs and Benjamin, seeks out
those traces of the past that constitute another form of evidence, opening up access to a past that is not officially scripted. He looks for voices
that have as yet played no part in forming the traditions of the collective memory and that with their different experiences and buried
hopes run counter to the framework of the established tradition.

To sum it all up, history (as critical historiography) is the product of a cultural process of differentiation. It has developed by way of
emancipation from memory in the sense of a normative tradition. This
differentiation in the structure of cultural knowledge, however, does
not necessarily lead – as some people have feared – to the decomposition and disappearance of living group memories. While the mutual
exclusivity of the two modes makes historiography irrelevant and memory mythical, their combination brings out the potential of each and
may create a corrective balance that is beneficial to both. Functional
memory cut off from the historical archive degenerates into fantasy,
whereas the archive cut off from practical use and interest remains a
mass of meaningless information. Just as storage memory can verify,
support, or correct functional memory, so functional memory can orient and motivate storage memory. The two belong together and form
part of an evolving culture, "which is open to the variety of interior
and exterior differentiations."[15]

A CONVERSATION WITH KRZYSZTOF POMIAN
ABOUT HISTORY AND MEMORY

The conversation took place on December 26, 1994, at the Getty
Center in Santa Monica, California, where a group of scholars and

---

[14] Ibid., 47.
[15] Ibid., 48.

artists were invited to discuss the subject of memory. (The discussion is reconstructed from memory.)

A.A.: I wonder whether one could find any points in common between the memory research projects being carried out in Paris, Budapest, and Bielefeld. I should add that I'm about to join the research group of the German historian Jörn Rüsen, whose project focuses on "The Construction of Historical Meaning," at the Center for Interdisciplinary Research (ZIF) in Bielefeld, Germany.

K.P.: Isn't Jörn Rüsen the man who would like to equate history with memory? I don't think much of that idea. There are currently two trends that I think are equally off target. One wants to reduce history to memory, and the other to rhetoric. What's happening in both cases I regard as a flattening of history. Rüsen seems to be pushing the first, and Hayden White the second. Both deny in their own ways that there's a third – critical historiography as scholarly discourse. It might sound boring and old-fashioned, but there's no way in the world that I'd want to take leave of this achievement handed down to us by people like Valla and others. They developed criteria for historical accuracy and methods, and those enabled them to unmask documents as forgeries. If we turn our backs on this critical historiography, we'll be turning our backs on something that's absolutely vital for me – the criteria for objective, intersubjective truth.

By the way, it seems to me that these more radical trends towards reducing historiography to something else mainly exist in the realm of theory, whereas in practical, everyday academic life everything more or less continues along its usual path. And what chance would anyone have of getting a job if he refused to use the critical tools of the trade?

A.A.: I find this distinction very helpful, although I'd look at the problem rather differently. Historiography obviously has (at least) three very different dimensions: the scientific, the memorial, and the rhetorical. My only doubt is that they really exclude one another as you seem to assume. Don't the difficulties arise more because the individual functions and dimensions are made absolute, or confused, or played off against one another? You could say for example that the *Historikerstreit* [Historians' Dispute] in Germany was the result of confusion or absolutism. There were some who favored the memorial dimension and some who favored the scientific. The first wrote their history of the Holocaust in order to make a record of the greatest crime in human history and to fix it in the memory as such, whereas the others wanted to treat the event comparatively and explain its causes. But maybe these two dimensions, the scientific and the memorial, need not be separated so radically – and so damagingly from each other. Aren't there similar tendencies in France, to play off history against memory? I'm thinking of Pierre Nora and his big project *Lieux de Mémoire* – isn't that the return of the memorial dimension in opposition to the scientific? I'm thinking of a text he wrote in which he set both terms off against each other and kept stressing the fact that history erodes living memory.

K.P.: You can't look at it that way. There are two things to be said about it: 1. Nora doesn't play memory off against history, because he bases all his thinking on scientific historiography. His originality consists in the fact that he discovered the history of monuments as a new subject area for historiography. I worked right from the start on the project that ran from about 1978 to 1992 and resulted in a total of seven volumes, each longer than the other (Vol. 1 *La République*, Vols. 2–4 *La Nation*, Vols. 5–7 *La France*), and know from many conversations and seminars exactly how the whole thing was conceived. 2. In order to understand what he means by the "erosion of memory through historial scholarship," you have to know what preceded Nora's project: The Annals School. Braudel, who was my teacher but not Nora's, studied history without any reference at all to memory. He specialized in processes that are bound to be imperceptible, unmemorable, and so unclassifiable – things like population structures and price fluctuations. He studied history as it were behind the backs of the people who took part in it. The end effect was that this sort of history became a highly specialized subject that was totally irrelevant to lay people. The price for this new knowledge was high: history disappeared from the consciousness of the people, and was gradually excluded from school syllabuses. That's where Nora stepped in. He wanted to bring history back into consciousness, into memory, into the memories of ordinary people, and so that's how he began to concentrate on symbols and monuments, in other words on those forms in which history was actually present in people's minds and maybe still is.

PART TWO

MEDIA

7

Metaphors, Models, and Media of Memory

> The images of the past cannot be counted on the fingers of one hand, or even on those of two hands.
>
> Mario Bretone, *Zehn Arten mit der Vergangenheit zu leben,* 1995

The main argument of this chapter is that the four "M"s in the title are bound together in a relationship of mutual enlightenment. It has often been maintained that we cannot approach the operations of memory directly, but are dependent on intermediary levels of reflection. Because the media of memory provide the most important metaphors and models of memory, it is not surprising that human memory co-evolves with the technical progress of media history.[1] Thus the media of writing, photography, and electronic forms of storage provide consecutive metaphors and models for the internal mechanisms and dynamics of memory. Our tour of the imaginary museum of memory images does not follow a historical itinerary. Nor does it attempt an exhaustive presentation of the virtually infinite inventory of possible metaphors of memory. Instead, it tries to systematize them by organizing them in two groups: metaphors of space and metaphors of time. The former include two-dimensional carriers and three-dimensional places. The underlying concept of memory becomes much more complex, however, when moving from "structured" to "unstructured"

---

[1] Douwe Draaisma, *Metaphors of Memory. A History of Ideas about the Mind,* Cambridge 2000.

spaces. Here, the metaphors emphasize what is hidden and out of reach rather than what is revealed and available. I argue that this new notion of hidden depths brings the spatial metaphors very close to the temporal notion of latency and thereby creates a bridge from spatial to temporal metaphors of memory. Because remembering is an essentially temporal phenomenon, it can scarcely be defined without taking into consideration the dimension of time. It is impossible to capture the transience, elusiveness, and constitutive time lag with purely spatial metaphors. The temporal metaphors of memory, which revolve around images of sleep/awakening and death/rebirth, present complex models of latency and reinforce the concept of a discontinuous presence of the past.

In one of her early novels, George Eliot ruminated on the meaning, changeability, and inescapability of metaphors. The images she had in mind were an attempt to explain the workings of the human mind. As a comment on the metaphors of memory, the following passage is doubly striking: first, because it concerns the effect of metaphors in general, and second, because the images she mentions are also used as central metaphors for memory:

It is astonishing what a different result one gets by changing the metaphor! Once call the brain an intellectual stomach, and one's ingenious conception of the classics and geometry as ploughs and farrows seems to settle nothing. But then it is open to someone else to follow great authorities, and call the mind a sheet of white paper or a mirror, in which case one's knowledge of the digestive process becomes quite irrelevant. [...] O Aristotle! If you had had the advantage of being "the freshest modern" instead of the greatest ancient, would you not have mingled your praise of metaphorical speech, as a sign of high intelligence, with a lamentation that intelligence so rarely shows itself in speech without metaphor, – that we can so seldom declare what a thing is, except by saying it is something else?[2]

The deep sigh with which Eliot ends her reflections may be taken as our own starting point, because we can safely say that no one can declare what memory is without using metaphors. This does not apply only to literary, pedagogical, or prescientific concepts, because even in science every new memory theory tends to be accompanied by new key images.

[2] George Eliot, *The Mill on the Floss* (1860), New York 1964, 117–118.

As the phenomenon of memory defies direct description, metaphors offer new access to it; they act as figures of thought rather than of speech, providing model frameworks for concepts and signposts for theories. In this context, therefore, we should take "metaphor" not as an indirect description of the phenomenon but as its cognitive and linguistic construction. In studying memory images, then, we also study memory models, their historical contexts, and their cultural requirements and patterns of meaning.

In a brief but pioneering essay on the subject, Harald Weinrich observed that in the field of memory metaphors, contrary to what one might have expected, we do not encounter a vast and colorful range of images.[3] In his view, there are in fact only two basic metaphors: the store and the tablet. Each of them has its specific origin and belongs to its own particular tradition. The store metaphor was derived from sophistry and rhetoric, which taught the pragmatic processing of eloquence and memory capacity. The tablet metaphor, as developed by Plato, was related to natural memory as opposed to one that was artificially enhanced. This appears to be a mysterious gift from the gods and has its seat deep in the human soul.

Weinrich summarizes his results as follows: "The duality of memory imagery is a fact of the western history of ideas. It is probably connected with the duality of the phenomenon of memory itself: storage metaphors accumulate mainly round the pole of *Gedächtnis* [the repository of memories], whereas tablet metaphors accumulate round the pole of *Erinnerung* [the act of remembering]."[4] One has to ask whether the "duality of the phenomenon of memory" is really as polarized as Weinrich makes out. The two German words are often used synonymously, but there have also been many attempts to assign terminological differences to them. However, the moment one settles on such a distinction, it is obvious that these so-called poles cannot be so neatly separated. Instead of defining them as opposites, we should rather regard them as complementary aspects of a complex process.

[3] Harald Weinrich, "Typen der Gedächtnismetaphorik," *Archiv für Begriffsgeschichte* (1964), 23–26.
[4] Ibid., 26.

WRITING METAPHORS: TABLET, BOOK, PALIMPSEST

Before the invention of electronic writing, there were only two basic writing techniques: one consisted in the application of pigments to a smooth surface, and the other in scratching or carving signs onto a suitable material. As paper did not come into widespread use until the 13th century, and papyrus and parchment were rare and expensive, ancient civilizations wrote on wax, clay, and stone. This form of writing was equated with engraving, and indeed the Greek word *kharaktēr* means "a tool for marking." Plato compares memory to a wax tablet – the instrument on which children learned to write in Antiquity. In the dialogue *Theaetetus* (191 C ff.) Socrates uses the image of the wax tablet, the gift from Mnemosyne, to describe the connection between memory (the original picture) and perception (the copy) that is a precondition for reliable remembering as recognition. The accuracy of the impressions in "the marrow of the soul" depends on how precise or confused that recognition is.[5] It is only one small step from engraved writing to the seal, which is Aristotle's metaphor for memory. His use of this image is particularly revealing, because it can help not only to explain the way memory functions but also to delineate its borderlines and its omissions:

For it is obvious that one must consider the affection which is produced by sensation in the soul, and in that part of the body which contains the soul – the affection, the lasting state of which we call memory – as a kind of picture; for the stimulus produced impresses a sort of likeness of the percept, just as when men seal with signet rings. Hence in some people, through disability or age, memory does not occur even under a strong stimulus, as though the stimulus or seal were applied to running water; while in others owing to detrition like that of old walls in buildings, or to the hardness of the receiving surface, the impression does not penetrate. For this reason the very young and the old have poor memories; they are in the state of flux, the young because of their growth, the old because of their decay.[6]

---

[5] Plato, *Theaetetus*, in *The Dialogues of Plato*, trans. B. Jowett, Vol. III, Fourth Edition, Oxford 1968, 191–319; here 191 c, d. In the dialogue *Philebos*, Socrates compares the soul to a book in which a writer has written true or false speeches that are linked to true or false images; Plato, *Philebos*, in *The Dialogues of Plato*, trans. B. Jowett, Vol. III, Fourth Edition, Oxford 1968, 531–630; here 40 a, d.

[6] Aristotle, *Parva Naturalia*, in *On the Soul, Parva Naturalia, On Breath*, with an English translation by W. S. Hett, London 1957, 205–427; here 450 a, 25–450 b, 10, 293f.

The idea that a good memory was a question of physiological consistency persisted in the world of medicine until the 17th century. In Shakespeare we still find indirect references to the Aristotelian principle, for example, in *The Tempest*, when Prospero complains that all his efforts to educate and teach the slave Caliban have proved futile because of his lack of receptive qualities: "Abhorred slave, / Which any print of goodness will not take" (I, 2, 351–352). Because the savage is incapable of learning and developing in the way his master wants him to, Prospero, the colonial ruler of the island, feels justified in subjugating him as a slave.

In biblical language, committing something firmly to memory is often linked with the image of writing it in the heart. Jeremiah is thinking of the "tablets of the heart" when he quotes God as saying: "I will put my law in their inward parts, and write it in their hearts" (Jer. 31: 33; see also Deut. 6: 6). The concept of the divine book of the world, first put forward in Mesopotamia, symbolizes absolute memory as a complete book.[7] Unlike chronicles and accounts, this book does not confine itself to the past, but also includes all data from the future. There is something similar in Psalm 139, which speaks of God's omniscience and also uses the metaphor of the book. What God writes with His quill on the papyrus has the power of deciding between existence and nonexistence. What is real is only that which is recorded in His book and what is left out or erased from His annals is not real – it is as if it never happened.

I must mention in passing that the writing metaphor has definite sexual implications. The writing instrument itself denotes masculinity (pen = penis), whereas the writing surface is the "matrix," and the white paper is virgin – therefore, feminine.[8] The following lines by

---

[7] The Jews were able to take over this book metaphor from Mesopotamia; Leo Koep, *Das himmlische Buch in Antike und Christentum*, Bonn 1952. See also Hans Blumenberg, *Die Lesbarkeit der Welt*, 22ff. (see Chapt. 3, n. 24) on the concept of the great account book in Judaism, and the connection between divine planning and historical fulfilment in the context of the divine book of the world. Borges elaborated on this image in his description of a mystic vision of God in the form of a round "cyclical book."

[8] In some languages, the words for remembering and forgetting have specific sexual connotations. Concerning Hebrew, Jakob Taubes writes: "Remembering is the positive principle, against which forgetting stands as the negative principle. Remembering belongs to Israel, the masculine pole, whereas forgetting corresponds to the feminine pole. Sikaron, memory, is related to sakar, masculine; and nakab, containing many

Oscar Hammerstein II from the Richard Rodgers musical *The Sound of Music* sum up this image perfectly:

> You wait, little girl, on an empty stage
> For fate to turn the light on,
> Your life, little girl, is an empty page
> That men will want to write on.

Although writing as a metaphor for memory is indispensable and highly evocative, it is also incomplete and misleading. The permanence of the written word is in striking contrast to the structure of remembering, which is always discontinuous and inevitably includes gaps, or nonpresence. And one cannot "remember" something that is now present – remembering can only take place when the item has become temporarily absent and left in a place from which it can be fetched again later. Recollection does not require permanent presence or absence but interaction between the two. The writing metaphor, which combines fixed signs with permanent readability and availability, is lacking in precisely this element of interaction between the present and the absent. To come closer to a true parallel, one would have to devise a form of writing that, once written, was not immediately readable but could only be read later under special conditions.

In one of his essays, Thomas De Quincey actually devised just such an image when he compared the human brain to a palimpsest. He described the technical process of the latter, which entailed using the costly parchment several times as the bearer of different writings: what might in Antiquity have held, say, a handwritten Greek tragedy could be carefully cleaned and then in Late Antiquity might have contained an allegorical legend, followed in the Middle Ages by a courtly epic. De Quincey observed that in his own day, sensationally, thanks to the combined efforts of chemistry and philology, it had become possible to go back in a reverse direction along the path of forgetting. For this miraculous backward movement of memory, De Quincey did not have our modern equivalent of the rewind; therefore he had to use images from poetic myth: "In a long regression we have gone behind every phoenix, and forced it to reveal its phoenix ancestor that rests in even

holes like a sieve, is related to nkeba, feminine." Jakob Taubes, *Occidental Eschatology*, Stanford 2009, 14.

deeper layers of its ashes."[9] Going back behind the beginning is the magic art of the philologist, who reverses chronology and is able to read backward. From this process, De Quincey derives an image for the retrograde, explosive force of memory: "What else than a natural and mighty palimpsest is the human brain? [...] Everlasting layers of ideas, images, feelings, have fallen upon your brain softly as light. Each succession has seemed to bury all that went before. And yet, in reality, not one has been extinguished."[10]

What fascinates De Quincey is "the possibility of resurrection for what had so long slept in the dust." In his view, memory does not spring from an act of the will nor is it a technique that can be learned; it simply arrives unsummoned when the circumstances are right. Layer by layer writings are stored one on top of another in the mysterious palimpsest of the human mind, which makes the new the grave of the old. "But by the hour of death, but by fever, but by the searchings of opium, all these can revive in strength. They are not dead, but sleeping. [...] In some potent convulsion of the system, all wheels back to its earliest elementary stage. [...] Alchemy there is none of passion or disease that can scorch away these immortal impresses."[11]

For De Quincey, memory is a hoard of undying and everlasting impressions. Although these remain basically inaccessible to people, because they cannot control or regulate them, the impressions are inscribed into human bodies anyway. This concept of permanent but inaccessible traces of memory is quite different from Wordsworth's "recollections," which entail imaginative reconstruction. De Quincey's concept, on the contrary, anticipates Proust's *mémoire involontaire*, which is also linked to the idea of lasting, somatic traces. Proust considered it "quite possible that [...] the philosophy of the journalists, according to which everything is doomed to oblivion, is less true than a contrary philosophy which would predict the conservation of

---

9 Thomas De Quincey, "The Palimpsest of the Human Brain," in *Essays*, ed. Charles Whibley, London no date, 272.
10 Ibid, 273.
11 Ibid., 276. De Quincey is giving voice here to a widespread conviction that "in the normal case [...] the whole biography only emerges in the last seconds of someone's life, in the famous deathbed scene. Only then does one know who one is." Heiner Müller, *Jenseits der Nation*, Berlin 1991, 71.

everything."[12] He speaks of a "reality we run the risk of never knowing before we die but which is our real, our true life." People do not see this real life: "they do not see it because they do not seek to illuminate it. As thus their past is encumbered with innumerable 'negatives' which remain useless because the intelligence has not 'developed' them."[13]

The coexistence in memory of ephemeral traces and lasting "impresses" was a problem that also intrigued Freud. He reformulated the problem of the alternating presence and absence as a paradox: how could one conceive the simultaneity of the opposed memory functions of preserving and extinguishing? How could one reconcile its "unlimited receptive capacity" with the "retention of permanent traces"?[14] Derrida has tracked the path taken by Freud from the neurological trace to psychic writing.[15] Freud finally succeeded in reconstructing the psychological process with the aid of an object that served him as a heuristic model. This object was the so-called magic pad, a simple toy – still found in the rooms of many children – which he made famous throughout the scientific world. The puzzling co-presence of lasting traces and the *tabula rasa* became clear to him through the three layers of which this writing instrument was composed: the surface was a sheet of celluloid that could be written on and written over, below was a sheet of fine wax paper that stuck to the written letters, and below that was the supporting tablet, which retained the lasting traces that under the right lighting conditions could still be discerned as fine grooves.

[12] Marcel Proust, *In Search of Lost Time*, Vol. 2, *Within a Budding Grove*, trans. C. K. Scott Moncrieff and Terence Kilmartin, London 1996, 57.

[13] Marcel Proust, *In Search of Lost Time*, Vol. 7, *Time Regained*, transl. by Stephen Hudson, (Project Gutenberg File), 417.

[14] Sigmund Freud, "A Note upon the 'Mystic Writing-Pad,'" in *The Complete Psychological Works of Sigmund Freud*, Vol. XIX, London 1964, 225–232, here 227; see also Sigmund Freud, "The Interpretation of Dreams (Second Part)," in *The Complete Psychological Works of Sigmund Freud*, Vol. V, London 1964, 538: "A trace is left in our psychical apparatus of the perceptions which impinge upon it. This we may describe as a 'memory-trace' [. . .] But [. . .] there are obvious difficulties involved in supposing that one and the same system can accurately retain modifications of its elements and yet remain perpetually open to the reception of fresh occasions for modification."

[15] "In letter 52 (6 Dec.1896) the entire system of the *Project* is reconstituted in terms of a graphic conception as yet unknown in Freud. It is not surprising that this coincides with the transition from the neurological to the psychical." Derrida, *Writing and Difference*, 258 (see Chapt. 4, n. 39).

Freud's description of the magic pad as a model for memory comes very close to De Quincey's palimpsest. Both use the writing metaphor to show the complexity of a phenomenon that combines reliable storage ("immortal impresses") and unlimited receptivity ("everlasting layers... softly as light") with temporary unavailability. Proust and Benjamin both focused their memory studies on this element of unavailability, absence, or, to be more precise, latency – Proust doing so autobiographically and Benjamin from the perspective of a philosophy of history. Benjamin expressed the indeterminacy of the moment of deciphering or readability with the formula "the now of recognizability." His 20th-century replacement for the writing image was the simile of photography: "As one looks upon history as a text, then one can say of it what a recent author has said of literary texts – namely, that the past has left in them images comparable to those registered by a light-sensitive plate. The future alone possesses developers strong enough to reveal the image in all its details[...]."[16] With the photograph as with the palimpsest, chemicals play their role in making invisible writing or an invisible picture visible. Neither De Quincey nor Freud thought of writing only as a code of signs; they broadened the notion to include "traces." This inclusive spectrum of "inscriptions" was also able to cover new recording techniques in the history of media technology, such as photography. In Susan Sontag's description of photography, for instance, one can discern a continuation of the oldest of all memory metaphors: it is "not only an image ... an interpretation of the real, it is also a trace, something directly stencilled off the real, like a footprint or a death mask."[17]

After World War I, the psychiatrist Ernst Simmel described war traumas in terms of photography; the self-inscription of a traumatic experience into the matrix of the unconscious corresponds to the photographic self-inscription of a section of reality into the silver bromide of the photographic plate. Simmel wrote: "The flash of terror makes a photographically precise impression."[18] The English psychotherapist William Brown, who also specialized in the treatment of war traumas,

---

[16] Walter Benjamin, *Selected Writings.* Vol. 4, 1938–1940, ed. Marcus Bullok and Michael W. Jennings, Cambridge, London 2003, 405.

[17] Susan Sontag, *On Photography*, New York 1979, 154.

[18] Quoted from Wolfgang Schäffner, "Der Krieg als Trauma. Zur Psychoanalyse der Kriegsneurose in Alfred Döblins Hamlet," in M. Stingelin and W. Scherer (eds.),

compared the latent traces of memory that he reactivated through hypnosis "to the successive photographic views in a cinematographical film."[19] This description not only reads like a technological version of De Quincey's palimpsest, but it also illustrates the precise correspondence between the history of technology and the theory of memory. As long as photographic and film analogies engraved their images through traces onto material carriers, memory theory as represented from Proust and Warburg to Freud was dominated by the idea that such traces were solid and inextinguishable. In this age of digital media, however, which no longer engrave but coordinate wires and set impulses in motion, we are swiftly moving away from such theories. Memory is no longer viewed as trace and storage, but as a malleable substance that is constantly being reshaped under the changing pressures and perspectives of the present.

SPATIAL METAPHORS OF MEMORY

From classical mnemotechnics (which fortified the unreliable natural memory with a dependable artificial one) onward, there has been a strong alliance between memory and place. The technique of the *ars memorativa* consisted of *imagines* – the codification of content in terms of meaningful images – and *loci* – the setting of these images in specific, structured places. The most popular medieval metaphor is the memorial storehouse or rather storebox; Mary Carruthers lists as synonyms of thesaurus in the context of memory: cella, cellula (the cell), arca (the arc), sacculus (the money pouch), and scrinium (letter case, book box).[20] Both sets of images, the tablets or papers and the boxes and rooms, have one thing in common: they suggest a solid and permanent presence of what has been singled out for preservation. In this sense, they represent memory as a material carrier or container

---

Hard War / Soft War. Krieg und Medien 1914–1945, Munich 1991, 34. I am grateful to Irene Albers for this reference.

[19] William Brown, "The Revival of Emotional Memories and Its Therapeutic Values," *British Journal of Medical Psychology* I, 1920, 17; quoted from Ruth Leys, "Traumatic Cures, Shell Shock, Janet, and the Question of Memory," in Paul Antze and Michael Lambek (eds.), *Tense Past. Cultural Essays in Trauma and Memory*, New York, London 1996, 111.

[20] Mary Carruthers, *The Book of Memory. A Study of Memory in Medieval Culture*, 34 (see Chapt. 5, n. 4).

of information. John Locke summed up the standard theory when, in his *Essay Concerning Human Understanding* (1690), he defined memory as a "Store-house of our Ideas."[21] The image of the storehouse illustrates less how memory operates and more what is demanded of it. Such images express a wish rather than provide an accurate psychological description, which is why images of inscription and storage are so closely connected to the concept of mnemotechnics, also known as "the art of memory" (F. A. Yates).[22] The *ars memorativa* is a pragmatic strategy, developed by Cicero and many after him, to stretch the capacity of human memory. The idea is to transform the fickle and vague human memory into a reliable tool by deploying structured imaginary spaces that provide pegs for various semantic units to be remembered. To memorize, according to Cicero, is to "write" images directly into the brain as though it were a wax tablet.

From boxes and storage space we move to places and buildings. This topological orientation leads logically to architectural complexes as embodiments of memory. An exemplary fusion of memory and architecture can be found in temples of fame, memorial theaters, and libraries.[23] The library is a vivid metaphor for cultural memory for Edmund Spenser, whom we have already quoted in relation to poetry and *fama*. In Book 2 of his allegorical verse epic *The Faerie Queene* (1596), the hero – a wandering knight – visits a castle. This is the Castle of Alma, a personification of the pure soul, unsullied by passions, who dwells in an equally healthy body, that is, the castle. After various physical functions have been admired during the tour of this allegorical building, the knight finally climbs into the tower, where there are three chambers, one behind the other, occupied by three men. The front room looks toward the future; it is filled with all kinds of chimeras, illusions, and half-baked ideas that buzz around like a swarm of bees. The inhabitant of this room is young, with a melancholic, saturnine face, and he looks like a madman.

The man in the second room is mature and is portrayed as the embodiment of wisdom. His domain is the present and evinces his

---

[21] John Locke, *An essay concerning human understanding* (1700), ed. P.N. Nidditch, Oxford 1979.

[22] Frances A. Yates, *The Art of Memory*, London 1966.

[23] The epic poet and theorist for this metaphor is J. L. Borges (*The Library of Babel*); in the 1920s T. S. Eliot and E. M. Forster also referred to the library as a synchronistic tradition. See also Ulrich Ernst, "Die Bibliothek im Kopf," *LiLi* 105 (1997), 86–123.

literal presence of mind – the images on the walls record official
actions, judgments, and decisions.

The third room lies behind the second and gives an impression of
decay. The plaster is flaking, the walls are crooked,

> And therein sate an old old man, halfe blind,
> And all decrepit in his feeble corse,
> Yet liuely vigour rested in his mind,
> And recompenst him with a better scorse:
> Weake body well is chang'd for minds redoubled forse.
>
> (II, IX, 55)

The mental alertness applies especially to his memory, which is
described as "infinite," and all things reside there in an "immortal
scryne [shrine], / Where they for ever incorrupted dwell'd." The
old man is called Eumenestes. Because he is older than Nestor and
Methuselah put together, he has witnessed every event since time
immemorial. He lives in his cell surrounded by the documents of the
past, which bear the traces of venerable age: the dusty folios, codices,
and scrolls are worm-eaten and mildewed. There he sits in the midst
of his treasures, leafing through the pages ("tossing and turning them
withouten end"), but as he is too decrepit to fetch the volumes from
the shelves himself, he has a boy working for him as a library assistant.
This nimble lad, who can also find lost and displaced books, bears the
name Anamnestes.

Through this description it is easy to recognize the Aristotelian
psychology of faculties, which distinguished between fantasy, reason,
and memory as three aspects of the human mind, located one behind
the other in three chambers of the brain. Spenser blurs the borders
between individual and collective, internal and external, by visualizing
the memory as a library that is stocked with ancient documents. The
power of conservation here is not due to any supernatural force or any
act of evaluation, but to the books themselves and to those who collect
and look after them – the librarians. Books and scrolls as data-carriers
relieve the professional bards in oral cultures of their task, which was to
construct and preserve the collective memory. In Spenser's allegorical
room in the tower the whole of human memory is stored forever.

In Spenser's memory metaphor there are two elements that may be
distinguished as passive and active, and may be linked to our earlier

discussion on the complementary nature of the (passive) repository of memories and the (active) act of remembering. "Passive" stored memory is called Eumenestes, a figure embodying the infinite supply of accumulated data. "Active" recollection is called Anamnestes, embodying the mobile energy associated with finding and fetching, that is, bringing data out of their latent presence and into concrete manifestation. The passive body of memory, then, is the store from which active recollection selects, actualizes, and uses memory.

The building metaphors are linked to different forms of memory. The temple of fame elevates and monumentalizes exemplary characters and deeds in a pantheon of fixed and timeless values. There is a shortage of space in this temple, which makes the criteria for acceptance all the stricter. On the other hand, the store of records preserved in the library can expand indefinitely. It represents knowledge of the past, which incorporates everything that has been rescued from time. Whereas the temple demands future recollection, the library allows access to the past and the present. One may associate the former mode of cultural memory with the functional memory or the canon, and the latter with the storage memory or the archive.

In their different ways, both canon and archive presuppose systematic organization, economy, and accessibility – all of them aspects that distinguish artificial from natural memory. Order is the hallmark of a mnemotechnically trained memory, whereas the ordinary memory has no such structure. Parts of our memory can be systematically structured to act as a store, but other parts, which record our sensual perceptions and biographical experiences, generally remain in a productive or destructive state of unmastered disorder. In contrast to our learning (or "semantic") memory, that of experience (known as "episodic") remains unsystematic, contingent, and incoherent. What holds it together is the magic web of variable, individual associations. Virginia Woolf was fascinated by the unpredictable contingency of experiential memory, and the terms that she associated with it were "muddle and mystery."[24] Her emphatically feminine memory metaphors are the seamstress and the clothesline. In both images, she stresses erratic association as a structural principle of memory: "Memory is the seamstress, and a capricious one at that. Memory runs her needle in and

---

[24] Virginia Woolf, *Orlando. A Biography* (1928), London 1989, 37.

out, up and down, hither and thither. We know not what comes next, or what follows after." The most commonplace actions may unexpectedly "agitate a thousand odd, disconnected fragments, now bright, now dim, hanging and bobbing and dipping and flaunting, like the underlinen of a family of fourteen on a line in a gale of wind."[25]

Another spatial metaphor for chaotic experiential memory is one devised by the Polish writer Andrzej Szczypiorski. In a text that we look at later in more detail, he describes himself as a gray-haired man carrying "a sack of personal experiences on his shoulders after having lived through most of his life on Earth" (225). Concerning memories of his youth, he writes: "The experience of my childhood days do still live on in me, but they are well hidden somewhere in the full and dusty attic of memory, where one seldom ventures." What is stored in the attic exists "unnoticed, silent through the years, not needed."[26] The attic once again is an image for latent memory. It has the character of the remnant, a storage memory with no illuminating meaning but not yet made totally inaccessible by forgetting and suppressing. Like the junk in the attic, which is still present but rarely seen, this memory remains in the shadows of our consciousness. F. G. Jünger, whose study of *Gedächtnis* and *Erinnerung* distinguishes between a destructive and a conservative form of forgetting, calls the latter "preservative forgetting." Terms like "latent memory" and "preservative forgetting" can be subsumed under the heading of storage memory; for instance, a stock of unattached elements that have no part in any narrative. In turning now to the metaphor of excavation, we move from one spatial metaphor that emphasizes the art of stored memory, to another that emphasizes the act and power of remembering.

Excavation

In one of his essays, Freud compared the work of the psychoanalyst, who uses signs given by the patient to reconstruct and interpret what has been forgotten, to that of the archaeologist, who excavates

some dwelling-place that has been destroyed and buried or some ancient edifice. [. . .] But just as the archaeologist builds up the walls of the building

[25] Ibid.
[26] Andrzej Szczypiorski, *Notizen zum Stand der Dinge*, Zürich 1992, 225.

from the foundations that have remained standing, determines the number and position of the columns from depressions in the floor and reconstructs the mural decorations and paintings from the remains found in the debris, so does the analyst proceed when he draws his inferences from the fragments of memories, from the associations and from the behaviour of the subject of the analysis. Both of them have an undisputed right to reconstruct by means of supplementing and combining the surviving remains.[27]

With this metaphor of excavation, Freud emphasizes the creative role of (re)construction in the memory work of the psychoanalyst. But he also sees significant differences between the two occupations. The archaeologist very rarely comes upon remains that are virtually intact, such as Pompeii or the tomb of Tutankhamun, whereas according to Freud, in the archaeology of the soul everything essential has normally been preserved, "even things that seem completely forgotten are present somehow and somewhere, and have merely been buried and made inaccessible to the subject."[28]

The image of archaeological excavation, like that of the palimpsest, introduces the concept of depth into memory theory. Depth is linked to a spatial model that has nothing to do with storage or order, but entails inaccessibility and unavailability. De Quincey spoke of "everlasting layers of ideas, images, feelings" that seemed to cover and bury one another, though in reality remaining preserved and unextinguished. He was as certain as Freud that there could be new life for what had been psychically buried: "the possibility of resurrection for what had so long slept in the dust." His image is the shroud of forgetting: "a pall, deep as oblivion, had been thrown by life over every trace of those experiences; and yet suddenly, at a silent command [...] the pall draws up, and the whole depths of the theatre are exposed."[29]

Proust's *mémoire involontaire* is also defined in terms of depth. In his famous episode of the *madeleine*, it is in the depths of the sea, not

---

[27] Sigmund Freud, "Constructions in Analysis," 259 (see n. 14). C. G. Jung recorded one of his dreams in which he found himself in a house where he gradually descended lower and lower. From the living room on the top floor, which was furnished in Rococo style, he went down to medieval rooms on the ground floor, then to a cellar from Roman times, and finally into a prehistoric cave in the rock. In this dream he combined ontogenetic with phylogenetic memories. Aniela Jaffé, ed. *Erinnerungen, Träume, Gedanken von C.G. Jung*, Freiburg 1984, 163.

[28] Freud, "Constructions in Analysis," 260.

[29] De Quincey, in *Essays*, ed. Charles Whibley, 245 (see n. 9).

of the earth, that the forgotten lies buried. A simple taste, released by a spoonful of tea and a softened cake, can suddenly establish new contact with hidden layers of memory. The body is thus transported into a hitherto unknown state of euphoria: "I had ceased now to feel mediocre, contingent, mortal."[30] For a second, the narrator overcomes the human condition of temporality, and he experiences a moment of anamnesis, of mystic universality, of being all in all, the complete presence, restoring and "re-membering" the missing parts that had been taken away by time. But this is not the end of the episode. After the body, the mind too must play its part in this act of remembering: "I put down the cup and examine my own mind. It alone can discover the truth." The mental work of memory proves to be difficult, strenuous, tiring – but in the end it is successful, because for Proust too it turns out that everything essential has been preserved. This intensive memory work is very different from mnemotechnics; it is much closer to meditation in the sense of religious, spiritual exercises. It requires a long sequence of probings that will weigh the anchor of memories in the depths of oblivion and help them to rise to the surface of consciousness. Proust describes with incomparable accuracy a process in which the rememberer is both active and passive at the same time: "I place in position before my mind's eye the still recent taste of that first mouthful, and I feel something start with me, something that leaves its resting-place and attempts to rise, something that has been anchored at a great depth; I do not know yet what it is, but I can feel it mounting slowly; I can measure the resistance, I can hear the echo of great spaces traversed."[31]

Even though the rememberer here is an isolated individual, there is nothing solipsistic about Proust's memory work. This form of memory also interacts – in the Halbwachs sense – with social frameworks, calling upon an external world through which it seeks to gain reassurance about itself. Only when this *milieu de mémoire* is lost or unresponsive, does memory lose its constructive social counterpart and become a fragile fantasy. The seismographs of the senses still function and register shock waves, but the memory of which the isolated individual is the

[30] Proust, *In Search of Lost Time*, Vol. 1, *Swann's Way*, 51 (see n. 12).
[31] Ibid., 53.

last carrier has lost its substance. The following passage is in complete contrast to Freud's archaeological optimism:

But when from a long-distant past nothing subsists, after the people are dead, after the things are broken and scattered, taste and smell alone, more fragile but more enduring, more immaterial, more persistent, more faithful, remain poised a long time, like souls, remembering, waiting, hoping, amid the ruins of all the rest; and bear unflinchingly, in the tiny and almost impalpable drop of the essence, the vast structure of recollection.[32]

Freud's parallel between analyst and archaeologist has the disadvantage of involving a division of labor between the active work of the analyst and the passive work of the patient. Walter Benjamin, one of whose "thought images" is contained in the title *Excavation and Memory*, avoids the opposition between active and passive by introducing a third category: the medium. His image of digging incorporates both active reconstruction and passive disposition:

Language has unmistakably made plain that memory is not an instrument for exploring the past, but rather a medium. It is the medium of that which is experienced, just as the earth is the medium in which ancient cities lie buried. He who seeks to approach his own buried past must conduct himself like a man digging. Above all, he must not be afraid to return again and again to the same matter; to scatter it as one scatters earth, to turn it over as one turns over soil. [...] In this sense, for authentic memories, it is far less important that the investigator report on them than that he mark, quite precisely, the site where he gained possession of them.[33]

Benjamin's image makes it clear that memories have no objective character; even after they have been rescued from the hidden depths, they can never be fully extracted from their past surroundings. In Proust's *madeleine* episode, the description of the process of remembering takes up twice as much space as the result of that process. The path to memory, the active probe, the "cautious, groping dig of the spade," the chance find remain inseparably linked to the target, the trophy, which is catalogued and then placed in the collection. A similar path was followed by Seamus Heaney, who forty years later described writing poetry as working on individual and cultural memory. He too uses the

[32] Ibid., 54.

[33] Walter Benjamin, "Excavation and Memory," in *Selected Writings*, Vol. 2, 1927–1934 (1999), 576 (see Chapt. 7, n. 16).

image of digging: "Poetry then is digging, a digging for discoveries which in the end prove to have been planted. 'Digging' was actually the title of the first poem that I thought put my feelings into words. [...] This was the first time I thought I had done more than just arrange words on paper: I had the feeling that I had sunk a shaft into real life." The last verse of this poem (1964) reads:

> Between my fingers and my thumb
> The squat pen rests.
> I'll dig with it.[34]

TEMPORAL METAPHORS OF MEMORY

The images connected with excavation already create a strong link between space and time, and the more prominent the time element becomes, the greater grows the emphasis on forgetting, discontinuity, decay, and reconstruction. This means that the focus shifts increasingly to the basic unavailability and suddenness of memory – qualities that also link memory to a perception of the new.

Swallowing, Ruminating, and Digesting

"Once call the brain an intellectual stomach," wrote George Eliot, and other images lose their potency. The stomach image goes back to St. Augustine, who in the 4th century wrote in his *Confessions*:

Doubtless therefore memory is as it were the belly of the mind, and joy and sadness like sweet and sour meat; which when they are committed unto the memory, be as it were passed away into the belly; where stowage they may have, but taste none at all. [...] Perchance, therefore, even as meat is by chewing of the cud brought up again out of the belly, so by recalling are these brought up again out of the memory. Why therefore does not the disputer perceive the taste of it in the mouth of his musing? Why does not the rememberer feel (I mean) the sweetness of joy, or the bitterness of sorrow? Is the comparison unlike in this, that it is not every way alike?[35]

Augustine gives vivid expression here to what it means to rethink things through memory with the aid of images. For him, the latter are

---

[34] Seamus Heaney, "Digging," in Seamus Heaney, *Opened Ground. Poems 1966–1996*, London 1998, 4.

[35] St. Augustine, *Confessions II*, trans. William Watts, London, Harvard 1961, Book X, chapter XIV, 113.

experimental – they expose aspects of something but at the same time may cover up something else. The stomach is the counterpart to the thesaurus: it is a place of passage, not of permanence, and things are processed and transformed there, not preserved. As a metaphor for memory, it can only be used under particular physiological conditions. The Latin *ruminare* means both to contemplate and to re-chew, and the word certainly makes us think more of a cow's stomach than a human being's. The phenomenon of regurgitating undigested food back into the cow's mouth for further processing is a remarkable image for memory that, unlike the widespread metaphors of writing, rooms, and buildings, highlights the time dimension involved in the act of remembering. Through this focus on time, new aspects are brought to the fore, in particular that of loss or of reduction. In contrast to Proust, who laid emphasis on taste during his somatic process of remembering, St. Augustine's memory loses its taste: the sweetness of joy and the bitterness of sorrow are sensual qualities of experience that are bound to the present and cannot be rescued from time. There is, then, an unbridgeable gap between current and remembered experience, and St. Augustine's image accentuates this gap. Finally, the action of ruminating brings out the productive element of memory, which is very different from the mnemotechnical process of retrieval. The stomach image again relates to latency as an intermediary realm between absence and presence.

Nietzsche reuses the stomach image, but against a different theoretical background. In his second treatise on the genealogy of morality, he develops his argument about the positive power of forgetting, with which he counters the overloaded, over-refined historical consciousness of the late 19th century. He talks of "forgetfulness" as a "counteractive force," which is

no mere *vis inertiae* (inert force) as the superficial believe; it is rather an active – in the strictest sense, positive – inhibiting capacity, responsible for the fact that what we absorb through experience impinges as little on our consciousness during its digestion (what might be called its "psychic assimilation,") as does the whole manifold process of our physical nourishment, that of so-called physical assimilation.[36]

---

[36] Friedrich Nietzsche, *On the Genealogy of Morals. A Polemic.* A new translation by Douglas Smith, reissued, Oxford 2008, 39.

Metabolism, which the body controls and which functions perfectly without any input from our conscious mind, is Nietzsche's image for mental processes of transformation, which he would like to regard as happening with similar unthinking reliability. Digestion, however, is an image not only for the relief of consciousness but also for the removal of a burden of memory that grows beyond measure. Nietzsche compares someone who lives with this ever increasing load, and has no means of periodically getting rid of it, to a dyspeptic. Such a person can never get over the past and thus "never gets anything done." Historicism, idleness, and boredom are the result of cultural indigestion. "In the end modern man drags around with him a huge quantity of indigestible stones of knowledge, which then, as in a fairy tale, can sometimes be heard rumbling about inside him."[37]

According to Nietzsche, the infallible method of getting the digestive juices working again is "a vehement passion."[38] In the light of such a passion, which he links to the paradigm of male sexuality, the world regains its shape. Such passion reignites the certainties of instinct, and within it stir the forces of power, forgetfulness, and injustice. "It requires a great deal of strength to be able to live and to forget the extent to which to live and to be unjust is one and the same thing."[39]

Freezing and Thawing

There are other memory metaphors that also lay emphasis on latency as a central feature. In order to clarify this term, one must distinguish between two forms of forgetting: one is disintegrative and destructive, and the other conservational. Latency, as has already been pointed out, belongs to the latter category, or what F. C. Jünger calls "preservative forgetting." When Hegel talked of the "shaft of forgetting," he was thinking of an intermediate depot where memories were temporarily inaccessible but not essentially beyond recall and reproduction.

How this aspect can be captured through metaphor is shown by a passage in Ruth Klüger's autobiographical novel *weiter leben* (Still Alive – A Holocaust Girlhood Remembered), in which fifty years later

[37] Nietzsche, "On the Uses and Disadvantages of History," 78 (see Chapt. 3, n. 6).
[38] Ibid, 64.
[39] Ibid, 76.

she commits to paper her memories of the time she spent in different concentration and death camps. While writing, she suddenly found herself confronted with an unexpected barrier: she could no longer remember the assumed name she and her mother adopted when they were on the run in Lower Silesia toward the end of World War II. Her mother, now 87, still knew it and, after a moment's hestitation, called up the stored name onto the screen of her memory: "Kalisch was the name on our forged papers. [...] At first the name means nothing to me. Kalisch. It's like a dish that one takes out of the freezing compartment, with no smell and no taste. As it thaws, it gives off a gentle aroma. From quite a distance away, I try it – just a taster. Because it was frozen and has now thawed, it has retained the smell of the February wind of 1945, when everything went well for us."[40]

For Klüger as for Proust, smell and memory are inseparable. For both, the senses play a vital, active role in the process of recalling lost memories, and for both they endow these memories with the stamp of authenticity. In fairy tales, food and taste are often connected with forgetting and remembering. We will now take a leap from these contemporary examples back into Late Antiquity and look at the way in which a Gnostic myth has couched the temporal metaphor of memory in a gripping story.

Sleep and Awakening

Around the beginning of the Common Era, there was a wave of apocalyptic, Gnostic hostility to the values of this world that spread from the Mediterranean to the Far East, equating the world with degeneration, disintegration, evil, darkness, and death. Against this background was staged the Gnostic drama of salvation. The principal antagonists in this drama were Forgetting and Remembering.

> With their wiles they made my acquaintance;
> Yea, they gave me their victuals to eat.
> I forgot that I was a King's son,
> And became a slave to their king.
> I forgot all concerning the Pearl

[40] Ruth Klüger, *weiter leben. Eine Jugend*, Göttingen 1992, 179–180; Engl. *Still Alive: A Holocaust Girlhood Remembered*, New York 2001.

> For which my Parents had sent me;
> And from the weight of their victuals
> I sank down into a deep sleep.[41]

The motifs of this spiritual drama come from fairy tales and folklore. The danger of forgetting is caused by a demonic enemy power who uses it as a cunning strategy. "Eating" here would rhyme with "forgetting." Through force and subterfuge, the protagonist is held in a world where he does not belong; noise drowns the cry from another world, and drunkenness is used to befuddle his consciousness. Hope resides in the possibility that the noise itself will rouse the victim from his lethargy and force him to wake up.

The Gnostic drama of forgetting and remembering, of sleeping and waking, of exile and homecoming, of death and life forms the archetypal background to each and every tale of alienation. It was also an effective element of political rhetoric. Revolutionary movements have always regarded themselves as "a wake-up call from the other side,"[42] an attempt to help the new and living to break into an evil, ossified world. National movements exemplify this in their efforts to usher in the new through a freshly forged link to the old. In an article about the monumental value and mobilizing memory of the Battle of Leipzig (1813), Joseph Görres reconstructed the history of the German nation in a narrative of forgetting and remembering. It was structured in three stages that neatly corresponded to the Gnostic drama of salvation:[43]

1) *Idea and Promise* – the medieval kingdom in which the Germans were united under King and Kaiser and were superior to all other nations in size and importance;

---

[41] The "Hymn of the Pearl" from the *Acts of Thomas*, trans. G. R. S. Mead, "The Hymn of the Robe of Glory," in Mead, *Echoes from the Gnosis* Vol. X, 1908, 18 (stanza VII). See also Hans Jonas, *Gnosis und spätantiker Geist*, Göttingen 1934, 114; Hans Leisegang, *Die Gnosis*, Stuttgart 1955, 365ff.

[42] Jonas, ibid., 124, see also 126. "I am the call of the sleep-awakening in the aeon of the night." This call is defined as serving to "rouse the sleeping and make them rise. They are to waken the souls that have stumbled away from the place of light. They are to wake them and rouse them, so that they may raise their faces to the place of light."

[43] See Volker Sellin, "Nationalbewusstsein und Partikularismus in Deutschland im 19. Jh.," in Jan Assmann and Tonio Hölscher (eds.), *Kultur und Gedächtnis*, Frankfurt a.M. 1988, 244f.

2) *Curse and Forgetting* – the political fragmentation that weakened the Germans during the 17th and 18th centuries and made them the plaything of hegemonic dynasties;

3) *Recovery and Fulfillment* – driving out Napoleon and shaking off the yoke of foreign conquerors through the unity of the nation.

The realization of political ends requires a vision, and revolutionary force requires a potent myth. According to this scheme, the present is described as a negative interim between a great past and an equally great future, the link between them being memory and hope. Memory becomes a political force maintaining norms that run counter to the present, and this energy will overcome the evils of the present and bring in the new age. For Hegel, and later for Benjamin, awakening is the "exemplary case of remembering."[44]

The motif of awakening dominated political rhetoric to such a degree that Werner Conze actually spoke of a "wakening nationalism."[45] The same applied to the literary historiography of the 19th century, which saw many variations on the theme of forgetfulness/sleep and memory/awakening. Max Schneider was only one voice among many that described World War I as "an almost metaphysical awakening from the dull state of a leaden sleep."[46]

How are these myths of political awakening related to Jewish and Gnostic memories in Late Antiquity? One common factor is that they describe the workings of memory within the framework of a particular genre of histories – namely histories of salvation. Against this background, the present is depicted as an unholy age that is to be overcome with the aid of memory. The difference between national myths and Gnostic myths lies in the fact that religious salvation is directed toward a non-historical future, whereas political legitimization aims to achieve salvation within historical time. For histories of political salvation, Emanuel Sarkisyanz has suggested a distinction between

---

44 Hegel, *Gesammelte Werke*, ed. H. Büchner and O. Pöggeler, Hamburg 1969, Vol. 4, 491.

45 Werner Conze, "Ethnogenese und Nationbildung – Ostmitteleuropa als Beispiel," in *Studien zur Ethnogenese*, Opladen 1985, 202, 204.

46 Max Scheler, *Der Genius des Krieges und der deutsche Krieg*, Leipzig 1917, 4. For other instances of sleep and awakening in politico-historical contexts, see H. D. Kittsteiner, "Walter Benjamins Historismus," in Norbert Bolz and Bernd Witte (eds.), *Passagen*, Munich 1985, 163–197.

"revolution myths" and "re-volution myths" (i.e., with or without a hyphen), the first relating to Jewish salvation, which looks forward to the coming of a Messiah, whereas the second refers to Gnostic salvation, which looks backward.[47] As in Gnostic myths, which describe a step-by-step undoing of the story of the Fall, leading to an eventual homecoming to heavenly origins, in political re-volutionary myths the wheels are turned back to an ideal origin.

Conjuring up Ghosts

The Jewish-Gnostic-Christian metaphor of awakening has its "heathen" equivalent in magic reanimation and resurrection. There are two particular elements that are believed to have regenerative powers in the context of memory: water and fire.

In the ancient classical world, the image of drinking is connected both to forgetting and to remembering. *Water* has a similar ambivalence: Lethe is the river that carries everything away forever and so separates us from all the earlier phases of our lives, just as the Styx separates us from earthly life. The waters of life and memory, however, spring from a single source. Castalia, the sacred source of the Delphic oracle, was regarded in Roman times as the seat of poetry, and its waters were prophetic,[48] thus blurring the borders between prophecy and memory. What the poets have to tell the world is given to them by the Muses, the daughters of Memory. In the old world, there is no creative utterance without memory, and no poetry outside tradition without a drink from the fountain of the Muses.

Book XI of *The Odyssey* describes the descent into the Underworld, which was an obligatory features of the epic hero's itinerary. From Homer to Hegel and from Freud to Jung, the adventure of memory has entailed a journey into the depths. This perilous descent into the realm of darkness, right through to Faust's descent to the Mothers, is connected with the idea of a different kind of knowledge that lies between memory and prophecy and is perhaps best described, using Walter Benjamin's paradoxical expression, as "memory of the new." The dead that Odysseus meets are dumb, and with their loss of language

---

[47] In an unpublished lecture.
[48] *Der kleine Pauly*, Vol. 3, Munich 1979, 150.

comes loss of memory. In order to communicate with them, he must temporarily restore their speech and memory. He slaughters some sheep, whose black blood fills a pit dug for sacrifices to the dead, and he guards this with his sword to ensure that only those dead spirits drink from it to whom he wishes to grant this favor. Teiresias is to be the first, because Odysseus hopes to learn from the seer whether he will ever reach his home. But before he is allowed a glimpse into the future, the past speaks to him in the form of his companion Elpenor, whose soul can find no rest because he has remained unburied and unmourned. After Odysseus has promised to give him a grave, the soul of his mother wishes to be the second to speak to him, but she must wait until Teiresias has revealed his fate to him.

Odysseus's necromantic ritual takes us right to the heart of another cluster of images for memory: resurrection and reanimation. One might say that the Renaissance humanists chose the theme of resurrection as the motto for their epochal project, their central concern being to revive a past age. In one of his poems (*Canzoniere*, 53) Petrarch evokes the spirit of ancient Rome, which has fallen into a deep slumber: he is surrounded by ruins, graves, and crumbling walls. But he discovers that within these fallen monuments the spirit of the old world still resides, waiting to be set free. In this situation, no normative wakeup call can fully restore the forgotten past. We are dealing here not with a religious myth of origin but with the cultural project of connecting the dead with the living across the abyss of time.

This descent into the depths of the past is also the one followed by philology and archaeology. One must dig in order to bring to light the lost or hidden layers. During what we know as the Renaissance, the images of excavation and necromancy were connected to the cultural vision of resurrection and rebirth.[49] Breaking through the different layers (as with De Quincey's palimpsest) is like traveling through time, but the action of digging is not limited to layers of earth. The philologist is the archaeologist's accomplice, and both see themselves as opponents of time and virtuosos of memory, for

---

49 "The image that propelled the humanist Renaissance and that still determines our perception of it, was the archaeological, necromantic metaphor of *disinterment*, a digging up that was also a resuscitation or a reincarnation or a rebirth." Thomas M. Greene, *Light in Troy. Imitation and Discovery in Renaissance Poetry*, New Haven 1982, 92.

they both heal the wounds that time has inflicted on monuments and texts. The bookseller and copyist Vespasiano da Bisticci was celebrated by his contemporaries as a second Aesculapius. Just as the latter was deemed to be able to resuscitate the dead, the former helped ancient authors to enjoy a new life. "Because of you, Greece can now disdain the waters of Lethe, nor does the language of Romulus fear the god of the Styx. Happy the man who can recall to the light of the living so many dead monuments of the ancients; happy he who has been able to snatch from the flaming pyre the lost names of divine poets."[50]

The task of resuscitation through memory also fell to the reader of those works that in the Renaissance had been elevated to the normative status of classics. This new form of hermeneutics made the reader into an "animator" of the past, to whose spiritual power and mnemonic charisma the dead owed their life. The background to this demanding task was a new consciousness of "past-ness": in order to bring the past back into the present, there had to be a necromantic power of resuscitation, the symbol of which was the *spark*. Plato describes the meaning of the spark in his "Seventh Letter" (341b-c) as a leap of understanding in communication: "but after much converse about the matter itself and a life lived together, suddenly a light, as it were, is kindled in one soul by a flame that leaps to it from another, and thereafter sustains itself." The fire symbolizes a sudden, inaccessible item of knowledge that is ignited on the basis of a material remnant or a latent memory. As a symbol of memory, fire is just as ambivalent as water, because it can denote destruction and oblivion through time ("scorching flames") as well as the remembrance and renewal of things lost.

The spark that kindles forgotten memories stands for a form of energy that is as subjective as it is sudden, and as selective as it is precarious. Memory as an "awakening" was a paradigmatic image for the European embrace of the ancient classical world, and the euphoria of Goethe's *Römische Elegien*, for instance, continues to feed on this magic of memory – the past lives so long as the spark leaps and the enthusiasm does not fade. The metaphor of awakening entails a new historical consciousness, evident in two more examples.

---

[50] Politian's Latin text is quoted by Thomas M. Greene, ibid., 165. There were similar Promethean self-presentations by English printers, editors, translators, and booksellers in the 15th and 16th centuries.

The major work of the historian of law Johann Jakob Bachofen, *Gräbersymbolik* (Sepulchral Symbolism), deals with ancient beliefs concerning the dead. In his research, he discovered a new access to Antiquity that did not require the aid of texts. In an autobiographical sketch he gives a vivid insight into the revivalist magic of which memory is capable. "There are two ways to all knowledge: the long, slow, painstaking one of reasoned combination, and the shorter one that is completed with all the power and speed of electricity – the way of imaginative intuition, which is inspired by the sight and direct touch of ancient remains, and grasps its truth directly without the help of any mediators."[51]

Bachofen's short route to knowledge may have inspired art historian Aby Warburg, who also worked on a theory of memory that was sparked off by images and symbols rather than words and texts. Warburg, who was well acquainted with the philological business of reconstructing long-lasting and elaborate lines of tradition, was equally interested in the phenomenon of direct contacts and electrical discharges. He coined the term *Anteic Magic* to describe a discharge of latent memories released by direct contact. In brief, the longer the route through historical time grew, the more tempting became the imaginative investment in shortcuts. The fire symbol for memory – from the spark and the lightning bolt through to the electric shock – took on new life against the background of historicism with its growing and long-winded processes of erudite scholarship.

The period of latency is a little like an hourglass, except that one can neither determine nor control precisely when the time will eventually arrive. Until the moment comes that releases a pent-up memory, this takes the form of forgetting. If the particular memory contains an emotional potential that cannot be incorporated into preservative forgetting, but has to be excluded from consciousness by suppression, then its return will take the form of a demonic event. In this case, the deliberately controlling mechanisms are put out of action, and the process of remembering follows the rhythms of immanent energetics. This involuntary and inescapable course of remembrance is captured by the image of ghosts.

[51] Johann Jakob Bachofen, "Lebensrückschau," in H. G. Kippenberg (ed.), *Mutterrecht und Urreligion*, Stuttgart 1984, 11.

According to Freud, the act of suppression will inevitably be followed by the return of whatever has been suppressed. The embodiment of this "unpacified forgetting" (Harald Weinrich) is the restless
dead – those who have been murdered or have not received a proper
burial.[52] They are doomed to return as ghosts. In this context, the
primary cultural obligations have to be respected. In other words,
first things first: before he is allowed to attend to his own affairs during his visit to Hades, Odysseus must first promise to take care of
unfinished business in the form of a proper burial for his companion
Elpenor.

An "unpacified" past is unexpectedly resurrected and like a vampire sucks the blood out of the present. For Heiner Müller, the ghost
of Banquo haunting Macbeth and that of Hamlet's father demanding
vengeance are both metaphors of memory, again signifying unfinished
business that may remain an unarticulated taboo from one generation
to another. Nietzsche considered the burden of the past to be remov-
able by means of a powerful and self-conscious effort to forget, but
Heiner Müller seeks out the traumatic past as the material from which
not only nightmares but also literature is made. His theme is collective
trauma, the guilt that is suppressed by society, but that in his plays he
seeks to force back into the consciousness of a present that has forgotten its past and its ancestors. He stages the return of the suppressed
in the style of a horror story, with the dead returning as ghosts, or
revenants, threatening the living.

> For ghosts do not sleep,
> And their favourite food is our dreams

he writes in the poem *Mommsens Block*.[53] But it is not only ghosts that
haunt the living. The poet does so too, in his pursuit of the ghosts:
on the one hand he seeks the bloodstained tracks of the "forgotten ancestors," and on the other he tries to free himself "from this
nightmare of dead generations."[54] Like Walter Benjamin before him,

---

[52] On the term "unpacified forgetting" see Harald Weinrich, *Lethe*, 132–136 (see Chapt.
3, n.10).

[53] Heiner Müller, "Mommsens Block," in *Sinn und Form* 2 (1933), 201. My thanks to
Hendrik Werner for this reference.

[54] Müller, *Rotwelsch*, Berlin 1982, 105.

Heiner Müller is interested in the political dimension of cultural memory; for him remembering is revolutionary and forgetting is counter-revolutionary – an assessment in keeping with Jewish and Gnostic tradition, which equates assimilation with forgetting and guilt, and exile with remembrance and redemption. But Müller does not stop at politicizing cultural memory – he also demonizes it. His necroromantic metaphors dramatize Benjamin's philosophy of history through the addition of horror, violence, and passion. "The dead are not dead in history. One function of drama is to conjure up the dead – the dialogue with the dead must not break off until they have yielded the future that had been buried with them."[55]

"The terror of which I write comes from Germany." With these words, Müller has twisted a statement made by Edgar Allan Poe in the foreword to his *Tales of the Grotesque and Arabesque*: "My horror is not of Germany but of the soul." The Romantic Poe meant that his horror did not emerge from a literary genre but emanated directly out of the human psyche. Ruth Klüger's horror, however, felt both physically and mentally when she was deported as a child to Theresienstadt and Auschwitz, was indeed made in Germany. She too was haunted by ghosts, and the words with which she articulates her memories in *still alive* alternate between narration and conjuration:

Remembering is a branch of witchcraft; its tool is incantation. I often say, as if it were a joke – but it's true – that instead of God I believe in ghosts. To conjure up the dead you have to dangle the bait of the present before them, the flesh of the living, to coax them out of their inertia. You have to grate and scrape the old roots with tools from the shelves of ancient kitchens. Use your best wooden spoons with the longest handles to whisk into the broth of our fathers the herbs our daughters have grown in their gardens. If I succeed, together with my readers – and perhaps a few men will join us in the kitchen – we could exchange magic formulas like favorite recipes and season to taste the marinade which the old stories and histories offer us, in as much comfort as our witches' kitchen provides. (Still Alive, 69)

As this exploratory comparison clearly shows, images are not just descriptions but also media for remembering, and more besides: they are instruments for memory therapy. The domesticating power of words and images could scarcely be more significant than it is in these

---

55 Müller, *Gesammelte Irrtümer 2*, Frankfurt a.M. 1990, 64.

lines, in which Klüger builds a delicate and ironic bridge from the
wounds of the trauma to the ceremonies of exorcism in the "comfortable" kitchen.

Her conjurations and her ghosts have little in common with those
of Heiner Müller. Klüger's images are feminine and invoke matriar-
chal domains – the saucepan, the witches' cauldron, and scenes that
conjure up an atmosphere of female solidarity. Whenever Müller sees
ghosts, he slips into the morbid fantasy world of the murderous Macbeth. His ghosts feed on collective guilt, whereas hers dwell on individual grief, for "where there is no grave, the work of grieving does
not end" (Still Alive 94). Her focus is on close relatives, the unburied
murder victims, the father and brother, for whom she seeks with her
words to create places where they might rest for a while, although she
knows very well that her literary magic will only achieve short-lived
effects of self-comforting.

As seen from the list and the variety of examples, the problem
of memory necessitates images, and these "thinking-images" (Walter
Benjamin) represent a constant attempt to illuminate an extraordinarily complex phenomenon from new angles. Their quantity is theoretically unlimited, even if their typology is within bounds. The wax
tablet, for instance, the Platonic image of anamnesis, was joined in
medieval times by the mirror, the metal of which kept tarnishing, thus
becoming opaque and requiring constant polishing.[56]

The imagery varies according to whether it refers to the qualities
and procedures of "artificial" or "natural" memory (*ars* or *vis*). The
differences are fundamental. The art of mnemotechnics and the technical procedures of storage aim to ensure that what is recalled will be
identical to what was stored; in natural memory, the two actions are
quite separate. Experience and remembrance can never be brought
completely into line, because there is always a gap between them, and
in this gap the substance of the memory will be shifted, forgotten,
distorted, reshaped, or reconstructed. The more the metaphors take
these immanent dynamics into account, the more they have to lay
emphasis on time as a decisive factor, and so reproduction of memories becomes a problem in itself. Between the spatial and the temporal

[56] I am grateful to the Islamicist William Chittick for this reference to the mirror as a
metaphor for memory.

models are those based on writing and traces. These are timeless in so far as they presuppose the making of permanent tracks, but they are also temporal in that they focus attention on the problem of temporary loss and forgetting, as well as on the effort required in order to reproduce the memory. Time-oriented images accentuate the discontinuity of time, and they start out from the predominance of forgetting and the unavailability of memory. This problem marks the beginning of the psychic history of memory, to which Augustine and Nietzsche, Wordsworth and De Quincey, Freud and Proust have all contributed important chapters.

In retrospect, it is striking that the metaphor of writing and of traces in general runs through all the different phases of cultural history with remarkable continuity. At the same time, though, it is evident that with the culture of materialism and the changing nature of technology, this image too has changed. With constant modernization, the metaphor of alphabetical writing was followed by the light and shade of photography, but that has now been superseded by images related to electronic writing. What has remained and what has changed has been summed up by J. F. Lyotard:

We can say with certainty that inscribing (*inscrire*) has to be done, whether through the cortex or through what – translated into sociocultural terminology – we have called writing (*écriture*). Thinking or inscribing, i.e. without support, doesn't work. This support can be anything at all. There are momentary changes in supports. Perhaps one doesn't yet have the "right" kind of support. Perhaps all the screens are still bad supports, because they are still too analogous to handwriting and tablets. [...] Nevertheless, the minimal precondition lies in inscription.[57]

With electronic, digital writing we have reached the most minimalist extreme of writing imagery. Indeed it is no longer an image that can stimulate our senses, and so at this point we leave behind the productive collection of metaphors assembled by George Eliot, and change our paradigm to the web, which by comparison is structural and "desensualized." The web reduces writing to the manipulation of electronic impulses – and this applies as much to the neural fabric of the human brain as it does to the computer. It may be that after

---

[57] Lyotard, *Statement in Kultur-Revolution* 14 (1987), 10f.

technology and physiology have come so close to each other, they have already virtually closed the gap that all the images strove to bridge. As an externalized, global nervous system, the web transcends and yet at the same time falls short of all the metaphors that have long translated the phenomenon of memory into concrete, technical, practical terms. It has brought such imagery to a point at which the imagination implodes, and anyone who starts out from this point will find our tour of the Imaginary Museum of Memory Metaphors even more remarkable.

8

Writing

> Literature is the fragment of fragments; only the least amount of what has happened and has been spoken was written down, the least of what has been recorded in writing has survived.
>
> Goethe, *Maxims and Reflections*, No. 512

> Hail to the inventor of rag paper; wherever he lies buried, hail to him! He has done more than all the monarchs of the Earth for our literature, the whole business of which proceeds from rags and so often ends in wastepaper!
>
> Herder, *Briefe zur Beförderung der Humanität*

> "Write!" said that voice, and the prophet answered: "For whom?" The voice spoke: "Write for the dead! For those you love in the previous world." – "Will they read me?" – "Yes, for they will return, as posterity."
>
> Herder, *Briefe zur Förderung der Humanität*

> No Geist without ghost.
>
> T. E. Hulme, *Speculations*

> Wer schreibt, der bleibt. [He who writes remains]
>
> Deutsche Post A. G.

In the first sentence of his book *Shakespearean Negotiations* Stephen Greenblatt confesses: "I began with the desire to speak with the dead."[1] This statement is a reminder to his colleagues – that is, the salaried

---

[1] Stephen Greenblatt, *Shakespearean Negotiations*, Oxford 1988, 1.

professional readers and professors of literature – of something they have completely forgotten: that deep down they are shamans who are holding a continual conversation with the voices of their ancestors and with ghosts from the past. They are not merely dealing with technical media, such as texts and performances – they are themselves media in the occult sense of the word, because for the general good they establish contact with the transcendent world of yesteryear and help to preserve it. In the course of this stimulating essay, Greenblatt focuses on the technical medium through which the voices of the dead continue to speak to us, if only in fragments. He speaks of "textual traces" in which "social energy" circulates – the energy that makes up the "life" that literary works preserve after the death of their author and the passing of their contexts. In his description of the "after*life* of textual traces from the Renaissance," he uses a metaphor that suggests that the black letters contain an immanent seed of life. His aim, however, is to replace the biological metaphor of the "life" of literary texts with a language of "energy," which he links back to social relations and the liberal economy of a free market. Using terms like negotiations, exchange, and trade, he describes the general cultural practices and material interests in which the promulgation of art is always embedded.

Greenblatt's reference to the conversation with the dead involves not only the arts but culture in general: the channels of communication and mediation, the anatomy of tradition, and the structure of cultural memory. These are not new questions but they are questions that each succeeding generation has to ask in its own new way. Of special significance are his "textual traces," that is, the letters or *litterae* that perform their unobtrusive work right at the heart of literature and constitute a forgotten dimension in the discourse on literary transmission.[2] Any study of the media of memory must start out with writing, not just in its social and technical context, but also in the context of what it achieves for memory, which of course will be judged differently from one culture and one era to another. The ideas, hopes, and disappointments tied up in these letters are an important

---

[2] Jacques Derrida in his *Grammatology* (1967) points out the philosophical significance of writing, but in the context of philosophical discourse he considers this to be a suppressed and not a forgotten dimension.

indication of the structural changes that have taken place in the modern era. We will therefore look first at concepts of writing in the Renaissance – the period in which celebration of this cultural medium was to reach a peak. We will then look briefly at the decline in the estimation of letters that set in during the 18th century – a decline that certainly did not apply to their social importance but simply to their cultural value – and finally, I speculate on the fate of letters and of cultural memory in a world of mass media and electronic technology.

WRITING AS A MEDIUM OF IMMORTALIZATION AND AN AID TO MEMORY

We have already looked at the *fama* function of poetry but we must not forget that in addition to the poet's art, the material medium has an important part to play in the process of immortalization. The Ancient Egyptians held writing to be the most secure medium of memory. The sages of the Middle Kingdom could already look back over more than a thousand years of culture, knowing full well that great buildings and monuments would eventually become ruins, whereas texts from those times were still being copied, read, and learned. They realized that traces of black ink on fragile papyrus represented a more lasting monument than elaborate tombs with lavish furnishings. Such a papyrus from the 13th century BCE compares the durability of graves and books, and concludes that writing is a far more effective weapon against the second or social death, which is general oblivion. Concerning the dead authors, it reads:

> For sure they are invisible, but their magic
> Still touches all that read from their books.[3]

This discovery enhanced the self-esteem of a new elite – the restricted class of the literate – who thrived on their awareness that they could ensure immortality independently of state-monopolized, Pharaonic memory politics.

---

[3] Papyrus Chester Beatty IV, verso 3, 9–10; see Jan Assmann, *Stein und Zeit. Mensch und Gesellschaft im Alten Ägypten*, Munich 1991, 177. For a different English translation cf. Miriam Lichtheim, *Ancient Egyptian Literature II, The New Kingdom*, Berkeley 1976, 177.

For later literates, the idea that writing remained untouched by the destructive forces of time, and thus provided a unique medium of immortalization, became a solid topos. In his 55th sonnet ("Not marble, nor the gilded monuments / Of princes, shall outlive this powerful rime"), Shakespeare follows the example of Horace, who in one of the poems that end his *Odes* writes:

> I have built a monument stronger than bronze
> and more sublime than the royal pyramids,
> one that rain cannot erode
> nor raging wind, the endless procession
> of years, or the flight of ages destroy.[4]

He continues with the claim that "not all of me will die" ("*non omnis moriar*"). The chance to separate an everlasting part of himself is offered by writing that as a medium of memory can ensure immortalization through continuous readability. Horace, who resorts to mythic language to refer to Melpomene and Delphic laurel wreaths, does not yet spell out this material condition explicitly. It is referred to far more directly by Ovid, who in the closing lines of his *Metamorphoses* invokes Horace's metaphysics of the "*opus exegi*"– the poetic work as an everlasting creation that defies the wrath of Jupiter, the sword, the fire, and time itself. But despite this grand defiance, Ovid ends not with unqualified self-glorification but with a cautious proviso:

> Wherever through the lands beneath her sway
> The might of Rome extends, my words shall be
> Upon the lips of men. If truth at all
> Is established by poetic prophecy,
> My fame shall live to all eternity[5]

According to the Latin text "*ore legar populi*," Ovid will be read through the ear and not the eye. The question of orality versus writing as media of fame is briefly discussed in a scene from Shakespeare's *Richard III*.

---

[4] Q. H. Flaccus Horatius, *Horace's Odes and Epodes*, translated with an Introduction and Commentary by David Mulroy, Michigan 1997, 168 f. On the connection between *fama* and the media, see Georg Stanitzek, "Fama/Musenkette. Zwei klassische Probleme der Literaturwissenschaft mit 'den Medien,'" in Ralph Köhnen (ed.), *Philologie im Wunderland. Medienkultur im Deutschunterricht*, Frankfurt a.M., Bern 1998, 11–22.

[5] Publius Ovidius Naso, "Epilogue," in *Metamorphoses*, translated by A. D. Melville, Oxford/New York 1986, Book XV, p 379.

There is a conversation between the young Prince of Wales, Bucking-ham, and Gloucester, who is about to usurp the throne as Richard III. In order to achieve this end, he has the boy taken to the Tower, where he will later be murdered. The Prince wants to know whether Julius Caesar built the Tower. Buckingham informs him that Caesar began it, but in later times it had to be renovated, or "re-edified." The Prince then wants to know whether this information is based on written or oral knowledge: "Is it upon record, or else reported / Successively from age to age, he built it?,"[6] and is told: "Upon record, my gracious lord." This reply motivates the boy to ask a new, though rhetorical question:

> But say, my lord, it were not register'd,
> Methinks the truth should live from age to age
> As twere retail'd to all posterity,
> Even to the general all-ending day.[7]

At this point Gloucester intervenes with a sarcastic aside: "So young, so wise, they say, do never live long." But when the Prince asks what he has just said, he replies: "I say, without characters, fame lives long." This does not seem to satisfy the Prince, who changes his mind and now gives his support to writing. He does so by praising his hero Julius Caesar, though little does he know that the only thing he has in common with Caesar is the fact that he is going to be murdered:

> That Julius Caesar was a famous man:
> With what his valour did enrich his wit,
> His wit set down to make his valour live;
> Death makes no conquest of this conqueror,
> For now he lives in fame, though not in life.[8]

The Prince, so wise and so young and due to be so short-lived, has summed up the nature of eternal fame and its media: oral tradition ("report") and written history ("record"). The comparison with Caesar exposes the helplessness of the doomed child, for he will never have the chance to perform immortal deeds or to have them recorded in

---

[6] Shakespeare, *King Richard III*, III, 1, 72–73, (see Chapt. 3, n. 8).
[7] Ibid., 75–77.
[8] Ibid., 84–88.

the annals of fame. Caesar was not only his own historiographer, but he also had Lucan, the epic poet of the Roman civil war, to commemorate him. In the ninth book of his history, Lucan laid great emphasis on the inseparable cooperation between hero and bard:

How mighty, how sacred is the poet's task! He snatches all things from destruction and gives to mortal men immortality. Be not jealous, Caesar, of those whom fame has consecrated; for, if it is permissible for the Latin Muses to promise aught, then, as long as the fame of Smyrna's bard endures, posterity shall read my verse and your deeds; our Pharsalia shall live on, and no age will ever doom us to oblivion.[9]

"*Venturi me teque legent*" – the poet's confidence in the attention of future generations is firmly based on the traditions of a written culture. Writing is the dependable medium of fame but it is far from being self-sufficient. This eternity is subject to certain conditions: fame can only endure as long as the traditions of reading are maintained. Heroes depend on poets, but poets depend on readers, and it is they who decide whether fame will last or not. Ovid and Lucan both recognized three preconditions for fame: first the work of art, second the fact that it is written and thus allows for lasting readability, and third the continued political authority of the Roman Empire. The European culture of the Renaissance, however, created conditions under which Roman authors remained readable even after the fall of the Roman Empire.

Writing is not only a means of immortalization; it is also an aid to memory. The process of writing on something, or inscribing into something, is the oldest and – despite the long history of all media – still the most salient metaphor for memory. However, although writing is both a metaphor and a medium for memory, it has also been seen as its enemy and destroyer, for the very act of writing creates the danger of eroding memory by handing over responsibility to the external medium. Plato was the first to express these doubts about the medium. It was he who taught us to think of writing and memory as opposites. In a famous narrative at the end of the *Phaidros* dialogue, Theut, the inventor of writing, proudly presents the alphabetic letters as a

---

[9] Lucan, *The Civil War / De Bello Civili*, with an English translation by J. D. Duff, London/Harvard 1969, Book IX, 980–986, p 579.

medicine for wisdom and memory. The far-sighted, skeptical King Thammus rejects the claim:

And in this instance, you who are the father of letters, from a paternal love of your own children have been led to attribute to them a quality which they cannot have; for this discovery of yours will create forgetfulness in the learner's souls, because they will not use their memories; they will trust to the external written characters and not remember of themselves. And so the specific which you have discovered is an aid (*pharmakon*) not to memory (*mneme*), but to reminiscence (*hymomnema*).[10]

The two key words *mnēmē* and *hypomnēma* can be equated with the distinction between the power of remembering (*vis*) and memory as storage (*ars*) that was discussed earlier. When it functions as storage, writing can outdo *ars*, but according to Plato it can never take over the function of remembering. The dynamic, productive, and inaccessible part of memory that Plato linked to the term *anamnēsis* cannot even be touched by writing, let alone replaced by it. Theut's claims are misleading, for instead of leading to true wisdom, writing can only lead to the appearance of wisdom, and instead of true powers of recollection, it can only offer a meager ersatz. The promise is therefore an illusion, for all that writing can do is remind someone who already knows – it cannot teach the ignorant. At this point Socrates, who takes over the role of the skeptical Thammus, compares writing to painting. Both are silent: "For their creations also stand there as if alive, but if you ask them something, there a dignified silence reigns. This is exactly how written words behave: you might think they speak like sensible beings, but if in your eagerness to learn you ask them something, they will always tell you only one and the same thing."

Plato's critical view of writing has been countered by many an author who has celebrated both writing and books. One of them was Richard de Bury who refuted Plato's criticism in his *Philobiblon* (1345). Whereas Plato saw writing as externalization and trivialization, Bury lauded its visibility and sensuality: "truth latent in the mind is wisdom that is hid and treasure that is not seen; but truth that shines forth in books desires to manifest itself to every impressionable sense."[11]

---

[10] Plato, *Phaedrus* in *The Dialogues of Plato in Four Volumes*, trans. B. Jowett, Fourth Edition, reprint, Oxford 1968, Vol. III, 275, p 184.
[11] Richard de Bury, *Philobiblon*, ed. M. Maclagan, Oxford 1960, 19.

Bury also reversed Plato's second objection. Books are by no means silent; indeed they are better teachers, "who instruct us without rod or ferule, without angry words, without clothes or money. If you come to them they are not asleep; if you ask and inquire of them, they do not withdraw themselves; they do not chide if you make mistakes; they do not laugh at you if you are ignorant."[12]

To Renaissance humanists, Plato's dichotomy between writing and remembering, between externalization and internalization, would have seemed largely incomprehensible because they were convinced that the one stabilized the other. There was not only an optimistic faith in the conservational powers of writing, which nourished aspirations to glory and to a spiritual afterlife, but there was also a staunch belief in the pragmatic function of writing as an aid to one's powers of memory. Shakespeare elaborates on this pragmatic power in his 77th sonnet:

> Thy glass will show thee how thy beauties wear;
> Thy dial how thy precious minutes waste,
> The vacant leaves thy mind's imprint will bear,
> And of this book this learning mayst thou taste.
> The wrinkles which thy glass will truly show,
> Of mouthed graves will give thee memory;
> Thou by thy dial's shady stealth mayst know
> Time's thievish progress to eternity.
> Look what thy memory cannot contain,
> Commit to those waste blanks, and thou shalt find
> Those children nursed, delivered from thy brain,
> To take a new acquaintance of thy mind.
> These offices, so oft as thou wilt look,
> Shall profit thee and much enrich thy book.[13]

This sonnet is to be seen as an accompaniment to a "table book," that is, a book with empty pages in which the owner may enter his or her own thoughts or those of someone else. The poem puts together three objects that are also frequently to be found in still-life paintings

[12] Ibid., 21.
[13] Shakespeare's Sonnets, *Complete Works*, Oxford 1952, 1116–1117.

connected with time: a mirror, a clock, and a book. It formulates instructions on how to use and evaluate these objects.

The first quatrain introduces them, devoting one line each to the mirror and clock, and two to the book. The first two items are clearly symbols of vanity but they also expose vanity, because "beauties wear" and "minutes waste." Both instruments therefore run counter to their everyday practical function: the mirror serves a cosmetic function, but here reveals the fading of beauty; and the clock is normally an aid to temporal discipline and the coordination of actions, but here serves as a warning signal that time flies. Thus the practical meaning of these two objects gives way to their emblematic meaning as a counter to vanity.

They are joined by the third object, a book with "vacant leaves," which is meant for both writing and reading. The verse speaks of "imprint," which, however, does not refer to the printer's plates but to the mind of the owner. The book is an instrument for the externalization of that which is internal, shut off, and inaccessible. This can be revealed with the aid of the empty pages and made readable. Just like with the other emblematic objects, the mirror and the clock, the book's pragmatic function gives way here to something of deeper significance, which is alluded to, though not yet developed, in the fourth line: "And of this book this learning mayst thou taste." In much the same manner as a still life presents objects for meditation, the second quatrain contemplates the symbolic meaning of these objects. What initially was compressed into just two lines is now developed over twice that number, endowing these signs of vanity with a greater vividness, immediacy, and urgency. The stress in the second and fourth lines of this second quatrain ironically falls on the words "memory" and "eternity," the meaning of which is annulled by the glass and the dial as symbols of transient vanity.

The third quatrain, which focuses exclusively on the book, brings a change in the argument.

The repetition of the word "memory" links the second and third quatrain, but also highlights their difference in meaning. Whereas the former "memory" is related to death, the second is related to life. From the traditional sphere of vanity we now return to the previously excluded realm of pragmatic action. Nothing would have been more natural at this point than to have referred to the book as a further symbol of vanity, as contemporary still lifes very often did.[14] The book, however, is cleared of its emblematic value and instead presented in terms of its pragmatic function. What exceeds the capacity of memory is to be taken over by the empty pages of the book. The injunction "Look... and thou shalt find" is followed by the most astonishing lines of all: for the writing down of thoughts is translated into terms of birth, nursing children, and new acquaintance. Writing is not associated here – as has been familiar to us since the days of Rousseau, Hegel, de Saussure, and Husserl – with death and stasis, but on the contrary with new life and growth.

The perspective of *vanitas* that is always linked to transience, death, and the grave is suddenly switched as it turns to writing and books that strikingly detach themselves from this background as forces of life and continuity. The empty pages become a different kind of mirror: whereas the face is destined irreversibly to age, the mind can recall and hence renew itself when it reads what it once wrote. Writing and books are also better clocks because they register profit and not loss. Writing is clearly removed from vanity and transience: in the context of inevitable decline and disappearance, it offers the chance of a productive renewal of time.

In Shakespeare's sonnet, writing is more than a mere aid. In contrast to Plato, it is not represented as a technical means of recording but as a medium of communicating with and relating to oneself. Although the written thoughts go from inside to outside, just as Plato argued, this does not cause them to die or to become incomprehensible; instead, by the process of externalization, they become a new means of confronting and forming the self. Writing does not destroy conversation – it facilitates an internal dialogue that may transcend

---

[14] Jan Bialostocki, "Books of Wisdom and Books of Vanity," in *In Memoriam J. G. Van Gelder 1903–1980*, Utrecht, 37–67. I am grateful to Moshe Barasch for this reference. "The ambiguity is inherent in the book as an object. [...] An image of the book may mean a religious book of truth – the Bible, it may mean books of human learning, appreciated as erudition and culture, but it also may mean human learning despised as fickle and transient, having no real lasting value and passing away with time. Therefore on the one hand books appear in the intricate allegories of transience, but on the other they are also shown held by the Saints and philosophers" (42).

long periods of time. Plato believed that externalized writing replaced and thus destroyed memory, whereas for Shakespeare its interaction is a stimulus for memory. The poet made meat out of the philosopher's poison.

ON THE COMPETITION BETWEEN WRITING AND IMAGE AS MEDIA OF MEMORY

Writing as Conserved Energy

In his book *Truth and Method* (1960), the philosopher Hans-Georg Gadamer discusses writing's conservational power: "This is like nothing else that has come down to us from the past. The remnants of the life of the past, what is left of buildings, tools, the contents of graves, are weather-beaten by the storms of time that has swept over them, whereas a written tradition, when deciphered and read, is to such an extent pure mind that it speaks to us as if in the present."[15] This concept of writing as "pure spirit" has traveled a long distance. It originated in Renaissance discourse on the competition between writing and image as media of memory. Those who stressed the uniqueness of writing pronounced it as the clear winner of this contest. The argument of many Renaissance humanists was that paintings and sculptures could not effectively protect whatever they represented against the ravages caused by the "storms of time," whereas in the dimension of writing there was no equivalent to such ruins, because its signifiers were subject to no comparable process of erosion.

The key term in this context is spirit. Writing was regarded as the most congenial medium of the spirit, whose immateriality is paralleled by the transparency of the arbitrary letters that in the reading process "fall off like dross." What is ignored in this affinity between spirit and letter, however, is language, the verbal medium that is codified in writing and that in turn codifies thoughts and information. Whereas letters remain the same, language is susceptible to change

[15] Hans-Georg Gadamer, *Truth and Method.* New York 1988, 145.

and, over time, can become alien, inaccessible, and incomprehensible. The Renaissance humanists do not mention the obscurity and unreadability of ancient texts, for their focus is entirely on the miracle of writing as a potentially revivable and thus eternal message. Whereas the spirit (represented in writing) exists outside of time, the body (represented in images and buildings) is affected and eventually destroyed by time. Writing therefore supports the claim to immortality, for it underpins both imperviousness to time and time's restorative power.

These, in brief, are the basic elements of the metaphysics of writing that underlie Gadamer's argument and link him to Renaissance discourse. The passage quoted testifies to the continuity of this metaphysics, showing how ideas developed during the Renaissance are still active and effective today in certain contexts. In the 18th century, however, this line of thought was interrupted. Writing was separated from the spirit and even became its utmost other. It was relegated to the status of an inert container, a waste product, an empty husk that could not secure let alone guarantee the live feelings and energy of the spirit, but in fact threatened to erode it from within.

The competition between the media of memory has a long history. In one of his *Odes* (IV, 8) Horace claims that verse as a medium of memory is superior to great monuments, and in his sonnets Shakespeare develops this argument still further. These poems are virtuoso variations on the paradoxical theme that the hardest materials such as bronze and marble are eroded by time, whereas fragile paper and a few drops of black ink are able to defy it. The more "immaterial" the medium, the greater evidently are its chances of immortality.

Francis Bacon and John Milton

Francis Bacon also wrote about the mnemonic powers of letters, but his perspective was that of the scientist, not the poet. His starting point was the need for continuity and durability as an anthropological universal. He declared the desire for immortality to be of the most basic of human aspirations, and regarded writing as the outstanding medium for its fulfillment. At the end of Book I of *The Advancement of Learning*, he deals with letters in some detail, picking up on the familiar theme of durability. He wonders how far the monuments of wit and learning are more durable than the monuments of... power or of the hands. For have not the verses of Homer continued twenty-five... hundred years, or more, without the loss of a syllable or letter, during which time... infinite palaces, temples, castles, cities have been decayed and demolished?[16]

Here Bacon is focusing on writing as the material guardian of tradition. Homer's verses have lasted "twenty-five hundred years," not because people have continuously memorized them, but because they were physically fixed and preserved "without the loss of a syllable or letter." Bacon's view of the written work as superior to that "of the hands" (e.g., the painted image) may have come from the dedication that George Chapman wrote to his translation of *The Iliad* in 1611:

> A Princes statue, or in Marble carv'd.
> Or steele, or gold, and shrin'd (to be preserv'd)
> Aloft on Pillars, or Pyramides,
> Time into lowest ruines may depresse:
> ... But, drawne with all his vertues in learn'd verse,
> Fame shall resound them on Oblivions hearse,
> Till graves gaspe with her blasts, and dead men rise.[17]

Although Chapman does not explicitly refer to writing, that is clearly what he has in mind. The life-giving power of poetic verse that resounds like the trumpet call of fame deep into the sarcophagus and thus can make dead men rise, is further enhanced by its material codification. Images and buildings are destroyed by time, but it is the verses of Homer, which are fixed in the form of writing, that can destroy time and are guaranteed an eternal afterlife. By comparison with Chapman's verses, Bacon's prose is striking in the precision of its argument and its freedom from the usual declarative pathos. In the passage that follows, explaining the difference between

---

[16] Francis Bacon, *The Advancement of Learning*, Book I, VIII, 6, *The Advancement of Learning and New Atlantis*, ed. Thomas Case, London 1974, 70. On Bacon's theory of memory, see Detlef Thiel, "Schrift, Gedächtnis, Gedächtniskunst. Zur Instrumentalisierung des Graphischen bei Francis Bacon," in Jörg Jochen Berns and Wolfgang Neuber (eds.), *Ars memorativa. Zur Kulturgeschichtlichen Bedeutung der Gedächtniskunst 1400–1750*, Tübingen 1993, 170–205.

[17] George Chapman, *Homer's Iliad* (1611), Epistle Dedicatory, lines 62–68.

image and writing as media of memory, his argument goes into further detail:

It is not possible to have the true pictures or statues of Cyrus, Alexander, Caesar, nor of the kings or great personages of much later years; for the originals cannot last, and the copies cannot but leese of the life and truth. But the images of men's wits and knowledge remain in books, exempted from the wrong of time and capable of perpetual renovation. Neither are they fitly to be called images, because they generate still, and cast their seeds in the minds of others, provoking and causing infinite actions and opinions in succeeding ages.[18]

As far as Bacon is concerned, then, letters are of far greater value than pictures as media of memory. Images that refer to something in the past can only offer a weakened copy of the original, whereas writing captures a living emanation of the mind and carries it intact into the future. What loses life and truth in visual media remains preserved by writing, which is itself an instrument of reproduction that not only has the remarkable ability to preserve the old, but at the same time is able to "cast seeds" and hence produce something new. To define writing as an external means of storage is inadequate, because it also activates the memory. For both Shakespeare and Bacon the "live" nature of writing is an effect of an interactive process: an idea conserved is inevitably an idea renewed. Thus letters not only store thoughts, but they also bring them afresh into the world. The disassociation between recording and knowing, of which Plato was so wary, is explicitly excluded from such descriptions, which proceed from the conviction that writing is a power of memory and a conserver of energy.

The conservational power of writing is just as great as its basic power to renew old thoughts. There is a pictorial equivalent of this concept in some of the still lifes of the period. I am referring to a painting by David de Heem (reproduced on the cover of this book): a child on the right and the classical head of a young man on the left frame a skull in the middle, which is slightly enlarged, is farther in the foreground, and is the only one of the three to face the observer front on. The skull is decorated with a laurel wreath, into which ears of ripe corn are loosely

---

[18] Bacon, *Advancement*, 70.

woven, touching the books that along with a quill are piled up on its right. A piece of paper at the bottom of the skull bears the inscription: "NON OMNIS MORIAR"[19] This is an illustration of the line from Horace: "not everything of me will die," as long as my books contain the seeds for renewed reading. As in the writings of Bacon, there is no room in this pictorial version for the Pauline letter, which kills. On the contrary, de Heem's painting draws our attention to the magic of the letter as a seed with the power of life. This was indeed the only kind of magic that the enlightened humanists could allow. It consisted in giving new life to something dead, and in effecting the continuity of knowledge and experience across centuries of forgetting. This was the ambitious project or, to be more precise, the epochal myth that lay at the heart of the Renaissance. Whereas Italian painters adopted a different position in this Renaissance media contest (*paragone*), English scholars and poets believed that the magic of rebirth could not be entrusted to images but only to verses and the letters with which they were written. Bacon saw pictures as mere copies; they were as external and lifeless for him as letters were for Plato, who argued that they could not grasp the live *logos* and therefore were comparable to pictures that could only suggest the illusion of life but in reality were deaf and dumb. In contrast to Plato, Bacon regarded writing as a medium for the individual and collective memory because it was not limited to pure recording but also acted as a stimulus to thought. What he says about hieroglyphs is also true of letters in general: "they do retain much life and vigour."[20] He reinforces his argument with a striking comparison:

So that if the invention of the ship was thought so noble, which carrieth riches and commodities from place to place, and consociateth the most remote regions in participation of their fruits, how much more are the letters to be magnified, which as ships pass through the vast areas of time, and make ages so distant participate of the wisdom, illuminations, and inventions, the one of the other?[21]

[19] Bialostocki, 37–67; here, 45 f. (see Chapt. 8, n. 14); see also R. Wittkower, "Death and Resurrection in a Picture by Marten de Vos" (1949), in Wittkower, *Allegory and the Migration of Symbols*, London 1977, 159–166 (see n. 52).

[20] Bacon, *Advancement*, II, IV, 3; 98.

[21] Ibid., I, VIII, 70.

Today we are more aware that the construction of transport and communications networks has not only furthered interaction and the dissemination of knowledge but has also brought about new forms of oppression, colonialization, and exploitation. Whereas Shakespeare still spoke of black ink when he proclaimed the power of (hand)writing to immortalize, Bacon was already thinking of printer's ink. Along with the compass and gunpowder, he hailed the technology of the printing press as one of the three pillars of the new age. The secular Bacon used religious images to point up the achievements of print. He called libraries "the shrines, where all the relics of the ancient saints, full of true virtue, and that without delusion or imposture, are preserved and reposed." For him the delusions of religion were followed by the truths of science, and the magic of letters relieved that of rituals. This magic was no longer performed by dubious priests, but by the scholars of the new discipline that was called "philology." Instead of the canonized saints there were now canonized texts or, as he put it, "new editions of authors, with more correct impressions, more faithful translations, more profitable glosses, more diligent annotations, and the like."[22] "Philology" means "love of words"; in Bacon's time it was less a matter of logocentrism than of graphocentrism and bibliolatry. In the arrival of the print age Bacon saw an end to the danger of a second Middle Ages, with "alarms about the loss of mankind's memory." The ground had now been prepared for a progressive accumulation of knowledge, that is, for a linear "Advancement of Learning."[23]

The speech in favor of the freedom of the press that John Milton delivered to Parliament in 1644 also praised the immanent power of books. He elaborated on the affinity between the spirit and the letter when he proclaimed that books contained their own form of vitality that could be used for good or ill: "For Books are not absolutely dead things, but do contain a potency of life in them to be as active as that soul was whose progeny they are; nay they do preserve as in a vial the purest efficacy and extraction of that living intellect that bred them."[24]

---

[22] Ibid., II, I, 74.

[23] See Elizabeth Eisenstein, "Clio and Chronos," *History and Theory* 5 (1966), 46–48.

[24] John Milton, "Areopagitica," in Malcolm W. Wallace (ed.), *Milton's Prose*, London 1963, 279–280.

Here Milton is using the language of alchemy to describe writing as the distillate of the mind – the "purest" and most concentrated form of energy. For him too, letters are not just an abstract system of notation but a magic source of energy, and in order to underline this concept he moves from alchemy to mythology: "I know they are as lively, and as vigorously productive, as those fabulous Dragon's teeth; and being sown up and down, may chance to spring up armed men."[25] Like Bacon, he emphasizes the immanent productivity of the written word, whose seeds survive time and may germinate over and over again. As the book is the living imprint of the mind, the mind may rise again at any time, though this may also represent a danger that is hard to avert. Milton was convinced, however, that censorship was not the right way to deal with this problem, for it was all too likely that many good books would fall victim to it. He regarded a good book as a sacred object, and he chose the most powerful rhetoric in defense of such a book:

[...] who kills a Man kills a reasonable creature, God's image; but he who destroys a good Book, kills reason itself, kills the image of God, as it were in the eye. Many a man lives a burden to the Earth; but a good Book is the precious lifeblood of a master spirit, embalmed and treasured up on purpose to a life beyond life.[26]

Again like Bacon, Milton sees good books not just as the most precious of cultural commodities but as something to be revered. This goes considerably beyond the humanistic view of writing and books as positive cultural symbols. Milton brings to his humanism a reformational zeal, which in the new print age sets up books (and not just the Bible) as a challenge to the authority of governing institutions. In this he exceeds even Bacon, as he shows that writing as "pure spirit" (Gadamer) has its origins in a very specific historical context. The theme itself was part of a conflict between the Protestant culture of writing and the Catholic culture of the image. In the age of print, the book became the most powerful weapon against the Church, and Milton's speech took sides in this political-cum-religious clash. The cult of the book was set squarely against that of the image, and it

25 Ibid., 280.
26 Ibid., 280.

was writing that assumed the magic cloak. Under such polemic conditions, it was clearly far more than a set of arbitrary symbols – here it
became equivalent to the essence of life, a sacred quintessence, and
immortality. Milton even goes so far as to call the destruction of books
"homicide." Anyone who attacks books "ends not in the slaying of an
elemental life, but strikes at that ethereal fifth essence, that breath of
reason itself, slays an immortality rather than a life."[27]

THE DECLINE AND FALL OF LETTERS – BURTON AND SWIFT

The Protestant English authors of the Renaissance whom I have been
quoting promulgated the idea of living letters, which did not separate
writing from memory as an adversary but regarded the two processes
as an interlinked and stimulating record of thoughts, as a trace of
the spirit, and as a store of energy. However, even in the Renaissance
there were other, less enthusiastic evaluations of writing that followed
the Platonic tradition of disparagement. One text that holds out very
little hope for resuscitation and lays great stress on destruction and
irretrievable loss is a sonnet cycle by Du Bellay entitled *Les Antiquitez
de Rome* (1558). The cycle is dedicated to the King of France, with the
admonition that he should take up the heritage of Roman culture,
and it describes with obsessive monotony how the former greatness of
Rome has now crumbled into ruins.[28] Now that the remains of this
culture lie in eternal dust, the *manes* [spirits of the dead] are conjured
up in a necromantic ceremony consisting of three invocations, so that
they may enjoy an afterlife of fame and glory (Sonnet 1). Only one of
the sonnets that follow, depicting the fall of Rome and its landscape
of desolate ruins, deals with the conservational power of writing that
survives this destruction (Sonnet 5). Here Rome is described as a
living being with body and mind, and it is *both* components of this
personification that have gone forever into their earthly grave. All
that lives on after this ending is writing (*ses escripts*) and fame (*son loz*).

[27] Ibid., 280.
[28] "May the gods one day grant you the glorious chance / To rebuild a grandeur like
theirs here in France." Joachim Du Bellay, *Les Antiquitez de Rome*. See Barbara Vinken,
"Die endlich begrabene Stadt. Du Bellays Antiquitez de Rome," in Aleida Assmann
and Anselm Haverkamp (eds.), *Stimme, Figur*, Sonderheft der DVjS, Stuttgart 1994,
36–46.

Neither, however, guarantees any substantial "afterlife," but instead they invoke a ghost:

> But his writings, which snatch his glorious fame
> In defiance of time out of the tomb,
> ... wander the world, conjuring up his ghost.[29]

The philologists of the Renaissance focused not only on the life-giving power of letters, but also on their powers of deception. Vala and Casaubon used new philological methods to unmask foundational documents and supposedly archaic records as forgeries. The antiquarians, who worked alongside the philologists, also began to pay less attention to writing as traces of "pure spirit" and more to the historical materials in which it was couched. There are some skeptical passages even in Shakespeare that directly contradict his glorification of writing as a medium of fame. In a speech of Lucrece's, he shows how fragile the materials of books can be:

> [time's glory is]
> To fill with worm-holes stately monuments,
> To feed oblivion with decay of things,
> To blot old books and alter their contents.[30]

Here writing does not enjoy any miraculous exemption from the ravages of time. However, in general it is not just the material survival of writing that is thrown into doubt, but authors are also concerned with the danger of forgery and/or change. Yellowed pages may be a symbol for venerable age and an all the more authentic truth, but this association is shattered if there is express talk of altering the contents of old books – hence Spenser's rhyming of "memory" and "forgery."

This skeptical approach was countered by a new professional group that lent its full weight to the conviction that writing guaranteed the lasting quality and authenticity of human memory. The credo "NON OMNIS MORIAR" and the proclamation "VERBA VOLANT – SCRIPTA MANET" were appropriated by printers and publishers and used as their trademarks. The claim that the durability of printed texts put all other cultural traces in the shade gave loud expression to their

---

[29] Du Bellay, *Rome*, 22 f.
[30] William Shakespeare, *The Rape of Lucrece*, 946 ff.

pride in their new profession. They placed a new commercial emphasis on the humanist credo, making the ideal of writing and printing,
as the indispensable bearers of tradition and culture, into an adver-
tising strategy. The publisher of a collection of 17th-century baroque
German dramas, for instance, boasted:

> Bearing in mind that pyramids, columns and images made from all kinds of
> materials are damaged by time or destroyed by violence or simply decay... that
> whole cities go down, sink, and are covered with water, by contrast writings
> and books are spared such destruction, for whatever goes up or down in a
> country or place will easily be found again in many other innumerable places,
> and so to speak of it in more human terms, there is nothing more lasting and
> more immortal than books.[31]

Thomas Jefferson, who put together a collection of historical
sources in drafting the laws of Virginia, also distinguished very precisely between the conservational power of (hand)writing and that of
printing. He asked: "How many of the precious works of antiquity were
lost while they existed only in manuscript? Has there ever been one
lost since the art of printing has rendered it practicable to multiply and
disperse copies?" From this he drew the conclusion that democratic
duplication and distribution offered the best guarantee for texts: "the
lost cannot be recovered; but let us save what remains: not by vaults
and locks that fence them from the public eye and use, in consigning
them to the waste of time, but by such a multiplication of copies, as
shall place them beyond the reach of accident."[32]

With the growing market, the book – which had been cherished
as a sacred object by many a Renaissance humanist – turned into a
commodity. In the foreword to his *Anatomy of Melancholy*, the doctor and encyclopaedist Robert Burton viewed the increased output of
the printing presses from the perspective of a reader who was overwhelmed by the mass of new books, and feared that there would be
a confusion of knowledge: "New books every day, pamphlets, curran-
toes, stories, whole catalogues of volumes of all sorts, new paradoxes,

[31] Jakob Ayrer, *Dramen*, ed. Adelbert von Keller, Vol. 1, Stuttgart 1865, 4; quoted from
Walter Benjamin, *Ursprung des deutschen Trauerspiels*, Frankfurt a.M. 1963, 153.

[32] Thomas Jefferson, Letter to George Wythe, quoted from Elizabeth I. Eisenstein, *The
Printing Press as an Agent of Change. Communications and Cultural Transformations in
Early-Modern Europe*, 3 vols, Cambridge, London, New York 1979, 115 f.

opinions, schisms, heresies, controversies in philosophy, religion etc."
And he sums up the situation: "What a catalogue of new books all this
year, all this age (I say), have our Frankfort marts, our domestic marts
brought out!"[33]

Burton quotes various authorities to list the drawbacks of the new
print age that he calls "this scribbling age": some are "bewitched with
the desire of fame," and "even in the midst of illness [. . .] and scarce
able to hold a pen, they must say something and get themselves a
name." (22) "They have to write to keep the printers occupied, or
even to show that they are alive." (23) The printing industry made the
exclusiveness of *fama* into a universal rush for self-immortalization.
The printed paper so venerated by Milton became wastepaper under
the critical gaze of Scaliger and the satirical gaze of Burton. Not only
were the libraries and bookshops full of such soiled paper, but so
too were the commodes and latrines. People were not writing for
the sake of knowledge and scholarship, but out of vanity, avarice,
and sycophancy. And what went down on paper was "trifles, trash,
nonsense." (23)

In the camp of the Anglicans and the loyal subjects of the King,
even a century and a half after the arrival of the print age, the belief
that textual traces could preserve and renew past life took a severe
beating. For them, the great promise made by Shakespeare to his
lover in Sonnet 55 became empty rhetoric:

> Gainst death, and all-oblivious enmity
> Shall you pace forth, your praise shall still find room
> Even in the eyes of all posterity
> That wear this world out to the ending doom.

Posterity began to change from being the guarantor of immortality
to being an acute threat to it. In a bourgeois age of economics and
industrialization of print culture, the new conditions of literary writing
and reading also changed those of fame. The context in which texts
were written became less and less that of *fama* and *memoria*, and more
and more that of the literary market, with its short-lived trends. The
printing industry continually adjusted itself to the changing demands

---

[33] Robert Burton, *The Anatomy of Melancholy*, 3 vols, ed. Holbrook Jackson, London
1961, Vol. I, 18, 24.

of its anonymous readers, and in such an environment the vision of a "literal" potential for survival dissolved into thin air. The promise of everlasting glory disappeared beneath the rapid cycles of innovation and "antiquation." In the foreword to his *Essays* of 1625, Bacon had still been able to proceed on the assumption that these (in their Latin version) would last as long as there were still books on Earth.[34] But in the foreword to his *A Tale of a Tub* (1710), Jonathan Swift's hopes were rather less ambitious: "The Book seems calculated to live at least as long as our Language, and our Taste admit no great Alterations."[35]

Such reservations suggest a different awareness of time. The change that threatens Swift's text may come from one day to the next; writing can no longer offer protection against the storms of time but in fact becomes their target. Because of this exposure, it now requires the support of various "paratexts," like forewords, justifications, dedications, and epistles. One such text in *A Tale of a Tub* is an epistle of dedication to "His Royal Highness, the Prince Posterity." This prince, as we learn from the epistle, is still a child who is living under the guardianship of a cruel governor who turns out to be none other than Father Chronos – the personification of time – whom Swift decks out with all the splendor of baroque symbolism:

I beseech You to observe that large and terrible *Scythe* which your *Governour* affects to bear continually about him. Be pleased to remark the Length and Strength, the Sharpness and Hardness of his *Nails* and *Teeth*: Consider his baneful abominable *Breath*, Enemy to Life and Matter, infectious and corrupting: And then reflect whether it be possible for any mortal Ink and Paper of this Generation to make a suitable Resistance.[36]

The old opposition between time's destructiveness and poetry's aspirations to immortality is mediated in Swift's text by posterity, represented as the young prince who, when he is old and mature enough, is to take over from his terrible guardian Father Time. In this way Swift replaces poetry's traditional aspirations to eternity with an appeal to posterity. "We confess Immortality to be a great and mighty goddess,"

---

[34] Francis Bacon, *Essays*, in *The Works*, ed. James Spedding, Robert Leslie Ellis and Douglas Denon Heath, 14 vols, London 1857–1874, Vol. VI, 373.

[35] Jonathan Swift, *A Tale of a Tub. Written for the Universal Improvement of Mankind* (1710), ed. A. C. Guthkelch and D. Nichol, Oxford 1958, 3.

[36] Ibid., 32.

he writes, "but in vain we offer up to her our devotions and sacrifices." In less mythological terms, this means that the durability of the written word can no longer be achieved by heroically defying a mythical god of time, but requires a social alliance with a later readership. Even though literary works are "light enough to swim upon the surface for all eternity," they lack any innate ability to last. They therefore depend on a social construction, on a pact across generations that will lend them support. It is not, then, the immanent power of texts but the decision of posterity that will ensure whether they will survive or not.

Until the prince reaches maturity, however, it is the terrible governor Father Time who will be in charge – this cruel, arbitrary despot whose "inveterate malice is such to the writings of our age, that of several thousands produced yearly from this renowned city, before the next revolution of the sun, there is not one to be heard of."[37] It is clear that with the traditional image of all-consuming time, *tempus edax*, Swift is caricaturing a very modern institution: the book market, with its organized transience. He had hoped, as we learn next, to put together a list of new publications for the prince, but after just a few hours he could find no trace of them.

I enquired after them among Readers and Booksellers, but I enquired in vain, the *Memorial of them was lost among Men, their Place was no more to be found*: and I was laughed to scorn, for a *Clown* and a *Pedant*, without all Taste and Refinement, little versed in the Course of *present* Affairs, and that knew nothing of what had pass'd in the best Companies of Court and Town.[38]

Then he turns the satirical screw even tighter. He asks "what is then become of those immense Bales of Paper, which must needs have been employ'd in such Numbers of Books?" The answer is that books, just like people, only have one way to come into the world, but can leave it in many different ways. The material remains disappear silently and permanently in many places: they are, for instance, used in public places of need, they are burned in ovens, they are stuck over the windows of brothels, or used for patchwork lampshades.

Swift's ironic portrait of the book market shows all too clearly that writing in itself has no inborn powers of resistance against decay and

---

[37] Ibid., 33.
[38] Ibid., 34–35.

oblivion but, as noted, is dependent on social agreements. The aspiration to and the promise of immortality rest on two basic assumptions: the material substance and the readability of the texts. Swift shows that in the middle of the 18th century neither of these could be taken for granted. The high rate of innovation, which went hand in hand with accelerated production, and the experience of historical change made the survival of texts in cultural memory increasingly unlikely. Instead of the universal erosion by time, from which writing was supposed to be miraculously exempt, written and printed material now found itself subject to the laws of historical change in a dialectic between renewal and obsolescence, production and waste. As Emerson was to point out a century later, the written word was now "tumbling into the inevitable pit which the creation of new thought opens for all that is old."[39]

Swift could still vouch for the fact that what he was writing was "literally true this minute I am writing: what revolutions may happen before it shall be ready for your perusal, I can by no means warrant." In much the same way, a century later, the essayist Charles Lamb expressed his awareness of the ephemeral nature of the written word, when under the title *Distant Correspondents* he wrote about his correspondence with a friend in Australia. "Indeed, it is no easy effort to set about a correspondence at our distance. The weary world of waters between us oppresses the imagination. It is difficult to conceive how a scrawl of mine should ever stretch across it. It is a sort of presumption to expect that one's thoughts should live so far. It is like writing for posterity."[40]

Lamb too considers it unlikely that what is true at the moment of writing will still be true when it reaches the addressee, but he must also be prepared for a complete invention to ripen into a plausible truth during its long journey. From now on, truth exists in time and has a tendency "to unessence herself."[41] Lamb's essay is a remarkable reversal of Bacon's concept of letters, which he

---

[39] Ralph Waldo Emerson, *Circles* (1841), in Joel Porte (ed.), *Essays and Lectures*, New York 1983, 403.

[40] Charles Lamb, "Distant Correspondents" (1823), *The Essays of Elia*, London 1894, 142–148; here, 142.

[41] Ibid., 143.

saw as heroic voyagers on the sea of time, and which he trusted would guarantee a direct relationship between the authors of the past and the readers of the future. With Lamb, letters have completely lost their aura as stores of energy that might be reactivated at another place and another time. Whereas Bacon stressed the binding effect of letters, Lamb saw their effect as distancing and "alienating."

FROM TEXTS TO TRACES

The relationship between an epoch and the past depends to a great extent on its relationship to the media of cultural memory. During the Renaissance there was still a strong belief that through texts a small but decisive section of the past, the immortal spirit of the author, could be preserved intact. As long as there was some kind of spiritual kinship, a later reader could communicate with the author across a wide expanse of time, because the writing could synchronize their communication. In the 18th century, however, this confidence in the unlimited conservational power of texts evaporated. Writing could no longer establish the synchronization that transcended history and that was the hallmark of the phenomenon of "the classics."[42] But the loss of simultaneity still did not mean that the past had become a foreign country to which the present had no right of entry. The experience of loss was once more countered by new experiences of immediacy, and once more a bridge was built across the gulf of oblivion. This time, however, the pillars holding the bridge were not texts, but relics and traces.

William Wordsworth

In the 19th century, implicit trust in the durability and reproducibility of letters had faded to nothing. Bacon had been convinced that the invention of printing had saved the world from a second Middle Ages and "the alarms about the loss of mankind's memory;"

---

[42] For more detailed discussion of this subject, see A. Assmann, *Zeit und Tradition. Kulturelle Strategien der Dauer*, Vienna 1998.

but, around 1800 these "alarms" were more of a threat than ever before. For the Romantic poet William Wordsworth the difference between lasting, two-dimensional texts and vanishing, three-dimensional monuments has disappeared. According to him, books are exposed to the same fate of destruction by time, whereas the privilege of immunity to time is passed on to Nature. The divine soul and the immortal spirit of man find their counterpart in timeless Nature, not in temporal and temporary culture:

> [. . .]man
> As long as he shall be the child of earth,
> Might almost "weep to have" what he may lose,
> Nor be himself extinguished, but survive
> Abject, depressed, forlorn, disconsolate.[43]

Wordsworth is here quoting Shakespeare's 64th sonnet, the last lines of which are:

> This thought is as a death, which cannot choose
> But weep to have that which it fears to lose.

This is the baroque mood of transience, but it is not the same as the Romantic mood, for between mutability and historicism there are substantial differences that can be grasped not least through the evaluation of writing as a medium of memory. Around 1800, writing was no longer seen as a stable bearer of information. Wordsworth was in no doubt about the historicity and transience of human culture. As far as he was concerned, the power of rebirth belonged only to Nature, which he assumed would miraculously reestablish itself even after a cosmic catastrophe. Nature, permeated by a divine essence, would slowly but surely and successfully restore its own "living presence," whereas culture, the works of the human mind, would have no chance of a similar renaissance. Milton praised writing as "the purest efficacy and extraction of that living intellect that bred them," Gadamer proclaims it as "pure spirit," whereas Wordsworth complains that this mind has no lasting, congenial medium to support it:

> Oh! Why hath not the Mind
> Some element to stamp her image on

---

[43] Wordsworth, *The Prelude*, V, 18–28, 137 (see Chapt. 4, n. 35).

In nature somewhat nearer to her own?
Why, gifted with such powers to send abroad
Her spirit, must it lodge in shrines so frail?

(V, 45–49)

He sees writing not as a miraculous weapon to fight the erosion of time, but as something particularly fragile. The dream that follows this reflection paints it in apocalyptic colors: an Arab flees through the desert with two books that in the language of the dream are visualized as a stone and a shell. The stone symbolizes the solid knowledge of numbers, and the shell the harmony of epic song. By burying both books, he hopes to save them from an approaching, apocalyptic flood – an impossible task that makes the Arab into a sort of quixotic adventurer. The dreamer painfully witnesses the fact that human knowledge and culture cannot be saved in any lasting form from time and destruction.

Thomas Carlyle

The insight that texts could not guarantee any reliable connection between past, present, and future was emphasized more and more by historians, who questioned the reliability of written sources just as much as they questioned their own conventions of representation. In an essay on historiography written in 1833, Thomas Carlyle gave clear expression to this new view of history: "Of the thing now gone silent, named Past, which was once Present, and loud enough, how much do we know? Our 'Letter of Instructions' comes to us in the saddest state; falsified, blotted out, torn, lost, and but a shred of it in existence; this too so difficult to read or spell."[44]

The lucidity of the past, then, was due to solid texts in an established tradition that had guaranteed their continuous readability. To deviate from this royal path was to find oneself, as Carlyle did, in the wilderness of opaque history, the complexity and density of which remained hopelessly inaccessible. The images Carlyle uses to refer to the past are

---

44 Thomas Carlyle, "On History Again" (1833), in *Critical and Miscellaneous Essays in Five Volumes*, Vol. III, London 1899, 168. In the 17th century, there had already been a similar approach, which was to become known as "historical Pyrrhonism." See Arnaldo Momigliano, *Wege in die Alte Welt*, Berlin 1991, 88.

those of a magic web, a complex aggregate, an obscure palimpsest.[45] For Carlyle, history is made up less of what is preserved than of what is lost: "Well may we say that of our History, the more important part is lost without recovery."[46] Faced with the ruins of Palmyra some eighty years earlier, Robert Wood had also spoken of "this silence of history."[47] The gaps that the Romantics endeavored to fill with their imagination are for Carlyle a constituent element of the text that we call history. What we are used to refer to as "history" is the result of a thoroughgoing compression of data that is achieved not by conscious selections but by temporal decay. Although Carlyle describes history as "a miserable defective shred," he is far from regretting this state of affairs. If all the data of the past could be reliably stored, this would mean the end of cultural memory. For events to fit into the necessarily confined space of memory, decay and oblivion must do their work of destruction and reduction. Without the assistance of these operators, cultural memory would be exploded with the events of an hour.[48] "Memory and Oblivion," Carlyle continues, "like Day and Night, and indeed like all other Contractions in this strange dualistic Life of ours, are necessary for each other's existence: Oblivion is the dark page, whereon Memory writes her light-beam characters, and makes them legible; were it all light, nothing could be read there, any more than if it were all darkness."[49]

Without "the grace of lost information" (Harald Weinrich), neither memory nor historiography would be possible. This insight points to a radical change in the concept of cultural memory. Previously, memory had been defined in terms of tradition, inscription, and storage, whereas the new historical consciousness defines it in terms of erasure, destruction, gaps, and forgetfulness. This in turn leads to a significant shift of emphasis "from texts to traces" as media of

---

[45] Carlyle, "On History" (1830), in *Critical and Miscellaneous Essays in Five Volumes*, Vol. II, 86.

[46] Ibid., 87.

[47] Wood, *The Ruins of Palmyra* (1753), I, quoted from Peter Geimer, *Die Vergangenheit der Kunst – Strategien der Nachträglichkeit im 18. Jahrhundert*, Dissertation, Marburg 1997, 64.

[48] Carlyle, "On History Again," 172.

[49] Ibid., 173.

cultural memory. With letters and texts, one could assume the complete reactivation of past information, but with traces only a fraction of past meaning can be restored. In this respect, traces are two-edged, because they link memory inextricably with forgetting. It is this inbuilt forgetting that breaks the traditional line from the past through the present to the future, and that turns the past into a foreign country.

Traces open a very different path to the past from that of texts, because they entail nonlinguistic signs of a bygone culture – ruins and relics, shards and fragments – as well as the remains of oral traditions. "What ancient historians omitted could be saved by modern antiquarians."[50] I have already briefly referred to the historian Jacob Burckhardt, who defined his cultural history project in terms of the distinction between texts and traces. By "texts" he understood coded messages in the sense of conscious expressions of a period together with all its associated, tendentious (self-)deceptions. By "traces," however, he meant unprocessed information that renders a more immediate image of the reality of an age because it remains outside intentional and conscious articulation. Much in the mode of Marcel Proust, the cultural historian's search for traces concentrates on the involuntary memory of a past society. Traces are more precious to him than texts, because their silent, indirect testimonies contain a higher degree of truth and authenticity – and indeed for Burckhardt the highest degree: "primum gradum certitudinis."[51]

WRITING AND TRACES

Writing and traces are often used synonymously, but they are in fact very different. Writing is language codified in the form of visual signs. This definition cannot be applied to traces, which relate neither to language nor to codified signs. They are, nevertheless, semiotically readable as indexical signs without any underlying

---

[50] Momigliano, "Alte Geschichte und Antiquarische Forschung," *Wege in die Alte Welt*, Berlin, 85–86.
[51] Jacob Burckhardt, *Die Kunst der Betrachtung. Aufsätze und Vorträge zur Bildenden Kunst*, ed. Henning Ritter, Cologne 1984, 175.

code.[52] The written, representative sign is therefore replaced by the directness of an impression.

In memory metaphors, the concept of the trace has played an important part since Antiquity:

> When the wax in the soul of any one is deep and abundant, and smooth and perfectly tempered, then the impressions which pass through the senses and sink into the heart of the soul, as Homer says in a parable, meaning to indicate the likeness of the soul to wax: these, I say, being pure and clear, and having a sufficient depth of wax, are also lasting, and minds such as these easily learn and easily retain, and are not liable to confusion, but have true thoughts.[53]

However, if the "heart of anyone is shaggy [...] or muddy and of impure wax, or very soft, or very hard," these impressions will be unclear and will soon become unrecognizable. If someone has no clear image of the original scene imprinted on the wax of his soul, and therefore cannot remember it accurately, he will not only see and hear wrongly, but he will think wrongly too.

In the 19th century, the concept of the trace enjoyed a new and enhanced status through the experimental psychology of memory. Plato's metaphysics of anamnesis gave way to a physics of the real. The assumption was that the real "inscribed" itself on the substance of the brain just as it did on the silver bromide of the photographic plate. "Trace" thus became a generalized term both for writing and for picture, and it extended especially to those physiological processes in which the human hand and mind no longer played any part. Richard Semon coined the expression "Engramm," which was productively taken up by the art and cultural historian Aby Warburg.[54] In 1877, Karl Spamer defined the trace as "an effect of power on an inanimate object" that contained this energy within itself. Memory and trace thus became synonymous. One can, wrote Spamer, "speak of a memory of all organic materials, indeed of materials in general, in the sense that certain effects leave more or less lasting traces on them. Stone itself

---

[52] Charles Sanders Peirce defines the indicative sign as "a sign which refers to the object that it denotes by virtue of being really affected by that object." *Collected Papers*, 8 volumes, ed. A. Burke, Cambridge, Mass., 1966, Vol. 2, 248.

[53] Plato, *Theaetetus*, in *The Dialogues*, Vol. III., 298, here, 194 d (see Chapt. 7, FN 5).

[54] Ernst H. Gombrich, *Aby Warburg. An Intellectual Biography*, London 1970.

retains the trace of the hammer that struck it."[55] According to this concept, as with Plato's wax tablet, some materials are more capable of traces – and hence of memories – than others. Fluids are normally not capable of any traces, because their surfaces automatically become smooth again, filling and closing any gaps. That is why Lethe became a central metaphor for oblivion. (Today, however, physicists assure us that there are also liquids that are actually capable of traces and/or memories [i.e., the so called non-Newtonian liquids].)

The concept of the trace extended the spectrum of "inscriptions" beyond texts to photographic images and the effects of force on and by means of objects. The step from texts to traces and relics as significant witnesses to the past was a step from intentional linguistic signs to material imprints that, though not meant to be signs, later become readable as such.

If we look at the long history of writing, we can see that it has gone through four decisive stages though none of them have automatically effaced the earlier ones. The steps are from *pictographic* to *alphabetical* writing, then to the *analogous* writing of the trace, and finally to *digital* writing. The latter brings us back to a codified script, even if this is only minimal, consisting of just two elements. Perhaps it would be better to speak of it as a "structural script," because it is composed of impulses that do not have the character of signs and do not themselves represent anything. By comparison to pictographic writing, alphabetical writing already marked a radical increase in the degree of abstraction: thanks to the massive reduction in the quantity of signs, it became possible to represent any natural language through this medium, thereby overcoming the earlier need to link a specific writing to a specific spoken language. Digital writing has developed this process of abstraction even further: it has once more reduced the number of elements and is able to codify a variety of media. If alphabetical writing may be called *translinguistic*, digital writing is *transmedial* – it uses the same code for pictures, sounds, speech, and writing.

As we have seen, scholars in the Renaissance regarded writing as an energetic medium. One may ask whether these authors – for whom the thought of dead letters was so alien, and who set such store by the

---

55 Karl Spamer, *Die Physiologie der Seele*, Stuttgart 1877, 86, quoted from Manfred Sommer, *Evidenz im Augenblick*, Frankfurt a.M. 1987, 149 f.

intrinsic powers of the written word – actually anticipated the concept of electronic writing in some form. There is certainly a similarity in so far as with both concepts writing is not reduced to "post-scription" but maintains the quality of "pre-scription" and so may be equated with programming. Textual traces are not confined to following an idea; they may also precede it as a signal, activation, or instruction.

The difference, however, becomes very clear if one considers the mnemonic power of letters. The alliance between writing and memory that was so crucial to Renaissance theorists is dissolved by electronic writing. This means that the role of writing as a servant and instrument of the human mind is reversed, and it is now writing that instrumentalizes the mind. The hierarchy between man and technology has changed completely since the Renaissance. The energy of electronic writing goes its own way and is no longer confined to its function as a means of human communication, as writing indisputably was for the Renaissance.[56] At that time it was a tool that helped man to extend the range of his thoughts and actions, and to fulfill his lofty hopes and ambitions. But above all, it facilitated and preserved human communication across the gulf of oblivion – in other words, it always functioned as an aid to memory, exactly as prescribed by its inventor Theut in the Platonic myth. Electronic writing, however, has cut the bond between writing and the human body and memory. What is written electronically can only be read electronically, and man has become a peripheral figure in this process, because he is reliant on retranslations back into the anthropocentric, codified forms of pictures and writing. In this respect, electronic writing has moved out of the Platonic scenario and creates traces of which neither Theut nor Thammus (the inventor and the critic of writing in Plato's dialogue *Phaedro*) would ever have dreamed.

Thanks to its "immateriality" or electronic energy, digital writing is fluid, which means that it loses the most important features that made writing into such a fertile metaphor for memory. Instead of fixed

---

[56] It must be stressed that the authors named here represent a humanistic view of writing that was developed during the Renaissance, but was not totally dominant. One very different concept was that of the kabbalistic models, which attributed divine energy to letters and so withdrew them from human access and communications.

engraving there are cascades of images and floods of information that, to quote S. J. Schmidt, "aim at intensively forgettable seriality." And instead of the vertical layers of overwriting that permit states of latency, there is now nothing but the flickering surface without depth, background, or subtext. The functions of storage and deletion are extremely close to one another in digital writing – literally just a click away. In this process writes S. J. Schmidt, "an evaluating memory, a memory that presupposes a break in the informational continuum, becomes improbable and disturbing."[57] No doubt this memory still exists, but under electronic conditions it can no longer reflect itself metaphorically – as it did before – in the technical process of writing. In the digital framework it is defined only in a negative form as "a break in the informational continuum."

TRACES AND WASTE

The problem of tradition – and with it, that of cultural memory – became considerably more complicated when the project was no longer to counter forgetting, but forgetting itself became part and parcel of the process of tradition. As interest shifted from "texts to relics," the media of memory changed from "speaking" to "silent" witnesses that could be made to speak again. When the focus moved from "relics to traces," the past had to be reconstructed above all through records that were not intended for posterity or even for durability. Their task was to communicate those things about which tradition was silent: the inconspicuous details of daily life. This takes us one step further from "traces to waste."[58] With his "reverence of the insignificant,"[59] the cultural historian or "detective of the past" turned

---

57 Siegfried J. Schmidt, *Die Welten der Medien. Grundlagen und Perspektiven der Medienbeobachtung*, Braunschweig/Wiesbaden 1996, 68.

58 Michael Thompson, *Rubbish Theory. The Creation and Destruction of Value*, Oxford 1979. He develops this theory from the perspective of sociology, and a detailed review is to be found in Jonathan Culler, *Framing the Sign. Criticism and its Institutions*, London 1988, 168–182. For a history of rubbish from a literary perspective, see Christian Enzensberger, *Grösserer Versuch über den Schmutz*, Munich 1968.

59 This is part of the title of a book by Roland Kany: *Mnemosyne als Programm. Geschichte, Erinnerung und die Andacht zum Unbedeutenden im Werk von Usener, Warburg und Benjamin*. Studien zur deutschen Literatur, Tübingen 1987, 93.

waste into information. I illustrate this last step through a novel by Thomas Pynchon, thereby bringing the theme of the mnemonic power of letters to the threshold of the present.

In western civilization, as we have seen, the problem of cultural memory has become more acute under the pressure of new media, which provide hitherto unimaginable storage capacities and distribute information at hitherto unheard-of speeds. Increasingly dense communication networks bring the most distant regions into direct contact, including radio and television that transmit their programs without a pause and as fast as light, thanks to satellites circling the globe. The storage capacity of new data-carriers and archives has shattered the confines of cultural memory. The flood of TV images has made writing obsolete as a central medium of memory, and new kinds of storage and information technology (IT) are based on a different kind of writing – namely digital, whose fluid form no longer has any connection with the old technique of inscription. This writing no longer allows for a clear distinction between remembering and forgetting.

The idea of a total media regime that governs social remembering and forgetting provides the plot for Thomas Pynchon's novel *The Crying of Lot 49*. The novel poses the question whether in a culture that draws its media network ever tighter there are still traces of unprogrammed life. The answer lies in the waste.

The electronic mass media have strengthened certain tendencies that were already apparent in the print culture. They include Swift's dialectic between innovation and "antiquation," or production and waste. However, Swift had not yet given up hope of being able to speak through time to the dead by making a pact with posterity.[60] In Thomas Pynchon's description of a world crisscrossed by mass media we search in vain for any such hope. In one respect the opposed systems of a mass media culture and a totalitarian state coincide: they pose a threat to memory, be it through a vast excess of information or through a drastic reduction of it. In Orwell's *1984* scenario of a totalitarian world even the tiniest cracks had to be blocked in case they afforded a glimpse of

---

[60] Nietzsche defined "'fame" as the "belief in the solidarity and continuity of the greatness of all ages" and as "a protest against the passing away of generations and the transitoriness of things." "History," in *Untimely Meditations*; here, 69, (see Chapt. 3, n. 6).

the past, because such a view might lead to a revision of the absolutist present. In the world as organized by western mass media, memory is dissolved in accelerated cycles of production and consumption.

Pynchon depicts the world of mass media as one of organized amnesia in which it is the media that produce the collective imaginary. By contrast, though, memory is linked to two opposed faculties: the sense of personal identity and the sense of reality. The heroine of the novel assiduously collects clues and traces that step by step uncover an alternative network named W.A.S.T.E – an unofficial counter-culture, secret, unpublished, and silent, outside of the official channels of communication. Oedipa Maas embraces her heroic destiny, which is to remember in a world of forgetting: "She was meant to remember. She faced that possibility. [. . .] She tested it, shivering: I am meant to remember."[61]

Her situation is comparable to that of Orwell's archivist Winston Smith, who also sets out in search of a past that has been destroyed. Significantly, both he and Oedipa concentrate on waste as the most reliable bearer of unofficial memory. Winston Smith discovers a scrap of paper here and a piece of refuse there that have somehow escaped the "memory holes" – the gigantic subterranean machines for the destruction of traces. Oedipa Maas also discovers a piece of rubbish that becomes an emblem for memory in general. It is the mattress of a dying sailor, the "inexhaustible stuffing" that suddenly becomes a precious treasure for her "that could keep vestiges of every nightmare sweat, helpless overflowing bladder, viciously, tearfully consummated wet dream, like the memory bank to a computer of the lost."[62]

Oedipa finds the traces she is looking for, not in cultural relics and fragments left over from a past era but in bodily remains and excretions: bones, sweat, semen, and chemical salts transform the stuffing of the old mattress into a data bank of everything that has been lost. In an age of rapidly developing storage technologies, Pynchon's heroine devises a seismograph to record what cannot otherwise be preserved because it cannot be encoded: the irreducible ephemera of life. Her discovery is a moment of revelation, a fleeting glimpse that gives her

---

[61] Thomas Pynchon, *The Crying of Lot 49*, Philadelphia, New York 1965, 118.
[62] Ibid., 126.

an intense contact with reality. The data bank, an emblem of remembering, turns into an emblem of forgetting. With the disappearance of the mattress, the world would lose every trace of this life, and "the set of all men who had slept on it, whatever their lives had been, would truly cease to be, forever, when the mattress burned. She stared at it in wonder. It was as if she had just discovered the irreversible process."[63]

The desire to speak with the dead is as old as humanity. Modern theorists, however, urge us to suppress such atavistic desires. Roland Barthes, for instance, criticizes a form of reading that tries "at all costs to make the dead speak," and Michel Foucault argues against the "historical-transcendental nineteenth-century tradition" that proceeds from the assumption "of the survival of the work, of its continuation beyond death, of its mysterious surplus."[64] However, the problem takes on a different guise if one considers the materiality of memory media as well as the cultural expectations, hopes, and disillusions that every era invests in them. Our historical survey has taken us from the immortalizing letters to traces and to waste; on the way, we have focused on important shifts of emphasis in the conception of cultural memory. These different media of memory do not simply take one another's place in a linear development. They continue to co-exist, representing different forms of continuity and discontinuity in cultural memory. The link with the past is not in any way or at any time uniform, but it becomes an ever more complex structure of overlapping and intersecting layers of memory, identified as texts, relics, traces, and waste.

It is not, however, only the media of memory that play the decisive role; just as important are the different discourse and hermeneutics that develop with them. We might describe them as paths that offer access to different pasts. There is the path of classic texts that are assured of conservation through the everlasting immateriality of letters and are read uniformly in a *transhistorical frame of synchronicity*. This is a path that was originally laid by the Renaissance humanists

---

[63] Ibid., 128.

[64] Roland Barthes, *Critique et vérité*, translated into English as *Criticism and Truth* (trans. Katrine Pilcher Keuneman, intro. Philip Thody), London 1987. Michel Foucault. "What Is an Author?," in Ed. Vassilis Lambropoulos and David Neal Miller (eds.), *Twentieth-Century Literary Theory*, Albany 1987. 124–142, quote "Was ist ein Autor?," in *Schriften zur Literatur*, Munich 1974, 14–15.

and can still be taken by the philosophers of today. Then there is that of *critical historiography*, which places texts in the category of relics and reads them with an awareness of an ever growing gap in time. There is also the path of *historical imagination*, which "reanimates" these relics through poetic reconstruction. And there is the path of *electronic information technology*, which facilitates increasingly simple and comprehensive techniques of recording, while at the same time sharpens perception of whatever cannot be stored and will be lost forever.

What we can draw from this history – if indeed we can call it such – is the fact that there has been a growing consciousness of the complex interaction between remembering and forgetting. The situation of cultural memory in the age of digital media appears to be that the boundaries between remembering and forgetting are becoming more and more blurred. In this respect, the structure of cultural memory will come closer and closer to that of the unconscious, which is generally noted for the collapse of leading distinctions. It is a state already anticipated by James Joyce, who staged the indistinctness in his world of unconscious linguistic productivity, as highlighted by word play, slips of the tongue, and puns. It was Joyce who reminded us that the word *letter* was closely related to the word *litter*.

9

Image

> The photograph of the missing being will touch me like the delayed rays of a star.[1]
>
> Roland Barthes, Camera Lucida

> Isn't it like a curse, this kind of remembering, this holding onto images that turn the gaze away from the here and now.
>
> Jürgen Becker, Der fehlende Rest

Let us summarize the main Renaissance arguments concerning the qualities of writing and images as media for storage. Bacon had no faith in images as means of providing accurate reproduction or stable conservation of the originals. He saw the two media in a totally different relation to time: pictures were considered to be material objects and so subject to temporal destruction, whereas writing was viewed as immaterial and thus either outside time or part of its generative dimension. Added to this was the fact that two- and three-dimensional images were seen as mere copies of the original, and so right from the start there was an ontological gap that material erosion by time could only widen. Writing, on the other hand, was seen as an emanation of the mind and a means of mental reactivation. Unlike the image, it was not the product of a single, irreversible "excarnation," but allowed an unlimited number of repeatable "reincarnations," as was made

---

[1] Roland Barthes, *Camera Lucida. Reflections on Photography*, New York 1981, 80–81.

clear by the widely used metaphor of the seed. The Renaissance debate mirrored both the lively competition between the different arts (paragons) and the protestant/catholic conflict between writing images as the central mass medium of culture. Bacon's bias in this cultural-political struggle was that of a scientist: his advocacy of writing was accompanied by hostility toward images, which he rejected as supports for an archaic, anthropomorphic mentality. Milton's position, on the other hand, was theological: he believed the democratization of the spirit was effected through the medium of writing; whereas images which were associated with idols offered no comparable potential for enlightenment and, therefore, in the hands of the Catholic Church could all too easily be used for the purposes of mass propaganda.

It was, then, the qualities of readability and transparency that made writing the preferred medium for cultural transmission in the eyes of Protestant, "enlightened," Renaissance humanists. This preference for letters, texts, and the cognitive function in the transmission of cultural memory became a persistent feature of western culture, and it even found its way into the definition of what we understand by "history." For instance, Ranke in his *Weltgeschichte* claimed that history only begins "where monuments become comprehensible and there are credible written documents at our disposal."[2] During the last few decades, however, we have witnessed an iconic turn in historiography; historians today focus increasingly on the seminal function of images in the production and reconstruction of history. Reinhart Koselleck has studied the monuments and rituals of the political cult of the dead and the transformation of the military hero on horseback from an aristocratic to a middle-class monument. Pierre Nora wished there were "ways to a new form of history that would focus on the symbolic and on the world of images."[3] With the

---

[2] Leopold von Ranke, *Weltgeschichte*, Part One, Leipzig 1881, 2nd edition, Preface IV.
[3] Reinhart Koselleck and Michael Jeismann (eds.), *Der politische Totenkult*, Munich 1994; Arthur E. Imhoff, *Geschichte sehen*, Munich 1991, and also *Im Bildersaal der Geschichte*, Munich 1991; Pierre Nora, "Between Memory and History" (see Introduction, n. 10), here 7–24. See also Aleida Assmann: "Im Zwischenraum zwischen Geschichte und Gedächtnis: Bemerkungen zu Pierre Noras "Lieux de mémoire," in Ètienne François (ed.), *Lieux de mémoire, Erinnerungsorte. D'un modèle français à un projet allemand*, Les Travaux du Centre Marc Bloch, Cahier 6, Berlin 1996, 19–27.

rise of cultural studies, new genres and media have become legitimate sources and objects of historiography. Oral history too in its own way has played its part in the rehabilitation of the image. Lutz Niethammer analyzes mental images as unprocessed and hence original raw material for recollection, and so as a kind of hard core for memory:

> Routines and conditions that were once so important that they were stuck in the memory, are obviously remembered as images. Therefore they can often be described with great precision to an interested observer, whose inquiries lift them out of the insignificance of their everyday context and may even facilitate [. . .] their reconstruction. Stories may be associated with them, but such descriptions in themselves have no narrative structure and do not tend towards a coherent meaning.[4]

Even in Ranke's time, however, there were counter-movements. Under the banner of an integral history of culture, some critics began to distrust the written tradition and to discover new forms of access to the past through pictures and monuments. The notion of immediacy that had been developed with respect to writing was claimed by historians such as Jacob Burckhardt and Aby Warburg for images. This immediacy, however, was no longer linked to transparency; pictures and symbols now entailed the opposite and were associated with nontransparency of irreducible ambivalence. Whereas writing supported a clearly legible tradition, the image was perceived as connected with emotion and the unconscious. The power (*vis*) of images, derived from their affective charge, made them the preferred medium for memory and the cultural unconscious in the eyes of those who mistrusted texts as carriers of intentions and propaganda. The textual tradition was one of clarity and light, and that of pictures and traces was dark and enigmatic – unlike texts, they were silent and yet at the same time over-determinate; they could be hermetic, or as eloquent as any text. The two media were in fact seen as incommensurate, each untranslatable into the other and yet at the same time stimulating acts of translation. This ambivalence between the two has its physiological

---

[4] Lutz Niethammer, "Fragen – Antworten – Fragen," in Lutz Niethammer and Alexander von Plato (eds.), "Wir kriegen jetzt andere Zeiten." *Auf der Suche nach der Erfahrung des Volkes in nachfaschistischen Ländern. Lebensgeschichte und Sozialkultur im Ruhrgebiet 1930–1960*, Vol. 3, Berlin and Bonn 1985, 405.

counterpart in the left and right hemispheres of the brain that process language and images. This double yet interactive structure is responsible not least for the complexity and productivity of both individual and cultural memory, which constantly move between the layers of the conscious and the unconscious.

Images arise in memory especially in those areas that cannot be accessed by verbal processing. This applies above all to precognitive and traumatic experiences. When the doctor and painter Carl Gustav Carus (1789–1869) wrote his memoirs, he was struck by the fact "that from the earliest times nothing was left except disconnected images" from which he concluded "that the earliest memories will never bring to light a thought but only one or the other sensual impression which, like a daguerreotype, has fixed itself particularly firmly."[5] Here again it is evident how closely connected the description of memory is with media technology: just like writing, the image is both a metaphor and a medium for memory, as the "daguerreotype" impressions relate both to mental images and to early forms of the photograph that provided an important new external support for memory.

Shortly before the invention of photography, De Quincey thought of the human mind as a palimpsest, in which the images of life stored themselves layer by layer and then later, suddenly, became readable again through the chemicals of the restorers. What for him seemed like a miracle became everyday technology thanks to photography that, as Roland Barthes reminds us, is also based on chemistry. The miracle of photographic emulsion consists in the fact that it gives material form to light radiated from an object. Just as De Quincey wrote of the resuscitation of dead pictorial traces in the hour of death or fever, or under the influence of opium, thus Barthes writes of the magic of photography as a resurrection of the dead. In his view photography does not function only as an analogy to memory, but also as the most important medium for memory, in so far as it provides the most reliable record of a past that no longer exists – it is the lasting impression of a moment that has gone forever. The photograph preserves this trace of

---

[5] Carl Gustav Carus, *Lebenserinnerungen und Denkwürdigkeiten*, Leipzig 1865/66, Vol. 1, 13. Also: Anton Philipp Knittel, "Bilder-Bücher der Erinnerung. 'Jugenderinnerungen eines alten Mannes' im Kontext ihrer Zeit," *Weimarer Beiträge. Zeitschrift für Literaturwissenschaft, Ästhetik und Kulturwissenschaften* 42 (1966), 545–560.

reality, and it provides a tangible connection between now and then: "The photograph is literally an emanation of the referent. From a real body, which was there, proceed radiations which ultimately touch me, who am here."[6] In this respect, photography transcends every preceding medium for memory because as an indexical sign it delivers absolute proof that a particular past once existed. This memory aid may, then, be pinpoint accurate, but nevertheless it remains mute; consequently, the simultaneously precise and vague memory of the image will take on a phantom life of its own as soon as it is separated from its framing narrative, for it is only the text that can translate external images back into the language of living memory.

IMAGINES AGENTES

Images and writing have been linked with memory ever since Antiquity. Plato emphasized the link between memory and writing, but it was the Roman art of memory that strengthened the connection with images. This subsystem of rhetoric developed a visual script to strengthen and enlarge memory capacity. Unlike alphabetical script, it was purely ideographic, consisting not of letters but of *imagines* that were "inscribed" into concretely visualized places or *loci*, just as letters are inscribed on or into a neutral surface. This ideographic art of memory was conceived as an alternative to alphabetical script, and indeed Cicero explained that the mnemotechnical *imagines* were written into the mind as "letters on a wax tablet." The unknown teacher of the Roman art of memory, whose work has come down to us under the title *Ad Herennium*, also compared the two acts involved in the process of remembering – imprint and recall – to those of writing and reading.[7]

---

[6] Barthes, *Camera* (see n. 1), 80. See also Anselm Haverkamp, "Lichtbild – Das Bildgedächtnis der Photographie: Roland Barthes und Augustinus," in A. Haverkamp and R. Lachmannm (eds.), *Memoria.* (see Chapt. 1, n. 1), 47–66. Reflections on the theological premises of Barthes' "ontological realism of the photographic image" are to be found in Gertrud Koch, "Das Bild als Schrift der Vergangenheit," *Kunstforum* 128 (1996), 197–201.

[7] Cicero, *De oratore II*, 86, 350–360. Eng. trans., *On the Ideal Orator*, 260 (see Chapt. 2, n. 4).

After the decline and fall of Egyptian hieroglyphs, the inventors of rhetorical mnemotechnics once more reinvented an ideographic script. They "psychologized" this script by inscribing it directly into the memory instead of on stone or papyrus, paying special attention to the affective charge of the images used. They chose images that made a particular impact on the imagination and could thus imprint themselves all the more effectively. In this respect, their images followed a different logic of representation from that of writing, the vital distinction no longer being between the arbitrary and the motivated, the similar and the dissimilar, but between the vivid and the pallid. This was what classical mnemotechnics meant by the term *imagines agentes* – actively effective and affective pictures that would make an indelible impression and could therefore be used as memory aids for concepts that in themselves were not striking. Affect was elevated in Roman mnemotechnics to the most important memory aid:

When we see in everyday life things that are petty, ordinary, and banal, we generally fail to remember them, because the mind is not being stirred by anything novel and marvellous. But if we see or hear something exceptionally base, dishonourable, extraordinary, great, unbelievable, or laughable, that we are likely to remember for a long time. [...] We ought, then, to set up images of a kind that can adhere longest in the memory. And we shall do so if we establish likenesses as striking as possible; if we set up images that are not many or vague, but doing something ('*si non mutas nec vagas, sed aliquid agentes imagines ponemus*'); if we assign to them exceptional beauty or singular ugliness; if we dress some of them with crowns or purple cloaks, for example, so that the likeness may be more distinct to us; or if we somehow disfigure them, as by introducing one stained with blood or soiled with mud or smeared with red paint.[8]

The somewhat surreal hieroglyphs of Roman mnemotechnics, which illustrated "poison" by way of a chalice, or *testis* (witness) by way of testicles (*testes*) – purely because the words sounded similar! – are astonishingly akin to the symbols and syntax of dreams. Both use processes of replacement, distortion, and hidden similarity for the purpose of intensification. These processes, which in a dream

---

[8] *Ad C. Herennium, De Ratione Dicendi* (*Rhetorica Ad Herennium*), with an English translation by Harry Caplan, London and Harvard 1964, Book III, XXII, 35–37, 219–221. See Frances A. Yates, *The Art of Memory*, London 1992, 25–26.

provide means of escaping the censorship of the conscious mind, in mnemotechnics serve to enhance the impression and deepen the impact of the signs. What made the *imagines agentes* – which were defined as "active" or "affective" pictures – superior to writing was not their naturalness or their directness (later attributed to hieroglyphs), but their immanent power to aid the memory. Unlike the Freudian unconscious, however, this affective power was not only released in the art of memory but also strictly instrumentalized by it. The testicles that were introduced as a reminder of a witness appearing before the court made for an extraordinary and therefore unforgettable image. After the sound of the word had built an infallible bridge to the targeted concept, the additional associations attached to the image had to be neutralized. The images were therefore not "active" because of their explosive powers of evocation, but solely because they could perform a single linking function in that act of remembering. If space had been allowed for individual interpretation and free-running association, the art of memory would very soon have turned into a psychedelic trip, a dream, or a text by James Joyce. In other words, the Roman art (*ars*) of memory used the power (*vis*) of memory, but it did so in such a way that the *ars* carefully controlled and dominated the *vis*.[9]

The *imagines agentes* still play a role in modern rhetoric. Thomas De Quincey defined rhetoric as the "art of aggrandizing [...] by means of various and striking thoughts, some aspect of truth which of itself is supported by no spontaneous feelings, and therefore rests upon artificial aids."[10] At a time when feelings were in danger of being exhausted, he interpreted style as an artificial stimulus that could thus compensate for the non-arousal of emotion. For De Quincey, style fulfilled the task of regenerating "the normal power and impressiveness of a subject which has become dormant to the sensibilities."[11]

Baudelaire – himself an enthusiastic reader of De Quincey – attributed this decline in the vividness of emotions to technical innovations and a concomitant acceleration of time. He defined modernity as

[9] We look in more detail at the emotional potential of pictures in the chapter on the body as a medium of memory, because the relevant emotions always have a somatic basis.

[10] *Collected Writings of Thomas De Quincey*, ed. David Masson, 14 vols, Edinburgh 1889–1890, Vol. 10, 92.

[11] Ibid, 260–261.

a new relationship with time – as "the ephemeral, the fugitive, the contingent," and as "one half of art whose other half is the eternal and the immutable."[12] Roman mnemotechnics had filtered out time and made space the central dimension of memory. Baudelaire, on the contrary, asked how, under the pressure of time and the impact of the modern technological images of photography, perception and memory had changed. He discovered a new form of mnemotechnics, consisting of a new interaction between memory and imagination, and a new *vis* or power of memory, which asserted itself in the flow of fleeting time. In an essay on Constantin Guy, whom he described as a "painter of modern life," Baudelaire developed his concept of modern mnemotechnics. Constantin Guy, he writes, brings "an instinctive emphasis to his marking of the salient or luminous points of an object [...] or of its principal characteristics, sometimes even with a degree of exaggeration [mnémonique si despotique] which aids the human memory; and thus, under the spur of so forceful a prompting, the spectator's imagination receives a clear-cut image of the impression."[13] Exaggeration is the signature both of ancient and modern mnemotechnics, but in the one case it is based on language and emotions, whereas in the other it highlights the neurological mechanisms of perception and attention in the environment of a modern metropolis.

SYMBOLS AND ARCHETYPES

The inherent energy of images is also at the heart of 19th- and early 20th-century theories of the symbol. These theories move from the individual psyche to concepts of a trans-individual cultural memory that reaches back into prehistory. Here we return once more to the cultural historian Johann Jakob Bachofen, and in particular to a biographical letter he wrote to his teacher Savigny. While studying the legal records of ancient cultures, focusing especially on traces of an archaic level, he discovered the power of the symbol in the context of burial sites. He noted that in this domain of "the sanctum, the

---

[12] Charles Baudelaire, "The Painter of Modern Life," in Charles Baudelaire, *The Painter of Modern Life and Other Essays*, translated and edited by Jonathan Mayne, London 1964, 1–40; here, 13.

[13] Ibid., 16.

unmovable, the irreversible," cultural forms had been firmly fixed and had acquired the status of a taboo. "In the context of graves the symbol was formed and has its longest history. What is thought, felt and silently prayed at the grave transcends the power of words; it can only be alluded to and evoked through the symbol with its perpetual form of enduring solemnity [. . .]. The fact that the Romans removed symbolism from their legal proceedings shows how young they are by comparison with the thousand-year-old culture of the East."[14]

As the reconstructed lines of tradition could not reach back to the realm of primordial culture, so fantasy had to take over. We need once more to recall the polarity between writing and traces, together with Bachofen's distinction between the short path of intuition and the long road of reason: "There are two paths to this knowledge – the longer, slower, more difficult one of reasoned combinations, and the shorter one on which we are propelled with the power and speed of electricity, the path of fantasy, which is stimulated by the sight and direct touch of ancient remains, grasping the truth at a single go without any intermediaries." (11) Bachofen's two paths are linked to two models of tradition and two media of memory: direct anamnesis through sensual contact, which works through the *contiguity of images*, and mediated tradition, which depends on the *continuity of texts*. The weaker the latter form becomes, the greater the appeal of the former.

The immanent mnemonic power of images was also central to the research of Aby Warburg and the circle of scholars around him. With its basic premise of the "inextricable interweaving of the image with culture in general," this approach distanced itself from the trend toward the autonomy of aesthetic form prevailing in contemporary art history.[15] Unlike the majority of scholars in his field, Warburg did not take the existence of images for granted, but instead inquired into the conditions that underlay their origin and their survival. With likeminded friends and colleagues he worked on a theory of images that was meant above all to illuminate their function as a medium

---

[14] Bachofen, "Lebensrückschau" (see Chapt. 6, n. 49).

[15] Edgar Wind, "Warburgs Begriff der Kulturwissenschaft und seine Bedeutung für die Ästhetik" (1931), in Aby Warburg, *Ausgewählte Schriften und Würdigungen*, ed. Dieter Wuttke, Saecula Spiritalia I, 3rd edition, Baden-Baden 1992, 401–417; here, 406.

of cultural memory. His projected history of European visual memory set out to "shed light on the psychological aspects involved in the problems of a cultural Renaissance."[16] He saw this "rebirth" and "afterlife" of classical Antiquity as underpinned not by texts but by images, and he sought to account for it in terms of a psychic disposition and desire rather than a conscious pedagogical intention within the frame of normative classicism. To follow this track, it was essential that one should detach oneself from all forms of conscious, subjective empathy ("Einfühlung"), and instead "plunge into the depths of the compulsive connections between the human mind and the layers of historic materiality. Only there can one perceive the deep impression made by the expressive values of heathen emotion that spring from the orgiastic primal experience: from Dionysian Thiasos."[17] Warburg pointed out that the artists of the Renaissance used antique formulas whenever they wanted to enhance the energetic expressiveness of their work, and this observation led him to a close analysis of antique forms of expression in the art of the modern era. He saw pictures as gestures frozen in time, which not only captured but also recharged and liberated anew the emotional impact of their underlying actions, whether cultic or violent.

For Warburg, images were the paradigmatic medium for memory. He himself spoke of "pathos formulas," the paradigmatic example of which was the classical moving figure of the veiled nymph, which with every reentry into a Renaissance painting would reactivate the emotional potential originally contained within it. The repetition of such a formula evoked far more than just a particular motif; it was accompanied by an embodied energy and impact that were released with its reactivation. He called the symbol, with its fundamentally ambivalent surplus of significance, an "canned energy." In the dynamic process of cultural memory, images fulfilled the function of a relay station in which they were energetically recharged, sometimes taking on the opposite meaning in a process of normative inversion. According to Edgar Wind, memory is the central historical-philosophical problem for the historian of symbols, "not only because it is in itself the organ

---

[16] Fritz Saxl, "Die Ausdrucksgebärden der bildenden Kunst" (1932), in Warburg, *Ausgewählte*, 426 (see n. 15).

[17] Ibid., 430.

of historical knowledge, but also because – through its symbols – it creates the reservoir of energy which is discharged in a given historical situation."[18]

Fritz Saxl has detailed the possibilities of such a new history of symbols. His words may remind us of Vico and Herder, but they are directly influenced by Darwin's *The Expression of the Emotions in Man and Animals* and his theory of rudiments:

> It is evident that in pictorial sign language, in contrast to normal speech, a vast reservoir of experience is transmitted from primal times to posterity. These primitive people, who were natural born mime artists, could vividly imitate whatever they wanted and thereby encode their own way of thinking. [...] From this lively tradition of mimicry and gesture have arisen the prototypes of the fine arts. This thought process is an indication of the vital role we can attribute to pictorial gesture in the history of human expression. It will always be a preserver of the early stages of human culture in history.[19]

The idea that cultural tradition not only continues through conscious formation but can also sink back into deeper, darker zones, where it branches out into a labyrinth full of inaccessible hollows, was one that even before Warburg and Bachofen had fascinated the Romantics. Such thought processes suggest themselves whenever one shifts from the text to images as the central cultural storage medium and purveyor of cultural transmission. Moving from texts to images – and this is the reason why Bachofen and Warburg focused on the symbol – led to a totally different theory of the dynamics of transmission. To put it simply, this theory was much closer to memory's powers of impression than to reason's powers of interpretation. The affective potential of images is far more difficult to channel and hence to chart. We can illustrate this imaginative surplus of image over text with a biographical anecdote from the essayist Charles Lamb, relating to a revealing experience with an illustrated children's Bible. The two-volume Stackhouse edition was kept in his father's bookcase. The pictures accompanying the biblical tales and the catechism made a far deeper and more lasting impression on the child's imagination than any text could have

---

[18] Wind, *Einleitung in die Kulturwissenschaftliche Bibliothek Warburg*, X.
[19] Saxl, "Ausdrücksgebärden," 425–426 (see n. 16).

done.[20] One picture that had a particularly powerful impact on the boy was of Samuel being conjured up from the depths by a witch:

[T]o his picture of the Witch raising up Samuel – (O that old man covered with a mantle!) I owe – not my midnight terrors, the hell of my infancy – but the shape and manner of their visitation. . . . All day long, while the book was permitted me, I dreamed waking over his delineation, and at night (if I may use so bold an expression) awoke into sleep, and found the vision true. . . . It is not book, or picture, or the stories of foolish servants, which create these terrors in children. They can at most but give them a direction.[21]

Pictures fit into the landscape of the unconscious in a way that is different from texts: as the boundary between the picture and dream is blurred, the picture is transformed into an internal "vision" that takes on a life of its own. Once this border is crossed, the status of the picture is changed from being an object of observation to an agent of haunting. Lamb was convinced that the primeval terrors of the soul were not created by individual pictures or stories, but preexisted and only took on their particular form from these stimuli. The force that "animates" images in a dream is what he calls "archetypes."

"Gorgons, and Hydras, and Chimeras – dire stories of Celaeno and the Harpies may reproduce themselves in the brain of superstition – but they were there before. They are transcripts, types – the archetypes are in us, and eternal." (94) After Plato's archetypes of reason (e.g., the *logoi spermatikoi* or "innate ideas") the Romantics discovered the archetypes of the imagination. Their most powerful effects derive not from concrete experiences of our own, and not from stories heard or pictures seen, but they go back even beyond our own bodies and have their roots – as part of the basic equipment of our psyche – in an "extraterrestrial" preexistence. (95) For Lamb, the archetypes are transsubjective, preformed pictures that are part of our human heritage. He claims that without them the effects of certain images and

[20] Thomas Stackhouse, *The History of the Bible*, 2 vols., 1737. The story of the witch of Endor is to be found in Samuel I 28, 7–21.

[21] Charles Lamb, "Witches and Other Night Fears" (1823), in *Essays of Elia*, ed. N. L. Hallward and S. C. Hill, London and New York 1967, 93.

ideas would be inexplicable, and he ascribes their force to the overlapping of concrete pictures and narratives with certain basic anthropological predispositions.

From this introduction to theories concerning the energetic potential of images, we now turn to three case studies in order to explore
their significance for both individual and cultural memory. In this
analysis, the common focus will be on the staging of women in the
male imaginaire.

IMAGES OF WOMEN IN THE MEMORIES OF MEN

Mona Lisa as *Magna Mater* (Walter Pater)

When William Butler Yeats was commissioned to edit *The Oxford Book of
Modern Verse*, he began his anthology with a poem entitled *Mona Lisa*.
This was not originally a poem, but was part of a text that he had found
in the chapter on Leonardo da Vinci in Walter Pater's book *The Renaissance* (1873).[22] The passage that Yeats selected stands out through its
dense and elevated style, which distinguishes it from the reflective
prose in which it is embedded. Pater's thoughts on the art of the Italian Renaissance, like the Warburg circle's studies of European pictorial
memory, start out from the assumption that there is such a thing as an
unconscious collective memory. From this perspective, individual and
cultural traditions are seen as elements of an all-embracing human
memory. While history moves forward in a linear direction as cultures
and epochs forget one another, they all accumulate in layers within a
universal memory, and can be brought together again in imaginative
acts of reminiscence. Pater called this archive of human memory the
"House Beautiful," in which were stored all the great works of art. In
the face of the Mona Lisa, the observer can find a concrete instance
of this accumulated memory, compressed into a single mystery. Pater
stages this female image as a palimpsest of various cultural eras, in
the same sense as De Quincey described the palimpsest of the human

[22] Walter Pater, "Leonardo da Vinci," in Adam Phillips (ed.), *The Renaissance. Studies in
Art and Poetry* (1873), Oxford 1998, 63–82. See Carolyn Williams, "Myths of History:
The Mona Lisa," in Williams, *Transfigured World. Walter Pater's Aesthetic Historicism*,
Ithaca and London 1989, 111–123.

brain: the cultural phases succeed one another, without forming the narrative of a conscious tradition, but also without being completely forgotten. "All the thoughts and experience of the world have been etched and moulded there, in that which they have of power to refine and make expressive the outward form, the animalism of Greece, the lust of Rome, the mysticism of the Middle Ages with its spiritual ambition and imaginative loves, the return of the Pagan world, the sins of the Borgias."[23]

The section of the text chosen and edited by Yeats follows immediately after this sentence:

> Mona Lisa
> She is older than the rocks among which she sits;
> Like the Vampire,
> She has been dead many times,
> And learned the secrets of the grave;
> And has been a diver in deep seas,
> And keeps their fallen day about her;
> And trafficked for strange webs with Eastern merchants;
> And, as Leda,
> Was the mother of Helen of Troy,
> And, as St. Anne,
> Was the mother of Mary;
> And all this has been to her but as the sound of lyres and flutes,
> And lives
> Only in the delicacy
> With which it has moulded the changing lineaments,
> And tinged the eyelids and the hands.[24]

This text, which was retrospectively broken up into verse and transformed into a poem, stands in the tradition of *ekphrasis* – a verbal description of a picture, which brings the pictorial medium back into writing, though in such a way that the text opens up the evocative potential of the picture. The object of the poem is not to describe the painting itself but to capture its effect on a receptive viewer, thereby constructing an image of the female in the male gaze.[25] From this

---

[23] Pater, *The Renaissance*, 80.

[24] *The Oxford Book of Modern Verse* 1892–1935, ed. W. B. Yeats, Oxford 1st edition 1936, 1966, 1.

[25] Ursula Renner, "Mona Lisa – Das 'Rätsel Weib' als 'Frauenphantom des Mannes' im Fin de Siècle," in Irmgard Roebling (ed.), *Lulu, Lilith, Mona Lisa. Frauenbilder der*

perspective, Leonardo's Mona Lisa is turned into a reflection of the cultural unconscious. The mysteriously smiling lady morphs into an occult medium that summons up the spirit of the eternally feminine through a litany of allusions.

The study of a painting here resembles a technique of meditation or even hypnosis, which is reminiscent of Warburg's descent into the subterranean regions of the unconscious collective memory. The observer is transported into a world of almost feverish fantasy, illuminated – to quote Pater himself – "as in some faint light under the sea." In this trance-like state, he will see the figure of Mona Lisa transformed into an incarnation of the *magna mater*. In total contradistinction to the masculine elements of culture, which are inscribed into conscious cultural memory with unmistakable names and historically recorded deeds – the poem is silent about these, but we need to keep them in mind as the poem's contrastive background – the text equates the feminine with something before and after history, everlasting, without a beginning, and without an end.

The first seven lines of the poem locate the lady in time and space – "She is older than the rocks among which she sits" – and move on to her power of rebirth, which overcomes oblivion in history and is seen here as an occult force, associating the Mona Lisa with the vampire, who returns again and again. All such figures are highly uncanny because they know the secrets of the grave and the hidden depths. In this link with darkness and the demonic lie the unfathomable strangeness and fascination of the feminine, which are like that of the deep sea that she has explored. The nine lines of the second part of the poem place her in the dimensions of myth and art. She embodies that which male cultural memory has pushed aside, lost, forgotten, or suppressed. But this is not the only thing that makes her different: she is above all else the eternal precursor, the force that can never be harnessed, the primal foundation on which all masculine empires and civilizations have been built. As Leda she "gives birth" to the fall of Troy and the founding of Rome; as St. Anne she "gives birth" to Christianity. The

---

Jahrhundertwende, Pfaffenweiler 1989, 139–156. She gives further examples of how the Mona Lisa has become established as an icon of the modern age. She writes: "Perhaps the 'Mona Lisa' is *the* example of the elevation of a portrait to being the projected image of the modern need for myth." (189)

cultural circles of Antiquity, the Middle Ages, and the Renaissance are concentric, all centered on this figure of the eternally feminine source of everything. She also connects the beginning and the end: "Here is the head upon which all the ends of the world are come" – a line that contains an allusion to 1 Corinthians 10,11. At this point primal beginnings merge with the retrospective gaze of aesthetic reflection, the effect being that all of the past is brought together as a simultaneous store of an eternal present.

The last lines of the poem introduce a change of perspective: when the viewer's gaze has dwelt long enough *on* the tired and heavy eyes of the Mona Lisa, he may finally for a moment look *with* her eyes. This is the view from an endless distance – a view that has witnessed the most profound upheavals of history and of the human psyche as cyclical rebirths, and that softens the experience of pain and violence into gentle sounds ("lyres and flutes" and decorative lines). In the end, history's suffering is transformed into art, which alone gives aesthetic justification to life. This is expressed by a return at the end to the delicacy and fine detail of the painting: "And all this [...] lives [...] / Only in the delicacy / With which it has moulded the changing lineaments, / And tinged the eyelids and the hands." This turn toward aesthetic sublimation, however, can also be interpreted in terms of Warburg's "heightened attention to the insignificant"; for instance, to a physiognomic study that seeks through inconspicuous details to plumb the unfathomable depths and essence of the strange presence of Mona Lisa.

Image and writing are linked here in a very special way: an *ekphrasis* like Pater's loads the painting with significance and weighs it down with memories. This kind of discourse selects particular paintings, endows them with meaning, and anchors them in the pictorial cultural memory. The Mona Lisa has been stylized into a secular icon of modern-day art. This means that she enjoys a sacrosanct status but has also been made. This very element of the sacrosanct has also made it the target of the iconoclasts, whose symbolic attacks only reinforce her place in the pantheon of masterpieces. When Marcel Duchamp painted a beard on a reproduction of the work and gave it an obscene title, he strove with one fell swoop to erase its accumulated cultural burden, to which texts like Pater's had made such a powerful contribution.

The Lover as Collector (Marcel Proust)

Pater was fascinated by Leonardo's painting as a picture puzzle halfway between dream and history. For him, however, this interweaving of reality and fantasy did not arise initially from the eye of the beholder but from that of the artist. In the accompanying commentary he wonders about the connection between painter and model: "What was the relationship between that living Florentine woman and the creature of his thoughts? And into what secret relationship did the person and the dream merge – so far from one another and yet so close together?"[26] This question applies equally to my next example of a pictorial memory, which is taken from the first part of Proust's *A la Recherche du Temps Perdu*. This section describes the love of the Jewish aesthete Swann for Odette. The novel draws the portrait of a lover as connoisseur and collector. What is special about his love for the not very well educated and aging cocotte is the fact that the source of his fascination is not the woman herself so much as the scenes in which he stages her in his imagination. One powerful spur to such imaginings is jealousy, which dramatizes the beloved as an agent in a secret plot; another is his idealization of her by means of art. When Odette is bending over an engraving that Swann has brought to her, it happens that this chance pose of relaxed contemplation suddenly changes her into a different person: "She struck Swann by her resemblance to the figure of Zipporah, Jethro's daughter, which is to be seen in one of the Sistine frescoes"[27] (See fig. 1). Thus the woman looking at a picture herself turns into a picture, and within this new frame of perception Swann now sees her in a new light: "He no longer based his estimate of the merit of Odette's face on the doubtful quality of her cheeks and the purely fleshy softness [...] but regarded it rather as a skein of beautiful, delicate lines which his eyes unravelled, [...] as though in a portrait of her in which her type was made clearly intelligible." (268 f)

Proust's "masterfully executed, beautiful work of lines" reminds one of Pater's "delicacy" and "changing lineaments," but this transformation of the woman into a work of art is not an idealization in

---

[26] Pater, *The Renaissance*, 131 (see n. 23).
[27] Marcel Proust, *In Search of Lost Time*, Vol. I, Swann's Way, 267 (see Chapt. 7, n. 12).

FIGURE 1. Sandro Botticelli, Zippora, daughter of Jethro at the well. Detail, Vatican, Sistine Chapel.

the sense that everything special to the individual is sacrificed for something general. If anything, what is special is elevated to the status of the general. The blending of art and life is made possible by the fact that artists too are aware of this strange characteristic of reality and life that the narrator describes as "a certain kind of modernity."[28] The imaginary interchange between painting and living person therefore applies both ways: the former can contain "anticipatory and

---

[28] It is striking that in the same context Pater also speaks of modernity. The paragraph from which Yeats extracted the poem ends with the sentence: "Certainly Lady Lisa might stand as the embodiment of the old fancy, the symbol of the modern idea." Pater, *The Renaissance*, 80.

rejuvenating allusions" to the latter, and the latter can attain "general significance" through the former (Proust 1981, 242–246). In this context, idealization does not mean a shift of meaning from A to B, but a reciprocal semantic or erotic exchange between both meanings: "although his admiration for the Florentine masterpiece was doubtless based upon his discovery that it had been reproduced in her, the similarity enhanced her beauty also, and made her more precious." (269) Love is ignited and renewed by these twists and turns between image and person. It is boosted by the fact that the male gaze does not confront the object of desire directly but frames it with imaginary scenes: Swann desires a being who seemed to Botticelli worthy of worship, and he finds satisfaction in the knowledge that his own desire echoes "his most refined predilections in matters of art." (296) What is forgotten, as the narrator remarks, is simply that the aesthetic and the erotic perspectives become mutually exclusive from the moment when seeing is exchanged for touching and aesthetic distance threatens to foreclose sexual desire. Swann "forgets" that art and life must, in certain domains, go their own separate ways.

The gain from iconization, however, is another story: this brings him a sense of possession, security and power in a field that is notoriously volatile. "The words 'Florentine painting' were invaluable to Swann." (269) Iconization is able to stabilize the disquieting many-sidedness of the living person, so that it can all be integrated in reassuring patterns arranged by the male imagination. It also entails a rise in value: he can be certain now that the object of his desire is of the highest worth, whereas conversely what is of highest worth is in his possession. Thus the fundamental incalculability of human relations is translated into bourgeois categories of value and ownership. This translation, however, also entails a mechanism of desire built on perpetual replacements:

He placed on his study table, as if it were a photograph of Odette, a reproduction of Jethro's daughter. [...] The vague feeling of sympathy which attracts one to a work of art, now that he knew the original in flesh and blood of Jethro's daughter, became a desire which more than compensated, thenceforward, for the desire which Odette's physical charms had at first failed to inspire in him. When he had sat for a long time gazing at the Botticelli, he would think of his own living Botticelli, who seemed even lovelier still, and as he drew towards him the photograph of Zipporah he would imagine that he was holding Odette against his heart. (270)

Here the text duplicates the gulf that the narrator had told us Swann had "forgotten" – that between enjoyment of art and the desire for love. Possession of the flesh is replaced by the collector's possession of art, the loved one is replaced by the original of the lover, and this is placed above the original of the artist. It could scarcely be more roundabout: Swann presses to his heart a photograph that copies the original painting; the original painting in his eyes, however, is nothing other than a copy of the original called Odette, who is a possession of the lover's. Thus in an age of technical reproduction art can become the embodiment of authentic experience.

Reconstructive and Explosive Iconic Memory (James Joyce)

In James Joyce's short story, "The Dead," from his collection *The Dubliners* (1914), the climax of the action comes about through a very different form of pictorial memory. With an affectionate attention to detail, the story describes a dinner party given in Dublin every New Year's Eve by two elderly ladies and their niece. The invitees are their friends, and among those eagerly awaited are Gabriel Conroy and his wife Gretta. Gabriel, an aesthete and provincial arts correspondent with aspirations to something loftier, is once again successfully playing his part in the evening's proceedings, looking after the somewhat eccentric guests, and providing the highlight of the party with a much admired speech in honor of the three hostesses.

In the last part of the tale, which focuses on Mr. and Mrs. Conroy, it is long past midnight and the guests are about to go home. Outside the house, a coach leaves amid much noise and laughter, while inside, already wrapped in scarf and coat, Gabriel stands at the foot of the stairs. At the top he sees in the half-light a figure and only when he takes a second look does he realize who it is. "It was his wife. She was leaning on the banisters, listening to something. Gabriel was surprised at her stillness and strained his ear to listen also. But he could hear little save the noise of laughter and dispute on the front steps, a few chords struck on the piano, and a few notes of a man's voice singing."[29]

While Gabriel strains to hear something of the melody that is being sung, he sinks into a pleasurable contemplation of his wife. "There was a grace and mystery in her attitude as if she were a symbol of something.

[29] James Joyce, "The Dead," in *Dubliners* (1914), Harmondsworth 1976, 207.

He asked himself what is a woman standing on the stairs in the shadow, listening to distant music, a symbol of. If he were a painter he would paint her in that attitude. Her blue felt hat would show off the bronze of her hair against the darkness and the dark panels of her skirt would show off the light ones. *Distant Music* he would call the picture if he were a painter." (207) When the front door shuts again, the music becomes more audible. It is an old Irish song that tells of rain, cold, love, and death. The tenor, who has a sore throat, had not wanted to sing at all, and so his voice is hoarse and also tentative, partly because he is not well and partly because he cannot remember all the words. When those returning from the front door start listening to the music, he abruptly breaks off. There follows a conversation about snow, the cold weather, and people catching a chill, but Gabriel does not join in because he is still lost in his thoughts about his wife. She seems to him strangely entranced, and for that reason all the more desirable.

The next step in the story is the journey home. The reader experiences it from the perspective of the erotically aroused Gabriel, whose associations and memories are now centered on forthcoming intimacy with his wife. But at the moment when they should both be drawn together, a gulf opens up between them. Gabriel endures the bitter experience of finding out that just when he himself feels most at one with the woman he loves, she is in fact miles away from him. It turns out that the old Irish song was once sung by Gretta's childhood friend when they were living in the country. The song has brought the long forgotten image of his eyes back into her mind – a deeply buried image that down through the years has not lost any of its poignancy. She sees the gentle youth in front of her. They were about to part, and he did not want to survive the parting, spent the night out in the rain, and it cost him his life. "I can see his eyes as well as well! He was standing at the end of the wall where there was a tree." (218) The tree seems like an irrelevant detail in the economy of the story, and yet in the logic of this "flashbulb-memory" it is important because it bears out the precision and unprocessed authenticity of a suddenly returning perception. Here I may once more quote Lutz Niethammer: deeply ingrained images can "often be described with great accuracy" even though they have "no narrative structure and tend not to express any meaning."[30]

---

[30] Niethammer, "Fragen – Antworten – Fragen," 405 (see n. 4).

Joyce's story is entitled "The Dead," and one of these dead is Michael Furey, the passionate young lover of Gretta's youth. By comparison with his intensity, it is the living who seem dead. Gabriel Conroy is the opposite of Michael, racked with insecurity and a need for self-protection and possession, possibly inspired by Chekhov's short story "The Man in a Case." Joyce creates a clash between two opposed forms of iconic memory, which we may link to Nietzsche's and Freud's concepts of memory. Gabriel's visual memory is processed according to a *mémoire volontaire*, shaped by conscious intentions and directed by the will. The transformation of his wife into a picture called *Distant Music* shows him to be a calculating compiler, whose erotic mood arranges the inner flow of images to fit in with the eagerly anticipated event. He remembers with relish all the scenes that nourish his present passion and is happy to forget those that might stand in its way. "Moments of their secret life together burst like stars upon his memory. [. . .] He longed to recall to her those moments, to make her forget the years of their dull existence together and remember only their moments of ecstasy." (210 f) Gabriel's choice of memories is geared entirely to his will and his desires – "quenching memory in the stronger light of purpose,"[31] as George Eliot once put it. This visual memory carefully selects those elements of the past that feed future expectations. Gabriel's desire controls his visual memory and maneuvers his feelings, recollections, and impulses like a skilled stage director. It is not by chance that Nietzsche defined the qualities of this form of memory through the paradigm of male sexuality. The desire for power and the desire for sex are not so very different: "imagine a man seized by a vehement passion, for a woman or for a great idea: how different the world has become to him! [. . .] As he who acts is, in Goethe's words, always without a conscience, so is he also always without knowledge; he forgets most things so as to do one thing, he is unjust towards what

---

[31] George Eliot, *The Mill on the Floss* (1860), Harmondsworth 1994, 315: "So it has been since the days of Hecuba and of Hector, tamer of horses: inside the gates, the women with streaming hair and uplifted hands offering prayers, watching the world's combat from afar, filling their long empty days with memories and fears; outside, the men, in fierce struggle with things divine and human quenching memory in the stronger light of purpose, losing the sense of dread and even of wounds in the hurrying ardour of action."

lies behind him, and he recognizes the rights only of that which is now to come into being and no other rights whatever."[32]

At the dramatic climax of Joyce's story, however, Gretta herself changes from the object of her husband's desires into a remembering subject or, to be more precise, into the object of her sudden eruption of memories. She is haunted by a *mémoire involontaire*, which intrudes into consciousness and shatters the frames of the will. The dynamic force behind this kind of memory is suppressed guilt. According to Freud, "[F]orgetting impressions, scenes or experiences nearly always reduces itself to shutting them off."[33] Whereas Gabriel's memories began with the fixation of an aesthetic image contemplated from a distance, Gretta's are stimulated by acoustic signals. Joyce stages these two forms of memory in gender-specific configurations, the deliberate one triggered by way of the male eye and the involuntary one through the female ear. The ear is the more passive organ; it gives entry to sensual impressions without mediation, whereas the eye is more at liberty to refashion the object it perceives. Just as irresistible as the acoustic impression is the long forgotten image that rises from the depths of the soul and, for a moment, is mirrored on the surface of the conscious mind. It had been shut away for decades until being released by a chance occurrence. Toward the end of the story, Gabriel wonders "how she who lay beside him had locked in her heart for so many years that image of her lover's eyes when he had told her that he did not wish to live." (219) The memory, without any support from the conscious mind, conserves what was once an experience of the utmost intensity, and it survives beyond the reach of the will as something forgotten until a sudden shock jolts it back into presence.

The visual memory is both a "creator of moods" and a "stimulator of moods."[34] With Joyce's Gabriel, who happily manipulates his memories, and Proust's Swann, who arouses himself by conjuring up imaginary scenes, memory is shown to be at the active disposal of a male hero. The opposite to this reconstructive memory is the eruptive, passive form exemplified by Gretta. Freud's theory begins at the point

---

[32] Nietzsche, *Untimely Meditations*, (see Chapt. 3, n. 6).

[33] Sigmund Freud, "Remembering, Repeating and Working-Through (Further Recommendations on the Technique of Psycho-Analysis II)," in *The Complete Psychological Works*, Vol. XII, London 1964, 148.

[34] Wind, "Warburgs Begriff der Kulturwissenschaft" (see n. 15).

where the memory is blocked by the gatekeepers of pain and guilt. Warburg joins Freud when he focuses on the energy of forgotten and suppressed memories, although Freud – apart from his late study of *Moses and Monotheism* (1939) – restricted his research to individuals, Warburg set out to investigate the collective side of this phenomenon. He replaced the formalist approach to the work of art with the imperative to uncover "a long buried complex." The art critic, he claimed, should not merely contemplate but he must also remember. Walter Pater's vision of the Mona Lisa as highlighted by Yeats may be regarded as a prime example of this approach to a work of art as a palimpsest of cultural memory. Pater described Leonardo's painting as the artistic projection of an image that the painter had engendered in his childhood and nourished throughout his life; this image, however, was not a subjective impression but "expressive of what in the ways of a thousand years men had come to desire." Pater was an early advocate of "the art of going deep," plunging into western visual cultural memory with instant visions and a "confidence in short cuts and odd byways to knowledge."[35] It was this quest for which one generation later Warburg and his circle set out to supply a new and systematic methodology.

[35] Pater, *The Renaissance*, 79–80, 66, 68 (see n. 22).

1 0

Body

The legs, the arms are full of blunted memories.

> Marcel Proust, *Remembrance of Things Past. Time Regained*

There is no escape from yesterday because yesterday has deformed us, or been deformed by us.

> Samuel Beckett, *Proust, Three Dialogues*

BODY WRITING

Earlier we learned of the story of Simonides, which Cicero made into the foundational legend of the new art of mnemotechnics. There is, however, another ancient story that is less well known but also combines the collapse of a house with an unusual feat of memory. So far, the tale of Melampus has never been linked to that of Simonides, but both deserve to be read together as stories that highlight different forms of memory. Melampus, who had the gift of prophecy, was asked by his brother to steal Iphiclus's cattle. He agreed, even though he must have known that this would result in a year's imprisonment. Apollodor's version continues as follows: "When the year [of this imprisonment] was nearly up, he heard the worms [conversing] in the hidden part of the roof, one of them [the worms] asking how much of the beam had already been gnawed through, and others answering that very little was left. At once he bade them transfer him to another cell, and not long after that had been done the cell fell in." Again the first part of the story describes the sudden collapse of a roof and a miraculous escape: it is followed by a second part that deals with a memory problem and its solution.

These events attract the attention of Phylacus, Iphiclus's father, and he promises the prophet his freedom on condition that he should find a means of curing Iphiclus's infertility. Melampus discovers that this has been caused by a suppressed memory, and is able to recommend an effective remedy:

Phylacus marvelled, and perceiving that he was an excellent soothsayer, he released him and invited him to say how his son Iphiclus might get children. Melampus promised to tell him, provided he got the kine. And having sacrificed two bulls and cut them in pieces he summoned the birds; and when a vulture came, he learned from it that once, when Phylacus was gelding rams, he laid down the knife, still bloody, beside Iphiclus, and that when the child was frightened and ran away, he stuck the knife on the sacred oak, and the bark encompassed the knife and hid it.

The prophet is able to reveal a traumatic experience from Iphiclus's early childhood – an experience that has been suppressed for many years and whose objective correlative is the knife enclosed in the oak. Just like the knife, which is present but invisible in the oak, the memory has stabilized itself inaccessibly within a "crypt" of the psyche. The visible trace of the hidden memory is the physical symptom of infertility, which is caused by the child's fear of castration. It is scarcely possible to describe this case of bodily memory without using Freudian terminology, but the therapy administered in the Greek story has very little to do with psychoanalysis: "He said, therefore, that if the knife were found, and he scraped off the rust, and gave it to Iphiclus to drink for ten days, he would beget a son. Having learned these things from the vulture, Melampus found the knife, scraped the rust, and gave it to Iphiclus for ten days to drink, and a son Podarces was born to him."[1]

Body marks may arise out of long physical habits, unconscious imprints, or the pressure of violence. Its common features are stability and inaccessibility. According to context, it may be judged authentic, persistent, or damaging. In any description of it, the material structure of the carrier of memory plays an especially important role. The metaphors of memory introduced by Plato and Aristotle connected

---

[1] Apollodorus, *The Library*, two volumes with an English translation by James George Frazer, London and Harvard 1961, Vol. I, IX, 12, 88–91.

the reliability and durability of an impression with the hardness of the material: wax could immediately be smoothed over to leave no trace, clay had to be burned, whereas stone was the most expensive but also the most durable carrier. However, even signs engraved in stone could weather or be removed by violence, although the act of removal would itself remain visible, as with the cartouches of Echnaton, whose name on all Egyptian monuments fell victim to a *damnatio memoriae*. In the Hebrew Bible, lasting marks of memory are to be inscribed on the "tablets of the heart" – God wants to write directly in the depths of the heart, where inscription is considered to be indelible and hence irremovable: "I will put my law in their inward parts, and write it in their hearts" (Jer. 31: 33; see also Deut. 6: 6).

In Shakespeare's *Hamlet*, this internalization is externalized in a dramatic scene that once more links remembering and forgetting to an act of writing. In this scene, however, the innermost thoughts are revealed as something external and indeed alien. In his famous "tables speech" Hamlet compares writing in the heart to a notebook carried by a student from Wittenberg, to be pulled from his pocket as an *aide mémoire*. When he meets the ghost of his father, he is given a complex message that culminates in the demand that he should take revenge. The ghost then takes his leave with the words: "Adieu, adieu! Hamlet, remember me." Hamlet is almost beside himself at this moment, and has to summon up all his strength and courage to stop his heart and body from bursting under the impact of this vision and its devastating message: "Hold, hold, my heart!" From the heart, as the deepest seat of memory, he shifts the focus to the head: "Remember thee! Ay, thou poor ghost, whiles memory holds a seat / In this distracted globe. Remember thee!" Nevertheless, the twofold repetition of the ghost's last words is still not enough – he must write the memory down:

> Remember thee!
> Yea, from the table of my memory
> I'll wipe away all trivial fond records,
> All saws of books, all forms, all pressures past,
> That youth and observation copied there;
> And thy commandment all alone shall live
> Within the book and volume of my brain,
> Unmix'd with baser matter. . . .
> My tables, – meet it is I set it down,

That one may smile, and smile, and be a villain;
At least I'm sure it may be so in Denmark:
Writing
So uncle, there you are. Now to my word;
It is, "Adieu, adieu! Remember me."[2]

The metaphor "the table of my memory" becomes a concrete object as he pulls his "tables" from his pocket – one of the notebooks that was used to write down memorable maxims and verses. But what exactly does he write down? Hamlet is overwhelmed with impressions and insights, such as "one may smile and smile and be a villain," which take him in many directions at once. In a state of utter distraction, he desperately tries to stay focused. What he eventually manages to write down are his father's final four words: "Adieu, adieu! Remember me." One may ask: Why this fuss about his father's final four words? An answer to Hamlet's problem may lie in a contemporary treatise about melancholy, which Shakespeare may well have been familiar with. This speaks of the cold, dry, and hard substance of the melancholic's brain, which "serveth well to retaine that which is once ingraven, so like adamant it keepeth, in comparison to other tempers, that which once it hath received."[3] Moreover, Hamlet's case is aggravated by the grotesque disproportion between the laconic message and the urgency with which it is written down, which makes the compulsive nature of this scene so striking. The message hits him with an excessive impact that penetrates the membranes of his memory and destroys its structure. In order to inscribe this one and only memory, he must "wipe away" every other memory that he has ever "written down." His whole past existence and identity are thus thrown into question by his father's injunction to remember him. This all-embracing, all-exclusive record refuses to integrate with past records, and indeed blots them out because it is clearly traumatic. The father's commandment transforms the son into a passive writing surface, a *tabula rasa*.

Whereas God's law was engraved on the tablets of Jeremiah's heart, it is the father's law that is engraved on Hamlet's, and it is clear that this traumatic inscription inflicts spiritual damage on him. The concept of internal writing on the heart underwent a radical shift through

---

[2] Shakespeare, *Hamlet*, Act I, Sc. 5, 97–110.
[3] Timothy Bright, *A Treatise of Melancholy* (1586), Chapt. XXII, 129.

Nietzsche, who provided this metaphor for memory with a totally new basis. He turned away from the traditional opposition of body and soul, with the latter being seen as a prisoner of the former, and instead saw the soul as the jailer of the body.[4] This had substantial consequences for his concept of memory because now it was the sensitive and vulnerable body that became the writing surface, instead of the heart and soul. In his famous treatise *On the Genealogy of Morals*, he asks how it is that people can develop a "memory of the will," which not only passively retains "a once engraved impression," but also actively links itself to a particular content. He calls this memory of the will "conscience," and sees in it the basis in which cultures anchor their sense of morality and responsibility. It does not record autobiographical experiences; it is, rather, a cultural script that is written directly and indelibly into the body. With this reversal, Nietzsche releases memory theory from its history of internalization and individualization, and links it for the first time to institutions of power and to techniques of violence.

Nietzsche developed his thesis of "pain as the mightiest aid in mnemotechnics" through a simple rhetoric of question and answer. The question he asks is: "How does one make a memory for the human animal? How does one impress something on this partly dull, partly scattered momentary understanding, this forgetfulness in the flesh, so that it remains present?" And the answer to this question is: "One burns something in, so that it remains in one's memory: only what does not cease *to give pain* remains in one's memory."[5] Among the cultural, corporeal inscriptions, then, in a broad sense we must include those brought about by supervisory and penal institutions, because these all seek to impose on humans particular norms and values of social life – Nietzsche speaks of "fixed ideas" – and to maintain them by means of memory. The ethnologist Pierre Clastres has pointed to the link between pain and memory with the particularly striking example of initiation rites. He also emphasizes that the scars and other traces establish an enduring physical memory: "But after the initiation, when

---

[4] According to Oscar Wilde, this idea harkens back to Giordano Bruno: "Was the soul a shadow seated in the house of sin? Or was the body really in the soul, as Giordano Bruno thought?," *The Picture of Dorian Gray* (1891), Harmondsworth 1994, 70.

[5] Nietzsche, *On the Genealogy of Morality*, trans. Maudemarie Clark and Alan J. Swensen, Indianapolis 1988, 37.

all the suffering is already *forgotten*, something remains, an irrevocable surplus, the *traces* on the body by the wielding of the knife or stone, the scars of the wounds received. An initiated man is a marked man. [. . .] The mark is a hindrance to forgetting; the body itself bears the memory traces imprinted on it; *the body is a memory*."[6]

What the ethnologist tells us here about initiation rites can also be applied to the body of the soldier, whose wounds and scars physically preserve the memories of battle. In *Henry V,* on the eve of the Battle of Agincourt, Shakespeare puts into the mouth of the king a patriotic speech that is calculated to rouse the most faint-hearted men to deeds of valor. Any wounds they might suffer, he assures them, will one day be the most precious of memories:

> This day is call'd the feast of Crispian:
> He that outlives this day and comes safe home,
> Will stand a tip-toe when this day is nam'd,
> And rouse him at the name of Crispian.
> He that shall live this day, and see old age,
> Will yearly on the vigil feast his neighbours,
> And say, "Tomorrow is Saint Crispian":
> Then will he strip his sleeve and show his scars,
> And say, "These wounds I had on Crispin's Day."
> Old men forget: yet all shall be forgot,
> But he'll remember with advantages
> What feats he did that day.
>
> (IV, 3, 40–51)

The body memory of wounds and scars is more reliable than that of the mind. Even when the latter fades with age, as is to be expected, the former will lose nothing of its power. "Old men forget: yet all shall be forgot, / But he'll remember[. . .]"!

For Nietzsche, the memory was associated with the problem not only of storage but also of continued presence. Whatever is entrusted to it must be forever unforgettable, which does not mean, however, that it is maintained as a perpetual presence. For this reason, commemoration rituals reenacted on a specific memorial day help to keep the memory alive through acts of remembrance. The embodied memory

---

[6] Pierre Clastres, *Society against the State. Essays in Political Anthropology*, New York 1987, 184.

of the wounds is thus periodically reconnected with conscious and communicative acts of remembering. By contrast, trauma is a form of embodied memory that is precisely cut off from such social ties of conscious and communicative acts of remembrance.

As well as writing, photography has been used as a metaphor to describe the phenomenon of bodily inscription. The metaphor of the photograph as a trace of the real lays emphasis on the immediacy of the imprint, and this directness was of particular importance for Proust. Using the protophotographic image of lightning, he was able to describe an impression "which had been neither traced by my intellect nor attenuated by my pusillanimity, but which death itself, the sudden revelation of death, had, like a stroke of lightning, carved upon me, along a supernatural, inhuman channel, a two-fold and mysterious furrow."[7] Proust calls upon the imagery of impressions and traces whenever he wishes to underline the indisputable truthfulness of a memory. By comparison with this somatic truth, that of the intellect is merely logical: "The ideas formulated by the intellect have only a logical truth, a possible truth, their selection is arbitrary. Our only book is that one not made by ourselves whose characters are already imaged. [...] The imprint alone, however tenuous its consistency, however improbable its shape, is a criterion of truth."[8] In its more radical forms, the metaphor of the photograph emphasizes not only the directness of the impression, but also the damage inflicted on sensitive material. There is thus a correspondence between photography and trauma: the inscription of a section of the real on the silver bromide of the photographic plate may be compared to the inscription of a traumatic experience on the matrix of the unconscious. I have already quoted the psychoanalyst Ernst Simmel, author of *War Neuroses and Psychic Trauma* (1918), who described the traumatic impact in photographic terms: "The flash of terror makes a photographically precise impression."[9] Paradoxically, the metaphor

---

[7] Marcel Proust, *In Search of Lost Time*, Volume IV, Sodom and Gomorrah (see Chapt. 7, n. 12).

[8] Proust, Vol. VI, "Time Regained" and "A Guide to Proust" (see Chapt. 7, n. 12).

[9] Quoted from Wolfgang Schäffner, "Der Krieg als Trauma. Zur Psychoanalyse der Kriegsneurose," in Alfred Döblins, *Hamlet*, in M. Stingelin, W. Scherer (eds.), *Hard War / Soft War. Krieg und Medien 1914–1945*, Munich 1991, 34.

of the photographic medium emphasizes the exact opposite of mediality – the absolute directness of impressions. Bereft of all intellectual technologies of interpretation and defense mechanisms, the soul or the body itself becomes a medium as pure as the photographic plate. Whereas for Proust this defenseless passivity of the recipient represents a criterion for truth, for the psychiatrist of his time it becomes the symptom of a pathology.

Body writing has constantly been focused on in very different contexts with a wide variety of interpretations and evaluations according to the metaphysics that guides it. Plato and Jeremiah both speak of writing directly into the soul or on the tablets of the heart, and their views are very much influenced by the ideal of an authentic, internal, unmediated, and indelible memory. By contrast, Nietzsche reverses the predominance of soul over body and speaks not of internalization and immediacy but of corporal punishment, pain, wounds, and scars.[10] These are interpreted by him as part of a strategy of cultural programming, guaranteeing permanent and reliable traces that are not affected by intermediate forgetfulness. For De Quincey, Proust, and Freud, the memories inscribed into the palimpsest of the human mind are just as indelible, although they are hidden deep down beneath layers of forgetfulness and are therefore inaccessible. The example of Hamlet shows that body writing may go back not only to archaic rituals of initiation but also to experiences of psychic violence. Whereas ancient initiation rites apply body writing to the forceful establishment of a new identity, the body writing of trauma has the opposite effect of destroying the possibility of identity-building. The following three sections look at affect and trauma as forms of memory that vary in the manner of their physical participation and in the degree of distance from reflective consciousness. One of these sections is devoted to stabilizers, and one to the distortion and unreliability of memories and to the different frameworks in which memories are socially reconstructed.

---

[10] Peter Sloterdijk, *Zur Welt kommen – Zur Sprache kommen. Frankfurter Vorlesungen*, Frankfurt a.M. 1988, makes these body writings into a poetological program. He writes: "Where there was branding, there should arise language!" See also Geoffrey Hartman, "Worte und Wunden," in Aleida Assmann (ed.), *Texte und Lektüren. Perspektiven der Literaturwissenschaft*, Frankfurt a.M. 1996, 105–141.

STABILIZERS OF MEMORY

In his novel *Das Geisterfest*, the Hungarian author György Konrád writes: "I give life to the stories that have survived in the amber of time."[11] Following on from this, I ask: Is there such a thing as the amber of time? What would be the media and mechanisms to conserve our memories in this way? If such stabilizers exist at all, we may suppose that they are highly exceptional, because – as we are all only too well aware – memories are among the most fleeting and most unreliable phenomena of all. That is why people of different cultures and living at different times have constantly had recourse to technical stabilizers ranging from material objects and pictorial mnemotechnics to the medium of writing. Having discussed these, we now focus mainly on the internal mechanisms that help to counter the general trend toward forgetfulness and to make certain memories less forgettable than those that immediately fade into oblivion.

From a theoretical perspective, the use of the term "stabilizers" may appear problematical. Recent neurophysiological brain and memory research has abandoned the theory of definitive localization and, since around 1970, has worked on the premise that "a leading role is played by information storage on the basis of 'channeling' neurological structures."[12] Constructivists have dramatized this shift in the theoretical paradigm by criticizing the usual memory metaphors of inscription and storage as unacceptable distortions. They replace the static storage model with a dynamically constructive one of continuous reorganization, according to which memory of the past is adaptive and malleable, so that it can fit in with an ever-changing present.[13] It may be that the power of the will or the demands of the present reshape memory continuously, but this endless flexibility is at the same time restricted by one other factor – that of the body. There are physically

---

[11] György Konrád, *Das Geisterfest*, Frankfurt a.M. 1989, 7.

[12] Hinrich Rahmann, "Die Bausteine der Erinnerung," *Bild der Wissenschaft*, Year 19, Vol. II, Issue 9, 1982, 75–86; here, 84.

[13] "Memory contents in this respect can no longer be retrieved as already codified information, but must rather be *produced* in the process of memory formation which depends on the present." [author italics.] Jürgen Straub, "Kultureller Wandel als konstruktive Transformation des kollektiven Gedächtnisses. Zur Theorie der Kulturpsychologie," in Christian G. Allesch, Elfriede Billmann-Mahecha, and Alfred Lang (eds.), *Psychologische Aspekte des Kulturellen Wandels*, Vienna 1992, 42–54; here, 50.

inscribed experiences and injuries that, we are told by the experts, defy deliberate manipulation. For this reason, it seems to me that the thesis of total flexibility and adaptability of memory goes too far and constitutes the other extreme of the storage model. Convincing and indeed undisputed though the claim may be that memories are constantly being reconstructed under the particular conditions of the present, the argument that memories depend exclusively on the present and "not on the past"[14] strikes me as a gross exaggeration. Such a concept would lead us to abandon the past as a reality that in many ways engenders or overshadows the present. I therefore take a different approach to the question of the (un)reliability of memory, focusing in particular on the stabilizing and destabilizing factors at work in the memory process.

First and foremost among these is language. This is the most powerful stabilizer of memory, for whatever we have captured in language is far easier to remember than something that has never been articulated. What we remember then is not the events themselves but our verbal account of them. Linguistic signs function like names through which we recall objects and facts. Christa Wolf describes this process perfectly: "It was eleven years ago and in another life. The memory of it would have faded completely from his mind if he had not captured it in words, with the aid of which he can now recall that event as often as he wishes."[15] Individual memories are stabilized and also socialized by language. Maurice Halbwachs stressed the fact that as members of a group we cannot perceive an object without giving it a name and thus subjecting it to the group's conventions and ways of thinking. Alongside language there are other psychic stabilizers of memory, which I discuss under the headings of affect, symbol, and trauma. In varying degrees of intensity, two of these involve the body as a medium, whereas the third – the symbol – entails the translation of physical experience into "meaning."

---

[14] Straub, 52.

[15] Translated from Christa Wolf, *Kein Ort. Nirgends*, Berlin/Weimar 1980, 25. Wolf has also criticized the verbal fixing of memories. In an essay on "Lesen und Schreiben" [Reading and Writing] (1968) she writes: "Thus childhood ends at that time, everyone believes it, it is polished through frequent telling till it shines, it is nicely self-pitying, it has its firm position in the shrine of the locket, and its caption is: 'End of childhood.' Christa Wolf, *Die Dimension des Autors. Essays und Aufsätze, Reden und Gespräche, 1959–1985*, Darmstadt and Neuwied 1987, 463–503; here, 479–480.

Affect

As we have seen, affect plays a major role in the tradition of mnemo-technics. Because this artificial technique of memory is designed to enhance the qualities of natural memory, it must start from its basic potential. The observation that if we see something unusually base, shameful, rare, large, incredible, ridiculous etc., it will imprint itself deeply on our memory, was the starting point of the treatise *Ad Herennium*. This suggests that one should choose striking images as props for memory: "We ought, then, to set up images of a kind that can adhere longest in the memory. And we shall do so if [...] we set up images that are not many or vague, but doing something."[16] In order to enhance the vividness of these images, the advice is to dress them royally in crown and purple, or to disfigure them with blood-stains, splashes of mud, or patches of bright red. This approach by the ancient mnemotechnicians coincides with astonishing precision to the findings of modern cognitive psychology. American psychologists have conducted an experiment in which they showed two groups of people identical series of nondescript slides. One group saw nothing but the slides themselves, whereas the other saw the slides accom-panied by a dramatic, bloodthirsty narrative. The result was that the second group retained a significantly higher proportion of the images than the first group.[17] Although in this example the bearer of the emotion was text and not an image, the experiment still confirms the importance of affect in establishing memorability.

Both ancient mnemotechnics and modern psychological experi-ments show the degree to which human memory can be manipulated. In both cases memory and emotion are not linked spontaneously, but are consciously and even arbitrarily connected. This changes, of course, if we move to autobiographical memories. In this con-text, memory and affect merge into an inseparable complex: the emotional content of particular memories is completely beyond our conscious control. It was precisely this element of uncontrollability that made the affect such a vital memory stabilizer for Rousseau. In his *Confessions* – a genre whose most important source is subjective

---

[16] *Ad C. Herennium, De Ratione Dicendi*, Book III, XXII, 37, 221 (see Chapt. 9, n. 8).
[17] Daniel L. Schacter (ed.), *Memory Distortion. How Minds, Brains and Societies Reconstruct the Past*, Cambridge and London 1995, 264–265.

memory – he appears to have been one of the first to question himself critically about his own credibility.[18] In the context of autobiography, this means that the writer actually has to investigate himself. But if there are no other witnesses to an event, and there is no external evidence to support or refute a view, what possible criterion can there be to establish the authenticity of memories? In search of such a criterion, Rousseau came upon the affect. It was clear to him that he could not reconstruct the events of the past with any precision, and so right from the start he acknowledged that his memories could make no claim to objective truth. What he could claim, however, was a truth that was anchored in "*la chaine des sentiments*" [the chain of emotions]:

All the papers I had collected to aid my recollection, and guide me in this undertaking, are no longer in my possession, nor can I ever again hope to regain them. I have but one faithful guide on which I can depend: this is the chain of the sentiments by which the succession of my existence has been marked, and by these the events which have been either the cause or the effect of the manner of it. I easily forget my misfortunes, but I cannot forget my faults, and still less my virtuous sentiments. The remembrance of these is too dear to me ever to suffer them to be effaced from my mind. I may omit facts, transpose events, and fall into some errors of dates; but I cannot be deceived in what I have felt, nor in that which from sentiment I have done.[19]

From emotion as an instrument to reinforce the memory as in classical mnemotechnics, we now find it in Rousseau as the hard core of memory. Jean Starobinski comments on this passage: "Feeling is thus the indestructible core of memory [...]. The truth that Rousseau wishes to communicate is not exactitude of biographical fact but accuracy in depicting his relation to his past. [...] We have moved from

---

[18] ... instead of adopting the usual method of putting the reader in charge and then undermining it through appropriate assertions. Augustine writes of his readers: "though I be not able to demonstrate whether I confess truly; yet give they credit unto me, whose ears charity hath set open unto me" (St. Augustine's *Confessions*, two volumes, with an English translation by William Watts, London and Harvard 1961 III, 79). Augustine, who wrote his confessions for God and not for his contemporaries or for posterity, presumed that falsification was impossible: "To thee [...], O Lord, I am laid open, whatever I am." (*Confessions*, Vol. II, Book X, II, 77). In these confessions he invokes Memoria as if she were a Muse; whether she sings the truth or lies is of no interest to him. As far as I know, right up until Rousseau no autobiographer had questioned the truthfulness of his own memories.

[19] Jean-Jacques Rousseau, *The Confessions of Jean-Jacques Rousseau*, 2006 [EBook #3913], Book VII, 242.

the realm of (historical) truth to that of authenticity (the authenticity of discourse)."[20]

The subjective authenticity of emotional memory rests on psychophysical experience that can be neither verified externally nor revised internally. This point is illustrated through another autobiographer who was equally self-critical about the reliability of her own memories. Mary Antin was born in 1881 in White Russian Polotzk, and at the turn of the century she emigrated with her family to the United States.[21] There in 1909 at the age of just twenty-eight she wrote her autobiography, the story of that part of her life that had taken place in a Jewish, East European environment and that came to an abrupt end when she emigrated.

Her memories begin at the age of four with the funeral of her grandfather. After a sketchy description of the wake, she suddenly interrupts herself with a question: "Do I really remember this little scene?" Then she goes on:

Perhaps I heard it described by some fond relative, as I heard other anecdotes of my infancy, and unconsciously incorporated it with my genuine recollections. [...] It is more likely, however, that I took no intellectual interest in my grandfather's remains at the time, but later on, when I sought for a first recollection, perhaps, elaborated the scene, and my part in it, something that satisfied my sense of dramatic fitness. If I really committed such a fraud, I am now well punished, by being obliged, at the very start, to discredit the authenticity of my memoirs.[22]

In passages such as this, Antin plays ironically with her memories, unnecessarily arousing the reader's suspicions and bringing to the foreground the reconstructive quality of her personal recollections. In other passages, however, she insists with surprising pertinacity on their truthfulness. In this respect, she goes one step further than

---

[20] Jean Starobinski, *Jean-Jacques Rousseau. Transparency and Obstruction*, trans. Arthur Goldhammer, Chicago and London 1988, 197 f.

[21] Mary Antin's *The Promised Land* was first published in serial form by *The Atlantic Monthly* in 1912, and the first book edition did not appear until 1940. The quotations are taken from the second edition, Boston 1969. My attention was drawn to her work by Monica Rüthers. See Monica Rüthers, *Tewjes Töchter. Lebensentwürfe ostjüdischer Frauen im 19. Jahrhundert, Lebenswelten osteuropäischer Juden*, 2, Cologne, Weimar, Vienna 1996.

[22] Antin, *Promised Land*, 80.

Rousseau, as she actually asserts this truth *in defiance of the facts*; to be specific, going against the empirical evidence. She explains this problem through one particular memory relating to the dark red dahlias that were said to have bloomed in the neighbor's garden:

Concerning my dahlias I have been told that they were not dahlias at all, but poppies. As a conscientious historian I am bound to record every rumor, but I retain the right to cling to my own impression. Indeed, I must insist on my dahlias, if I am to preserve the garden at all. I have so long believed in them, that if I try to see *poppies* in those red masses over the wall, the whole garden crumbles away and leaves me a gray blank. I have nothing against poppies. It is only that my illusion is more real to me than reality.[23]

Poppies or dahlias – why does Antin pick on this minor point, which has absolutely no bearing on the course of her story? I do not see her as an advocate of postmodern epistemology, holding her "subjective" truth to be superior to an objective, empirically authenticated one. It seems to me, rather, that her comments concern not the structure of reality but the structure of memory. When she insists on *her* dahlias, she is in fact emphasizing the apodictic quality of affective memories. These are incorrigible, because they stand or fall by the intensity of live connections, of immediate impressions. If one dispenses with these, then all is lost.

This live link with the past also has value as historical testimony, albeit in a different manner from that of historians, with whom the autobiographer, Antin, compares herself: "You can come to me with the most precise description of Polotzk and show me where I have gone wrong – but I shall still remain the better guide. You might prove to me that my road of adventure led to nothing, but with my accelerating pulse and my living chain of associations I can prove that things happened to me here and there – and *I* am the one who will be believed, not you."[24]

Symbol

In his pioneering study of memory and its social frames, Maurice Halbwachs wrote: "Every personality and every historical fact, as soon as it enters into this [i.e., social] memory, is transposed into a lesson,

[23] Ibid., 81.
[24] Ibid., 84.

a concept, a symbol; it takes on a meaning and becomes an element in a society's system of ideas."[25] What Halbwachs applied to the collective, socially communicated and shared memory can also, in my opinion, be applied to that of the individual. In a piece entitled *Memories of an Old Man*, the Polish author Andrzej Szczypiorski describes the role of symbols as stabilizers of memory. The old man he is referring to is the Capuchin friar Anicet, whose civil name was Albert Koplin. He was born in 1875 in Friedland, Eastern Prussia, entered the Order of the Capuchins in Alsace in 1893, and was ordained into the priesthood in Krefeld in 1900. In 1918, he went to Warsaw, where he remained as a Polish citizen by choice. He was actively engaged in welfare and social work, and was one of the most respected priests in Warsaw. In 1940 he presented himself to the Nazi authorities as a Pole, was sent to Auschwitz in 1941, and died in the gas chambers that same year.

As he explains in his introduction, Szczypiorski has set his personal recollections in a very special institutional framework. A conference was held at the palace of the Primate of Poland in memory of the friar, and the background to this was a particular situation: the Order of the Capuchins was proposing that the Vatican should begin the process of beatifying Father Anicet. Szczypiorski was just a boy when he first met Father Anicet, and between 1938 and 1942 he helped as a server at Mass. He knew nothing about the origin, importance, or fate of this man, and the memories of images, scenes, and conversations that remained from this time were from the very restricted perspective of a young boy. The unprepossessing collection of memories was disproportionate to the importance these meetings assumed in the retrospective revision of Szczypiorski's life story, and so he warns his readers right from the beginning: "Basically, everything I say here will be a confession – the depiction of my spiritual destiny."[26] He has very little to say about Father Anicet and a great deal to say about himself. He distinguishes very precisely between the memories of his youth and those of the gray-haired old man who he has become and who, as he repeatedly tells us, "carries a heavy sack of his own experiences on

---

[25] Halbwachs, *Das Gedächtnis*, (see Chapt. 6, n. 7).
[26] Andrzej Szczypiorski, *Notizen zum Stand der Dinge*, Zürich 1992, 224. All other quotations are translated from this edition.

his shoulders, with the majority of his earthly life placed behind him." (225) Of these youthful memories he writes:

The experiences of early childhood did indeed continue to live on in me, but very well hidden somewhere in the crammed and dusty attic of memory, which one seldom enters. [...] Certainly somewhere in there was Father Anicet, but unnoticed, silent across the years, not needed. In my memory [...] if he was there at all, he was a small, bent old man in a rather dirty habit, with sandals on his bare feet. And I literally knew nothing more about him. (225)

The attic is a vivid image for latent memory: untidy and neglected, objects lie scattered all around – simply a load of junk that has no purpose and no apparent value. And just like junk, these latent memories lie in an intermediate state from which they will either sink into the darkness of total oblivion or be brought out again into the daylight of remembrance. Each little anecdote that Szczypiorski is still able to recount bears the stamp of a particular emotion: ambition, humiliation, surprise, alienation, and mystification – all come into play where perceptions have solidified into experiences and experiences were consolidated into memories.

Szczypiorski is careful to distinguish between the recollections of his old age and those of his youth:

Only in later life did he return. Today he is for me a central or at least a very important figure in my spiritual adventure [...]. One might indeed say that Father Anicet in my memory, in the process of my spiritual maturing, is to a certain extent a hero staged ex post facto; he fills a gap in the imagination rather than in the reality I have experienced. Anicet is a kind of spiritual need, a moral imperative of – to tell the truth – my somewhat complicated existence. (225 f)

What had been *affect* in the memories of youth became a *symbol* in the memories of age. Affect and symbol are stabilizers of a very different kind. The memory that takes on the force of a symbol is formed by retrospective interpretation of the past, and is set within the framework of a determinate meaning. Szczypiorski tells us quite specifically that the Anicet of his later, processed memories is not a restitution of the real, historical person, "his life, his actions or his influence, but Anicet as a particular symbol, as a destiny raised by my imagination to the level of a symbol. [...] What I now have is important for me, is my affair, is *my* Anicet, but not the true, the real Anicet who once walked through the streets of Warsaw and died behind the barbed wire of Auschwitz." (226 f) Once again it would be premature to dismiss this now symbolic memory as fiction or as a lie just because the author himself has admitted that it has no connection with the historical truth. One should not underestimate the importance of such memories that have been processed "through patterns of interpretation which have been acquired at a later date."[27] Reinterpretations of this nature play an important role in stabilizing memories and hence fashioning the identity of the individual. Unlike emotions, however, they are not rooted in perceptions or actual memories, but are added on later. The stability of a large proportion of our memories depends on whether or not such reinterpretations can be formed as an integrating frame. The process itself is part not only of our human needs, but also of our self-determination. In a novel that we have already quoted from, György Konrád writes: "To the question what is the meaning of life, everyone answers with his own curriculum vitae [c.v.]."[28] A c.v. is composed of objectively verifiable data, but a biography depends on interpreted memories that are connected in a memorable and narratable form. It is this form that is called meaning, and is the backbone of living identity.

Trauma

The literary critic Lawrence Langer would probably classify Szczypiorski's transformation of memories into symbols as "heroic memory." Langer, who comments on the video testimonies of Holocaust survivors, contrasts "heroic memory" with "unheroic memory." The former – which should not be confused with Nietzsche's concept of greatness and "monumental memory" – presupposes an integral self that is possessed of attributes such as self-respect, free will, intellectual options, a future, positive values, and the rhetoric of salvation,

---

[27] "Perhaps it is not at all important what role he played in my life in 1940 or 1941, but all that matters is the role he plays today, who he is for me today, and who he will remain for me until the end of my days, this bent old man of whom I knew nothing before, and whom I have later put together from the fragments of my memory as a symbol of my own transformation and spiritual maturation." Szczypiorski, 235.

[28] Konrád, *Das Geisterfest*, 7 (see n. 11).

whereas the latter is irreversibly deprived of all such resources. This is what Langer calls a "diminished self," which has lost all physical and mental control over its environment, and whose language has lost all connotations of agency. In the testimonies of Holocaust victims, Langer found "an abandonment of the entire vocabulary of the integral self, anchored in such terms as choice, will, the power of deliberation, and future security."[29] He argues that unheroic memory bears witness to the fact that any retrospective conquest of terror is out of the question because the necessary mental and spiritual preconditions and values have also fallen victim to Nazi brutality. Langer's prime concern is not therapeutic rehabilitation for the traumatized individual, but social recognition of his or her status. According to him, the diminished self "calls for an entire complex of redefinitions and new perceptions, a modernized or modernistic view of ethical discursive possibilities and limits that need not confine themselves to the reality of the Holocaust."[30]

Terms such as "unheroic memory" and "diminished self" are related to traumatic experiences that cannot be transformed into redemptive symbols. They result from experiences the intensity of which exceeds the capacity for cognitive and emotional integration. Trauma stabilizes an experience by encrypting it, that is, by keeping it inaccessible to conscious inspection and reconstruction.[31] Ruth Klüger, who survived the concentration camps at Theresienstadt, Auschwitz, and Christianstadt, repeatedly struggles with the problem of how to translate traumatic

---

[29] Lawrence Langer, *Holocaust Testimonies. The Ruins of Memory*, New Haven and London 1991, 177.

[30] Ibid. I would not wish here to delve into the problem whether it is possible to generalize from the exceptional circumstances surrounding the experience in the death camps, identifying the survivors of the Holocaust as a kind of paradigm for "modern man." This classification in another way also depends on the strategy of the symbol, which makes a particular remembered situation into a sign for something else that is not directly connected to it.

[31] With regard to the trauma that goes back to early childhood experiences, it is generally the fragmented nature of the events but not their context that stays in the memory. The fear-ridden associations cannot be located in a particular place or time, but are stored on a sensory and neurological level. This makes it extremely difficult to translate them into symbols and to retrieve them through language. Bessel A. van der Kolk, Onno van der Hart, and Pierre Janet, "Breakdown of Adaption in Psychological Trauma," *American Journal of Psychiatry* 146: 12 (December 1989), 1530–1540; here, 1535.

experiences into language. At the very beginning of her autobiography she writes about her cousin Hans, who was tortured by the Nazis. She lets him describe and demonstrate every detail, but then goes on: "And yet the details smoothe out this torment, and it is only from the tone of his voice that one can discern the otherness, the extraordinariness, the evil. For the torture does not leave the tortured, never, not for the rest of his life."[32] Words cannot capture the trauma. Because they belong to everyone and everything, words cannot encompass something incomparable, something unique, let alone the uniqueness of unending terror. And yet it is precisely such traumas that are in need of language, although it is not the language of memory and narrative: "Memory is conjuration, and effective conjuration is witchcraft." (79) She is not concerned with memories but with ghosts. "Where there is no grave, the work of mourning never ceases." (94) In her words and poems Klüger creates places where she can lay to rest the unburied victims, her father and her brother, although as she is well aware, this ultimately serves the purpose of providing her with peace.

This power of words and verses was tested by herself as a 12-year-old when she wrote a poem in Auschwitz about the death machine. Later she comments: "One must understand the cleverness that inspired me to condense the trauma of those weeks in Auschwitz into verses. These are children's poems whose regular beat tries to create a counter to the chaos – a poetic, therapeutic attempt to balance out this senseless circus of destruction, in which we were dying, through a linguistic, rhyming unity; in fact, then, the oldest of aesthetic preoccupations." (125)

The memory that Ruth Klüger names as the harshest and most vivid concerns the humiliation of her mother, which she was forced to witness. After she describes it in her own precise and succinct style, she adds: "I thought I would not be able to write about it, and instead I was going to insert at this point the reflection that there are things I cannot write about. Now that they are down on paper, the words are just as common as others and they were not hard to find." (137) This example shows very clearly the discrepancy between intersubjective words and subjective experiences. What for the writer is the most terrible experience becomes merely one episode among many for the

---

[32] Ruth Klüger, *weiter leben*, Göttingen 1992, 9.

reader. "The words are just as common as others" (i.e. they draw a veil of generalization and trivialization over the unique and the profound, blunting instead of sharpening, as one would expect of any memory that never ceases to cause pain). Words cannot represent this physical wound of the memory. The relationship of language to trauma is ambivalent: there are magical, aesthetic, therapeutic words that can be effective and life-giving because they banish terror, but there are also pallid, vague, and superficial words that convey only the empty shell of the terror.

Ruth Klüger also delves into the problem of the unheroic memory that blocks integration of the traumatic experience and prevents the possibility of constructing an identity. For instance, she resists the close association of her name with Auschwitz, because the trauma has a different impact from that of one's personal background:

The word Auschwitz has an aura today, albeit a negative one, which largely determines how one thinks of a person that one knows was there. People who want to say something important about me also include the fact that I was in Auschwitz. But it's not as simple as that, because whatever you may think, I do not come from Auschwitz; I come from Vienna. Vienna can't be bypassed – you can hear it from my accent – and Auschwitz was as alien to me as the moon. Vienna is part of the structure of my brain and it speaks through me, whereas Auschwitz was the most remote place I ever went to, and the memory of it remains like a foreign body in my soul, rather like a bullet that can't be taken out of the flesh. Auschwitz was nothing but a terrible act of chance. (138)

The image of an inoperable bullet in the flesh vividly illustrates the paradoxical contradictoriness of the trauma: even though it is an irremovable part of oneself, it cannot be assimilated into one's identity, but remains an intruder that shatters the categories of traditional logic: it is both internal and external, present and absent. The French philosopher Jean-François Lyotard also underlines the paradoxical nature of trauma when he focuses on the problem of its representation in a collective and historical context. His historical and psychoanalytical essay on *The Jews* deals with the (im)balance between the murder of European Jews, how it is described, and how it is collectively remembered. He refers to Freud's concept of suppression, which is not a form of forgetting but, on the contrary, a particularly obstinate mode of conservation.[33] However, Freud takes repression to be an outcome that he hopes to nullify through therapy, whereas Lyotard – again paradoxically – raises it to the level of a norm by his claim that traumatization is the only adequate way of relating to the Holocaust. He reaches this conclusion at the end of his search for the most reliable stabilizers of memory. He regards monuments as mere "representations," which as such are meant to relieve the memory and therefore in fact are strategies of oblivion. Written records do not provide any effective defense against forgetfulness either, as was already argued by Plato, who saw writing as a mode of forgetting. What is written down can be altered or erased, whereas what has never been fashioned into a sign or a memorable symbol cannot – according to Lyotard – be denied or forgotten. He writes:

Whenever one represents, one inscribes in memory, and this might seem a good defense against forgetting. It is, I believe, just the opposite. Only that which has been inscribed can, in the current sense of the term, be forgotten, because it could be effaced. But what is not inscribed, through lack of inscribable surface, of duration and place for the inscription to be situated, what has no place in the space nor in the time of domination, in the geography and the diachrony of the self-assured spirit, because it is not synthesizable – let us say, what is not material for experience because the forms and formations of experience, be they unconscious (those which are produced by secondary repression), are inapt and inept for it – cannot be forgotten, does not offer a hold to forgetting, and remains present "only" as an affection that one cannot even qualify, like a state of death in the life of the spirit.[34]

[33] More recent psychotherapeutic studies dispense with the term "repression" (already discredited in the False Memory Debate) and prefer to describe the process as "dissociation." The instinctive strategy for survival under such circumstances is splitting off. The victim of a traumatic experience separates that part of himself that cannot be accommodated, hovers above the events, and produces covering memories that can be integrated into the constitution of the self. In the long term, the affect whose force was too great to be integrated into the cognitive and emotional system still remains present, and over time makes that presence felt through the formation of symptoms and related actions. The task of the therapist then consists in reestablishing unity between those parts of the psyche that have been separated by the trauma, and restoring a balance between the affective and the cognitive levels.

[34] J. F. Lyotard, *Heidegger and "the Jews,"* trans. Andreas Michel and Mark S. Roberts. Minneapolis and London 1990, 26. R. Barthes adopts a similar approach when he distinguishes between "studium" and "punctum": "What I can name cannot really prick me. The incapacity to name is a good symptom of disturbance." Barthes, *Camera Lucida*, 51 (see Chapt. 9, n. 1).

The catalogue of negatives – absence of space, time, signs, and so forth – that for Lyotard describes the only adequate way of relating to the trauma of the Holocaust reaches its apogee in the mystical formula of death in the midst of life. The formula carries with it a certain religious connotation and is itself a kind of symbol, though in this instance it symbolizes resistance to any construction of meaning – an indefinable relic, or what he calls an *oubli inoubliable*. His concept of trauma is, then, very different from that of Langer. While Langer is concerned with the "ruined" memories and states of impaired consciousness among real Holocaust survivors, Lyotard (in a paradoxical gesture) prescribes trauma for the western mind as the only adequate way of relating to the collective crime of the Holocaust. For him the trauma created by the most extreme act of disempowerment itself becomes the most suitable stabilizer for remembrance. Through this collectivization and ennoblement, Lyotard's concept of trauma has become a metaphor, and in this form it has entered into literary theory, where it signifies a general "crisis of representation." His analysis reflects a change of paradigm in memory theory. He advocates trauma as the form of a placeless and restless present that prevents closure, thus guaranteeing a stable continuation of the Holocaust within western cultural memory. Although the individual is entitled to a therapeutic processing of his or her traumatic experiences, such alleviation is excluded on the collective level. In direct opposition to the aim prevalent in the 1960s of "mastering the past," the focus in the post-traumatic age is on the "preservation of the past."[35] The construction of symbols and the erection of monuments, which present themselves as means of holding onto the past, are criticized from this perspective as a mode of closure and forgetting, an externalization, a memory screen.

In order to describe flashbacks of traumatic situations, a victim of child abuse resorts to metaphor: "Throughout such memories I am there, not here [. . .] reliving something clearly not understood, not given meaning – just lived and recorded, as if in amber, now suddenly

---

[35] For typical examples of this elevation of the concept of trauma outside the sphere of literary studies, see Michael Roth, *The Ironist's Cage. Memory, Trauma and the Construction of History*, New York 1995, and Antze and Lambek (eds.), *Tense Past* (see Introduction, n. 14).

cracked open."[36] The three key terms that we have been discussing have led us to different forms of stabilization, which may be set down in triangular form:

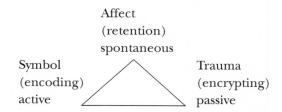

Affect
(retention)
spontaneous

Symbol
(encoding)
active

Trauma
(encrypting)
passive

The affect works as a magnifier of perception, retaining vivid scenes and acute images in the shape of disconnected fragments.[37] Without the affect, there are no memories; it highlights a few moments of our experience and retains them against the background of our continuous forgetting. The affect-memories bear the stamp of authenticity, which is why they are cherished by individuals as inalienable private property. Such vivid, somatic, and pre-verbal memories retain isolated scenes without a before or after. In their fragmentary character, they may be considered as protonarrative kernels. Memories charged with an affect hold a middle position between the active encoding of a symbol and the passive encrypting of trauma. From this middle position, the dynamics of memory can move in two directions. If the affect-memories are integrated into a framework of values and encoded in a narrative (as we have seen in the example of Szczypiorski), they become part of the stock of conscious memories that support the structure of an identity. If, however, the affect exceeds a certain limit

---

[36] Roberta Culbertson, "Embodied Memory, Transcendence, and Telling: Recounting Trauma, Re-Establishing the Self," *New Literary History* 26 (1995), 169–195; here, 187.

[37] From a psychoanalytical standpoint, however, the stabilizing role of an affect (especially a negative one) is judged somewhat differently. The point here is that this "process of suppression – like very many mechanisms that create unconsciousness during situations of conflict – consists in separating the affect from the scene related to it. The affects then attach themselves to what one might call 'false' scenes, and this leads to symptoms of neurosis. Only through the process of analysis can these 'false' associations be put into reverse." This quotation is from a letter written by Ilka Quindeau; see Quindeau, *Trauma und Geschichte. Interpretationen autobiographischer Erzählungen von Überlebenden des Holocaust*, Frankfurt a.M. 1995. A similar conclusion was reached by a postgraduate discussion group in Hildesheim, which I whould like to thank at this point for a number of illuminating suggestions.

of intensity, it shatters memory and threatens identity. This is what happens in trauma. The event that is neither remembered nor forgotten is encrypted and remains inaccessible to conscious inspection and retrospective interpretation.[38] Trauma is the impossibility of narration. Symbolic encoding and traumatic encrypting are the opposite poles between which our memories are reconstructed.

We can now return to our initial question concerning the stability or malleability of memory: its plastic nature stems to a large extent from the fact that it is reconstructed not only under the pressures exerted by the present, but also within particular institutional frameworks that guide selection and fix contours. We have worked our way through a series of these – autobiographical, ecclesiastical, juridical, therapeutic, testimonial, and historiographical. Because the frameworks can never all be made to coincide, memories will always transcend their social and cultural borders, and therefore alongside their plasticity we must also take into account their unwieldiness and their resistance to confinement, which run counter to the idea that the smooth path of consensus can lead to a simple and neat "construction of a new past."[39] Our awareness that interpretation and processing of the past are never closed is no justification for disputing the actual matter of fact of past injustices and sufferings or the after-effects of events imprinted on the mind, soul, and body.

FALSE MEMORIES

The (in)stability of memory is inseparable from its (un)reliability. In this context we must therefore consider the problem of "false memories," which in recent years has become the focus of increasing attention. We are constantly being reminded of the fact that memories are unreliable, and this is due not only to deficiencies in the faculty itself but also, and at least as much, to the active forces that work to distort it. Theorists stress that the process of remembering is always under the pressure and demands of the respective present. Current

---

[38] R. Culbertson distinguishes between "encoding" and "encrypting," *Embodied Memory*, 194 (see n. 36); R. Leys, "Traumatic Cures," in Antze, Lambek (eds.), *Tense Past*, 120 (see n. 35) distinguishes between "traumatic" and "narrative" memory.
[39] Straub, *Kultureller Wandel*, 52 (see n. 13).

affects, motives, and intentions are the guides to remembering and forgetting. They determine which memories are accessible to an individual at any given moment and which are not, and they also produce specific values between the extremes of moral repugnance and nostalgic delight, between relevance and indifference. This theory of retrospective transformation is not the recent discovery of our modern neuro-psychologists. According to Freud, the distortion goes back to "guilt," which is the dominant factor in the economy of memory. Consequently psychoanalysis is the "art of memory," which can bring back the lost or deformed memories from their state of repression and distortion. According to Nietzsche, the central agent of memory formation is the "will." Nietzsche is the theorist of a memory that serves the action-oriented purposes of the conscious mind, presenting the man of action as always *gewissenlos* [without conscience] in the sense of *wissenlos* [unknowing, or unconscious].[40]

What he means by this is that at a given moment, it is always just a part of his knowledge and memory that is available to "the man of action." "He forgets most things so as to do one thing, he is unjust toward what lies behind him, and he recognizes the rights only of that which is now to come into being and no other rights whatever."[41] Nietzsche argues that culture has constructed morality and conscience to counter this unjust forgetting, but these are not much more reliable themselves. Conscience needs the support of memory, but memory shows itself to be too weak for the purpose. In a famous passage, he compresses this whole problem into a miniature psycho-drama:

> "I did that," says my memory.
> "I can't have done that," says my pride, and remains unshakable.
> In the end, memory gives in.[42]

This pattern of psychomachia Nietzsche might well have found in Montaigne: "*chaque person d'honeur choit de perdre son conscience que de son honeur*" [every person of honour chooses to lose his conscience rather than his honor]. These aphorisms are part of the moralist tradition;

---

[40] Nietzsche, *Untimely Meditations* (see Chapt. 3, n. 6).
[41] Ibid.
[42] Nietzsche, *Jenseits von Gut und Böse*, in Sämtliche Werke, Band V, 86.

they are based on a skeptical anthropology and describe humans with all their contradictions.

The problem of false memories is of vital practical importance to those concerned with the credibility of eyewitness accounts – for example, lawyers and experts in oral history. In the meantime, the technical problems of memory verification have entered also the field of psychotherapy, and they are also relevant to literature. Questions that arise in these different contexts include the following: Are there universal standards by which to measure the truthfulness of memories? Is there such a thing as a specific truthfulness for subjective memories? How do differing memories relate to the ideal of a single, authoritative, historical truth? Does the plasticity of memory stand for a "postmodern" epistemology that questions the "modern" predominance of a monolithic truth? Or does the relevance of false memories consist rather in our increasingly skeptical basic assumptions concerning our capacity to grasp the fullness of human experience in a world that has become so confused and confusing?

The American "False Memory Debate"

When we think of the body as a medium for memory, we rule out the freedom of the will and assume that such memories cannot be arbitrarily manipulated. We all know that to err is human and we all know that memory is fallible, but these clichés take on a different slant when scientists demonstrate that even those memories that concern basic or traumatic experiences may turn out to be false. Referred to here are events that made the headlines in the United States as the "False Memory Debate," and it is well worth recalling some of the details.[43] At the center of the debate was the question of how reliable or unreliable memories were. In this case, a private memory problem escalated

---

[43] The final rounds of the debate were reported, for example, in three editions of *The New York Review of Books* in 1994–1995. Frederick Crews rekindled the fire with his essay "The Revenge of the Repressed"; *The New York Review of Books*, XLI, no. 19, Nov. 17 (1994), no. 20, Dec. 1 (1994), and XLII, no. 1, Jan. 12 (1995). The debate, however, reached further back into the past; a comprehensive account of the opposing positions was already published in the leading organ of American family therapy, *Family Therapy Network*, in September and October 1993. This is the source of my references, and I am grateful to Helm Stierlin for pointing it out to me.

into a public legal battle, in which two enemy camps opposed one another. They can be identified by means of their appropriate abbreviations. On the one side was the MPD party of psychotherapists, working under the umbrella term Multiple Personality Disorder syndrome, which boils down to a pathological disintegration of the components of personality. A particularly important cause of this disintegration is "post-traumatic stress disorder," which can be the long-term effect of a traumatic experience. The official terminology for this condition has only been in existence since 1979, when it was included in the *American Handbook of Psychiatry*. It was to have far-reaching legal consequences. In 1980, twenty-one states raised the seven-year limitation on certain claims for compensation. First and foremost, this applied to crimes whose victims were not adults but children; consequently, at the time there were no plaintiffs because the criminals might, for instance, have terrorized their victims into secrecy or the children might have suppressed their traumas for decades. And thus the limitation on crimes such as incest and child abuse was raised in 1980. Parallel to this legal recognition came the "Incest Recovery Movement," which aimed to bring out the suppressed memories through therapy sessions, self-help groups, and also suitable reading materials and even television programs.[44]

The opposing camp also identified itself by its initials. This was an organization known as FMSF: the False Memory Syndrome Foundation. Its members were mainly parents who had been accused by their children of sexual abuse and who vehemently denied the charges. They saw the new Incest Recovery Movement as a modern variation on the early modern witch hunt, but here instead of the Inquisition it was the guild of psychotherapists that was pulling the strings. Their complaint was that the psychotherapists were inducing illnesses instead of curing them; they were engaged in "confabulation" to generate false memories in their patients, so that they could use these as a convincing, blanket explanation for every problem. Thus uncovering experiences of sexual abuse during early childhood became the therapeutic key to all kinds of later behavioral disturbances and sicknesses,

---

[44] Ellen Bess and Laura Davis, *The Courage to Heal. A Guide for Women Survivors of Child Sexual Abuse*, 3rd ed., New York 1994.

from an unhappy marriage or depression right through to temporary eating disorders.

The confrontation between children and parents, underpinned by the participation of the legal profession as well as the lurid interest of the media, caused a rift in the middle-class white American family. However, my own interest is not in the politicization of this subject but in the different theories of memory that came into conflict with one another during these proceedings. On the side of the FMSF were not only the accused parents, such as those directly affected by the Incest Recovery Movement, but also memory researchers and critics who mounted a major offensive against what they called the "myth of repressed memories." Elizabeth Loftus, the most prominent founding member of the organization, joined the group in her capacity as a researcher on the subject. Her special field was cognitive psychology, and she was regarded as the leading American authority on experimental research into memory. As such, she took part in court proceedings as an expert on matters pertaining to the truthfulness of witnesses' accounts. Her own particular area of research was the unreliability of memory, which she had tested through a wide range of ever more original experiments under laboratory conditions. She proved over and over again how imprecise the human memory is, and how subject to change and to outside influence. In her laboratory she even succeeded in implanting into an adult the false memory of a traumatic experience he was supposed to have undergone at the age of five.[45]

It is obvious that in the rapidly expanding area of psychotherapy, as in any profession, there will be cases of malpractice and that such incidents – especially as they may have serious individual and social consequences, above all on those directly involved – must be subject to the most stringent examination. However, from the standpoint of research into the nature of memory, the American "debate" interests me for another reason. It shows that memories are reconstructed in particular institutional frameworks according to widely differing rules and standards.

[45] Elizabeth Loftus et al., "The Reality of Illusory Memories," in D. Schacter, *Memory Distortions*, 47–68 (see n. 17).

The *therapeutic framework* is characterized by closure, cooperation, and a form of detached empathy. The trained wariness of the analyst is not directed toward unmasking the client, but toward providing therapy. He must find his way through barriers and distortions in order to expose a person's subjective truths, the objective form of which is the manifestation of his or her suffering. The most important criterion for truth is the pressure of this suffering, which can be measured by its effect on the human psyche. Opposed to this is the *juridical framework,* whose main features are its public nature, its distrustfulness, and its critical approach. A precondition of the legal discourse is the clear alternative of truth versus lies, which is established with the aid of external evidence and has to lead to a decision in the form of a verdict of innocent or guilty.

In other words, the legal framework leaves no room for therapy, and the therapeutic framework has no place for judgment. Memories, then, are reconstructed differently in different environments according to a different ethos. This can be illustrated by the response of a therapist who was challenged to exclude from his work memories that could not be subjected to external verification. He wrote:

I have interest in such a task. I am a therapist, not a detective. When clients come to me and genuinely risk disclosing and exploring their life's issues, the therapeutic relationship must be, as it always has been, a sanctuary – confidential, private, and safe. I work in the aftermath of shattering experiences. I am less interested in the pinpoint accuracy of each detail of clients' memories than I am in the chronic, debilitating aftereffects. I am not piecing together legal evidence. It is well beyond the usual clinical covenant for therapists to enter into their clients' lives as researchers, detectives, solicitors or professional chroniclers.[46]

Our glance at the American debate shows that even the most private memories when reconstructed within particular institutional frameworks can have considerable social and political consequences. It also shows opposing approaches toward the question of stability: trauma therapists start out from the fact that memories can be preserved for decades and then rediscovered, whereas cognitive psychologists basically question the very possibility of such durability and, like the

---

[46] David Calof, "Facing the Truth about False Memory," *Family Therapy Networker*, Sept. and Oct. (1993), 44.

constructivists, consider memory to be subject to unlimited changes of form and substance.

Criteria for the Credibility of Memory in Oral History

Whereas autobiographers such as Rousseau and Antin have little difficulty living with the separation of objective truth and subjective authenticity, this is quite untenable for another group of professional specialists – namely, oral historians. As these have expanded their historical sources to include personal memories and have developed the "memory interview" into a new instrument of research, they are dependent on objective criteria for verification. As interviewers they take over *two* roles that, as seen in the case of the false memory debate, are quite diverse and even incompatible: on the one hand, they must establish an empathetic, intersubjective relationship with their interviewees, and on the other, they must probe the memories critically, testing their historical value. Lutz Niethammer, a leading pioneer in German oral history research, writes that memories

are not objective reflections of past realities or perceptions. The memory interview is determined, rather, by the fact that the memory selects and condenses, that elements are newly combined and verbally articulated through more recently acquired patterns of interpretation or modes of communication, and that they are influenced by changes in socially accepted values and by the socio-cultural interaction that takes place during the interview itself.[47]

As the truthfulness of subjective memory is notoriously unreliable, no historian would use interviews as a method of establishing facts if there are more objective sources available. Oral history is based on an irreducible gap of uncertainty between the truths of the interviewer and those of the interviewee. The interrogator cannot give unconditional credence to his partner, nor can he simply discount whatever information he is given. What he is concerned with above all is the participant's subjectivity, which has always been eliminated from the abstract, academic construction of history. His aim is to incorporate this subjectivity, with the calculated effect of shattering the concept

---

47 Lutz Niethammer (ed.), *Die Jahre weiss man nicht, wo man die heute hinsetzen soll. Faschismuserfahrungen im Ruhrgebiet. Lebensgeschichte und Sozialkultur im Ruhrgebiet 1930–1960*, Vol. I, Berlin, Bonn 1983, 19.

of history as a unified whole under the pressure of a plurality of histories.[48] In order to show its importance as an "intervention of the memory into historical research," oral history requires a specific critical approach to its sources, and a methodological way of processing and evaluating its material; but above all the interviewer must recognize that he himself, by his very presence, his questions, and his reactions, is also taking an active part in the (re)constructive work of remembering.

In addition to a properly structured critical and hermeneutic approach to texts, Niethammer recommends a few rules of thumb to act as criteria of verification:

- Inconsistencies or striking discrepancies in emphasis or matters of detail on the one hand and the situational framework on the other can be taken as indicating the spontaneity and authenticity of "encapsulated memories."

- One device by which the interviewer may get at an authentic memory is to ask about the *first time* something was experienced. It may be supposed that the freshness of the first experience will have resulted in a stronger impact and it can consequently count as a more reliable recollection.

- However, according to researchers into oral history, the authenticity of a memory is reinforced not only by the affective power and extraordinariness of an experience, but also by its opposite, namely routine and repetition. The very ordinariness of everyday life seals memories by keeping them below the surface of verbal articulation. What has never been discussed will never be reinterpreted; it congeals in a state of latency that preserves the "innocence" of memory.[49] In this state routines and situations that were once important are remembered as images without the addition of a narrative structure or an articulated meaning.[50]

- On the other hand, a well-structured memory suggests that it has been transformed by retrospective processing and adaptation to current value systems.

---

[48] Niethammer, "Fragen – Antworten – Fragen," 405 (see Chapt. 9, n. 4). I am grateful to Ute Frevert for this reference.

[49] Niethammer, *Die Jahre weiss man nicht . . .*, 29.

[50] Niethammer, "Fragen – Antworten – Fragen," 405.

The secret patron saint of research into oral history is Marcel Proust, who introduced the basic opposing categories of *mémoire volontaire* and *mémoire involontaire*. For historians who work with oral sources, as for Proust himself, the reliability of memories depends on their stability and their intactness. The historian – and also, incidentally, the psychoanalyst – can make best use of those memories that have been least shaped by consciousness and instead have been stabilized by affect or by their state of latency.

Interest in the *mémoire involontaire* is, however, perfectly compatible with constructivist premises in oral history. Like Halbwachs, who introduced the social frameworks of memory, Niethammer speaks of "settings" and the "specificity of socio-cultural arrangements," in which memories are interactively produced and evaluated. With his systematic description of these frameworks, Niethammer confirms the observation that the status of memory changes from a psychoanalytical context to a legal one. Characteristic of the *psychoanalytical setting* is the fact that it is

shut off and sheltered from the public, in order to promote perception of the unconscious and the process of transference. The relationship is established at the desire and the cost of the patient; the service of the analyst consists in a dual role, which he is qualified to fulfill by his theoretical training and, above all, by his own intensive experience in this situation. [...] The truthfulness of the memory of the person under analysis consists in an extended self-perception of parts of his (usually childhood) life history and in agreement with the analyst as to their meaning.

Cross-examination in court, on the other hand, is

an information process relating to a particular set of facts and conducted by agents of the state who in this process exert their monopoly on state power, to which those affected must generally subjugate themselves against their will. [...] The truthfulness of the memory is established independently of the person remembering, in a regulated process of investigation and provision of evidence, by way of multiple documents and plausibility.

In an *interview for social research*, the initiative depends "on the researcher, who in accordance with the public response and the specialized equipment or purposes of evaluation, sets out to produce a suitable text. The interviewee is not questioned as a unique person, but as a representative of social status and opinions, modes of behaviour or forms of expression. [...] All statements made in interviews involve acts of remembering, though for the most part their content is interesting not for the subjective rendering of the past, but for its social relevance to the current situation."[51]

The "Truth" of False Memories – Four Examples

FIRST EXAMPLE: Let us return once more to Mary Antin, the Jewish immigrant to the United States from Polotzk, who stuck so obstinately to her "false" memory. Looking back at an important point in her life – the death of her grandfather – she reflected self-critically on her first memory. However, when she came to the seemingly insignificant detail of the flowers in the neighbor's garden, she defended her memory most emphatically against the possibility of error. Dahlias or poppies – why such emphasis on a minor detail? Dahlias have to be planted and are to be found in rural or Biedermeier-style flower gardens, whereas poppies bloom in the fields or wherever the wind blows them. In defending the flowers of the garden in Polotzk, Antin is emphatically defending the garden of her memory, around which she has built an invisible fence. Nothing must intrude on it from a later time to change the image, least of all poppies, which are a familiar symbol of forgetfulness. To her, remembering means first and foremost preserving at all costs, holding onto a sensuous experience that is forever lost, even at the expense of objective verification (see p. 243 with the full citation).

When I referred to this example in a lecture at the Getty Center in Santa Monica, I provoked a storm of controversy. Susan Sontag, who was in the audience, took up a very definite position: she was vehemently opposed to the erosion of objective truth by subjective memories, which she regarded as being bound to their historical value as eyewitness accounts. With typical forthrightness she declared: "If the garden crumbles without dahlias, then let it crumble!"

There is a great deal to say in favor of this viewpoint. The point here is certainly not to go in for a subjective relativization of reality and discard the norms of an objectively valid and generally acknowledged truth. This was a discussion, however, not about the nature of reality

---

[51] Ibid., 397, 435.

but about the nature of memory. Antin's emphatic championship of dahlias against poppies seems to harbor a truth about the way memory functions, which cannot be uncovered if the problem is stated in the simple terms of true versus false. The truth that we can derive from Antin's false memories, as I suggested earlier, lies in the apodictic nature of affective memories. They are incorrigible and nonnegotiable, because they stand or fall by the vividness of their emotional impact.[52] It was the discussion in Santa Monica that set me off on the trail of the paradoxical truth of untrue memories. Once I had embarked on such a quest, my ears remained pricked for similar cases in which manifestly false recollections are combined with a certain claim to truth, and I now offer three more examples that have come to my attention.

SECOND EXAMPLE: Dori Laub, a psychoanalyst who worked as an interviewer for the "Video Archive for Holocaust Testimonies" in Yale, recounts the following story. He was conducting an interview with a Jewish survivor who had been deported to Auschwitz and told him of her experiences there. The woman was in her late sixties, and told her tale in a monotonous voice, but when she came to the uprising of the prisoners in October 1944 her whole countenance changed. Intensity, passion, and color animated her narration. "All of a sudden," she said, "we saw four chimneys going up in flames, exploding. The flames shot into the sky, people were running. It was unbelievable."[53]

At this point, Dori Laub, the professional analyst and interviewer, changed into a subjectively involved listener who complemented the report with his own imaginative support. In fact, he turned into a witness for the witness. These are his words:

There was a silence in the room, a fixed silence against which the woman's words reverberated loudly, as though carrying along an echo of the jubilant sounds exploding from behind barbed wires [...] It was no longer the deadly timelessness of Auschwitz. A dazzling, brilliant moment from the past swept through the frozen stillness of the muted, grave-like landscape with dashing

---

[52] See Martin Walser, who emphasizes the fact that it is not possible for him to "instruct his memories with the aid of later acquired knowledge." In *Über Deutschland reden*, Frankfurt a.M. 1988, 76.

[53] Shoshanna Felman and Dori Laub, *Testimony. The Crisis of Witnessing in Literature, Psychoanalysis, and History*, New York and London 1992, 59. Dori Laub's chapter has the heading: "Testimony and Historical Truth."

meteoric speed, exploding it into a shower of sights and sounds. Yet the
meteor from the past kept moving on. The woman fell silent and the tumults
of the moment faded. [. . .] The gates of Auschwitz closed and the veil of
obliteration and silence, at once oppressive and repressive, descended once
again. The comet of excitement and alertness, the explosion of animation
and resistance, faded and disappeared into the distance. (59)

Here, Dori Laub's description provides an impressive enhancement
of the witness's account. Not only are the scenes of the uprising painted
in vivid colors for the reader, but Laub also records a precise correspondence between the drama of the report and the animation of the
reporter. This animation in turn is described in terms of an impact,
which hits the woman with the force of a meteor and makes her
relive the past moment in the present. Metaphors like meteor, comet,
and explosion on the one hand, and frozen, tomblike stillness on
the other, underpin the account of the uprising with a mimetic gesture, thus reenacting the recounted events in the interview room and
passing the emotional impact onto the reader.

A few months later, Laub had an opportunity to present this testimony at a conference. The historians who were present, however,
responded in a very different way, and argued that the testimony of
this witness was not correct. It was not four chimneys that had been
blown up in Auschwitz, but only one. In view of revisionist propaganda,
they felt obliged to protect historical truth from being compromised
by false testimony. Against this verdict of the historians, Laub tried to
plead for the truth of the woman's false memories: "The woman was
testifying," he claimed,

not to the number of chimneys blown up, but to something else, more radical,
more crucial: the reality of an unimaginable occurrence. One chimney blown
up in Auschwitz was as incredible as four. The number mattered less than the
fact of the occurrence. [. . .] The woman testified to an event that broke the
all compelling frame of Auschwitz, where Jewish armed revolts just did not
happen, and had no place. She testified to the breakage of a framework. And
that was historical truth. (60)

He then goes on to draw very precise borderlines between the psychoanalytical and the historical interview. A decisive point is how to
deal with silences. As an analyst he is careful to adapt to the limitations of the interviewee's knowledge and feelings and not to confront
her with the more comprehensive knowledge he has gained from

hindsight. Only by preserving this dividing line between the knowledge of the interviewer and that of the interviewee is it possible to elicit genuine testimony: "It was clear to me that only if this price of respect was paid, respect towards the compulsions and borders of silence, could that which the woman knew in a manner that none of us knew, that is to say her own particular testimony, be put into language and heard by us." (61)

THIRD EXAMPLE: This, too, is an interview, though of a very different kind. On May 7, 1995, a day before the 50th anniversary of the end of the war, Hendrik Werner – a postgraduate student in Konstanz – spoke with Heiner Müller. His subject was the mechanisms and constraints of private and public memories. In this context, Werner asked Müller about the possibility of his writing an autobiography. The answer was as follows:

Real memory needs the work of formulation. It is possible that in this process something emerges that may not stand up factually, but is still a sort of real memory. For example: I remember quite clearly the moment described in *Krieg ohne Schlacht*, on 17 June 1953, when I saw Stephan Hermlin get out of the underground in Pankow smoking a pipe – but the underground wasn't running that day. And Hermlin maintains, as he has always done, and he is probably right, that on that day he was in Budapest and not in Berlin at all. [...] I can't explain it, but it's a memory that is probably composed of quite different impressions, recollections and facts, but this is more correct for me than Hermlin having been in Budapest on that day.[54]

In his approach to memory, Müller also explicitly dissociates himself from the historians. For him memories are not documentary fragments that can be put together in a coherent historical pattern, but they are experiences compressed under the emotional pressure of an historical moment. The truthfulness of memory can consist in the distortion of facts because, like exaggeration, memory records moods and feelings that cannot be described in terms of facts. Consequently, memories, even if they are manifestly false, may reveal a truth on another level. Of course atmospheric truth cannot simply take the place of factual truth. It is possessed of no comparable, indisputable evidence such as that which underpins historical truth, but it needs a psychoanalyst or an artist to grasp the essence of it.

---

[54] "Verwaltungsakte produzieren keine Erfahrung." Zum Supergedenkjahr: Heiner Müller in conversation with Hendrik Werner (May 7, 1995 in Berlin), Ms., 41.

FOURTH EXAMPLE: In a short essay on Saleem Sinai, the narrator of his novel *Midnight's Children,* Salman Rushdie takes an unusually direct look at false memories. He talks about himself and describes a personal experience in a language that might almost have been taken over from Heiner Müller and Mary Antin:

> I myself have a clear memory of having been in India during the China war. I "remember" how frightened we all were, I "recall" people making little nervy jokes about needing to buy themselves a Chinese phrase book or two, because the Chinese Army was not expected to stop until it reached Dehli. I also know that I could not possibly have been in India at that time. I was interested to find that *even after I found out that my memory was playing tricks* my brain simply refused to unscramble itself. It clung to the false memory, preferring it to mere literal happenstance. I thought that was an important lesson to learn.[55] (The italics are Rushdie's.)

Rushdie transforms into literature what he has learned from his own memories. He does not do this, though, with the deliberate literary subterfuge of the "unreliable narrator," but with a gradual, exploratory probing, such as might accompany the invention of new narrative techniques. At first he was annoyed by the mistakes in his text that were pointed out to him by readers, but then his attitude changed: "Its wrongness feels right," he says in the essay. He therefore left the mistakes as they were and even highlighted them and elsewhere he introduced new ones. "I went to some trouble to get things wrong." Whereas the unreliable narrator can be identified as such by the reader, who sees through him and can estimate the distortion of the narrative, Rushdie's narrator is unreliable in a very different way. The fact that he makes blunders about Hindu mythology and the Bombay bus system, rankings in the Pakistani army, and brands of cigarette, will not upset most of his readers because they will never know. And so it is hard for them to fully appreciate the method of writing that Rushdie has unveiled to us in this essay.

His concern here, though, is with something very important: he calls it "memory's truth": "It is memory's truth, he insists, and only a madman would prefer someone else's version to his own." (25) In

---

[55] Salman Rushdie, "Errata: Or, Unreliable Narration in *Midnight's Children*," in: Rushdie, *Imaginary Homelands. Essays and Criticism 1981–1991,* London 1992, 22–25; here, 24.

search of this he sees himself as a companion to Marcel Proust; but there is one major difference between the situation of the modern narrator as compared to that of the postmodern: whereas Proust was separated only by time from the experiences he wanted to describe, Rushdie is separated both by time and by space. The veil that stands between him and his past has thickened through migration, and the hope that individual memories might still be able to filter through this veil becomes ever more illusory:

When I began the novel my project was somewhat Proustian. Time and migration had placed a double filter between me and my subject, and I hoped that if only I could imagine vividly enough it might be possible to see beyond those filters, to write as if the years had not passed, as if I had never left India for the West. But as I worked I found that what interested me was the process of filtration itself. So my subject changed, was no longer a search for lost time, had become the way in which we remake the past to suit our present purposes, using memory as our tool. (24)

WAR TRAUMA IN LITERATURE

Trauma is understood here as a physical imprint of excessive affect that cannot be transposed into language; it resists shape and reflection and therefore cannot assume the status of memory. Remembering requires a certain degree of self-distancing that makes it possible to engage with the self, talk with it, double it, reflect it, distort it, stage it, and experience it; this is precisely what does not happen with trauma that binds an experience tightly, inextricably, and inextinguishably to the person involved. The metaphor I use for this complex state is "bodily inscription."

One specific variety of this is war trauma or "shell shock," which was first diagnosed and treated as an epidemic of male hysteria during World War I. In the 1880s and 1890s Charcot, Janet, Freud, and Breuer had experimented with hypnotherapy in the treatment of hysteria, but had then to a degree abandoned it in favor of talking cures. Twenty years later, however, hypnosis made a comeback when in World War I the aim was to send psychically disturbed soldiers back into battle and to help war veterans readjust to society. Such disturbances manifested themselves as varying states of amnesia, insomnia, disorientation, depression, and even blindness and deafness – all physical symptoms that could be traced back to repressed emotions. It was assumed that just like hysterics, soldiers traumatized in battle were suffering from specific memories that had made themselves inaccessible by splitting their personalities; these memories, it was thought, could be liberated through a trancelike repetition of the scenes of terror, and thereby definitively purged. This treatment did indeed result in a swift restoration of the "manly virtues," but it also caused controversy among the specialists, because many considered this hypnotherapy and emotional catharsis to be not so much a matter of raising the patient's consciousness as exorcising memories, which thus constituted a therapy of forgetting.[56]

We now look at literary presentations of shell shock in two American texts set in World War II. One is by a man who lived on the East Coast of the United States and was descended from German immigrants, and the other is by a woman who lives in the region of the border between New Mexico and Arizona and is descended from Laguna Pueblo Indians.

Trauma and the Fantastic – Kurt Vonnegut's *Slaughterhouse Five*

"One of the main effects of war, after all, is that people are discouraged from being characters."[57] These are the words of Kurt Vonnegut in his novel *Slaughterhouse Five* – a literary reworking of his memories of World War II. We may define "characters" as "men of action" in the Bergsonian sense: "The man of action is characterized by the ability to invoke pertinent memories while maintaining an insurmountable barrier in his consciousness that separates him from his chaotic and incoherent memories."[58]

The man of action – and Bergson was certainly thinking exclusively of men – is distinguished by this ability to keep his memories under control, which Nietzsche described as the dominance of the will over memory. Kurt Vonnegut presents himself as just such a man in the first chapter of the novel, in which the narrator introduces himself and his project. As a young man he was posted to France as an infantry scout

---

[56] Ruth Leys, "Traumatic Cures," in Antze, Lambek (eds.), 103–145 (see Chapt. 7, n. 19).

[57] Kurt Vonnegut Jr., *Slaughterhouse-Five or the Children's Crusade. A Duty-Dance with Death* (1969), London 1991, 119.

[58] Translated from Henri Bergson, *Matière et mémoire*, Paris 1896, 166.

for the American forces, where he was captured by the Germans and taken with other prisoners-of-war to Dresden. Here, he lived through the bombing raids carried out during the night of February 13, 1945. It was inevitable that a writer such as Vonnegut would eventually give literary form to such biographical experiences. "When I got home from the Second World War twenty-three years ago, I thought it would be easy for me to write about the destruction of Dresden, because all I would have to do would be to report what I had seen. And I thought, too, that it would be a master-piece or at least make me a lot of money, since the subject was so big." (2)

The subject, as he was soon to discover, was in fact too big to pass through the needle's eye of memory and narrative. World War I techniques employed by Hemingway of precise, emotionless observation and reporting were no longer an option. The figure of the neutral observer had disappeared along with the ideals of tough masculinity, asceticism, and endurance. Vonnegut's novel is significant as an early example of how literature can process trauma. It was written during the 1960s after a cultural change of values connected to the "Peace Movement" and the war in Vietnam. This change brought an end to the postwar period, and the the war could be viewed and reconstructed in retrospect through different perspectives. The literary project is given a kind of baroque framework on the title page:

Slaughterhouse-Five / or / The Children's Crusade / A Duty-Dance with Death / by / Kurt Vonnegut / a fourth-generation German-American / now living in easy circumstances / on Cape Cod / (and smoking too much), / who, as an American Infantry Scout / *hors de combat* / as a prisoner of war, / witnessed the fire-bombing / of Dresden. Germany, / the "Florence of the Elbe," / a long time ago, / and survived to tell the tale. / This is a novel / somewhat in the telegraphic schizophrenic / manner of tales / of the planet Tralfamadore, / where the flying saucers / come from. / Peace.

He begins the novel with the failure of his project. Like Bergson's man of action, Vonnegut had first tried to take control of his memories. Because memories were the stuff out of which his novel was to be made, he first of all had to go in search of them. He made contact with a wartime colleague whom he hoped would help trigger his memories. Vonnegut describes how the two veterans try to gather their memories: "So we tried to remember the war [...] but neither one of us could remember anything good." (10) The net result of all their efforts was a handful of irrelevant details that were not "much to write a book about." The road from recollected memories to the novel had turned out to be a cul-de-sac. This was due partly to the scarcity of memories that they could conjure up spontaneously and partly to the rules that govern the writing of novels. Vonnegut's capacity as a professional writer had suddenly become an obstacle. He had not expected his attempts at fictionalizing the material of memory to result in such failure: "As a trafficker in climaxes and thrills and characterization and wonderful dialogue and suspense and confrontations, I had outlined the Dresden story many times. The best outline I ever made, or anyway the prettiest one, was on the back of a roll of wallpaper." (4)

The conventions and structures of fiction with which he was so familiar were simply of no use in this case. On the contrary, as became more and more apparent to him, they offered him a dangerous invitation to falsify. Not only did his tools of the trade now abandon him, but he also had to make himself abandon them if he wanted to write his Dresden book, because it obviously required a totally different method from those he had used previously. What path remained open to him, then, if those of personal recollection and fiction were now closed? Historical and biographical trauma clearly demanded a different literary technique, and it needed to be radically experimental – different even from those used in the "new" and "avant-garde" novel. Therefore he devised an original form, which "is so short and jumbled because there is nothing intelligent to say about a massacre." (14) In this introductory chapter he asks what one can expect of a book written by someone who has looked back and turned into a pillar of salt. Someone who continues to bear in him the silence that followed the massacre – a silence that only the birds could break. The last words of the novel are "Poo-tee-weet." And, yet, there is method in this mad way of describing trauma that we might summarize under two headings: collage and science fiction.

"Collage" – The tried and trusted backbone for fiction is a storyline – a constructed plot that moves phase by phase through a linear chain of events, which according to Aristotle is made up of beginning, middle, and end. This narrative structure is as basic as it is unavoidable; only with an enormous effort can one circumvent it, and in order to do so one requires some kind of counter-model.

Vonnegut's counter-model is the collage – a spatial arrangement that brings (or forces) heterogeneous elements into unexpected constellations. As a technique, the collage entails not only a degree of chance but also one of violence, which in terms of a narrative can be expressed verbally: it "breaks" the spine of narrative, which is the chronological sequence of events; it "disrupts" connections and casts the fragments into arbitrary patterns. Collage is not just a loss of order – it shatters order.

The main character that Vonnegut invents for his novel, Billy Pilgrim, is suffering from shell shock. His psychological condition manifests itself specifically in the fact that he has lost his sense of time. He finds it impossible to orient himself in time or remain continuously within one time frame. Uncontrollable somatic associations lead him from one period to another, and therefore past, present, and future are all the same to him. Thus the novel itself continually journeys forward, backward, and sideways through different layers of time, combining different threads and experiences in a kind of palimpsest, moving from one event to another with the speed of light: France and Germany – 1944 and 1945; a psychiatric hospital – 1948; when the hero's daughter gets married and he is robbed by the crew of a flying saucer – 1967; and the day of his death, February 13, 1976, which takes place on the 31st anniversary of the bombing of Dresden.

Vonnegut stages trauma as temporal rootlessness. The hero's first encounter with this strange affliction coincides with his capture by German soldiers just outside of a Belgian village. The trauma leads to an extension of perception that shatters the borders of consciousness and memory. At this moment Billy Pilgrim goes backward in time to before his birth, and forward to 1967 when he drives in his Cadillac to a Lions Club meeting. "Billy's smile as he came out of the shrubbery was at least as peculiar as Mona Lisa's, for he was simultaneously on foot in Germany in 1944 and riding his Cadillac in 1967." (43) The reference to Mona Lisa in a war novel at the dramatic moment when the hero is being taken prisoner is just one surprising detail among many that are typical of the carnivalesque style of this book. Mona Lisa's smile is not, however, just a comical intrusion on the grimness of war; if we bear in mind Pater's description of this smile, it is also a sign that the frontiers of historical time are being transcended.

As a "time spastic" – the name given to his illness – Billy Pilgrim cannot help sliding from one period to another. This shows just how violently the trauma has broken the continuum of time, which itself is an unstable social construct. Anyone who does this, and even steps beyond the boundaries of birth and death, has lost all connections, hopes, and fears. To use an expression coined by the philosopher R. W. Emerson, he has become a "transparent eyeball," with no anchorage in the body or the earth. On his freewheeling journey through time, Billy simultaneously has everything behind him and before him, including the catastrophes of the Dresden bombing, a later air crash, and his own death.

This state of fluctuating consciousness – not unlike an "LSD trip" – is linked to a principle of representation that condemns Billy to passiveness and makes him the helpless vehicle for involuntary memories and anticipations. Such inaction is precisely the opposite condition from that described by Bergson and Nietzsche in relation to their man of action. The power to conjure up memories deliberately has been completely switched off, and instead he is flooded with a plethora of uncontrolled and uncontrollable images. These move in and out of time and space as if passing through a revolving door. Some of Billy's memories function in just this manner as recurrent signals that are condensed into verbal leitmotifs. Examples of these are memories charged with an overdose of affect, such as the barking of a dog or feet blue with cold, which automatically propel the perception/memory/narrative off onto another time level.

"Science fiction" – The genre in which time travel appears commonplace is, of course, science fiction. Vonnegut does not shy away from associating the psychiatric syndrome of shell shock with the clichés of this genre, and he even adds to timelessness the phenomenon of weightlessness. Billy is temporarily abducted and taken to another galaxy, and as a result he is able to gain an overall view of the world from the perspective of a timeless extraterrestrial. The books that are written on this other planet are no longer held together by chronology: "There is no beginning, no middle, no end, no suspense, no moral, no causes, no effects. What we love in our books are the depths of many marvellous moments seen all at one time." (64)

Vonnegut has invented a childlike figure whom he makes into the defamiliarizing bearer of his own autobiographical experiences. This character confronts the whole world of war as a complete outsider. Dissociation, as staged in his psychic drift through time, is symptomatic of trauma. It is, however, as mentioned earlier, given an almost carnivalesque stylization, which makes it part of a trauma therapy conducted through the literary medium. It is through this playful defamiliarization that Vonnegut is able to allow the events of war to come close to him while at the same time keeping them at a distance.

In the middle of the book, the focus switches to the connection between literature and trauma. In 1948 Billy Pilgrim spends a few months in an American military hospital where his roommate, who reads nothing but the science fiction of one particular author, keeps him supplied with plenty of reading material. We are told that "they were re-inventing themselves and their universe. Science fiction was a big help." Why this insistence on science fiction in the novel? The genre takes on a special role in a world that – under the impact of trauma – has lost its realistic shape and is therefore constantly being fictionalized. To put this in more general terms, the trauma of the world war has shattered the structures of real-life experience and the standards of normality; in order to go on living, it is essential to find new means of orientation. A patient in the book holds the psychiatrists responsible for this task: "I think you guys are going to have to come up with a lot of wonderful new lies, or people just aren't going to want to go on living." (73)

Wonderful new lies are indeed mass produced by science fiction, with its promise of new depths, of simultaneity, of transcending death.[59] Vonnegut used this uncommitted fiction of fantasy as a kind of alibi, as a "heterotopos" that enabled him to write down his own trauma and that of the war itself.

Trauma and Ethnic Memory – Leslie Marmon Silko's *Ceremony*

Our second literary example of war trauma is *Ceremony* by an author who is a Laguna Pueblo Indian and lives in a reservation on the border between Arizona and New Mexico. Once again the main subject is

---

59 What was called esotericism in the 18th century (Emanuel Swedenborg) became science fiction in the 20th. The borders of discourse and the standards of truth had shifted.

the trauma of a war veteran who undergoes therapy that initially is unsuccessful but is later successful. This therapy focusses on the link between trauma and identity. The trauma dramatically highlights the identity problem of the hero, who is of mixed race: during the war he is made to feel like a full American, but afterward he returns to being one of a discriminated minority.

They were America the Beautiful too, this was the land of the free just like teachers said in school. They had the uniform and they didn't look different no more. They got respect. [...] The war was over, the uniform was gone. All of a sudden that man at the store waits on you last, makes you wait until all the white people bought what they wanted. And the white lady at the bus depot, she's real careful now not to touch your hand when she counts out your change.[60]

After the war, these former heroes are broken men, alienated from their origins, and given over to alcohol, violence, and crime. After unsuccessful psychiatric treatment by white doctors in white hospitals, who try to individualize the trauma and keep it on a purely psychological level, the hero Tayo decides to try out the talents and practices of the native shamans.

The novel begins with the nightmares and hallucinations that Tayo suffers on his return from a Japanese prisoner-of-war camp. He had been incapable of carrying out an execution order in the jungle of a Pacific island because he thought the Japanese soldier he was supposed to shoot was his uncle. Even though the difference between friend and foe was repeatedly explained and demonstrated to him, the logic had suddenly fallen apart in his eyes. In this situation a bodily reaction took control of him. "He felt the shivering then; it began at the tips of his fingers and pulsed into his arms. He shivered because all the facts, all the reasons made no difference any more; he could hear Rocky's words, and he could follow the logic of what Rocky said, but he could not feel anything except a swelling in his belly, a great swollen grief that was pushing into his throat." (8–9)

Tayo remains in thrall to certain traumatic scenes that unexpectedly keep coming back to him with all their original force through harmless, everyday images. Then and now cannot be separated

---

[60] Leslie Marmon Silko, *Ceremony*, Harmondsworth 1986, 42.

because the past is locked into the present and continually impinges on it. As with Billy Pilgrim, Tayo's shell shock is manifested through his loss of any sense of time: "Years and months had become weak, and people could push against them and wander back and forth in time." (18) The novel stages trauma therapy as a search for lost identity. In the end the healing process is indeed achieved, not by shock treatment or medication, but by a ceremony in which the mentally damaged individual finds himself again through an ethnic identity that transcends the individual. The connection between sickness and belonging is unfolded as a process of initiation, in the course of which the disturbed individual's identity is brought into contact with cultural memory. The oral transmission of the Pueblo Indians is similar to that of the Australian Aborigines in that it is not only anchored in their bodies but also inscribed in the topography of their land. The land plays a major role in the therapy. The loss of identity is equated with the loss of any sensual connection with the land, and a cure can only come about through the gradual restoration of this connection.

Tayo's search for his lost identity is a long and difficult one. He is tempted by his opponent Emo, another American Indian war veteran, who goads him on with alcohol-inspired vehemence:

"You know," he said, slurring the words, "us Indians deserve something better than this goddam dried-up country around here. Blowing away, every day. [. . .] What we need is what they got. I'll take San Diego. [. . .] We fought their war for them. [. . .] But they've got everything. And we don't got shit, do we? Huh? [. . .] They took our land, they took everything! So let's get our hands on white women!"

While the rest applaud him, the eyes of the equally intoxicated hero alight on the label of the beer bottle. It shows a foaming spring with the words "COORS BEER, brewed from pure Rocky Mountain spring water, Adolph Coors, Co., Golden, Colorado." "He looked at the picture of the cascading spring of the bottle. He didn't know of any springs that big anywhere. Did they ever have droughts in Colorado? Maybe Emo was wrong: maybe white people didn't have everything. Only the Indians had droughts." (55–56)

Laguna is a reservation that constantly suffers from drought. The division of land, with the rich and fertile areas going to the whites and the dried-up barren parts to the Indians, is blatantly unfair, but the novel makes it clear that even this perception is in line with the white perspective. It is this greed and possessiveness that destroy all connection with and understanding of the land. Such polarizations spark aggression and lead to endless conflict. In the novel, this kind of thinking is labeled "witchery" and presented as a mechanism that aims at universal destruction. The "ceremony" of the title mobilizes the forces that run counter to this destructive mechanism.

The hero gradually learns that there is a different quality in the land that goes beyond matters of barrenness and fertility and has nothing to do with its immediate usefulness. He discovers its life. The land lives in its animals, its sensual perceptions, and above all in its stories. Regaining the land means regaining its stories, which are written into its topography. The land is much more than the provider of materials; it is cultural memory, and it is with this that the protagonist must restore his bond. The land is filled with age-old tales, and Tayo learns to read and tell his own story as part of them. Indian folklore – myths, legends, songs, puzzles, prayers – permeates the novel like a web of interwoven threads. Wherever the trauma has torn holes in the pattern and damaged consciousness (the psychoanalyst Lyman Wynne speaks of "thought disorder"), these narrative elements restore a structured perception. The damaged psyche has to learn afresh how to form Gestalten, and this sense for patterns, connections, correspondences, and relationships builds up a web that gradually covers and closes the gaping wound of the trauma.

Just like the white doctors, the Indian medicine man is unable to heal the trauma. Old Ku'oosh, the shaman whom Tayo consults at the suggestion of the grandmother, has to admit that this case exceeds his powers. He can do no more than declare that the world order is as delicate and vulnerable as a spider's web, and he has to confess that he lacks the means of counteracting the destruction unleashed by the white man's power. In this posttraditional, qualitatively changed world, he can no longer repair the broken threads of cosmic symbols. However, Old Betonie is another medicine man, and his wisdom does not end where the white man's power begins. He does not try to resist this power, but instead integrates it into his stories and into the pattern of his cosmic vision. Indian traditions have been overtaken by western civilization, and so they can no longer provide stable, reliable structures; he therefore replaces the traditional rituals and ceremonies with the open form of a story that shifts and changes in its search for its own ending – an ending that is yet to be found or invented. The model form of "ceremony" thus does not yet exist – it must be found in the course of the quest. The crucial word within this context is "transition," which opens up a perspective that goes beyond established goals and values. In the novel, this perspective is shared by those who live in the space between races, languages, and cultures.

"'It strikes me funny,' the medicine man said, shaking his head, 'people wondering why I live so close to this filthy town. But see, this hogan was here first. Built long before the white people ever came. It is that town down there which is out of place. Not this old medicine man.'" (117–118) The cultural memory of the Indians, as embodied by the medicine man, goes back much further than that of the white immigrant. And this memory is a vital resource in dealing with the personality disintegration brought about by the trauma. Reactivating it entails breaking out of the vicious circle of destruction and exploitation and gaining a detached and superior vision. That is why Old Betonie can laugh in the midst of the no-man's-land between railway lines and rubbish dump: "He laughed. 'They don't understand. We know these hills, and we are comfortable here.' There was something about the way the old man said the word 'comfortable.' It had a different meaning – not the comfort of big houses or rich food or even clean streets, but the comfort of belonging with the land, and the peace of being with these hills." (117) This is a perspective that at the time the hero is still unable to share. He is not yet in a position to understand the new meaning of the old word "comfortable": "the special meaning the old man had given to the English word was burned away by the glare of the sun on tin cans and broken glass, blinding reflections off the mirrors and chrome of the wrecked cars in the dump below." (117)

From the Native American point of view, the war trauma is not written only in the bodies of the soldiers; the nuclear weapons industry, with its ever increasing potential for destruction, has also inscribed itself into the body of the earth. That is why trauma therapy can never be purely individual, but must encompass the macro-history of the equally traumatized land. As a result, the trauma of the young Indian soldier and the possibility of nuclear global destruction must be seen and treated as a single disease. The topography of the Laguna region, which is alive with Indian myth and history, is also the topography of nuclear research. The first atom bomb was detonated in Trinity Site, and the laboratories in which the foundations were laid for these weapons of mass destruction are situated in the Jemez Mountains, "on land the government took from the Cochiti Pueblo: Los Alamos, only a hundred miles northeast of him now, still surrounded by high electric fences and the ponderosa pine and tawny sandrock of the Jemez mountain canyon where the shrine of the twin mountain lions had always been." (246) Here, in one place, two worlds meet that are far apart: those of Indian mythology and western technology. The only vision of unity that Tayo sees at this moment is the catastrophic one of universal destruction:

From that time on, human beings were one clan again, united by the fate the destroyers planned for all of them, for all living things, united by a circle of death that devoured people in cities twelve thousand miles away, victims who had never known these mesas, who had never seen the delicate colors of the rocks which boiled up their slaughter. [. . .] He cried the relief he felt at finally seeing the pattern, the way all the stories fit together – the old stories, the war stories, their stories – to become the story that was still being told. (246)

The imminent danger of universal destruction, this buildup of the forces of "witchery," requires an even more comprehensive vision that must encompass the story of destruction to avert its otherwise fatal course. This story must be invented by humans who in turn must be invented by the story. This all-embracing tale activates the oldest of cultural memories – that of the cosmos, which man cannot have at his disposal because he himself is contained by it. The stages of the symbolic action that are to create the structure of the initiation ceremony finally converge in a consciousness that extends in ever wider circles. The Indians were there before the white man came, and the stars were there before the Indians came. The constellation of the stars is thus the signature of a cosmic memory that encloses all others: "The stars had always been with them, existing beyond memory, and they were all held together there. Under these same stars the people had come down from White House in the north. They had seen mountains shift and rivers change course and even disappear back into the earth, but always there were these stars." (254) The therapy consists in learning to form a new relationship to the world. In the case of the Indian war veterans, whose cultural traditions have already been destroyed by dispossession and extermination and whose individual identity has been shattered for a second time by the war, this means finding a perspective that will free them from their passive role as victims. The core of identity, of a new self-awareness and self-confidence, is not to be based on power but on meaning. At the end of the process lies the insight that the white settlers who drove away, dispossessed, or slaughtered the Indians have never succeeded in taking their land from them. It continues to belong to them so long as they continue to belong to the land and are "comfortable" there, so long as "the ear for the story and the eye for the pattern were theirs; the feeling was theirs; we came out of this land and we are hers." (255)

The two American novels, one from the 1960s and the other from the 1970s, look back on World War II traumas from a distance of more than two and three decades. The contexts of these memories clearly changed in the United States during those decades. Although both authors participate in the continuous unease relating to the collective American identity, the consequences of this disorientation take them in very different directions. Vonnegut was writing at the height of the anti-(Vietnam)-war protests, and his program of postheroic global pacifism is linked to an infantilization of culture in the male imagination. The men of action have been dismissed, and from Holden Caulfield to Billy Pilgrim the child emerges as father of the man. The carnivalesque hero Billy Pilgrim wanders like a Shakespearean fool or a latter-day Don Quixote through a world that has been destroyed by the militarism of the men of action. His trauma holds fast to memories that cannot give way to the normality of the postwar era, but instead they shatter the continuity of experience and thus the capacity to act and to form identity. Through allusions to the trivia and the clichés of popular science fiction (like being kidnapped by aliens in a flying saucer, or making love to a Hollywood sex kitten in outer space), the trauma is translated into phantasmagoric unreality. Fragmented experience and withdrawal from reality typify this drift through the world of the imaginary, which should also be seen against the background of the rapidly expanding drug culture of the time. Vonnegut does not necessarily suggest to his readers that Pilgrim's perceptible weakening of consciousness is to be regarded as a form of clairvoyance. Nor is it Vonnegut's aim to cure the trauma. His interest lies much more in creating a literary correlative through which the workings of the trauma might be manifested.

Silko, as a woman writer, deals with war trauma from the perspective of an ethnic minority in America, whose collective history has already taken on the features of a trauma. For her the individual's condition is bound up with the traumas not only of American Indian history but also of global nuclear destruction. She too develops new techniques to give literary form to the trauma. Instead of pop culture and its links with the imaginary, she turns to Indian folklore and its links with cultural memory. Just like Vonnegut, she departs from conventional linear narrative and structures her novel like a collage with an associative network of patterns. However, she goes even further by doing away with the organizational principle of dividing her book into chapters; instead of blank spaces and numbers she uses scraps of traditional Indian folklore signs, threads that are consistently woven into the web of the text.

Unlike Vonnegut, Silko presents not only the manifestations of the trauma but also its cure, which gives her text the dynamics of a narrative and performative progression, that is, of the outer form of a story, even though there is nothing predetermined about the manner in which it unfolds and which indeed remains open right to the end. The healing process is staged as a search for and discovery (or invention) of identity; the decisive orientation for this lies in the hero's own forgotten traditions anchored in the cultural memory of his tribe. The renewal of this identity is linked to his bond with the land, which is to be restored not through reconquest but through narrative and memory. Silko is not concerned with the weakening of consciousness but with its expansion, and she presents this change as an open process – open for the hero to explore and for the reader to participate in.

11

Places

"The soil is sacred," he said. "But I wish it grew more potatoes."

Ernest Hemingway, *A Farewell to Arms*

If we elide both voice and look, or allow them to slip away as purely phe-
nomenal, what is left? What "demeure," substance, rock, foundation,
house, path?

Geoffrey Hartman, *Saving the Text*

When people fall silent, the stones will cry out.

J. G. Herder, *Briefe zur Beförderung der Humanität*

THE MEMORY OF PLACES

The expression "the memory of places" is both convenient and evocative. It is convenient because it leaves open the question of whether
this is a *genetivus objectivus*, meaning that we remember places, or a *genetivus subjectivus*, meaning that places retain memories. It is evocative
because it suggests the possibility that places themselves may become
the agents and bearers of memory, endowed with a mnemonic power
that far exceeds that of humans. Starting out from the evocative powers of this ambiguous expression, I take a closer look at what "memory
of places" might entail.

"Great is the power of memory that resides in places (tanta vis
admonitionis inest in locis)" wrote Cicero, thereby providing us with

a starting point for our investigation.[1] The great theorist of Roman mnemotechnics had a very clear notion of just how important places were in the structure of memory. As its building blocks he introduced images and places (*imagines et loci*), with images being used for the affective imprinting of particular forms of knowledge, and places for their order and their recoverability. Cicero himself made the step from mnemotechnics as the art of recollecting to a culture of remembrance based on concrete historical sites when he discovered that impressions received at a particular historical location were "more vivid and sensual" than those created by hearsay or reading.

Even if places themselves have no innate faculty of memory, they are of prime importance for the construction of cultural memory. Not only do they stabilize and authenticate the latter by giving it a concrete setting, but they also embody continuity, because they outlast the relatively short spans of individuals, eras, and even cultures and their artifacts. An entry into this complex field can be provided by a letter that Goethe wrote to Schiller on August 16, 1797.[2] In this, Goethe introduced his friend to ideas that he later summed up in his theory of the symbol. The background to this letter was a deep anxiety that haunted Goethe; it concerned the painful abyss between man and world, subject and object, meaning and being, which left him with the unhappy choice between phantoms to be "brought forth" from his own innermost depths, and the "million-headed Hydra of empiricism." In his search for something to bridge this yawning gap, Goethe devised the symbol. This is a category that extends beyond literature and applies to "fortunate objects" that are able to generate particular feelings in the observer. Goethe was convinced that he owed deep intuitions of generality, "one–ness and all–ness" to the aura of certain objects, and he insisted that it is not the observer who loads them with meaning but that they are significant in themselves.[3]

---

[1] Cicero, *De finibus bonorum et malorum*, with an English translation by H. Rackham, London and Cambridge, reprint 2nd Edition 1961, 392f.

[2] Translated from the correspondence between Schiller and Goethe, Vol. 1, Jena 1905, 415–418.

[3] In his answer, dated September 7, 1797, Schiller disagrees with Goethe: "You make it seem as if this depended very much on the object, with which I cannot concur. Of course the object must mean something, just as the poetic object must be something; but ultimately it depends on the mind whether or not an object is to mean something." Correspondence, 438.

Of particular interest are the two examples that Goethe introduces for such symbolic objects. These in fact are not objects but places: "the square on which I live," and "my grandfather's house, courtyard and garden." The symbolic power that Goethe attributes to these places seems to be connected with memory. Both places embody memories that he shares as an individual but that far transcend his own life. Here, the individual memory gives way to that of the family, and the context of an individual life is inextricably bound to that of people who were once within that context but are now no longer there. Thus in both places, individual memory merges with one that is more general.

Goethe makes it clear that his concern is indeed with the places themselves and not with material objects that still exist as relics of the past. His grandfather's house, which is now nothing but a pile of rubble, is of no importance in itself. In emphasizing this, Goethe suddenly lapses into the language of the property speculator: the building "crumbled under the bombardment but is now, mainly as a pile of rubble, nevertheless worth double what the present owners paid eleven years ago to my family." Just like financial capital, Goethe's symbolic capital lies not in buildings but in land. In order to reveal the capital that lies in the land, however, one needs special training. Goethe describes how systematically, step by step, he seeks to enhance his sensitivity to such symbolic places. He begins with those to which he has close personal ties, for example, those that start him off with "a loving memory." Gradually he intends to move from the "remarkable" to the "significant," whereby the proportion of private memories will decrease and the aura of a particular place will increase:

I am trying to find out here what I can regard as symbolic, training myself especially in strange places that I am seeing for the first time. If one can succeed in this, one should be able – without pursuing the experience far and wide, but by delving into the depths of every place and every moment – still to extract enough booty from familiar countries and regions.

Goethe's symbol theory initially has the character of an open experiment. Having discovered and opened up the horizontal space, he sets out to discover the symbolic depths inherent in the vertical. *Spaces*, in the sense of "familiar countries and regions," are examined, measured, colonized, annexed, and integrated. *Places*, however, where one can "delve into the depths of every location and every moment," still preserve a secret. "Space" becomes a neutralized, desymbolized category of functionality and availability, whereas "place" is charged with mysterious and unspecified significance. These secrets hidden within particular places are what Goethe wants to uncover and carry away with him as booty, like silver extracted from a mine.

GENERATIONAL PLACES

The quality that endows particular places with their special power of memory is, above all, connected to their firm and long-established ties with family histories. The phenomenon of these "family" or "generational" places (as I prefer to call them) has been described by Nathaniel Hawthorne in the autobiographical sketch that precedes his novel *The Scarlet Letter* (1850). There we read:

> This long connection of a family with one spot, as its place of birth and burial, creates a kindred between the human being and the locality, quite independent of any charm in the scenery or moral circumstances that surround him. It is grounded less on love than on instinct. The new inhabitant – who comes from a foreign land, or whose father and grandfather came – has [...] no conception of the oysterlike tenacity with which an old settler, over whom his third century is creeping, clings to the spot where his successive generations have been imbedded. [...] The spell survives.[4]

There is, then, an unbroken generational chain here; although Hawthorne describes the cohesive power of place very clearly, there are also hints that he sees this phenomenon as archaic and out of step with his time. Modern ways of life no longer favor such "oysterlike tenacity" that makes people cling to a particular patch of land; the stubbornness of the old settlers is no longer acceptable when it goes against the modern need for mobility and flexibility. Such generational places are a hindrance to progress. Hawthorne highlights the obsolescence of the territorial way of life by connecting it with instinct. In this context, instinct is part of human nature and it signifies conduct that has not been elevated to the stage of cultural reflection. His

---

4 Nathaniel Hawthorne, *The Scarlet Letter*, New York 1962, 22.

use of language suggests that endurance and continuity are not in themselves civilized values – they establish themselves naturally and are not the product of cultural formation and processing. And so the magic of the place is out of date: the archaic man, the old settler, is not a self-determined individual but is ruled by fate and external forces.

From this negative assessment of the archaic, place-bound settler emerges Hawthorne's contrary image of the mobile modern man. He detaches himself from the old and obsolete power of instinct, and turns away from a value system based on age, tenacity, and continuity. The bond between man and place must be broken, emotional ties cut, and the magic spell of the land overcome if man is to fulfill his civilizing potential. The very choice of his words and images enables Hawthorne to free himself from the old-fashioned structures of thought. With the lightest of touches he switches from the language of land and instinct to that of agriculture and exploitation: "Human nature will not flourish, any more than a potato, if it be planted and replanted for too long a series of generations in the same worn-out soil. My children have had other birthplaces, and, so far as their fortunes may be within my control, shall strike their roots into unaccustomed earth."[5] Anyone who adopts this functionalist perspective will have little sympathy for the principle of continuity, which is here denounced as archaic and instinctive. Modern America must free itself not only from its own past, but also from its ties to tradition in general, such as characterize ancient Europe as well as the American Indian, whose culture is anchored in places and nurtures contact with ancestral spirits. The latter, in general, are not mobile. But modern civilization demands a flexible consciousness that will break free from the forces that bind man to his locality. The binding power of places of memory must be overcome and replaced by neutral space that will lend itself to new quests of exploitation.

The example of Leslie Marmon Silko's novel *Ceremony*, which we discussed in the context of body memory and trauma therapies, shows that a new literature has emerged in the United States that fundamentally opposes this approach and rediscovers the spiritual power of the land. This form of literature, which has nothing to do with

[5] Ibid., 23.

the descriptive "local color" movement, is primarily concerned with recording loss. It gives a platform to those who owned the land before the white settlers took possession of it, and it draws attention to the ways of life, the values, and the myths that were destroyed by colonial invasion. In this context, one might speak of a returning sense of place and its symbolic power – a sense that had been suppressed by the process of modernization. The cultural memory of the Laguna Pueblo is inscribed into the topography of their land, and as Silko's novel sets out to demonstrate, it can be reactivated through the land. Novels like this engender a growing sensibility toward those places that fell victim to white domination. "Dominion and oppression, by subtle or brutal methods of intervention in the lives of people whom the oppressor does not know or understand, destroy the places which are the literal ground of understanding. The Navajo woman who says to developers who have come to take her land, 'If you move me, what will I teach my children?' knows that wisdom and survival are fruits of continuity."[6]

HOLY PLACES AND MYTHICAL LANDSCAPES

Places are regarded as holy if the presence of gods is to be experienced there. Such places are endowed with special taboos. The voice of God speaks to Moses from the burning bush, saying "[...] put off thy shoes from off thy feet, for the place whereon thou standest is holy ground" (*Exodus*, 3, 5). A holy place is a contact zone between God and man.

Before the monotheistic God revealed himself in books, the pagan gods revealed themselves in the world. Their home was not only the heavens, but could also be mountains, caves, groves, springs, or wherever places of worship were erected. The gods of polytheistic religions wished to be approached and worshiped in their own settings, and so people had to go on pilgrimages to the sacred places that were

---

[6] Reyes Garcia, "Senses of Place in Ceremony," *Melus – The Journal of the Society for the Study of Multi-Ethnic Literature of the United States*, 10 (4) (1983), 37–48; here, 37. The essay, which deals with Leslie Marmon Silko's *Ceremony*, describes the theme of the novel as follows: "In *Ceremony* the feeling of being at home and of belonging to the land realized by Tayo derives from a special sense of place that is also participation in culture and community." (40)

their "fixed abode." Outside their territory and its sacred topography, the gods could not be addressed. The concept of an omnipresent God transcending locality (already hinted at in polytheistic religions) is one of the preconditions of monotheism. A particularly impressive instance of sacred topography is the mythical landscapes of the Australian Aboriginals. Their various tribes live in a space that has been precisely marked out, not to say prescribed, by their totemic ancestors. For the inhabitants, this area of land is a sacred text, which is not read and interpreted, but is memorized and periodically recited. The units of the text are the so-called songlines of which each individual and each group possesses and protects fragments of the whole.[7]

In the course of migrations, wars, and conquests an earlier memory is extinguished by "overwriting." This mode of inscribing places is described in the closing chorus of T. S. Eliot's *Murder in the Cathedral.* The lines spoken by the women of Canterbury recall how the sacred landscapes of heathen Antiquity, of which nothing remains except fragmentary relics ("the broken imperial column"), were overwritten with a new memory in the medium of martyred Christian blood:

> We thank Thee for Thy mercies of blood, for Thy redemption by
> blood.
> For the blood of thy martyrs and saints
> Shall enrich the earth, shall create the holy places.
> For wherever a saint has dwelt, wherever a martyr has given his blood
> for the blood of Christ,
> There is holy ground, and the sanctity shall not depart from it
> Though armies trample over it, though sightseers come with
> guidebooks looking over it;
> From where the western seas gnaw at the coast of Iona,
> To the death in the desert, the prayers in forgotten places by the
> broken imperial column,
> From such ground springs that which forever renews the earth

---

7 Bruce Chatwin, *The Songlines,* Harmondsworth 1988, 13: "Each totemic ancestor, while traveling through the country, was thought to have scattered a trail of words and musical notes along the line of his footprints, and [...] these Dreaming-tracks lay over the land as 'ways' of communication between the most far-flung tribes. 'A song', he said, 'was both map and direction-finder. Providing you knew the song, you could always find your way across the country'. [...] In theory, at least, the whole of Australia could be read as a musical score. There was hardly a rock or creek in the country that could not or had not been sung [...] every episode was readable in terms of geology. 'By episode', I asked, 'you mean "sacred site"'? 'I do.'"

Though it is forever denied. Therefore, O God, we thank Thee
Who hast given such blessing to Canterbury.[8]

We can see from this speech how important holy places and sacred
landscapes are in the context of Christianity. The basic human need
for sites and settings that bear the promise of miracles, atonement,
healing, and spiritual renewal has produced institutions like pilgrimages and the cult of relics.[9] Chaucer described one of these groups of
pilgrims, whose destination is the same place of memory immortalized
by Eliot: Canterbury, and the grave of the martyr Thomas Becket.

EXEMPLARY PLACE OF MEMORY – JERUSALEM AND THEBES

In Ancient Israel there were no holy places in which God's permanent
presence could be guaranteed. The only biblical sacred sites were
those of historical memory relating to single encounters with God.
These sites that preserved the memory of historical events were made
into places of memory that gave concrete form and authentication to
the story of God and His chosen people. For instance, after Jacob had
wrestled with the angel, he changed the name of the place to "Peniel"
(the face of God); thus, through the symbolic gesture of giving it a
name, the place was written into the group memory.[10]

The city of Jerusalem is an exemplary place of memory, and it is
particularly instructive for two reasons. First, we can see how such a
location can vary between the sacred and the historical; and second,
how it can become a battleground for rival memory groups.

Dry with thirst, oh let my tongue cleave
To my palate – let my right hand
Wither off, if I forget thee
Ever, O Jerusalem[11]

---

[8] T. S. Eliot, *Murder in the Cathedral* (1935), London 1969, 93 f.
[9] See Friederike Hassauer, *Santiago. Schrift. Körper. Raum. Reise. Eine medienhistorische
     Rekonstruktion*, Munich 1993.
[10] See Geoffrey Hartman's interpretation of Genesis 32:1–23 and 33: "The Struggle for
     the Text," in G. Hartman, Sanford Budick (eds.), *Midrash and Literature*, New Haven
     and London 1986, 3–18.
[11] Heine, *Romanzero* (see Chapt. 5, n. 11).

wrote Heine, echoing Psalm 137. But Jerusalem had not always been a place of obligatory memory. It was David who first made it so when he captured it from the Jebusites and founded David's City on Mount Zion. When he made Jerusalem his new capital, he had the Ark of the Covenant – which until then had been kept in a private house – brought amid much pomp and circumstance to his city. Then his son Solomon built the Temple on Mount Moria ("place of seeing"), this being the historic site where Abraham's sacrifice of Isaac was forestalled at the last moment. With the Temple as the home of God, Israel received its first holy place of divine presence that was no longer simply a commemorative site: "And I will dwell among the children of Israel, and will not forsake my people Israel," God promises in 1 Kings 6:13. With worship now centralized in the Temple of Jerusalem, the other holy places lost their importance. After the destruction of the Temple, however, it was the Torah that took over this function of a central symbol. The scriptures were not confined to any location, and so they became a mobile temple or, as Heinrich Heine called it, a "portable Fatherland," that made possible the survival of Jewish communities in exile. Until Zionism once more turned it into a symbol, Jerusalem remained for the Jews a remote, eschatological place of death, judgment, and the long wait for the coming of the Messiah.

The Christian remembrance of Jerusalem developed quite independently of all this.[12] The "Church Fathers" thought little of the earthly city, and in the allegorical system of four levels of writing, they placed it on the bottom or literal level. When reading the Bible, one had to overcome such spatially concrete meanings in order to attain the heights of those that were more spiritual. Jerusalem was to be sought with the soul and not with the feet. Christian interest in Jerusalem as a holy place did not begin until the 4th century AD, after Saint Helen, mother of Constantine the Great, had discovered the tomb of Christ where she built the chapel of the holy sepulchre. This topographical interest was initially confined to Byzantium, until between the ninth and the twelfth centuries when the historical locations of "the Jesus story" also became important memorial sites for the Church in the western world. After Islam had taken symbolic possession of the city

---

[12] I am grateful to Wolf-Daniel Hartwich for a number of references.

in the 7th century and expressed its own universal claims, Jerusalem became the target for crusades organized jointly by ecclesiastical and secular powers. Only in the 13th century when Frederick II symbolically divided the city into Islamic and Christian places of worship were the Crusades brought to an end. Since then this sacred topography has seen a coexistence between the Christian *terra sancta* and the sacred sites of the Islamic and Jewish faiths.[13]

In Antiquity and during the Middle Ages, cities were rarely founded in neutral areas. The site needed to be endowed with certain advantages that included favorable transport conditions and symbolic importance. The most important sources of such symbolic significance were the localization of myths and the burial places of heroes.[14] *The Greek Alexander Romance* tells how Alexander conquers the city of Thebes and is preparing a bloodbath there. A local poet named Ismenias appears before Alexander to try and persuade him not to raze the city to the ground. He attributes the Emperor's bloodthirstiness to a mixture of blindness and forgetfulness, and so uses memory as a last resort to save Thebes. He begins by reminding Alexander that he himself is descended from the heroic sons of the city, Dionysus and Hercules, and therefore he cannot possibly want to destroy the city of his ancestors, which is a part of himself. At this point, the prose narrative is interrupted by a long poem in which the singer links the topography of the city to its mythical past. Time and space are coupled together through the deictic word "here," which is used to emphasize the rhythm as well as the location of the poem:

> This is the house of Labdacus. Here the unhappy mother
> Of Oedipus bore the murderer of his father.
> Here was the shrine of Hercules, formerly
> The house of Amphitryon; here Zeus slept,
> Joining three nights into one. [...]
> This is the house of Tiresias, the mouthpiece of Apollo.

[13] See Maurice Halbwachs, *La topographie légendaire des évangiles en Terre Sainte*, Paris 1941. Since the 13th century, Muslim families in Jerusalem have been employed as guardians over the sacred Christian sites.

[14] Jan N. Bremmer speaks of "polis talismans" in "Religious Secrets and Secrecy in Classical Greece," in Hans G. Kippenberg and Guy G. Stroumsa (eds.), *Secrecy and Concealment, Studies in the History of Religions* 65, Leiden, New York, Cologne 1995, 60–78; here, 62.

Here lived the thrice-old prophet,
Whom Athena once turned into a woman. [...]
From here blind Oedipus was driven out
... On Creon's orders, his daughter Ismene his only staff.
This river which flows down from the Cithaeron
Is the Ismenus, and its water is Bacchus. [...][15]

However, this mythological tour of the city fails to achieve the desired
effect, for the old stories make as little impression on Alexander as
fabulous genealogies. This is his stern answer:

Do you think you can deceive Alexander by telling
These clever fabrications of mythology?
Now I am going to destroy the whole city by fire
And turn it to ashes; [...]
I order you, Ismenias, the best of the pipers,
To stand beside the houses as they burn
And accompany the destruction of your city
... With the shrilling of your instrument's double reed.[16]

This tale of brutality is relevant to our subject for several reasons.
Alexander is by no means as indifferent to the power of cultural memory as the scene may lead us to believe. With regard to Thebes, he
appears to be dismissive of past memories, genealogies, and myths,
but his attitude changes completely when it comes to his own future
commemoration. He is extremely concerned about his *fama* and, as
we have seen earlier, he is anxious to find a poet who will capture his
immortal glory in verse. Here too, then, we have imperial acts that
overwrite cultural memory, for the conqueror has to create a *tabula
rasa* before he can engrave it with the tale of his own glory.

PLACES OF COMMEMORATION — PETRARCH IN ROME, CICERO IN ATHENS

The importance of generational places arises from the longterm link
between families or groups and a particular location. This also brings
about a close relationship between individuals and the geographical

---

[15] *The Greek Alexander Romance*, 46, ed. Richard Stoneman, Harmondsworth 1991,
81–82.
[16] Ibid., 83–84.

site, for the latter helps to determine their way of life and the nature of their experiences, just as the people impregnate the place with their traditions and their histories. The situation is quite different, however, with places of commemoration, that are marked by rupture and discontinuity, signaling an abyss between past and present. Such places show that a particular story, far from continuing, has come to a sudden, perhaps even violent end. This abrupt discontinuation has its material form in ruins and relics, which stand out against their surroundings – alien structures, fossilized, unconnected to the local life of the present, which has not only moved on but has trampled heedlessly over these disconnected remnants.

Pierre Nora uses two expressions to capture this shift from a place where traditional ways of life were once stable to a place where nothing remains but shattered material links to the lost way of life: it is a change from the *milieu de mémoire* to the *lieu de mémoire*.[17] A place of commemoration is what remains when a tradition has ended and an event has lost its context. In order that such a place may survive and maintain its relevance, it requires a story to support it that can replace the lost *milieu*. The shattered fragments of a lost or destroyed way of life are used to authenticate stories that in turn become reference points for a new cultural memory. The places require explanation, and their relevance and meaning can only be maintained through stories that are continuously transmitted.

The continuity that has been broken by conquest, loss, or forget-fulness cannot be retrospectively restored; however, in the medium of memory we can connect with it. Places of commemoration – where something has been preserved from what has gone forever but can be reactivated through memory – are therefore markers of discontinuity. Something is still present here, but what this demonstrates above all is absence: the present relic denotes an irretrievable past. The sense of the past that arises from places of commemoration is quite different from that which pertains to the firmly established place of genera-tional memory. The former is based on experience of discontinuity, and the latter on experience of continuity.

This truncated past, which can only be grasped by way of remnants and traces, may be of great importance to later times if it can provide

[17] Pierre Nora, "Between Memory and History," 7 (see Introduction, n. 7).

a normative, knowable, recognizable link to the present. Ruins and relics that have survived in the form, say, of piles of rubble that have lain unnoticed and unheeded over a long period of time may suddenly become visible again if a new interest invests them with new relevance. The journeys undertaken by humanist scholars of the Renaissance to sites of Greek and Roman Antiquity are a case in point. "Everything is animated in your holy walls," wrote the tourist Goethe in his *Roman Elegy*, thereby following the humanist instruction that in such places the past is to be encountered as a living presence. This approach embodied in antiquarian tourism was described with great precision by the humanist Justus Lipsius in a letter written in 1578 to a friend who was about to embark on a journey to Italy:

A special emphasis is on the eyes, which in this case are the only true guides to knowledge. Look, you are now off to Italy, which is adorned with fruits, men, cities, famous for speeches and writings. There you will not set foot anywhere or turn your eye, without coming upon some monument or acquiring the memory of some ancient custom, some old story [...]. How great and mysterious is the pleasure of such a view! When those great men enter not only into the mind but almost into the eye, while we step on the ground on which they themselves so often trod.[18]

The long road of the written tradition is brought to vivid life by the short road of autopsy; the spiritual legacy of the past becomes accessible to the senses through the informed eye, as it alights upon visible relics. Through this process – so runs the expectation – a mysterious spark will leap from the past to the present, crossing the gap of time and forgetfulness. Renaissance means rebirth in cultural memory, aided not only by the original texts of classical authors but also by historical sites and their relics.

A few generations before Lipsius and his friend, Petrarch also undertook an educational journey to historic sites of commemoration. In April 1341, he and his friend and patron Giovanni Colonna

---

[18] Letter of April 3, 1578 from Justus Lipsius to the young Philippe de Cannoy, *Justi Lipsi Epistolae, Pars I: 1564–1583*, ed. A. Gerlo, M. A. Nauwelaerts, and H. D. L. Velvliet, Brussels 1978, 199–200, ll. 64 ff. I am grateful to E. A. Schmidt for the reference and German version on which this translation is based.

went for a walk in Rome.[19] Six months later, Petrarch wrote a letter in Latin reminding his friend of their conversation on this occasion:

while we wandered not only in the city itself but around it, at each step there was present something which would excite our tongue and mind: here was the palace of Evander, there the shrine of Carmentis, here the cave of Cacus, there the famous she-wolf and the fig tree of Rumina (better named Romulus), here occurred the death of Remus, here the circus games and the rape of the Sabines, there was the marsh of Capri and the place where Romulus vanished [...]. Here Caesar triumphed, here he perished. In this temple Augustus viewed the prostrate kings and the whole world at his feet [...]; here Christ appeared to his fleeing Vicar; here Peter was crucified; there Paul was beheaded; here Lawrence was burned, and here was his tomb that was opened to receive the body of Stephan the Martyr.[20]

For the two walkers, time is now condensed into space; what time has made invisible through removal and destruction is still mysteriously retained by place. Chronology is turned into a topology of history, and one can make one's way through it step by step over the very ground where it all happened. Through the substance of its material structures, the city of Rome preserves the continuity of its two cultures – the ancient heathen and the modern Christian. Both worlds intersect and merge in this historic site. Petrarch's preference for ancient Rome is balanced by Colonna's love of the Christian city, and the two perspectives blend into a single sacred landscape.[21]

If Antiquity and Christianity blend easily, the same cannot be said for two other worlds: the past and the present. Between them lies an enormous gulf that invisibly cuts the city of Rome to pieces. "Who

[19] This was probably one of the walks they went on together in Spring 1341, after Petrarch had been ceremonially crowned poet there on April 8th. Colonna came from a powerful, aristocratic Roman family, but lived in Dominican monasteries in Avignon, Rome, and Tivoli. See Arno Borst, *Lebensformen im Mittelalter*, Frankfurt a.M., Berlin 1979, 41–46.

[20] Francesco Petrarca to Giovanni Colonna, Fam. VI, 2, in Francesco Petrarca, Rerum familiarum libri, I – VIII, translated by Aldo S. Bernardo. Albany, New York 1975, 291–293.

[21] Legends of the martyrs and saints associated with Christian places of memory are to be found in the *legenda aurea* collected by Jacobus de Voragine in the late 13th century. Concerning the later history of these places, see Karlheinz Stierle, "Der Tod der grossen Stadt. Paris als neues Rom und neues Karthago," in Manfred Smuda (ed.), *Die Grossstadt als "Text,"* Munich 1993.

today knows less about Roman history than the citizens of Rome?" Petrarch asks his friend, and he continues: "I hate to say this, but nowhere is Rome less known than in Rome." The city through which the two friends wander is not that of the contemporary inhabitants, who have lost all contact with the past. The humanist Petrarch, as Arno Borst puts it, lives "in search of lost time." Whereas the vast majority of Petrarch's contemporaries lived only in the present, he embodied a consciousness of broken traditions and forgotten memories together with the dream of a political and cultural rebirth of Antiquity. He was convinced that the loss of identity among contemporary Romans could be cured by the restoration of memory: "For who can doubt that Rome would rise again on the spot if it began to get to know itself?"[22] For Petrarch, cultural identity is based on the kind of cultural memory that he and his friend embody. They are the ones who are able to make the places as silent witnesses of the past speak again, restoring their lost voices. For the text of this memorial landscape can only be read by someone who already knows its content – it entails reading into and not out of the text. A memorial space is projected onto the ruins of the city, which amounts to a kind of screen memory: "the textual space of memory related to Rome is projected on the spot, in Rome, over the remains of the city."[23] The ruins are signs that encode both forgetting and remembering. They denote a past life that has been extinguished and forgotten, defamiliarized and lost in the abyss of history; and at the same time they denote the possibility of remembering, of an awakening in the dimension of memory that brings back to life what time has snatched away and destroyed.

Petrarch and Colonna were not the first to visit historic places and feel a reverence for the lost past. In his *De finibus bonorum et malorum* (45 BCE), Cicero describes how he and a group of friends visited Athens and its surroundings. They became aware that wherever they trod, they "set foot on historic ground." (V, 5) One of the fascinating places of commemoration they visited was the nearby Academy. They

[22] Borst, *Lebensformen*, 42 (see Chapt. 11, n. 19).
[23] Barbara Vinken, "Petrarcas Rom: Tropen und Topoi," in Gerhard Neumann (ed.), *Poststrukturalismus. Herausforderung an die Literaturwissenschaft*, DFG-Kolloquium XVIII, Stuttgart and Weimar 1997, 554.

chose a time when there were not likely to be any people around, because the less one is distracted by signs of contemporary life, the better one can read the traces of the past:

When we reached the walks of the Academy, which are so deservedly famous, we had them entirely to ourselves, as we had hoped. Thereupon Piso remarked: "Whether it is a natural instinct or a mere illusion, I can't say; but one's emotions are more strongly aroused by seeing the places that tradition records to have been the favourite resort of men of note in former days, than by hearing about their deeds or reading their writings. My own feelings at the present moment are a case in point. I am reminded of Plato, the first philosopher, so we are told, that made a practice of holding discussions in this place; and indeed the garden close at hand yonder not only recalls his memory but seems to bring the actual man before my eyes. This was the haunt of Speusippus, of Xenocrates, and of Xenocrates' pupil Polemon, who used to sit on the very seat we see over there. For my own part even the sight of our senate-house at home [. . .] used to call up to me the thoughts of Scipio, Cato, Laelius, and chief of all, my grandfather; such powers of suggestion do places possess [*tanta vis admonitionis inest in locis*]. No wonder the scientific training of memory is based upon locality."[24]

Cicero's interest in the mnemonic value of places clearly reflects his role as the pragmatist of mnemotechnics. In other writings he names images and places (*imagines et loci*) as the building blocks of the art of memory, with particular emphasis on the involvement of the emotions if images are to take up a lasting presence in the mind.[25] The impressions received at the scene itself more "strongly stimulate the imagination and vivify our ideas [*acrius aliquanto et attentius*]" than those received by hearing and reading. The memory of places, however, is very different from places of memory. Whereas the memory of places is firmly fixed to one particular location from which it cannot be separated, places of memory are distinguished by the very fact that they are transferable. The spatial structure of mnemotechnics functions like a plan or a map, released from its concrete place of origin. Through this abstract spatial power, mnemotechnics comes close to writing, albeit a writing that is composed not of letters but images.

[24] Cicero, *De finibus bonorum et malorum*, 390–393 (see n. 1).
[25] See Cicero, *De oratore II, On the Ideal Orator*, 218–221 (see Chapt. 9, n. 7).

The most famous scholar-tourist of Antiquity was a Greek who lived in the 2nd century AD. His name was Pausanias, and he was a citizen of the Roman Empire, which had long since taken over the great historical sites of Greek culture. In 146 BCE the city of Corinth was conquered and destroyed by the Romans, just as almost two hundred years earlier Alexander had conquered and destroyed the Boeotian city of Thebes. Such dates mark the turning points at which traditions and ways of life are suddenly and violently shattered. Pausanias's travels took him to what were once important sites of Greek culture, which now lay in ruins and had given way to fields and grazing sheep. He returned to the place where Cadmos had founded Thebes and by collecting antiquarian information restored the importance of the vanished city in memory. With meticulous attention to detail, he recorded both its historical and its mythical traces, and like an ethnologist traveling around with his tape recorder, he collected the legends that had remained alive there. Unlike the singer Ismenias, however, who tried to get Alexander to change his mind, Pausanias did not vouch for the truth of tradition. "Not far from the gate is a common tomb, where lie all those who met their death when fighting against Alexander and the Macedonians. Hard by they show a place where, it is said, Cadmus (he may believe the story who likes) sowed the teeth of the dragon, which he slew at the fountain, from which teeth men came up out of the earth."[26]

The intensive search for and preservation of such traces transformed the lost culture of Greece into a memory landscape, with the sites of past events becoming mnemotechnical *topoi*. These became places "of sacrifice, foundation, death and invocation. They localize and stabilize mythical memories of death, sacrifice, and bloody conflict, and hence also of the origin of the community as re-enacted in the cult."[27] The relics that Pausanias recorded in his ethnographic inventory once had the documentary importance of testimonials and certificates; they provided the basis for the holiness of temples, the

---

[26] Pausanias, *Description of Greece*. With an English translation by W. H. S. Jones, Vol. 4, London 1961, 213.

[27] Stefan Goldmann, "Topoi des Gedenkens. Pausanias' Reise durch die griechische Gedächtnislandschaft," in Anselm Haverkamp (ed.), *Gedächtniskunst: Raum – Bild – Schrift. Studien zur Mnemotechnik*, Frankfurt a.M. 1991, 145–164; here, 150. See also Christian Habicht, *Pausanias und seine Beschreibung Griechenlands*, Munich 1985.

legitimacy of dynasties, and the legality of possessions. In the 2nd century AD, these documents had irretrievably lost their importance, and yet they were not altogether deprived of their relevance. They became part of the cultural memory of a group that was able to raise its vanished culture to the status of a normative past. The memory work of Pausanias is a paradigmatic example of the dialectics between loss and return, between a historical break with its attendant oblivion and its restoration in memory. The culture that had perished in history underwent a metamorphosis: it became "classical," which means that it reemerged as a normative framework of reference in the cultural memory of a later age.

GENIUS LOCI — RUINS AND NECROMANCY

Peter Burke tells us that the medieval view of the ruins of Rome was different from that of the Renaissance. "They were thought of as 'marvels,' as *mirabilia* – they were taken as given. People seem not to have wondered how they had got there, when they were built, or why the style of architecture was different from their own."[28] In the Renaissance, perception of such ruins was sharpened. The gaze that fell on the fossils of a bygone era could, however, vary considerably. For Petrarch the ruins of Rome were transformed into a memorial landscape in which the history bound up with these places could once more come alive in the memory of the attentive and well-informed observer. As Walter Benjamin put it so elegantly, ruins show how "history wanders into the site."[29] As long as a story is handed down and remembered, ruins remain a support that underpins memory. This is also true of the stories that one invents about them and that wind around them like ivy. But if they are cut off from such forms of transmission, they become fossils and monuments of oblivion. Such ruins can take on a second life in the aesthetic frame of the picturesque.[30] In an age of rapid change and industrialization, the malleable ruins were withdrawn from history and assigned to Nature. At the end of

[28] Peter Burke, *Renaissance*, 2 (see Chapt. 2, n. 46).

[29] Walter Benjamin, *The Origin of German Tragic Drama*, translated by John Osborne, London 1977, 92.

[30] See Edgar Zilsel, *Die Entstehung des Genie-Begriffs*, Tübingen 1926, 62–70, 139–211; Rose Macaulay, *The Pleasure of Ruins*, New York 1966.

the 18th century there developed in England a romanticism of the ruin that aestheticized the architectural remains of past epochs. A distinction was drawn between Greek and Gothic. According to this aesthetic code, Gothic ruins signified the triumph of time over the power of man, which was regarded as a melancholy but not altogether unpleasant idea while Greek ruins denoted the triumph of barbarism over good taste, which was felt to be a discouraging and depressing phenomenon.

In his essays on the high art of "picturesque travel," William Gilpin considered ruins to be the meeting point between art and Nature: "the ruined tower, the Gothic arch, the remains of a castle, and abbeys [. . .] are the richest legacies of art. They are consecrated by time; and almost deserve the same veneration we pay to the works of nature itself."[31] For Wordsworth, ruins were settings purged of history and filled with eternity. In his description of a ruined abbey, the remains of the building have merged with Nature:

> . . . the antique walls
> Of that large abbey which within the Vale
> Of Nightshade, to St Mary's honour built,
> Stands yet a mouldering pile with fractured arch,
> Belfry, and images, and living trees,
> A holy scene![32]

In the midst of a lushly vegetated Nature, which after the rain is seething, dripping, rustling, sighing – in other words, pulsating with life – the song of the wren rings out through the open ruins of the nave transcending the cycle of growth and decay:

> . . . that single Wren
> Which one day sang so sweetly in the Nave
> Of the old church, [. . .] that there I could have made
> My dwelling-place, and lived for ever there
> To hear such music. (II, 125–135)

The picturesque, Romantic ruin does not denote the past so much as timeless continuity. In this state of decay, human culture comes

---

[31] William Gilpin, *Three Essays: on Picturesque Beauty; on Picturesque Travel*, London 1792, 46.
[32] Wordsworth, *The Prelude II*, 103–108.

closer to Nature. For ruins to be read as signs of a specific past, however, what is needed is not an aesthetic but a curious, antiquarian gaze. In this connection, a member of Cicero's touring party made a revealing comment as they wandered around together. He drew a distinction between an illegitimate and a legitimate view of the past:

> "Well, Cicero," said Piso "these enthusiasms befit a young man of parts, if they lead him to copy the example of the great. If they only stimulate antiquarian curiosity, they are mere dilettantism." (*studia . . . ingeniosorum / studia . . . curiosorum.* Cicero, de finibus, V.6).

A study of the past that aims only at knowledge is regarded as illegitimate; one should only retrieve the past from the depths of oblivion in order to revive and transmit it. Reverence is the approach that must be applied, whereas mere antiquarian curiosity is considered the opposite of restoring a living tradition. It is this reverence that guides the reading of the ruins by Petrarch and Colonna who, despite the growing darkness of the age, reanimate the past in their memories. They embody the classical approach of a culture that was able to build a bridge of tradition and memory across the dark chasm of forgetfulness.

If the link between memory and the lost past is broken, places of memory will become unreadable. Nevertheless, they may also give rise to totally new ways of reading. Reverence is then replaced by curiosity. Places of commemoration become archaeological sites, which are deciphered through the expertise of specialists. Where once there were pilgrims, now there will be epigraphers, archaeologists, and historians to take over the painstaking business of grasping the traces – all within the framework of an inquisitive quest for knowledge rejected by Cicero. The spirit of historical research advances at the expense of broken traditions and forgetfulness of the normative past. "The cultural clock," writes George Kubler in *The Shape of Time*, "runs mainly upon ruined fragments of matter recovered from refuse heaps and graveyards, from abandoned cities and buried villages."[33] Does this mean that the memory humans have lost has now been transferred to places? Is it possible that what can no longer be reached by memory can still be grasped indirectly through relics? This indeed is the faith

---

[33] George Kubler, *The Shape of Time. Remarks on the History of Things,* Yale: University Press, 1962, 14.

FIGURE 2. Giovanni Battista Piranesi, Le Antichità Romane (1756).

that underlies the methodical investigation of traces. It establishes an historical consciousness of the past across the gradual disintegration caused by time, which is quite different from Cicero's or Petrarch's emphatic embracing of tradition.

If, however, one looks at the early days of archaeology, the borderline between piety and curiosity easily becomes blurred. As an example, we can take the work of the Italian architectural painter Giovanni Battista Piranesi. In 1756, he published four folio volumes under the title *Le Antichità Romane*. His aim was no less than to "rescue the traces of the Eternal City from the desecrations and injuries of time" (VRBIS AETERNA / VESTIGIA / E RVDERIBVS / TEMPORVMQUE INIVRIIS / VINDICATA). In the Latin title, the words "traces" and "rescue" are placed on their own for emphasis; in the most succinct manner possible, these two terms denote an extraordinarily ambitious antiquarian project (as seen figure 2). With more than 250 etchings, the artist set out to reverse the remorseless march of time and resurrect Rome through his imagination. The enterprise was inspired by an acute experience of loss and destruction. Piranesi had found out that the extensive but already badly damaged burial grounds along the arterial roads of Ancient Rome were rapidly deteriorating. The speed with which they were disappearing sparked off an extraordinary burst of conservational zeal in him. The three-dimensional materials now exposed to their inexorable fate could, thanks to modern techniques of reproduction like printing and copper plate etching, at least be recorded in writing and image and thus preserved for posterity. Writing and image, monument and book were no longer in competition as media of memory, and indeed the book made it possible for the monument to have an afterlife, even if its actual materials vanished from the face of the Earth. In his foreword, Piranesi explains the purpose of his project as a memorial:

As I saw that the remains of the ancient buildings of Rome, many of which are scattered through gardens and other areas used for agriculture, were crumbling away day by day, partly through the ravages of time, and partly through the greed of the owners – who with barbaric lack of feeling secretly tear down the ruins and sell the stones to be used for new buildings – I set myself the task to preserve them in print. [. . .] And so in the present volumes I have depicted the above-mentioned ruins with the greatest possible care: with many, I have reproduced not only the outer appearance, but also the ground plan and the interior. I have distinguished between the individual parts through sections and elevations, and noted the materials and sometimes also the way in which the buildings were constructed, for which purpose I have acquired insights during long years of tireless and most precise observation, excavation and examination.[34]

Piranesi looked at the ruins of Ancient Rome through eyes that were very different from those of Petrarch and Colonna. The two friends confined themselves to the narrow topography of historical sites and legendary relics, assuming that these would be there forever; Piranesi's focus covered the whole area, including the unprepossessing and anonymous monuments of whose fragility and defenselessness he was well aware. For him, the ruin had lost its solid consistency as an allegorical symbol, and had become a transient object. It no longer provided secure support for an invisible past, but was now itself the fragile object of memory, of conservation, of recording and

---

[34] Quoted and translated from Norbert Miller, *Archäologie des Traums. Ein Versuch über Giovanni Battista Piranesi*, Munich 1994, 159.

reconstruction. No matter what we may think today of Piranesi's anti-quarian feat, the fastidious precision with which he collected and eval-uated written documents, and recorded measurements, plans, views, and details, leaves no doubt that his record of the monuments bore the hallmark of a pioneer archaeological publication.

What distinguishes Piranesi from modern archaeologists, however, is the fact that he attached as much importance to the imagination as he did to experience. The blending of science and fantasy was to function well in the work on which his subsequent fame was based. This was the extended version of the *Vedute di Roma*, which he pub-lished himself in 1760. Here he returned to the early cycle of the *Carceri* – fantastic prisons – that so inspired the Romantic imagina-tion. In this new edition, they were given a thorough stylistic rework-ing: the playful sketchiness generally gave way to clarification and an impressive increase in weight and power. But the most important change was the fact that these prison constructions, designed with all the latitude allowed by fantasy, were now provided with historical references and dated as belonging to the early days of the Roman Empire. They became a legendary milestone of the historical imagi-nation, greatly admired by the Romantics. These prison constructions present an "archaeology of the dream" (Norbert Miller), both as the virtual, labyrinthine architecture of the human soul and as the hid-den but permanent substructure of the Roman Empire – subterranean nooks and crannies that stay remote from historical consciousness and are only revealed to the historical imagination. In their new guise, the *Carceri d'Invenzione* present an impressive example of research into a "counter-reality buried beneath the surface of the empirical world."[35]

A hundred years later, when Edgar Allen Poe described his experi-ence of touring the past in Rome, contact with history was compressed into the aura of the relics. In the Colosseum, the visitor was no longer inspired by antiquarian curiosity or by conservational zeal. Among the stones and crumbling columns and pedestals, his one and only focus was his own imagination, as he gave himself over to a host of

[35] Ibid., 151.

vague emotions. Abstraction and emphasis are the obvious traits of this poetry as it strives to capture the feelings of the poet:

> ... grandeur, gloom and glory!
> Vastness! And Age! And Memories of Eld!
> Silence! And desolation! And dim Night![36]

Reverence mingled with a kind of mild horror puts consciousness into a trance, and in the course of the poem the voices of the past begin to speak to it. The stone witnesses break their silence. The poem describes a "Renaissance experience" in the spirit of the 19th century, in which it was no longer the classics and philology that created the links with the past, but a morbid, necromantic fantasy. The message delivered by the stones is awesome, but not particularly informative. In this invocation of the dead, the voice itself seems to be more important than what it has to say:

> We are not impotent – we pallid stones.
> Not all our power is gone – not all our fame –
> Not all our magic of our high renown –
> Not all the wonder that encircles us
> Not all the mysteries that in us lie –
> Not all the memories that hang upon
> And cling around us as a garment [...]

Poe's poem illustrates how in the 19th century the two sides of historicism, philology and fantasy, that Piranesi combined with such virtuosity have been separated. The more definitively the past is seen as being over and done with, the more intensely the imagination seeks to secure it by other means. The historical imagination became an important domain of writers, first and foremost among whom was Sir Walter Scott, the inventor of the historical novel.[37] With his novels as well as his estate of Abbotsford in Scotland, where he amassed his collection of books and relics, Scott was the most active of antiquarians, and through his imagination he reconstructed a past that was able to provide a burgeoning Scottish national consciousness with a solid background and basis.

---

[36] Edgar Allen Poe, "The Coliseum" (1833, 1845), in *The Poems of Edgar Allen Poe*, ed. Floyd Stovall, Charlottesville 1965, 57 f.
[37] See Stephen Bann, *The Clothing of Clio*, Cambridge 1984.

The modern construction of abstract spaces was the most significant precondition for colonial geopolitics.[38] The land had to be stripped of its holiness and its demons before it could be measured out as an abstraction. Whereas past maps of the world converged upon Jerusalem as the holiest of holies, and other places were distributed over the area available, new maps for the first time laid emphasis on the precise specification of the spaces in between. The new organization of space on the abstract basis of a network of coordinates became the principle underlying maps, which could now serve for exact orientation.[39]

Romanticism countered this trend, and thereby brought new honors to the memory of places. Of course the gods were no longer to be found in their former residences – the grottos, springs, groves, mountain tops, or wherever else their temples and chapels had been built. Instead, these places retained their aura as settings in which a long-lost past unexpectedly came back into the present. Romanticism broke with a culture dependent on tradition and succeeded in creating a model of forgetfulness and the sudden return of the forgotten – a model that transferred the processes of culture to the unconscious. In this context, the genre of the Gothic novel provides an apt illustration. Here voices from the past, like that of Hamlet's father, suddenly and shockingly break into a present that has been determined by forgetfulness and repression. The authors of these novels were interested in Gothic ruins as witnesses to a lost feudal era that they were able to bring back to life. One meaning of the word "Romantic" was the imaginary visualization of a vanished age. One might call it galvanizing the past. What had irrevocably disappeared was once more filled with "infusory life."[40] In an increasingly enlightened world, the Gothic novel provided an entrance ticket to a lost world of enchantment where ghosts and signs and miracles were the order of

[38] Space becomes a kind of slate that is wiped clean of old signs so that they can make way for new. This symbolic revision of space as "a neutral grid on which cultural difference, historical memory, and societal organization is inscribed," is dealt with by Akhil Gupta and James Ferguson, *Culture, Power, Place: Explorations in Critical Anthropology*, Durham, NC 1997.

[39] On the subject of colonial space, David Harvey, *The Urban Experience*, Baltimore 1989, 176, writes: "the conquest of space first required that it be conceived of as something usable, malleable, and therefore capable of domination through human action."

[40] Norbert Miller, *Archäologie des Traums*, 100 (see n. 34).

the day. It has been rightly pointed out that the real heroes of these novels are the buildings that are haunted by the ghosts of the past.[41] The more people forget, the more auratic are the places and relics that are left behind. In Gothic novels and tales like those of Poe, buildings become the places of a memory that haunts to those who have lost it, creating stages for the return of the repressed.

GRAVES AND GRAVESTONES

In Romanticism, specific places were not only relevant as the sites for events, but they also took on a new significance as the settings for writing and reading. In the context of a new poetry of nature, wandering and writing complemented each other, with poetry seeking to provide authentic conservation of the specific qualities of a place. This gave rise to "*in situ* literature," whose basic principle is succinctly summed up by Thomas Gray: "Half a word fixed upon or near the spot, is worth a cart-load of recollections."[42] The same applies to reading, and especially to the churchyard poetry so popular in the 18th century. Detailed testimony to this is provided by a letter from Christian Fürchtegott Gellert, describing a painting in which are mixed all the colors of the "memory of places":

Never have I read *Young's Night Thoughts* and *Creuzens Gräber* with a soul so much in tune as during some summer nights, beneath a starlit sky, amid the silent bower of a little garden bordering a churchyard, where ancient sacred lime trees infused with the breath of night rustled shivers into the soul, and from the somewhat distant ruins of a sinking courtly castle, and from her dwellings in the old Gothic church tower the philosophical owl sometimes uttered her hollow cries – Then one finds oneself in a place where the storms of thought thunder down and come to rest, and the soul becomes still, like a still lake in a summer's night, and it is as if one could hear the voices from the graves of the dead which one fashions deep within.[43]

[41] Henry A. Beers, *A History of English Romanticism in the 18th Century*, New York 1899, 253.

[42] Quoted from Malcolm Andrews, *The Search for the Picturesque Landscape, Aesthetics and Tourism in Britain, 1760–1800*, Stanford 1989, 155.

[43] Quoted and translated from Johann Gottfried Herder, *Frühe Schriften 1764–1772*, ed. Ulrich Gaier, Deutscher Klassiker Verlag, Frankfurt a.M. 1985, 490.

The autobiographical writings of Johann Jakob Bachofen, which we have already quoted earlier, also belong in this context. In 1841 Bachofen was appointed to the Chair of Roman Law at the University of Basel, but just three years later he resigned and went on to earn his living as a private tutor. His approach to his special subject was clearly historical: "Antiquity was the attraction that held me, and not what is applicable today, and I wanted to study the true, authentic ancient Roman Law and absolutely not the Roman Law of today."[44] Authenticity, as he discovered, was not just a matter of philological scholarship but also of an intensely emotional study of art. Against the background of the "poverty and barrenness of our present-day world," he cultivated "a deep intensity of feeling" in his dealings with Antiquity. This came about not through classical texts but through material relics, which he called the "wholesome breath of antiquity" (3). For him it was above all the gravestones whose forms and images said more than any words: "What is thought, felt and silently prayed at the grave transcends the power of words; it can only be alluded to and evoked through the symbol with its perpetual form of enduring solemnity." (11) The clarity and the determinacy of the word are contrasted here with the richly suggestive symbol; the former leads to history and the latter to eternity, to the "oldest of peoples" and to "the Earth." As we have seen, word and symbol correspond to a slow and a fast route to knowledge. The slow and painstaking route is that of philology and historical scholarship, whose critical methodology disciplines reason and distances the past from the researcher. The short route is that of the imagination, which grasps what remains fundamentally inaccessible to historical study: the live and direct connection, thus turning the researcher into a medium of sorts. Piranesi knew both routes, developed them separately, and then linked them together – the ascetic way of patient collection, precise and detailed reproduction, and meticulous reconstruction; and the imaginary, illusory approach through the ghostly illumination of inspired subjectivity.

The *genius loci* encountered by Cicero and Petrarch was anchored in live memories of a normative past. The silent ruins could be brought to speak with the aid of traditions preserved by memory. The explanatory inscription attached to the place can help the memory, and its basic

---

44 Bachofen, "Lebensrückschau," 2 (see Chapt. 7, n. 49).

form is the inscription on the grave, with its unchangeable "Here lies . . . ," *hic jacet, po tamun.* Such writing cannot be removed from its specific location; it is itself the emblem of spatial permanence. The "indexical" writing of such an inscription articulates the same "here" that, like a litany, punctuated the wanderings of Ismenias, Cicero, Pausanias, and Petrarch: Xenocrates was *here* and his pupil Polemon was *here*; *here* Peter was nailed to the cross; *here* Paul was beheaded. The act of remembering at these places of memory is encapsulated by the pointing finger – the ruins and relics themselves being nothing but fingers pointing to the particular spot where once there was life and action. While these indicate something that is absent, the grave remains the resting place of the dead (like places that house material relics). It is a place of numinous presence.

In a chapter of Goethe's *Elective Affinities*, there is a detailed discussion of these same questions of fixed places and movable monuments, and of presence and absence. At the beginning of Book Two we read:

> We remember the change Charlotte had made in the churchyard. All the gravestones had been removed from their places and ranged along the walls and around the foundations of the church. The remaining space had been levelled; and [. . .] all the rest had been sown with different kinds of clover, which was now a lovely green and in flower. New graves were planned to start in a certain order from the farther end; but these plots were to be kept level and also sown with clover. No one could deny that this arrangement offered a pleasant and dignified sight to the churchgoers on Sundays and holidays.[45]

Even in the graveyard, Charlotte does not give death precedence over life. In the foreground of her modern order is the cheerful aspect confronting the churchgoer – who "instead of the clumsy gravestones saw

---

[45] Goethe, *Elective Affinities*, 148 (see Chapt. 2, n. 49). For many stimulating ideas concerning this excerpt, I am grateful to Eva Horn and her dissertation on *Trauer Schreiben. Die Toten im Text der Goethezeit*, Munich 1998. It is interesting to note that at around the same time Wordsworth was also preoccupied with the subject of gravestones, and wrote three *Essays upon Epitaphs*, in which he too reflected on modernization and the cult of the dead. For Wordsworth, the importance of epitaphs lay in their close spatial link with the bones of the person they referred to: "which record is to be accomplished, not in a general manner, but in *close connection with the bodily remains of the deceased*": William Wordsworth, *Essay upon Epitaph I (1810)*, in *Literary Criticism of William Wordsworth*, ed. Paul M. Zall, Lincoln 1966, 96.

before him a beautiful bright carpet" – and the practical benefits for the minister. But her enterprise falls afoul of some of the villagers, who in the shifting of the graves see nothing less than an act of *damnatio memoriae*. They object "that the marking of the plots where their forefathers rested had been removed, and that their memory had, as it were, been obliterated by this action. For although the well-preserved gravestones indicated who had been buried, they did not say where; and this where was, as many maintained, really the thing that mattered." (149)

The pros and cons of fixed places of commemoration are then discussed at length. One group argues for the remembrance of the dead, which remains stubbornly linked to the burial place; in a sense, the place of memory has become sanctified – consecrated through the actual presence of the dead person. The other follows the demands of modern life: this group is free from such local reverence for the dead, and prepared to dig up the headstones and transfer them to another monument. "Archaic" sentiment insists on the immovability of the symbol, its adherence to the authentic patch of earth that guarantees the presence of the loved one. It is this presence that is of prime concern, and not the wooden cross, iron cross, or slab of stone – as is explained by a young law student: "It is not the stone which attracts us, but [it is] what lies beneath and has been received by the earth. It is not only a question of the monument, but also of the person: not only of a memory of the past but also of the present. The beloved departed is much closer to us when we see the mound before us – the mound rather than the monument, which is in itself of small significance." (150) The memory of places guarantees the presence of the dead person; the monument, on the contrary, distracts attention from the place and onto itself as a representative symbol. Moving from the archaic monument, which only indicates the concrete place of burial, to the modern monument, which replaces what is lost by a symbol, for some constitutes an original sin and for others the progress of representation: the fetish being replaced by the symbol. In the modern age of mobility and renewal, the tenacious memory of places and the restriction to one spot have become obsolete. Just like Hawthorne, with whom we began this chapter, Goethe's Charlotte gives expression to the modern spirit: "But I must tell you quite frankly that your arguments have not convinced me. The pure feeling of a final, universal equality, at least after death, seems to me of greater comfort than this obstinate, rigid persistence upon our personalities, our attachments, and the circumstances of our life." (150)

The controversy developed in Goethe's novel concerns different cultural practices, linked to an archaic memory of places and a modern memory of monuments. In the former, the power of the monument arose from the deictic "here," whereas in the latter the memory is fashioned by artistic representation. With this move from index to symbol, the sign becomes independent of the place, for what it has to communicate can be expressed anywhere. We may speak of progress in this context if we view the release from binding locations and the resultant mobility as progress in rationality. The basic principles of a place-neutral art of memory via representation are subsequently explained by the architect in charge of the modern design:

"Do you mean to say that everything should pass away without a sign to evoke a memory?" Ottilie asked, in wonder. "By no means!" The Architect continued. "We should not give up the memorial itself, only its position. The architect and the sculptor are anxious to provide humans with enduring evidence of their lives through their art and their handicraft. That is why I should like to see well-designed and well-executed monuments, not standing by themselves or scattered here and there at random, but set up together in a place which promises permanence for them." (151)

The aura that sanctifies the place of memory cannot be translated into well-made monuments. These have been fashioned by the human hand and mind; their message is written in stone, like letters addressed to posterity. Goethe's problem of transferring the memory of places to the memory of monuments has taken on an unexpected relevance in our own time. The murder of European Jews under Hitler's regime has left white spaces all over the map of Europe. Together with the people, centers of Jewish life and culture were obliterated. Little reliance can be placed on an immanent "memory of places" after such violent annihilation and an enforced "forgetting of places." Just as the surface of the water immediately closes after a stone has been thrown in, the wounds of places also close over; new life and new uses soon make the scars invisible. One does not even need Charlotte's carpet of clover – the grass of oblivion grows naturally, and what is actually required is a superhuman effort to preserve the gaps and wounds that are left by destruction.

It is all too clear that a place will only retain its memories if people care enough to make that effort. Since the early 1980s, Eastern Europe has indeed seen an increasing desire to identify and preserve these places of memory in a landscape of oblivion. As the survivors of the Holocaust gradually pass away, the memory of the appalling crimes committed against them must be stabilized by other means. An important commemorative function has been taken over by the places of deportation and extermination. Two generations after the murder of the Eastern European Jews, the region has been transformed into a memorial landscape, visited by groups from Israel, America, and Western Europe. "When finished, these memorials become great tourist attractions, drawing hundreds of Western (mostly Jewish) tourists to villages with little else to offer but this memory of an absence. In lieu of waiting families and communities, monuments built for and often founded by Western visitors now invite survivors to return as tourists."[46]

"I embrace a departed loved one far more readily and more intensely in a burial mound than in a monument," says the law student in Goethe's *Elective Affinities*. But if graves can no longer be visited, because the people have been deported, their families murdered or scattered all over the world, the place memory disappears with them. What remain are relics that, by being processed into monuments, can stabilize a new form of place memory. In Kazimierz, a small village in Poland whose pre-war population was almost fifty percent Jewish, the graves from the Jewish cemetery have been "translated" into a monument.[47] Outside the village, a wall 3 meters high and 25 meters long was erected with a large crack in it. Plastered onto this wall is a frieze of Jewish memorial slabs. These were not only taken from the cemetery but were also dug up from the roads of a former Franciscan monastery that the Nazis had made into their Gestapo headquarters. When reused in the construction of roads, the gravestones had been laid out with their backs on top, thereby erasing all memory of their original form. However, this ensured that the inscriptions were protected from wear and tear, as was ascertained when the stones were excavated from the roads.

---

[46] James E. Young, "Jewish Memory in Poland," in G. H. Hartman (ed.), *Holocaust Remembrance. The Shapes of Memory*, Oxford and Cambridge, Mass., 1994, 228.

[47] Ibid., 215–231.

PLACES OF TRAUMA

Places of memory are those where exemplary deeds have been performed or terrible suffering has been endured. Bloodstained episodes of persecution, ignominy, defeat, and death have a prominent position in the mythical, national, and historical memory, and they become unforgettable if a group translates them into a form of binding remembrance. Places of trauma are different from places of memory because they block the path to such an affirmative interpretation. Religious and national memories are soaked with blood and sacrifice, but they are not traumatic because they have a normative quality and are incorporated into a positive self-image and endowed with collective meaning.

At this point we turn once more to Nathaniel Hawthorne, this time for an example of the traumatic place. As the saying goes, the criminal returns to the scene of the crime. This is the case of the heroine of *The Scarlet Letter*, who has been branded by Puritan society with the letter "A" for adulteress. She returns instead of using her chance to move elsewhere, which would have freed her from her memory and enabled her to forge a new identity:

It may seem marvellous, that this woman should still call that place her home, where, and where only, she must needs be the type of shame. There is a fatality, a feeling so irresistible and inevitable that it has the force of doom, which almost invariably compels human beings to linger around and haunt, ghostlike, the spot where some great and marked event has given the color to their lifetime; and still the more irresistibly, the darker the tinge that saddens it. Her sin, her ignominy, were the roots which she had struck into the soil.[48]

Whereas the place of memory is stabilized by the story that is told about it, with the place supporting and authenticating the story, the defining feature of the place of trauma is that its story cannot be narrated. The narrative is blocked either by psychological pressure on the individual or by social taboos within the community. Expressions such as sin, shame, compulsion, and the force of destiny are screen terms that reinforce the taboo – they indicate that something is not expressed but has been warded off as unspeakable, thus ensuring that it remains inaccessible.

[48] Hawthorne, *The Scarlet Letter*, 83 (see n. 4).

Hawthorne focuses on guilt and trauma as symptoms of a social and cultural "disease" that springs from hypocrisy and lack of self-knowledge. The circumstance that has given rise to all this – an illegitimate child – becomes a "crime" only through the stigmatization of the heroine, together with the repressions and the moral code of a Puritan society. Hester feels compelled to remain in her place of ignominy, where her adultery cannot become a thing of the past but will remain a painful present. The traumatic place retains the infectiousness of the "disease" as a past that will not go away or even fade into the distance. The narrative of Hawthorne's book is a process of working through the trauma, which entails a reversal of values and the construction of a new identity.

Auschwitz

The name Auschwitz has become synonymous with the Nazis' systematic mass extermination of the Jews and other defenseless minority groups. Whereas the verbal associations of the *name* are unmistakable, the meaning of the *place* is anything but clear. Auschwitz the place, according to Jonathan Webber, is "not a museum, even though it seems on the surface to be a museum; it is not a cemetery, even though it has some features of a cemetery; it is not just a tourist site, even though it is often full to overflowing with tourists. It is all these things at once. [. . .] We have no category in our language to describe what this place is."[49]

In order to dissect the elements that have given the name its fixed meaning, so that they can be reassessed in memory, we must as always return to the place itself and the problems connected with it. The many-layered complexity of this place of trauma arises not least from the heterogeneity of the memories and perspectives of those who claim the place as theirs and those who come to visit it. For the Poles who administer the camp in their own country and have made it a central place of memory in the history of their nation's suffering, its meaning is quite different from that of the Jewish survivors, whereas Germans and their descendants will again see it quite differently from

[49] Jonathan Webber, "The Future of Auschwitz. Some Personal Reflections," *Religion, State and Society*, Vol. 20, No. 1, 1992, 83 f.

the descendants of the victims. Different people are affected in different ways and with different emotions. As Ruth Klüger has rightly emphasized: "All those who live in the countries of the West after Auschwitz have Auschwitz in their history."[50] But we also know that the accompanying emotions are just as varied as the individual and collective stories that people associate with this place.

It is the variety of emotions rooted in one and the same place that creates its complexity. For groups of former inmates, the place is filled with suffering, and it provides the concrete basis of their shared experience. For the survivors and their children, who come here to mourn their murdered loved ones, it is above all a cemetery. For those who have no personal links to the millions of victims, Auschwitz is principally a museum that presents the crime scene by way of exhibitions and guided tours. For church or political groups it is a scene of saintly martyrdom, whereas heads of state use it as a platform from which they can deliver their public confessions, admonitions, declarations, aspirations. For historians, Auschwitz is an archaeological site that retains the traces of the past. The place is everything one seeks from it, knows about it, and associates with it. The perspectives are as many and as varied as the camp itself is real and solid. The time has passed when governments tried to transform places of trauma like Auschwitz and Buchenwald into memorial sites with a heroic symbolic choreography and a political message. As the varnish of official "meanings" cracks, a mass of variegated and often irreconcilable memories appears.

These places of trauma have been conserved and made into museums because of the conviction that the mass crimes of the Nazis, from which there can be neither legal limitation of accountability nor historical detachment, must be permanently anchored in historical memory. We expect places of memory to go beyond the provision of information, which we can get from memorials and documents that are independent of place – place should intensify the presence of a past reality through an immediate appeal to the senses. What cannot be conveyed through written or visual media should penetrate deep into visitors at the actual historical scene of the events; in other words, they should be struck by the unfathomable aura of the place. This

---

[50] Ruth Klüger, "Kitsch, Kunst und Grauen. Die Hintertüren des Erinnerns: Darf man den Holocaust deuten?," *FAZ*, No. 281, 2.12.1995.

approach corresponds not only to the age-old desire of pilgrims and travelers to see significant places for themselves, but also to a new form of museology that tries to convey history via lived experience. The purely cognitive absorption of historical knowledge needs to be supplemented and intensified by direct sensual perception and emotional coloring, so that that history is actually "experienced" in a direct and personal encounter.

Krzysztof Pomian, in his research into the collections and the history of museums, uses an example to illustrate the different phases through which an object of presumed historical value must go. His example is a factory, which initially is part of a productive and useful network, but whose machines eventually wear out or become uneconomical and therefore are discarded "after everything useful or sellable has been removed." Our factory, Pomian continues,

... is a ruin, a relic from the past. No consumer goods are produced in it now. It is put on display to the public. The public, sadly or indignantly, sees its walls and machines as a monument to the proletariat or to the captains of industry, to class warfare or to the owner's concern for his employees, a monument to the exploitation of the worker by the bourgeoisie, to the accumulation of capital or, the exact opposite, an image of the spirit of enterprise, the progress of technology, the triumph of the market. Our factory has become a subject of discussion and of gestures, the expression of different attitudes towards the past which it symbolizes. From now on, it functions within a semiotic cycle.[51]

Much of what Pomian says about his disused factory can also be applied to the death factory of Auschwitz. As a relic it is preserved under the condition that it becomes the bearer of new meanings and the concrete support of narratives. Like the objects in a collection, a place of memory also functions within a semiotic cycle. "The function of the factory now consists in its relation to a vanished past. It points to something that is no longer there; it refers to an invisible reality."[52] And again like the collected objects, such places become "mediators between past and present." We might even say they are media of memory, because they also refer to an invisible past and maintain present contact with it.

[51] Krzysztof Pomian, "Museum und kulturelles Erbe," 42 (see Chapt. 2, n. 41).
[52] Ibid., 43.

When Peter Weiss visited Auschwitz in the 1960s, like Cicero and Petrarch he tried to apply his existing knowledge to the place he was viewing. Even though the time gap was far smaller, the blending of then and now in the indexical or deictic "here" was extremely difficult for him, because despite meticulous reconstruction, the task exceeded the imagination of the latecomer to the scene of the past crime:

They came here, in slow procession arriving from all parts of Europe: this is the horizon they could still see, these are the poplars, these are the watchtowers, with the sun reflected in their windows, this is the door through which they went, into the rooms that were bathed in harsh light and in which there were no showers but just these rectangular metal pillars, these are the foundation walls between which they ended in sudden darkness, in the gas that streamed out of the holes. And these words and this knowledge say nothing, explain nothing. All that remain are piles of stones overgrown with grass.[53]

As a visitor after the event, Peter Weiss realizes the overwhelming difference between memory learned and memory experienced: "The living person who comes here from another world has nothing except knowledge of the figures, or written records, of eyewitness accounts – they are a part of his life that weighs heavily on him, but he can only truly grasp what he himself has experienced."[54] Ruth Klüger experienced Auschwitz herself. In her autobiographical novel *weiter leben*, she weighs up the pros and cons of transforming concentration camps into memorial sites. First and foremost, she sees them as a therapeutic aid for the survivors. The reverence, she argues, with which the survivors go on clinging to the place, the stones, and the ashes can be of no benefit to the dead but only to themselves: "The untied knot that is left behind by such a violated taboo as mass murder and infanticide changes into an unredeemed spirit to which we give a kind of home that it can haunt."[55] She does not believe that "one can exorcize ghosts in museums."[56] As a counter to Auschwitz she cites Theresienstadt, where she was able to follow the traces of her memories undisturbed by crowds of visitors and the zeal of the

---

[53] Peter Weiss, "Meine Ortschaft," in *Atlas, zusammengestellt von deutschen Autoren*, Munich 1968, 27–36; here, 35.

[54] Ibid., 36.

[55] Ruth Klüger, *weiter leben*, 70 (see Chapt. 10, n. 32).

[56] Ibid., 75.

conservationists. The little Czech town of Terezìn had resumed its old, humdrum homeliness, and it readily accepted her memories: "Then I wandered through the streets, where children were playing, and I saw my ghosts among them, very sharply and clearly, but transparent as ghosts are and should be, and the living children were solid, loud and sturdy. Then I went away, comforted. Theresienstadt had not become a concentration camp museum."[57]

Concerning those who travel to Auschwitz, Ruth Klüger writes: "Anyone who thinks he has found something there must have brought it with him in his luggage."[58] The survivors who return to this site of horror bring quite different luggage from that of visitors whose knowledge is gleaned only from books and pictures. What they bear is an infinitely heavier load of personal memories and loyalties. It is conceivable that the lighter the luggage, the greater will be the visitor's expectations of this place: what is missing must be offset by the immanent power and the overwhelming evocativeness of the place and its memories.

Underlying such places of memory that have been turned into memorials and museums is a deep-seated paradox: their conservation, which is meant to serve the purpose of authenticity, in fact leads inevitably to a loss of authenticity. By the very fact of their preservation, they have already been covered up and replaced. There is no other way for them to survive. Only a small part can be retained as representative, but even here the crumbling materials must be replaced or renewed. With the passage of time, authenticity must rely more and more on the simple "here and now" of location instead of on the actual relics. Anyone who attaches too much importance to the mnemonic powers of the location will therefore run the risk of confusing the refashioned place he is visiting with the historical place where the inmates lived and died. "I once visited Dachau," writes Ruth Klüger, "because some American friends wanted to go there. Everything there was clean and tidy, and one needed far more fantasy than most people are capable of just to imagine what had happened there forty years earlier. Stones, wood, huts, parade ground. The wood smells fresh and resinous, a fresh breeze is blowing over the parade ground, and those huts almost

---

57 Klüger, *Still alive*, 87–88.
58 Klüger, *weiter leben*, 75.

seem to invite you in. One might associate it with a holiday camp rather than a life of torture."[59]

For Klüger, the survivor who has lived through this life of torture, such places are not only devoid of any immanent memory, but they also distort memory itself. One needs imagination in order to see beyond them and not to succumb to these distortions. For her, the museum quality of the memorial site turns it into a screen memory. If it is not to present its visitors with a fake experience, the illusion of the authentic vision must be countered. The gap between the place of the crime and the place of the visitor must be made obvious, so that the emotional potential mobilized by the place should not lead to a merging of temporal horizons and an illusion of easy identification. "We have no category in our language to express what sort of place Auschwitz is," wrote Jonathan Webber. Klüger searched for a new word to describe Auschwitz, and suggested the following: "The concentration camp as a place? Cityscape, landscape, seascape – there should be a word timescape, to convey what a place is in time, at a particular time, neither before nor after."[60]

Involuntary Places of Memory – the Topography of Terror

In the country of the perpetrators, the towns – especially Berlin – are "an extraordinary storehouse of memories."[61] The American journalist Jane Kramer, who took a close and careful look at Berlin, writes: "Suddenly in the psychological archaeology of the city, which has once again become the capital of Germany, the past has replaced the wall, and nobody really knows what to do with this past, or how to address it, or where to begin with so many memories, while the people who are still able to remember are passing away."[62]

In Germany, "the past" is likely to stand for "the Nazi past." It is interesting to note that the wall, which divided the city horizontally, has been replaced by a vertical shadow line that separates the city's

---

[59] Ibid., 77.

[60] Ibid., 78.

[61] Bogdan Bogdanovic, *Die Stadt und der Tod. Essays.* Klagenfurt, Salzburg 1993, 22; also *Architektur der Erinnerung*, Klagenfurt 1994.

[62] Jane Kramer, *Unter Deutschen. Briefe aus einem kleinen Land in Europa*, Berlin 1996, 17.

present from its past. The marking of particularly memorable places of Nazi history was far from consensual until well into the 1980s; some memorial plaques had been put up on buildings through local initiative to indicate the part they had played in the administration of the Nazi regime, but many of them were soon removed and disposed of.[63] The former headquarters of the Gestapo in the center of Berlin offers a striking example of an involuntary place of memory.[64] Immediately after the war, the buildings that between 1933 and 1945 had housed the Gestapo, the SS, and the security services were demolished. From then on, it was impossible to identify Prinz-Albrecht-Strasse 8 – the official address of the NS headquarters – either on the spot or on maps of the city. The East Germans had renamed this street Niederkirchnerstrasse after the seamstress and Communist resistance fighter Käthe Niederkirchner, who had been murdered at the concentration camp in Ravensbrück. The West German side of the area had been used for many years to transform the remnants of the buildings into rubble: "*Erdverwertung*" [reutilization of earth] was the technical term. In 1981, Bazon Brock seized on this term when he included the area as part of a cultural tour and presented it to the historical imagination. He turned "the reutilization of earth" into an eloquent metaphor for historical change: "There the ruins of what had been were and are piled up, sorted out, and redesignated."[65] One result of this "redesignation" was that the rubble from the Nazi ruins was used for the foundations of Tegel Airport. This combination of demolition, waste, and covering up was later conceived to be highly symbolic. (Brock also noted that for decades the site had been used for driving without a license, *Führerschein*, in sharp contrast to the time after 1938 when "on this very place the *Führer* and his various *Unterführer*, at least were in possession of *Führerscheine* issued by the German people."[66])

---

[63] For example, the memorial plaque at the former Reichskriegsgericht, Witzlebenstr. 4–5, see Peter Reichel, *Politik mit der Erinnerung. Gedächtnisorte im Streit um die nationalsozialistische Vergangenheit*, Munich 1995, 191–192.

[64] *Bauwelt*, Issue 18 (1993), 916–917. See also Reichel, ibid., 196–202.

[65] Bazon Brock, "Geschichte als Differenz in der Gegenwart," in Nicola von Velsen (ed.), *Ästhetik gegen erzwungene Unmittelbarkeit. Schriften 1978–1986*, Cologne 1986, 191–197; here, 194.

[66] Ibid., 195.

In 1983, a competition was announced to turn this area of waste-land into a "memorial park for the victims of National Socialism." The design that won first prize, but was never built, would have sealed off the entrance to the historic site with an imposing structure of steel. The step from forgetting to symbolic remembrance is much shorter than that to the active processing of memory. The status of this site as an historical place of memory was not yet recognized: an application by the Opposition SPD party to excavate the remnants of the build-ings was rejected by the Berlin Parliament on January 31, 1985. A few months later, at a political ceremony to commemorate May 8th, Chancellor Kohl and President Reagan visited the military cemetery at Bitburg, while at the same time in Berlin a symbolic counteraction was taking place. A crowd of people with shovels dug up the land in dispute, thereby contradicting the popular opinion that "there was no longer anything to seek or find in the place of the SS and Gestapo headquarters."[67]

In summer 1985, a systematic examination of the site under the direction of the Berlin historian Reinhard Rürup uncovered the remains of a basement with washrooms and a kitchen area. This was a symbolic breakthrough that, in the very heart of Berlin, established material contact with the recent past and that has been on display since then beneath the roof of an exhibition hall, under the heading "Topography of Terror."[68] *Der Umschwiegene Ort* (the place not talked about), as this Gestapo site was called at an exhibition in Berlin, has become a test case for the way in which German history is to be approached. This archaeological securing of evidence shows clearly what a place of trauma is in the land of the perpetrators: materi-ally in immediate proximity, but worlds away in terms of conscious-ness. These are "stones of provocation," which were laid bare and offered to public view in the face of considerable opposition.[69] Unlike

---

[67] Sibylle Wirsing, "Die Freilegung des Gestapo-Geländes. 'Der umschwiegene Ort' – eine Berliner Ausstellung," *FAZ*, 24.12.1986.

[68] Reinhard Rürup, *Topographie des Anstosses – Gestapo, SS und Reichssicherungshauptamt auf dem 'Prinz-Albrecht-Gelände'. Eine Dokumentation*. Berlin 1987, 10th ed. 1995. See also the Internet page on the Stiftung "Topographie des Terrors."

[69] Jochen Spielmann, "Steine des Anstosses – Denkmale in Erinnerung an den Nation-alsozialismus in der Bundesrepublik Deutschland," *Kritische Berichte* 16/3 (1988), 5–16.

the places of memory marked out by the victims, the Gestapo site concerned a *mémoire involontaire*, a "rumbling" memory brought to light by a sudden act of uncovering. The power of memory in this case asserted itself against a strong desire to forget and to suppress. According to Heiner Müller, traumas are mnemonic dynamite, which sooner or later will explode: "The work of memory and of mourning proceeds from shocks," he said in an interview.[70] Like Nietzsche, Warburg, and Freud he advocates a memory theory that links lasting traces of memory to primal scenes of violence. For him, as for Walter Benjamin, memory is also a revolutionary force that "brings to the fore the blood of forgotten ancestors" together with residual, unresolved issues from the past. This act of revolutionary remembering is the most passionate objection to the suffering and injustice of history.

If Hitler had had his way, he would have followed up his Jewish genocide with a mnemocide. The German memorial landscape would then have looked completely different – Gestapo headquarters would be standing on this spot and there would be no trace left of the extermination camps. But after the collapse of this regime and all the values associated with it, the signs are reorganized: what was once central now becomes peripheral; everything is reversed; the official messenger falls silent, and those condemned to silence speak out; the persecutor and the persecuted exchange their roles and status. Sites of memory differ from monuments, memorials, and rituals in that they are never fully congruous with the meaning given to them in retrospect.[71] As historical sites with their sparse material relics, they are still, for all the symbolic interpretation and exploitation, more than just symbols because they are also themselves. While cultural symbols may be built up and pulled down, the durability of places – which cannot be made to disappear completely even in a new geopolitical order – demands a longterm memory, which provides normative points of reference for the present, but also forces us to be aware of how such norms have changed in historical memory.

---

[70] "Verwaltungsakte produzieren keine Erinnerungen," Interview on May 7, 1995 in Berlin with Hendrik Werner, Ms., I.

[71] This is a reference to the title of Reinhard Koselleck's "Kriegsdenkmale als Identitätsstiftungen der Überlebenden," 255–276 (see Chapt. 2, n. 17).

The Aura of Places of Memory

Human memory does not work according to the comforting and unerring chronological framework of the calendar. It can push the nearest of things into the remote distance, and it can pull the remotest of things into frightening proximity. Whereas chronologically ordered history books provide information for a nation's historical consciousness, the nation's memory finds its expression in the landscape of its places of remembrance. The strange bond between distance and proximity gives them their aura, and through them one seeks direct contact with the past. The "magic" of the place of memory results from its status as a "contact zone." Holy sites that establish a link with the gods have existed in all cultures, and places of memory may be regarded as their modern equivalent, because these too are expected to provide a connection with the spirits of the past. However, what builds such links is very different: in generational places it is the chain of kinship between the living and the dead; in memorial sites it is the reconstructed narrative passed on to new generations; in places of memory it is simply the antiquarian, historical interest; in traumatic places it is a wound that cannot heal.

Walter Benjamin took over the concept of the aura and developed it in his reflections on the connection between art, technology, and mass culture, although he used it to indicate the reverse of the phenomenon we are looking at. His famous definition is: "A strange tissue of space and time: the unique apparition of distance, however near it may be."[72] For him, the experience of an aura does not lie in the directness that brings things nearer, but on the contrary in their distance and unapproachability. What we might have imagined to be near suddenly appears in a different light that takes it away from us. Benjamin attributes the holy quality of the aura to the feeling of remoteness and strangeness. An auratic place in this sense does not promise an unmediated experience; it is, rather, a place where the unbridgeable gap between present and past can be experienced. The place of memory is indeed a "strange tissue of space and time," weaving sensual

[72] Walter Benjamin, *The Work of Art in the Age of its Technological Reproductivity, and Other Writings on Media.* Ed. by Michael W. Jennings, Brigid Doherty and Thomas Y. Levin, Harvard 2008, 14.

presence and historical absence together. Although the hallmark of full authenticity is the solid bond between here and now, the place of memory as a 'here without a now' can only be half authentic. Indeed if one tries to join these two halves together, the place of memory will stubbornly keep them apart as a 'here and then.' Thus the aura of such places lies in their alienation; it consists in a categorical gap that is more difficult to bridge than in an imaginative response to a book or film.

The step from places of generational memory to those of historical memory – from *milieu de mémoire* to *lieu de mémoire* – occurs through changed social contexts and broken cultural frames of meaning. Like tools and utensils that have lost their original function and links with daily life and have been collected as relics by museums, ways of life, attitudes, actions, and experience undergo a similar metamorphosis when they are taken from the context of contemporary life and turned into national and cultural memories. Objects that have lost their living context are similar to aesthetic artifacts that are void of context and disconnected from practical function. This latent aestheticization of objects in a museum corresponds to a latent "auratisation" of relics in places of memory. Nora attributes the transformation from *milieu* to *lieu de mémoire* first and foremost to the dialectic of modernization and historicization. In a process of accelerated renewal and obsolescence, the modern age reinforces permanent changes on the everyday world, which leads to an ever increasing number of museums and places of memory: "Our interest in *lieux de mémoire* where memory crystallizes and secretes itself has occurred at a particular historical moment, a turning point where consciousness of a break with the past is bound up with the sense that memory has been torn – but torn in such a way as to pose the problem of the embodiment of memory in certain sites where a sense of historical continuity persists. There are *lieux de mémoire* because there are no longer *milieux de mémoire*, lived environments of memory."[73]

Nora's paradigm is that of modernity, breaking with tradition, and historicism. However, German places of memory cannot be sufficiently described through this paradigm of innovation. There are today memorial sites of World War II that cover the whole of Europe

---

[73] Pierre Nora, "Between Memory and History," 7 (see Introduction, n. 7).

but have little to do with modernization and much to do with the atrocities of the Nazi regime, culminating in their crime of systematic mass murder. The extermination camps are places of trauma because the unbearable horror of what took place there exceeds the human capacity for understanding and for visualization. Owing to these unimaginable acts, the generational places of a long and live Jewish tradition have been replaced with memorial sites and places of memory. Places of trauma, of memory, and of generations are now superimposed in a memorial landscape like the different forms of writing on a palimpsest.

PART THREE

STORAGE

12

Archives

Ruin hath taught me thus to ruminate.

Shakespeare, Sonnet 64

We should learn to see ourselves as having been, and to see the present as a past.

Bazon Brock

What is a thing? What remains?
What, after all, of the remains?

J. Derrida

Beyond identity and difference lies the realm of the undifferentiated, indifferent, arbitrary, banal, unprepossessing, uninteresting, not-worth-considering, not-identical, and not-different.

Boris Groys, *On the New*

The word "archive" is derived from the Greek *arkhé*, which has a double meaning: "beginning" and "government." Derrida emphasizes this irreducible double meaning when he points out the connection between "commencement" and "commandment." Two further components in his definition of "archive" are "substratum" and "residence"; also integral is the institution of guardians, who watch over the law, recall it to memory, and interpret it. From the very beginning, the archive has always been linked to writing, bureaucracy, records, and administration.[1] Conditions for the existence of archives are

---

[1] Eckhart G. Franz, *Einführung in die Archivkunde*, Darmstadt 1974.

systems of recording that function as external means of storage, the
most prominent being the technique of writing, which takes memory
out of mental storage and fixes it independently of living bearers. In
the early, advanced civilizations of the Near East, writing was used
mainly for economic and administrative purposes; the scribe was a
civil servant *par excellence*, providing a solid base for the King's governance by means of bureaucracy, official records, and chancellorship.
In Egypt, writing helped to establish a complex system of economic
redistribution: all proceeds had to be handed over to the State that
as the central "provider" redistributed them. Thus writing formed the
organizational support for a large-scale network of storage and supply.
Under favorable conditions, certain documents do not decompose
after use but create a residue that can be collected and preserved for
a more or less indefinite future. When such materials are recollected
in a later period, the archive as a "political" memory of administration
and economic organization turns into the archive as an "historical"
witness to the past.

Archival memory of history, then, is preceded by archival memory as governance in the form of testaments, certificates, and documents that serve to authenticate claims relating to power, ownership,
and descent. In the Middle Ages, princes, monasteries, churches, and
cities preserved those documents that served to legitimize groups and
institutions. Derrida sees the archive as fundamentally political: "This
question will never be determined as one political question among
others. It runs through the whole of the field and in truth determines
politics from top to bottom as *res publica.* There is no political power
without control over the archive, if not of memory."[2]

Because control of the archive means control of memory, a political shift of power can lead to changes in the structures of legitimation
being accompanied by changes in the content of the archive. After
political change a new hierarchy of values is constructed and what
was once kept secret – for instance, the Stasi files – now becomes
accessible to the public. The French Revolution resulted in huge
archival changes. Because of this violent break with the feudal past,
previous legal and administrative structures were discredited and

---

[2] Derrida, "Archive Fever. A Freudian Impression," *Diacritics* 25.2 (1995), 9–63; here,
   10–11. Derrida's essay stems from a visit to the Freud Museum in London and is
   mainly concerned with the history of Freud and psychoanalysis.

along with them went the written documents that had authenticated the old order. However, the legal documents that had lost their authority were not destroyed but, on the contrary, collected, for now they took on a new, historical importance as a source of information for professional historians.

The archive is a collective store of knowledge that fulfills several different functions. As with every form of storage, it involves three main aspects: selection, conservation, and accessibility. As I deal with problems of conservation in the next chapter, I restrict myself here to the other two, beginning with *accessibility*. Archives can be either open or closed, and whether an institution is democratic or repressive can be gauged by their accessibility. Athens, for example, incorporated the laws and the citizens' rights that then were fixed and preserved in archives. Such foundational texts enable a group to define itself. In illiberal, totalitarian states the contents are kept secret, whereas in democracies – at least theoretically – they are public property that can be used and evaluated by individual citizens. As Derrida says, "There is no political power without control over the archives, if not of memory." But we have to add: without an archive, there is no public, no criticism, no *res publica*, no republic. Totalitarian regimes tend to limit their storage memory to the confines of their functional memory, whereas democratic regimes tend to expand their storage memory at the expense of their functional memory. Where the archive, like the museum, is public property, it stands under the protection of professional authorities who are responsible for safeguarding the contents through special security measures, such as "bans, inventories, checks, restoration."[3]

The status of the archive as the institutionalized memory of the polis, the state, the nation, or society therefore lies somewhere between function and storage, according to whether it is organized as a political instrument of government or an external depository of knowledge. In totalitarian states, which take central control of the social and cultural memory, or wherever the criteria for inclusion are very narrow the archive will be functional; but the same contents may switch

---

3 Pomian, 57, 59, (see chapt. 2, n. 41). It is, though, self-evident that even in democratic states, such security measures can be manipulated to safeguard the interests of the government, as opposed to those of the general public – for instance, under the cloak of "national security."

to storage mode if, as in the French Revolution, former documents of legitimization are reframed as sources of historical information. After their functional use had been lost they were not discarded and destroyed but submitted to a new critical assessment. "Archives that store material [must] be read and interpreted [...] if their content is to be recalled to memory."[4] As a potential memory or a material precondition for future cultural memories, the archive takes on enormous significance. Furthermore, there is a special functional memory that is part of the archive; it is called "cultural heritage" and is placed in the custody of the archivist, who has to secure it against potential natural or manmade catastrophes such as earthquakes and nuclear war.

The second keyword is *selection*. Initially, the focus was on collecting and preserving documents, but since the 19th century with its enormous increase in storage material the task of disposal has become equally important. Storage capacity is measured by shelf space, and this can be anything between 3 and 55 kilometers or more.[5] The percentage of what is deemed worth saving shrinks to the degree to which the avalanche swells. By the mid-1970s it was estimated to be around one percent.[6] Every period has its own principles of selection and evaluation although these are not always shared by subsequent generations. What is regarded as refuse in one age may be seen as containing invaluable information in the next. That is why archives are places not just of informational continuity but also of informational gaps, and these are by no means always the result of natural catastrophes or wars, but are caused by unavoidable acts of internal disposal which "in hindsight will often be deplored."[7]

The problem of selection plays a special role in two concepts of the archive that involve a metaphorical extension of the term. Neither has anything to do with the institutional safeguarding of material culture. The following definition of an archive offered by Michel Foucault

---

[4] Andreas Schelske, "Zeichen einer Bildkultur als Gedächtnis," in Klaus Rehkämper and Klaus Sachs-Hombach (eds.), *Bild. Bildwahrnehmung, Bildverarbeitung*, Wiesbaden 1998.

[5] Franz, 37.

[6] Ibid., 75.

[7] Ibid., 120.

explicitly excludes any ordinary notion of the archive: "By this term I do not mean the sum of all the texts that a culture preserves to document its own past, or as evidence of its continuing identity; nor do I mean the institutions, which, in a given society, make it possible to record and preserve those discourses that one wishes to remember and keep in circulation." After these negative definitions Focault adds his own:

The archive is first the law of what can be said, the system that governs the production of utterances as unique events. But the archive is also that which determines that all these things said do not accumulate endlessly in an amorphous mass, nor are they inscribed in an unbroken linearity, nor do they disappear at the mercy of chance external accidents; [...] The archive [...] is that which defines at the very root the embodied event of the utterance within *the system of its enunciability.*[8]

A material definition is not enough for Foucault's purpose, which is to highlight the power structure that is rooted in this institution of an archive. For him, it is not a depository of data shut away from social life, but an instrument of repression that restricts the scope of thought and expression. As "the law of what can be said," the archive has changed from being an inert memory of culture to being the program that governs cultural expression. At the same time, this definition is rather nonspecific; the archive as "the law of what can be said" could be easily replaced by the term "discourse." In the light of his transmedial and dematerialized concept of discourse, Foucault disregards the materiality of the archive.

Boris Groys, who sees the cultural archive as a referential framework for "the new," expresses the same reservations and criticizes Foucault's definition as being too immaterial. By contrast, he suggests that one should consider the archive as something real and existing, "and in this sense also threatened with destruction and thus finite, exclusive and restricted, so that one cannot find every possible statement preformulated in it."[9] In his concept of a cultural economy of art, Groys defines the archive (which he equates with museum and cultural memory, but not with the library) as the repertoire of everything within a culture

---

[8] Michel Foucault, *The Archaeology of Knowledge*, trans. A. M. Sheridan Smith, Pantheon Books, New York 1972, 128 f.
[9] Boris Groys, *Über das Neue. Versuch einer Kulturökonomie*, Munich 1992, 179.

that at a given point in time has been evaluated as new. For him the old and the new are dialectically linked, because innovation is the only route that leads into the archive. "Every occurrence of newness results basically from the drawing of a new comparison from something that until then had never been compared because this comparison had never before entered anybody's mind. Cultural memory is a memory of these comparisons, and the new only gains access to cultural memory if it is just such a new comparison."[10] For Groys, the archive is the memory of art into which innovative works have made their way and provide the yardstick by which the originality of new works is to be measured. In other words, he sees it as the basis of comparison by which one can gauge the difference of the new. I return later to Groys, because his interest lies not only in the border between the old and the new, but also in that between the archive and waste.

[10] Ibid., 49.

13

Permanence, Decay, Residue

Problems of Conservation and the Ecology of Culture

In a consumerist culture and with an economy that combines an ever increasing production of goods with an ever shorter cycle of renewal and disposal, the accumulation of discarded objects has become a major problem; the vast amount of highly toxic, nonbiodegradable materials makes this problem into one of ecological survival. Under these urgent conditions, words like "degrade" and "decompose" have acquired a positive connotation. A growing ecological awareness now insists that material products be designed in such a way that after use they no longer survive as relics but instead conform to the pattern of organic decay and renewal, or technological obsolescence and recycling. While in the field of culture men dream of permanence, in the field of waste disposal the dream is of total disappearance. The strong drive to stability, "le dur désir de durer" (Paul Eluard) is ironically counteracted by the ecological value of decomposition. Biodegradability refers to the process through which organic materials disintegrate: "Waste is called biodegradable if it is subject to decomposition through microorganisms."[1] A similar process for mass-produced technical goods is not so easy to devise, although it is the object of intensive research. Cultural creations, however, with aspirations to originality strive to make themselves permanent. What in one field (e.g., that of toxic materials) is a cause of the utmost concern is regarded in the

---

[1] Jay Benforado and Robert K. Bastian, "Natural Waste Treatment," *McGraw-Hill Yearbook of Science and Technology 1985* (New York 1985), 38.

field of culture as the ultimate aim, and art's longing for eternity finds its deadly fulfillment in nuclear waste. Poisonous materials of industry and the aesthetic materials of art are linked in a paradoxical structural homology.

This similarity becomes all the more striking if we consider the specific storage conditions that apply to valuable works of art and to radioactive substances. While cultural objects are to be conserved and secured for posterity, toxic objects are to be disposed of in a manner that will cause the least amount of damage to posterity. Geologists focus their attention and resources on the types of stone and the depths required to store the hazardous waste. This has its exact counterpart in the former silver mine at Oberried near Freiburg, Germany, which is now used as a depository for the "cultural heritage of the nation." Both the storage of hazardous waste and the national heritage are preserved with maximum security.

Deep in the mine, under a protective layer of several hundred metres of hard granite, in bunkers secure from radiation and nuclear attack, lie 750 million microfilms which, in case of catastrophe, will preserve records of the life, thought and effects of our civilization. In the jargon of cultural conservation, this is called "security film." The Oberried mine functions as the "central place of preservation" for the Federal Republic of Germany, and in the Federal Office of Civil Defence in Bonn, one speaks with pride of "the nation's treasure chamber."[2]

In high-grade steel containers sealed with sixteen lots of screws, the disaster-resistant treasure chamber contains a "representative cross-section" of cultural items in coded form: buildings, monuments, art-works, manuscripts, books, and other objects of aesthetic, archaeological, and historical interest are stored on space-saving rolls of microfilm. The containers are metaphorical messages in a bottle for anyone cut off from our world by a catastrophe and unable to view our realities with any other kind of continuity. When the original works and objects have long since disappeared, their images will survive on microfilm. Francis Bacon saw book printing as security against the loss of human memory. Wordsworth, who no longer shared such confidence in the

---

[2] Stephan Krass, "Alexandria – London und zurück. Via Oberried, Bukarest, Paris. Kleine Exkursion für Bibliothekare, Brandstifter und Bunkerspezialisten," *Kunstforum* 127 (September 1994), 126–133; here, 127 f.

memory powers of writing, could already visualize a complete loss of culture through catastrophe. That particular fear has now been assuaged: in the bunker, the dematerialized cultural memory can live on, ready to be resurrected in an unknown future.[3]

It is not, however, just cultural collections that are stored in this manner to protect them against catastrophe for the benefit of an indeterminate posterity. In the United States today there are companies that also make it possible for individuals to send their private bottled message into the distant future. So-called time capsules are enclosed in airtight aluminium containers complete with an official customs seal and holding personal items such as underwear, videos of fitness programs, and homemade cakes.[4] This is now a flourishing industry. Whoever opens these sealed containers will not receive a message, of course, but items that will enable them to reconstruct an everyday culture of the past. The preservation of one's name is thus no longer the privilege of the cultural elite, for even the man in the street now has access to the eternity industry and can fulfill humanity's great dream of communicating with the future. These time capsules demonstrate the extent to which the history of the archive has now become decentralized and democratized. It is not only institutions but also, and increasingly, private individuals that have become archivists and senders of time capsules.

Jacques Derrida, who has spent many years studying questions of being and passing, losses and remainders, has frequently discussed the materiality of information carriers.[5] At the turn of the year from 1988 to 1989, when he wrote a memoir on his late friend Paul de Man, he also articulated his basic thoughts on the problem of permanence and transience. He summarized the case with a question: what can it mean

---

[3] A similar deposit, under the name "The Crypt of Civilization," was made in 1940 by Thornwell Jacobs at Oglethorpe University. The poet and Presbyterian minister assembled a collection the size of a swimming pool. The collection consisted of microfilmed materials that were meant to cover more than 6,000 years of human history. This archive is not to be opened before the year 8,113. See *Newsweek*, April 14, 1997, 10 f.

[4] Ibid.

[5] Derrida, "Biodegradables. Seven Diary Fragments," *Critical Inquiry* 15 (1988, 1989), 812–873 and Derrida, "Archive Fever," *Diacritics* 25.2 (1995), 9–63. I am grateful to Rembert Hüser for these and other references drawn from conversations and from his essay "Art Ratlos," in Renate von Heydebrand (ed.), *Kanon Macht Kultur*, Munich 1998.

to kill a dead man again?[6] He then went on to reformulate the fundamental problem facing the cultural archive: "What will remain of all
this in a few years, in ten years, in twenty years? How will the archive be
filtered? Which texts will be reread?"[7] In this context he attaches particular significance to the waste disposal term "biodegradable," which
has a certain affinity with the term and process of "deconstruction."
Both are concerned with things falling apart, with processes of breaking up and reconstituting, and with a subliminal dissolution of the
borders between remembering and forgetting. The aesthetic "work"
that in the rhetoric of organic unity is held to be "alive," absolute,
individual, and eternal in Derrida's perspective appears as a "wreck"
that has sunk and become wedged into the seabed, covered with algae,
and scarcely visible let alone recognizable as its former self.

   This focus on the physical aspect of the aesthetic work draws attention to its fragility and destructibility. The work of art that has its social
existence between the cyclical poles of veneration and indifference
is equally subject in its material existence to the biocycle growth and
decay. Does this mean that art is on a par with Nature, and culture with
agriculture? Since Derrida distrusts organic rhetoric in all its forms,
he doubts it, and in this context warns against a return to the old
dichotomy of culture and Nature. He tackles the question of what
makes a text destructible or indestructible on the level of its intrinsic
quality. For him, this quality is self-contradictory: on the one hand,
it must be possible to take the work apart, evaluate, and assimilate it
in order to enrich the cultural soil of tradition, but on the other, it
has to preserve its identity and its uniqueness. And so the work of art
is situated at the point of intersection between two economies: that
of agriculture, which is based on assimilation and decay, and that of
culture, which resists decay. But even a Derrida does not abandon the
metaphysics of permanence for he still holds fast to the indestructibil-
ity of great works. For him there are two qualities that preserve a text

---

[6] My reduction of this problem does not do justice to the twists and turns of his prose.
Herewith another sample: "Yes, to condemn the dead man to death: they would like
him *not to be dead* yet so they could put him to death. [...] To put him to death
this time without remainder. Since that is difficult, they would want him to be *already
dead without remainder*, so that they can put him to death without remainder." Derrida,
"Biodegradables," 861.

[7] Ibid., 816.

from oblivion: its personal signature and the resistance created by its manner of writing.

For Derrida, it is already the very act of comprehension that endangers the integrity of a text in so far as it recomposes and metaphorically decomposes it. He therefore equates permanence with resistance to readability. He develops this idea with the aid of the leitmotif of biodegradability:

> In the most general and novel sense of the term, a text must be "(bio)degradable" in order to nourish the "living culture," memory, tradition. [...] And yet, to enrich the "organic" soil of the said culture, it must also resist it, contest it, question it, and criticize it enough (dare I say deconstruct it?) and thus it must not be assimilable ([bio]degradable, if you like). Or at least, it must be assimilated as unassimilable, kept in reserve, unforgettable because irreceivable, capable of inducing meaning, incomprehensibly elliptical, secret. [Such a text...] is proper to nothing and no one, reappropriable by nothing and by no one, not even by the presumed bearer. It is this singular impropriety that permits it to resist degradation – never forever, but for a long time. Enigmatic kinship between waste, for example nuclear waste, and the "masterpiece."[8]

In the cultural archive those texts are destined for permanence that have the erratically unmistakable quality of originality together with a resistant structure. Resistance and persistence, continuity and perpetuity belong together according to Derrida and to Harold Bloom, for whom "strangeness" is the most important feature of canonical texts.[9] Of course what is not mentioned in relation to such authors is who actually adjudges the texts to have these qualities and in what institutional contexts. Also omitted is the question concerning the material media. Derrida was conscious of this gap and noted the need eventually to come back to the materiality of the text: "But it is also necessary to take into consideration the 'supports,' the subjectiles of the signifier – the paper, for example, but this example is more and more insufficient. There is this diskette, and so on. [...] Official institutions are calculating the choices to be made in the destruction of nonstorable copies or the salvaging of works whose paper is deteriorating: displacement, restructuring of the archive, and

---

[8] Ibid., 845.

[9] Harold Bloom, *The Western Canon. The Books and School of the Ages*, New York 1994, 4 ff.

so on."[10] Indeed the practical problems of the present and the future relating to material data-carriers and their storage are so complex that one is inclined, like Derrida, to gloss them over with an "and so on." Archivists are the professionals who are entrusted with the task of selecting and conserving cultural memory. We must therefore consider the practical side of conserving cultural documents, in order to establish how the new electronic storage media will affect the relationship between permanence and decay, recording and conserving.

This development is nicely illustrated by an incident that took place in 1980. The semiotician Thomas E. Sebeok was given an unusual commission: a company that dealt with the storage of radioactive waste in the United States asked him to devise a sign system that would allow for error-free communication over a period of ten thousand years. The reason was clear: the company wished to encode information about hazardous materials and their physical qualities for the generations that would still be affected in ten thousand years' time. The desire to communicate with posterity was not, in this case, inspired by the need for self-immortalization but by the permanence of the danger. In the past, posterity was an authority to whose judgment one appealed and whose protection one solicited; now it became the addressee itself that was in need of protection. Sebeok did not meet the company's requirements; he could not devise a sign system that would be absolutely time-resistant. Instead he showed that such a message could only be given stable form if a "nuclear priesthood" of the relevant experts continually reencoded the information from generation to generation.[11]

This reaction by a semiotician has been confirmed in a different field. Archivists inform us that in their task of conservation they are now confronted by a new set of problems because the archive has become less and less of a storehouse and more and more of a gigantic mechanism of forgetfulness. The invention of writing and even more so of printing produced the vision of eternal communication on permanent material carriers; however, in the electronic age this dream has given way to growing concern over the means of preserving our cultural archive. Durability was once a matter of materials and climatic

---

[10] Derrida, 865.

[11] Manfred Schneider, "Liturgien der Erinnerung. Techniken des Vergessens," *Merkur* 8 (1987), 676–686.

conditions. Documents from Antiquity written on papyrus have only survived in exceptional cases, when the material has been preserved in tombs or caves in arid desert regions. The longterm stability of paper is also questionable. In 1995, the Bavarian State Library set up a department for preservation whose task is to counter the effects of paper disintegration on works dating from the 19th and 20th centuries. But far more dramatic is the problem of conservation in the field of analogue audiovisual media that has produced artworks, monuments, and books whose historical and cultural value has achieved general recognition. These documents can no longer be safeguarded simply because they are on record; they are subject to a creeping but entirely foreseeable process of erosion that has been vividly described as a "smouldering Alexandrian fire."[12] An arsonist is not needed now to extinguish the cultural memory because the data-carriers slowly but irreversably burn themselves up of their own accord.

Erosion in the field of audiovisual media raises another acute problem. It goes without saying that it was impossible for oral cultures to keep archives when writing was the only means of creating a permanent record. Analogue audiovisual media – which also capture dance and music, and thus document the direct sensuality of performance culture – are considerably less reductive. But these unique ethnographic data, which are safeguarding a hitherto undocumented "history from below," are particularly exposed to the process of erosion; after a short period of apparent security in the archives, these oral cultures are in danger of disappearing once more – this time through the transience of the media that have recorded them.

Much more radically than print, analogue media in the form of photography, tape recordings, cassettes, records, videos, and films illustrate all too clearly the problem of archival conservation. Both in their structural organization – low redundancy and high density of data – and in the nature of their material – chemical changes affect their technical quality – they require completely new methods of conservation. In this context there is now a clear change of direction in

---

[12] Dietrich Schüller, "Materialien und Reflexionen," *Das Audiovisuelle Archiv, Informationsblatt der Arbeitsgemeinschaft audiovisueller Archive Österreichs*, Heft 27 and 28 (1990–1991), 17–34; here, 30. My thanks to Herrn Hofrat Dr. Schüller for suggestions and information.

archiving: the search for a permanent data-carrier that will guarantee unending continuity has had to be abandoned, just like the hope for a time-resistant sign system. In its place is the permanent practice of transcribing information into the digital domain. Continuous copying into a never-ending succession of carriers means, of course, that the authenticity of the original material is lost and this in turn opens up a new perspective for cultural archiving:

Such a system is conceivable as a mass store of high capacity, in which every stored item of data can be accessed fully automatically. In times of low utilization, these systems, following prescribed criteria (the age and usage frequency of the data carriers), will test the integrity of the data and in the event of increased error-rates, using the error-correction capacity of fully automatic data carriers, will transfer them to new carriers before interpolations, i.e. concealed errors, can occur. If such a system after, say, ten years becomes obsolete because new mass storage systems work more efficiently and economically, the transmigration of data – transferring them into a new system – will then also follow automatically.[13]

Data that are to be conserved can no longer be conserved in a state of stasis, but must undertake an endless journey, like reincarnated souls, to be reembodied in an endless succession of data-carriers. Through this "transmigration of data" the archive, as the store in which documents are watched over, preserved, and arranged by its custodians, will be replaced in the future by a fully automatic memory that regulates itself because it has been programmed to recall what it permanently forgets. The model of material continuity will give way to that of a dynamic reorganization of data. A fully automatic archive that can forget and remember on its own initiative functions like a megabrain. Indeed in its technical structure it is astonishingly similar to the neuronal structure of human memory. Cultural memory will therefore be removed not only from human heads and bodies, but also from human care and maintenance, and instead it will become the province of technology. Under the influence of commercial developments this technology will keep changing both through the obsolescence of the

---

[13] Schüller, "Von der Bewahrung des Trägers zur Bewahrung des Inhalts. Paradigmenwechsel bei der Archivierung von Ton- und Videoträgern," *Medium* 4 (1994), Year 24, 28–32; here, 31.

hardware and through new storage formats. Thus the archive will eventually become a self-regulating, self-reading, and self-writing memory. The further it withdraws from human organization, the more accessible it will become; because access to all the information will be fully automatic, the data that find their way into the digital domain as writing, image, or sound will be subject to new ways of arranging and networking. Multimedia forms that combine one set of information with another via broadband networks and data highways will eliminate the boundaries between forms of archive, and will facilitate all kinds of navigational possibilities. Digital mass storage promises to free knowledge from its dependence on space and materials and to make access universal, and as we approach this scenario at ever increasing speed, we can already see that the image of the archive as a stable and self-contained place of memory is on its way out.

To come back once more to the specific problem of selection. There is much debate over just how great is the worldwide requirement for storage space "which is indispensable for the preservation of existing material as well as for the efficiency of the approaching age of information."[14] Some are concerned with the technical aspect of this worldwide information explosion, whereas others focus on viewing and securing the national cultural heritage in the light of spreading commercialization and the permanent material loss of cultural, media-related artifacts. In this context, a UNESCO (the United Nations Educational, Scientific and Cultural Organization) project "Memory of the World" was launched in 1992 with a view to examining documents and cultural objects of all kinds in order to set up an international archive and network of digitally stored data.[15] One example of such a project on a national level is that of the Australian National Library, with emphasis on film and sound. "Legal deposit is essential if Australia is to safeguard its published cultural heritage material through its collecting institutions."[16] The background to this initiative was as follows: "the irretrievable loss of a large proportion

---

[14] Schüller. "Jenseits von Petabyte – zum weltweiten Speicherbedarf für Audio- und Videoträger," in *18. Tonmeistertagung Karlsruhe 1994*, Munich 1995, 859.

[15] Schüller, "Datenreduktion und Schallarchivierung," *Das Audiovisuelle Archiv*, 33 and 34 (1993–1994), 4–5.

[16] National Film and Sound Archive, National Library of Australia, Submission to the Copyright Law Review Committee on Legal Deposit, August 1995, 2.

of Australia's audiovisual heritage shows the vulnerability of cultural objects for which there are no legal safeguards in the form of obligatory depositing of copies. Today only five percent of Australian silent film culture is left to us. Many early TV series and radio broadcasts, including almost every episode of the famous series *The Blue Mountains*, are lost to us forever."[17]

Here we have a new problem for cultural memory: what can or should be preserved from our radio, TV, and Internet culture? Is conservational thinking even appropriate in this electronic age, which venerates the principle of renewal and recycling? Where does necessary collecting end and legitimate forgetting begin? There is no simple answer to these questions, and they are a major source of controversy in our time. As far as selection is concerned, the secular democratic states, which have fought against centralized censorship and have generally left the regulation of cultural goods to the open market, now see themselves confronted by a new task and a new responsibility. They are charged with the duty of conservation, although not necessarily of selection. That is why the process must be accompanied by public discussion, bearing in mind the requirements of an increasingly multicultural society.

This situation has given rise to a new pragmatic approach to the conservative concept of "cultural heritage." Every year UNESCO stages a conference where new applications for entry into the list of world cultural heritage sites are discussed. In 1997, at the conference in Naples, thirty-eight sites and eight natural wonders in five continents were given special protection by the organization. These newcomers included the Austrian Salzkammergut (Salt Chamber), Lumbini (the birthplace of the Buddha), and the Sundarbans Mangrove Forest in Bangladesh. UNESCO also has a "red list" of world heritage sites that are under threat, and they aim to protect old city centers and monuments, such as the palace and gardens of Potsdam, from being swamped by the process of modern urbanization.

In hindsight, it is possible to discern a number of major turning points in the relationship between media technology and cultural memory. The archive arose out of writing. Illiterate societies have no remainders, and hence no archives. Only where there is writing can

17 Ibid, 7.

cultural memory differentiate itself into the old and the new, the past and the present, the background of stored memory and the foreground of functional memory. With the advent of writing as a means of recording, the range of political government, economic organization, and social communication was vastly expanded, but in addition material remains of verbal testimonies accumulated that could be discarded or preserved and used by subsequent generations for a variety of purposes. The invention of writing brought with it fulfillment of man's longing for a secular eternity, an afterlife in the memory of posterity. The archive offers an intermediate store for posterity's memory, and from it signs may be extracted that can be reconstructed as messages. This intermediate store has advanced in leaps and bounds with every new stage of development in the technology of recording media. This applies to books that have enlarged libraries, and papers and photographs that have expanded archives. New technologies have not only increased the quantity of documents, but they have also created new kinds of archives. Besides written and sound, there are visual archives that support a "visual memory" (André Malraux), including monuments and data banks for archaeological, medical, and criminological purposes.[18]

In the course of this technical evolution, the archival store has also expanded through the addition of film and sound recording. But an even more radical development than this material expansion is the reorganization of the archive through the new medium of digital storage systems. With material documents now being rewritten as electronic impulses, both writing and archiving have changed their character. They are no longer stable, tangible data-carriers, but have turned into a fluid system of international self-organization. With this the old dream of the early advanced civilizations, which saw writing as immanent transcendence creating a space for individual immortality, has reached its limits.

---

[18] See Herta Wolf, "Das Denkmälerarchiv Photographie," *Camera Austria International* 51 and 52 (1995), 133–145.

14

Memory Simulations in the Wasteland of Forgetfulness

Installations by Modern Artists

The artists I discuss in the following chapter belong to the generation of those who were born during or shortly after World War II and who grew up in an environment of ruin and reconstruction: Anselm Kiefer (1945), Sigrid Sigurdsson (1943), and Anne and Patrick Poirier (1941 and 1942). Central to all their art is the theme of memory or, to put it in a slightly different perspective, art as the outstanding and ultimate medium for memory in a world that has rid itself of its memory. Of course, they are not alone. I am taking them as examples of a general artistic preoccupation that began in the 1970s and became dominant in the 1980s. It may well be that we have not yet reached the peak of this movement, and it remains to be seen whether this fascination with memory undergoes further development. The motivation of the individual artists is, however, extremely varied. In Germany it is connected with the traumatic aftermath of a past that will not, cannot, and must not go away and that no pragmatic, social formulation of memory can ever assuage. But as Heiner Müller has shown in exemplary fashion, it also has to do with a political interest in the subversive powers of memory, which can be used to undermine the totalitarian and the restorative hardening of forgetfulness and repression. After the devastation of the war and in the shadow of the nuclear threat, it is also linked to an enhanced awareness of loss and of the potential for self-destruction that characterizes modern society. Finally, it reflects the precarious situation of memory in an age of an industrial mass culture of electronic storage and communication technology. It is almost as if a memory that no longer has any cultural form or social function may have to find its last refuge in art.

The artists who have taken memory under their wing, so to speak, have developed new and remarkable forms of "memory art." In the old tradition of the "art of memory," art lent a helping hand by offering technical support for its reconstruction and for guaranteed access to it. The new memory art has a different starting point. It does not come *before* but *after* forgetfulness, and it is neither a technique nor a preventive measure but at best a therapy, a careful collecting of scattered remnants, an inventory of losses. If we assume, along with Nietzsche, that man is an animal who remembers, then the art of memory helps him to enhance this capacity, whereas memory art reminds him that he has a cultural faculty that he is in the process of losing. Simonides, the legendary patron of the art of memory, was able to identify the dead people at the feast after the collapse of the roof because he had been on the spot before the disaster and had stored the exact setting of the feast in his head. The memory artists of the late twentieth century are in a totally different situation. They arrived at the scene only after the disaster, and there is no conceivable form of art that could provide a memory bridge between now and then. There is no longer anything for them to reconstruct – all they can do is collect, safeguard, arrange, and preserve whatever remains of the scattered relics. Instead of documenting with their work a death-transcending power of memory, these memory artists confine themselves to weighing, measuring, and recording loss.

ANSELM KIEFER

Since the early written cultures of Asia Minor and the Mediterranean, books and libraries have been the main media for memory. This remained the case during the Gutenberg era of book culture.[1] While books and libraries may have lost much of their social significance with the electronic cultural revolution, they have gained in artistic importance. Their dramatic functional decline has led to a new fascination

---

[1] See Uwe Jochum, *Kleine Bibliothekgeschichte*, Stuttgart 1993; Günther Stocker, *Schrift, Wissen und Gedächtnis. Das Motiv der Bibliothek als Spiegel des Medienwandels im 20. Jahrhundert*, Würzburg 1997.

with their nature as objects. Even though they have ceded their predominance as media of cultural memory to other data-carriers and banks, they have embarked on a new career as central metaphors for that memory. I illustrate this transition from the book's declining technical function to its artistic auratization through the work of two modern artists: Anselm Kiefer and Sigrid Sigurdsson. Both of them have discovered the materiality of the book at a time when image and writing have become increasingly virtual.[2]

Anselm Kiefer has repeatedly drawn attention to his own obsession with memory and its media. In his own words, he works "with a gigantic sack of culture on my back." Whatever is contained in this sack is largely inaccessible to the conscious mind and becomes visible only indirectly through its roundabout transformation into the materiality of the artwork. The memory artist Kiefer differs from the professional guardians of memory through his anamnestic sensibility; his own concern is to establish connections between what is temporally or spatially remote. When he succeeds in bridging this vast historical gap, he reveals himself to be – like Warburg – a seismographer of mnemonic waves in a cultural memory that, because of dramatic loss, violent disruption, and suppression, has lapsed into a cultural unconscious. He has linked his studio in a former brickworks, amid the beech trees of the Odenwald, anamnestically to the Palace Library of Assurbanipal (7th century BCE) in Nineveh. He sees distance in proximity and proximity in distance. In the crude, abandoned shelves of the storeroom he recognized the basic function of the archive: in the bricks he saw the clay tablets of the ancient library, and in the loam from which the bricks were made, together with water and fire, he discerned the material substrata of culture itself – its construction and its fragility both out of and on the everlasting earth.

These are some of the associations from which emerged his installation *Zweistromland* (Mesopotamia), which he began in 1985 and continued to develop as a work in progress (see figure 3). It consists of two colossal bookshelves measuring 4 × 8 × 1 meters, which themselves form the obtuse angle of an open book. The installation includes

---

[2] In this context I would like to draw attention to a fine essay by Monika Wagner: "Bild – Schrift – Material. Konzepte der Erinnerung bei Boltanski, Sigurdsson und Kiefer," in Birgit Erdle and Sigrid Weigel (eds.), *Mimesis, Bild und Schrift. Ähnlichkeit und Entstellung im Verhältnis der Künste*, Vienna 1996, 23–39.

FIGURE 3. Anselm Kiefer, "Mesopotamia." Double shelf with books of lead.

FIGURE 4. Anselm Kiefer, an opened lead book.

two test tubes full of water, which are ironically named "Tigris" and "Euphrates" and provide a kind of label for the two-winged structure. The double shelf contains approximately 200 lead books. This lead is not a raw material but is itself a cultural product that has been recycled by Kiefer: it stems originally from the roofs of Cologne Cathedral. Lead denotes print – the movable type with which Gutenberg revolutionized printing technology. After the switch to electronic technology, it has become an obsolete material, but in Kiefer's books the lead of the letters has now turned into the pages themselves.[3] Because of their size and weight they need several men to handle them, which makes them virtually unreadable. The opacity of the lead books is balanced by a large printed volume bound in lead-colored cloth that displays a small selection of photographs of things we cannot see: nine double pages from each of twenty-eight books are "published" here.[4] The obtrusive presence of the material suppresses the function of the book as a medium, but at the same time attention is directed to the lead books through the "catalogue," with texts and photographs. The compressed objects become accessible and readable through this metabook from which one may extrapolate information and a visual impression.

As far as the lead books themselves are concerned, however, one can only regard them as antibooks: they restrict the book to its material components and eliminate its dimension as a carrier of coded information. Instead of written signs, organic materials like peas, loam, water, hair, or wool are displayed and accompanied by photographs – generally aerial views – of landscapes, cityscapes, ruins, and railway lines. Corresponding to the pictures of civilizations at different stages of construction and destruction are cloud formations that create a natural pendant that is as ephemeral as it is eternal. Kiefer's books do not tell a single human story. Their tale is, rather, that of the Earth's history from a distant, nonhuman perspective that shows how the Earth is only

---

[3] I have taken over this observation from Reinhold Grether, to whom I am indebted for several valuable suggestions.

[4] Anselm Kiefer, *Zweistromland. Späte Plastik im Zweistromland*, Cologne 1989. Kiefer has also reinvented the historical painting, which in works like the *Hermannsschlacht* and *Nürnberg* bring out the cracks and crevices in an undermined national memory. When in 1993 he moved to Southern France where he rebuilt a farm in the Cévennes into an artistic landscape, his works took on a cosmic dimension. See Christoph Ransmayr, *Der Ungeborene oder Die Himmelsareale des Anselm Kiefer*, Frankfurt a.M. 2001.

temporarily in our possession. It is a tale that remains menacingly vague and full of unspoken meanings. And the meanings of these antitexts, which are not coded in signs, lie buried in their materials – enclosed in the heavy volumes as if laid to rest in lead coffins, in which they remain locked in forever. Thanks to the excellent preservative powers of lead, these books can withstand a worst-case scenario just as well as the clay tablets of the Assurbanipal library were able to survive the conflagration when Nineveh was seized by the Babylonians in 612 BCE. Kiefer's antibooks or book coffins fulfill absolutely the book's function of memory and immortalization, but they do so at the cost of information, duplication, and publication. They are not only a monument to memory and forgetfulness – as indicated by the two rivers of the title – but they are also a treasure chamber of recondite, occult knowledge, as suggested by the other title of the work: *die Hohenpriesterin* [High Priestess], a reference to the second figure in a pack of tarot cards.

Cees Noteboom, on seeing Kiefer's installation in the museum of the converted Hamburger Bahnhof in Berlin, associated the lead books less with a library than with an archive: "the books standing here seem to me more like the books of a land registry. Or a registry of births and deaths, or something like that."[5] His "something like that" is a reference to the illusory nature of the staging, as a simulated archive: "There should be lead names in these books, but they are chance names, just as the long bands of still photographs hanging from the semideformed video recorders on the top shelves show chance people, anonymous, contemporary – people who existed or exist and whose names will slumber on in these lead colossi, unseen because no one can read them."[6] For Noteboom, Kiefer's installation not only simulates but paradoxically also nullifies the archive for it depicts this as a storehouse of knowledge, but at the same time makes that knowledge unreadable and inaccessible.

SIGRID SIGURDSSON

Vor der Stille (Before Silence) is the title of a work in progress that Sigrid Sigurdsson began in the late 1980s at the Ernst Osthaus-Museum in

---

[5] Cees Noteboom, *Die Dame mit dem Einhorn. Europäische Reisen*, Frankfurt a.M. 1997, 250. I am grateful to Max Brocker for this reference.

[6] Ibid, 251.

Hagen, Germany (see figure 5). In this installation, the central focus also lies on a bookcase that is loaded with an increasing number of books created by the artist.[7] In the first phase, the work comprised a bookcase with seventy-two compartments that housed book objects and display units; in front of it was a square worktable, at which visitors could open and leaf through individual volumes. In 1993, after four years, the installation had grown to 12 bookcases with 380 compartments and 730 books containing some 30,000 documents of different kinds. Through "visitor books," which viewers could help to design, and "travel books," which were sent to 500 addressees and were sometimes returned to the museum, the size and scale of the work were once again substantially expanded. The books, which have been covered with cotton cloth and smeared with earth, give the impression of age. They include some that are locked and therefore inaccessible, and others that can be opened and looked at. However, the volumes in these bookcases, just like Kiefer's, are carriers not of information but of memory. The contents cannot be read or used – at best, they can be contemplated (see figure 6). They consist of various materials: photos, letters, postcards, newspaper cuttings, forms, official documents, plans, maps, drawings – in short, a veritable kaleidoscope of relics and fragments such as a person might collect in the course of a lifetime. These remnants have been placed in opaque constellations, and some of them have also been covered with filigree drawings. There is no textual commentary or heading that guides us through this labyrinth of memories with its collage-like arrangement of contiguous and contingent *objets trouvés*.

Sigurdsson's books convey no messages, but are simply a store of personal, biographical recollections. The relics that are collected and preserved in them are permeated with personal reminiscences, but they only record the fact that things happened, they do not tell the story. Contexts are withheld and meanings remain unclear. This absence of meanings is very different from Kiefer's staged esotericism; it is derived from the fragmentary nature of documentation and the unfamiliar quality of the material. Through this kind of record, however, the viewer gains insight into the manner in which the

---

[7] Michael Fehr and Barbara Schellewald (eds.), *Sigrid Sigurdsson: Vor der Stille. Ein kollektives Gedächtnis*, Cologne 1995. Matrina Pottek, *Kunst als Medium der Erinnerung. Das Konzept der Offenen Archive im Werk von Sigrid Sigurdsson*, Weimar 2007.

FIGURE 5. Sigrid Sigurdsson, "Before Silence." Installation at the Ernst Osthaus-Museum, Hagen, Germany.

FIGURE 6. Sigrid Sigurdsson, opened book in the installation "Before Silence."

abstract, collective dimension that we call history is refracted in the prism of individual lives and recollections. A large number of the documents stem from the Nazi era, and we see things through the perspective of both victim and perpetrator. The trivial snapshots, for instance, that capture a typical family idyll come from Bergen-Belsen, and are accompanied by envelopes addressed to a captain in the medical corps who worked there. Or the photo of an anonymous girl is stuck without any explanation to an official waybill. Everyday, normal things are thus connected directly with the unspeakable crime of the Holocaust. In these book collages, history is presented as personal memories incorporated into the fine-grained structure of individual lives and deaths. The memories are amorphous and fragmented – the flotsam and jetsam of forgetfulness, a filling-in "before the stillness" and the final, irrevocable loss. These books are not so much stores as graveyards of documents, and the message comes not through the medium but through the marked material. With this emphasis on their materiality, Sigurdsson's books are just as unreproducible as Kiefer's, but she has endowed them with a different quality – the uniqueness and authenticity of real-life relics. Nevertheless, she sees herself as more than the guardian of a heritage of biographical traces. This crystallization of her own memory works through a documentary, fragmentary montage designed to be infectious and to trigger associations that in turn will spark the memory processes of the viewer. One might say that in Sigurdsson's work, the emphasis has shifted from simulation to stimulation of memory. This has been confirmed by different projects she has since undertaken in various places such as a little village near Gdansk, Poland, as well as in Germany in Braunschweig, Frankfurt A/M., and Munich, where through the medium of art she has created social contexts in which to deal with individual and family memories.

ANNE AND PATRICK POIRIER

A key experience for the Poiriers was a visit in 1970 to the ancient royal city and temple of Angkor Vat, in Cambodia, where they found themselves gazing at an impressive, spiritual structure ravaged by tropical humidity, its walls burst apart by roots and overgrown with dense vegetation. Here, the problem of cultural memory was present in emblematic form before their very eyes. From that moment on, the question of how cultures could deal with their past became a shared obsession. Together the couple set off in search of the lost pasts of their own culture. They found their model in archaeology, whose task is to excavate what was once a living present. It was on archaeology that the Poiriers based their mode of perception, their stylizations, and their whole approach to memory. Their art became a kind of pseudo-archaeology, and their passion for it is somehow reminiscent of the French film *Les jeux interdits* in which the traumatized children play games of death and burial after the war.

Playfully the Poiriers erase the dividing line between art and science as they delve into memory and try to fix it. In their project *Ostia Antica* (1971–1972) they created an archaeological model in which reconstruction and construction blended into one another.[8] The archaeological skeleton of this once bustling port town is turned into a work of cultural memory. In *Mnemosyne*, the artists stage themselves in romantic fashion as fictive administrators of the estate, handling the papers of a dead friend. This friend is a commuter between archaeology and architecture, the latter building for the future and inscribing itself into space, while the former lays bare the traces of the past and makes the earth speak. For the Poiriers, the two belong together: the one is the shadow of the other. The fictitious project that they take over from their friend is the excavation of the city of memory, Mnemosyne. Unlike Atlantis, the utopian sunken city, Mnemosyne can be dug out and rescued anywhere and everywhere in its duality of present and past, living function and fossilized ruin, remembered and forgotten.

The expression "memory art" is particularly apt for the work of the Poiriers. There is no sign whatsoever of memory in the sense of biographical reminiscence, such as we find at the heart of Sigurdsson's work. They are concerned with the mysteries of cultural memory – its quality as an artistic resource and as *terra incognita*. The city of Mnemosyne is a psychic space, and every excavation down below the surface of its earth is a journey into the dark regions of the soul. Archaeology, which can shed only a partial light on the darkness of

---

[8] *Anne et Patrick Poirier.* Texts by Jean-Michel Foray, Lóránd Hegyi, Günter Metken, Jérome Sans, Milan 1994.

oblivion, offers more auratic images than the illuminated, plastic, colored brains of magnetic resonance pictures, which are devoid of all evocativeness. The following text appears in their fictitious diary of the excavation:

LE PAYSAGE
S'OUVRAIT DEVANT LUI
COMME UN CERVEAU
MIS A NU DONT
ON POUVAIT VOIR
LES FONCTIONS
MULTIPLES.

(The landscape / opened up before him / like an exposed / brain, in which / one could see / the various / functions.)

The art of the Poiriers competes with the "imaging" of neuroscience, which turns the brain inside out and with the aid of computer technology illuminates and measures every convolution. Once again it will be helpful here to glance back at the art of memory for in the Renaissance, too, models were developed to draw a map of the memory in order to measure, restructure, and colonize its capacity. Just like the Renaissance artists, the Poiriers construct spaces of memory; and just like the memory theater of Giulio Camillo (1480-1555) or the memory spaces projected in palaces, squares, and cathedrals, they build miniature or room-sized structures with ever new variations of a mythological, cosmological world memory. Today the physiology of the brain is providing the basis for computer technology, which means that the organic is no longer exclusively internal and the technological no longer exclusively external. The paradigmatic point of intersection between the technosphere and the biosphere is indeed the human brain, which is in the process of implementing itself technologically, whereas conversely technology is optimizing its efficiency following the physiological model. The memory art of the Poiriers implants architectural ruins into the human skull, which confirms this new interplay between the interior and the exterior, and excludes any possibility of the clear analogy that underlay the structure of the ancient art of memory (see figure 7). The stumps of columns and other fragments not only blend together psychic structures with those of cultural memory, but they also dissolve the borders between remembering and forgetting.

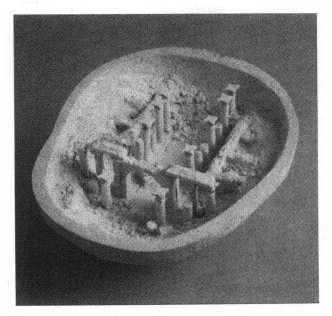

FIGURE 7. Anne and Patrick Poirier, cranium with a ruin from the installation "Mnemosyne."

FIGURE 8. Anne and Patrick Poirier, "De la Fragilité du Pouvoir" (The Fragility of Power).

This is the background against which, as I see it, the stylistic dimension of their work unfolds. Their art is characterized by meticulous order, aseptic purity, and classical perfection. There is none of the sensual rhetoric of Kiefer's materials, and none of the pointed authenticity of Sigurdsson's documents. The focus instead is on a precise and painstaking organization of the relics long after the disaster of forgetfulness. Authenticity is replaced by perfection, and in this context perfection means both a technique of conservation and a technique of remembering beauty. The loving care and attention lavished on the process of recording and arranging give to this memory work an affective quality that has less to do with internal shocks and aftershocks than with an aesthetic craftsmanship of the highest order. By comparison with the other memory artists, this marked absence of personal pathos endows the Poiriers' work with a smooth polish and a cool atmosphere, as seen in figures 7 and 8. These are fantastic constructs that have a (pseudo-)scientific purity and yet are filled to the brim with the mysteries of memory. The secrets cannot be brought to light, however they can be evoked through the reflections of an idealized art.

In complete contrast to the work of Sigrid Sigurdsson, that of the Poiriers avoids expression and instead seeks allegory. In an installation with the baroque title *De La Fragilité du Pouvoir* (On the Fragility of Power, see fig. 8), decoratively arranged fragments and stumps of columns are struck by huge metallic bolts of lightning. The arrow of destruction – Zeus's thunderbolt – becomes a kind of allegorical shorthand for catastrophic invasion. The only remaining witnesses to this sudden onset of violence are the ruins and the huge single eye in which the horror is still reflected. *LA PEUR DANS LES YEUX* (Fear in the Eyes) is the caption of another work showing the face of a statue. In the eyes wide with terror is concentrated the shock that set this memory work in motion and that the various objects have preserved, very much in the sense of Warburg's "canned energy." But the shock is not preserved through the authenticity of materials or collected objects, as with Kiefer and Sigurdsson. The new creation replaces the pathos of authenticity with an aesthetic fiction. It emphasizes the role of the imagination in the artistic act of constructing the past anew. One is almost reminded of Wordsworth's "emotion recollected in tranquility." Here, too, the work of art is a belated reconstruction, created in contemplation and imagination to replace a lost past.

We may refer to all the above artistic examples as memory simulations. Each installation in its own way represents a paradigmatic medium of cultural memory – books and libraries, but also maps, ground plans, and relics. They themselves store nothing, but they show us the significance of individual and cultural storage and archiving. The new art of memory works through metaphor; it holds up a mirror to cultural memory, opening up new access to it through artistic reflection. Here art lays emphasis on the solid materiality to which memory clings at a time when the mass of data is becoming more and more immaterial. In a culture that does not remember its past and has even forgotten its own loss of memory, it is artists who bring memory back vividly into the present by giving visible form to its lost functions through aesthetic simulation. One might say that art is reminding culture that it has lost its memory.

15

Memory as *Leidschatz*

The expression "memory as *Leidschatz*" (treasure trove of sufferings) became increasingly important for artists toward the end of the 20th century. It derives from Aby Warburg, the art historian and founder of the "Warburg Kulturwissenschaftliche Bibliothek." At the beginning of the 20th century, with his library and a circle of friends, Warburg established a line of research that opposed the restrictions of the academic disciplines and focused on basic questions concerning the transmission of culture. His own starting point was a repository of intensive, primal human experiences. It was on this archaic psychic level that he searched for the motor of the perpetual dynamics of human culture. However, at the same time he saw this psychic capital as something dangerously ambivalent. It could manifest itself in destructive affects as well as sublimate itself in the highest achievements of the arts and sciences. Warburg studied individual works of art in the context of this theory of energy, looking for links connecting great works with the "semi-subterranean regions" of the soul. He took the terminology for his psycho-energetic approach to cultural studies from Richard Semon, who had given scientific respectability to the term "trace." Powerful shocks, Warburg learned from Semon, imprint themselves on the "sensitive substance of the organism" in a trace, or "engram." Such traces are preserved for a long time in the subconscious, but can be reactivated and released on a later occasion. Warburg applied this model to the history of culture, in which he believed that shocks were stored as "mnemonic energy." The embodiment of such shocks were states of collective excitement such as occurred in archaic cults but also, for instance, in the mass celebrations of the Renaissance. But orgiastic and traumatic experiences – and this is an insight that Warburg shared with Freud and transposed to culture – can be neither remembered nor forgotten by the collective. They become part of a collective unconscious or, to be more precise, they form the substratum, the permanent trace of a social mneme that can be reactivated in changed historical circumstances. This memory of humanity that records the shocks of traumas, phobias, and cultic, orgiastic passions is what Warburg called the *Leidschatz der Menschheit* (treasure trove of humanity's sufferings).[1] It is very clear that he was greatly influenced by new ethnological research as well as by those culture theorists who in the course of the 19th century had brought to light the darker, "unclassical" side of ancient classical culture (from Creuzer, Bachofen, and Nietzsche to Usener and Rohde).

According to Warburg, art is linked to the driving force of the cultural unconscious. How this happens is explained in the following long and syntactically convoluted sentences, which show Warburg's difficulty in trying to endow his intuitive and experimental thoughts with the sanction of scientific articulation:

It is in the zone of orgiastic mass seizures that we must look for the mint which stamps upon the memory the expressive forms of these extreme states of emotion. Due to their high intensity, these engrams of passionate experience are communicated through gesture language and stored in human memory. It is the work of the artist that taps this transgenerational heritage and by releasing it recharges the intensity of the imprint.[2]

For Warburg, the symbol is "canned energy" in the long-term process of cultural transmission.[3] The same effect is ascribed to "pathos

---

[1] "Der Leidschatz der Menschheit wird humaner Besitz," Aby Warburg, announcement of a lecture given at the Hamburg Chamber of Commerce on April 10, 1928, London, The Warburg Institute, Archive No. 12, 27; see also Werner Hofmann, Georg Syamken, and Martin Warnke, *Die Menschenrechte des Auges. Über Aby Warburg*, Frankfurt a.M. 1980; Horst Bredekamp, Michael Diers, and Charlotte Schoell-Glass (eds.), *Akten des internationalen Aby Warburg-Symposions Hamburg 1990*, Weinheim 1991.

[2] Quoted from E. H. Gombrich, *Aby Warburg*, An Intellectual Biography, London 1970, 245.

[3] The formula "*Energiekonserve – Symbol*" is in the notebook of 1929, 21; quoted from Gombrich, 243.

formulae" that we referred to earlier in connection with mnemonically effective images (*imagines agentes*). Warburg sees these as "superlatives of the language of gesture," which keep an intense experience locked into a stylized icon.[4] They are transformations of cultural memory energy, which can be semantically reversed at turning points in human history (e.g., from paganism to Christianity) without losing their contact with the underlying current of energy. Warburg turned the faded topos of the "afterlife of Antiquity" into a theory of the dynamics of culture, even into a kind of demonology that he explored within the framework of a theory of a cultural unconscious.[5]

The works of the artist Sarkis (born in Istanbul in 1938 and domiciled in Paris since 1964) are inextricably linked to memory. Acknowledging this, Sarkis refers the complete history of mankind, although he tries to filter it through individual memory:

My work is always connected with memory. Everything that I have lived is in it. History is like a treasure. It belongs to us. Everything that has happened in history belongs to us. Everything that has emerged through humanity, in suffering and in love, is in us, and that is our greatest treasure. And everything that I have experienced, lived and made is my treasure.[6]

Sarkis borrowed the term *Leidschatz* from Aby Warburg, who regarded himself as the executor in charge of the estate of European memory. However, while Warburg saw this as a primeval energy that was encapsulated in certain images and could be reactivated, Sarkis thinks of it as the cumulative force of material objects:

With this concept I suddenly had the feeling of having come upon the inner accumulation of memory and the suffering associated with this memory, all

---

4 The art historian Wolfgang Kemp, "Walter Benjamin und die Kunstwissenschaft. Teil 2: Walter Benjamin und Aby Warburg," *Kritische Berichte* 3, Issue 1, 5–25; here, 24, note 45 speaks of a "rationalized fear of images" with reference to Warburg. This noteworthy feature of a Jewish art critic can be taken one step further, because underlying the fear of images is a fear of the body, and this is what constitutes the real "pathos" in his concept of pathos. See also Konrad Hoffmann, "Angst und Methode nach Warburg: Erinnerung als Veränderung," in Horst Bredekamp, Michael Diers, and Charlotte Schoell-Glass (eds.), *Akten*, 261–267.

5 Warburg uses the expression *energetische Metamorphose*, which is reminiscent of the term *Pseudomorphose* made current by O. Spengler. The latter borrowed it from geology, and also applies it to cultural typology. "Pseudomorphosis" is both distortion and preservation of a previous form.

6 Doris von Drateln, "Sarkis," *Kunstforum International* 114 (1991), 290–315; here, 295.

that had piled up internally. But in order for it to accumulate, things must take on a form – a form must be created so that memory, so that a treasure can emerge. And in this sense, it is extremely painful work. Dealing with suffering always entails developing an energy, finding a form through which one can deal with memory of suffering.[7]

Artists like Heiner Müller and Jochen Gerz also talk of a collective *Leidschatz* as being the source of their work. For Müller, the starting point of his work with memory and grief is shock.[8] Simply expressing it in language carries with it the danger of loss, as whatever has not yet been put into words remains in a state of pure energy. Suffering too is a treasure of which one can be robbed by language. This approach echoes Lyotard's theory, quoted earlier: trauma that excludes representation is preserved as virulent energy.

I now look at two artists whose work may be interpreted as *Leidschatz*; in both cases this historical treasure trove of suffering is derived from the Holocaust.

CHRISTIAN BOLTANSKI – *THE MISSING HOUSE*

Christian Boltanski was born in Paris in 1944 at the time of the German occupation. His Jewish father survived by hiding; this existential fear stimulated his artistic sensitivity, even though his works rarely make direct reference to the Holocaust. One of his central themes is the tracing of loss – the loss of objects, as in an installation of shelves filled with *objets trouvés*; the loss of memories, as in a dimly lit room plastered from floor to ceiling with large black-and-white photographs; the loss of knowledge, as in the narrow gangways through an archive piled high with tin boxes; the loss of bodies, as in rooms full of empty beds and stretchers. In some of his works, the process of forgetting is staged as a gradual fading away, while in others we see empty containers and remnants left behind after their vital link to human life and action has been cut. He furnishes rooms that the viewer can enter to experience a particular atmosphere and undergo subjective experiences of forgetfulness, loss, and death.

---

[7] Ibid., 295

[8] "Verwaltungsakte produzieren keine Erinnerungen," interview with Hendrik Werner on May 7, 1995. See also Michael Roth, *The Ironist's Cage. Memory, Trauma and the Construction of History*, New York 1995.

The works in consideration here are centered on visualization of something missing. The paradoxical artistic problem of making an absence present is not a new topic, for it was already being discussed some 400 years ago. In *The Advancement of Learning*, Francis Bacon sharply criticized the natural inclinations of the human mind. Without method and discipline, it was unreliable: "For the mind of man is far from the nature of a clear and equal glass, wherein the beam of things should reflect according to their true incidence; nay, it is rather like an enchanted glass, full of superstition and imposture, if it be not delivered and reduced."[9]

To illustrate this anthropocentric distortion of reality, Bacon gives an example that is particularly interesting in our context. He wants to prove that the human mind is far more attuned to the affirmative and the active than to the negative and the absent. He even argues that the human mind is incapable of coping with negativity. It automatically plays a trick whereby something absent is continually counterbalanced and replaced by something present: "So that a few times hitting or presence, countervails oft-times failing or absence." Bacon's example of the mind's inability to focus on gaps is the story of Diagoras, who in the Temple of Neptune is shown the many pictures of those who escaped from a shipwreck and expressed their gratitude for their rescue through votive tablets. In response to the question whether these symbols of grace did not make him believe in the power of prayer, Diagoras is said to have answered: "Yea, but [...] where are they painted that are drowned?"[10] What Bacon applies to the human mind is equally applicable to the human memory. Gaps and absences are far more difficult to codify and store than the exceptional experiences of survival and presence. Since the slaughter of six million Jews and other victims by the Nazi regime, the power of loss has become overwhelming, and we are faced with the question of what means can enable us to grasp, process, preserve, and pass on this loss in cultural memory.

The problem with memory of the Holocaust is the sheer number of those who disappeared. This leads to the danger described so accurately by Bacon that the human mind is liable to suppress a great

---

[9] Bacon, *Advancement*, 153, (see Chapt. 8, n. 16).
[10] Ibid.

FIGURE 9a. Christian Boltanski, "Missing House," Berlin, Grosse Hamburger Straße 15-16.

FIGURE 9b. Christian Boltanski, "Missing House," detail.

gap by representation, whether abstract or concrete. The artists who attempt the impossible and dedicate themselves to the painful task of working on this treasure trove of suffering, have to take hold of the traces, mark out the gaps, and focus on the mechanisms of memory.

How a gap can be marked out, and how absence can be made concrete without being transformed into a deceptive presence, is shown by Boltanski's *The Missing House* (see figure 9). In 1990, the Berlin Senate invited artists to create a work for the reunification of the capital city. On a World War II bombsite in the eastern part, Boltanski "built" his missing house by putting plaques on the security walls of the two adjacent buildings. Thanks to diligent research in the archives, where his helpers scanned vast numbers of address books, accounts of bombings, property deeds, records of fires, the Reich's department of genealogy, and documents relating to deportation, he was able to find the names of the former occupants, their professions, and some of their personal histories. On the level of each original floor, Boltanski put nameplates of the people and families who had lived in this house before and during the war. Also written on these plates was the time when individual tenants had lived there, right up until the house was destroyed by a bomb. Although most people had stayed there until 1945, two men – a civil servant named J. Schnapp and a lorry driver named R. Jaroszewski – had left at some time between 1939 and 1943. Neighborhoods were broken up at that time by forced emigration or deportation. This well-known fact takes on a different quality when it is linked to concrete places, names, and addresses.

With this work, Boltanski transformed an inconspicuous piece of land, now used mainly by pedestrians as a shortcut, into an historical site. With a bare minimum of symbols, he made it possible once more to read the signs of a history that had become invisible. Moreover at the same time he showed that memory is not possible without knowledge. Remembering becomes a process of searching – through books and archives – and it is by connecting the archival data with the concrete scene of events that abstract information on pieces of paper can point to the uniqueness of individuals and their personal histories. Boltanski's work shows how these personal histories intersected with that of National Socialism, which took hold of people's lives, distorted them, and cut them off. With his theme of "the absent, the lost body" embodied in the *Missing House*, he has created a space where he has refuted the scepticism of Diagoras and has made visible that which is no longer there:

The writing with the names gives the absentees a place, but it remains uninhabited. [...] The occupation of the empty space by names enables the gap to become material through the power of the place. Thus the presence of the absent and of the destroyed is inescapable.[11]

NAOMI TEREZA SALMON'S PHOTOGRAPHIC CYCLE "*ASSERVATE*"

"Don't bother to go in there," I heard a German visitor say to his companion in a brick building at Auschwitz. "There's nothing but shoes there." The blunt thoughtlessness of that statement draws attention to a problem that confronts all visitors to a place that is at one and the same time a museum, a crime scene, and a memorial. With what feelings and attitudes should we enter such a place? What ways of seeing are appropriate/inappropriate? How can any visitor do justice to a sight of such enormous complexity?

It is well known that when confronted with an excessively complex environment, people resort to mental strategies of simplification. They probably could not survive if they did not have at their disposal the art of foreshortening the world that also underlies every sign and symbol. Deep in our faculties of perception lie cultural patterns that teach us (even if we are unaware of them) to see the whole in the part, the sequence in the example, the general in the particular. When one has already seen one cubic meter of shoes in Auschwitz, why bother to go and see another heap at the end of the next corridor? Is the visitor therefore justified in taking a shortcut? This foreshortening process within the human mind, which otherwise takes place automatically, becomes a problem in Auschwitz. The normal shortcut to generalization becomes ethically intolerable when one knows that each shoe represents the death of a unique individual – a singular life and death in this gigantic killing machine. But how can the visitor's response do justice to such mountains of shoes? Our human mental and psychic faculties are hopelessly overstretched by this terrible display.

---

[11] Wagner, 28, (see Chapt. 14, n. 2).

FIGURE 10. Naomi Tereza Salmon, four photographs from the series "Asservate" (Evidence Objects).

Naomi Tereza Salmon's photographic cycle *Asservate* (*Asservate –
Exhibits – Auschwitz, Buchenwald, Yad Vashem* [Exhibition catalogue],
Ostfildern-Ruit, 1995) challenges the limitations and conventions of
our customary ways of seeing (see figure 10). Her artistic work began
as a purely technical commission: she was asked to photograph a number of objects from the Holocaust archive at Yad Vashem in Jerusalem
so that they could be put on record. But the photographer, a young
third-generation Israeli, gradually found the project developing into a
practical act of memory and of piety through her medium of photography. In creating the record of objects, she encountered the multi-
faceted dimension of the death camp as crime scene, museum, and
memorial.

While archaeological finds generally establish a direct material contact with the reality of a past world, the relics that were photographed in Yad Vashem, Buchenwald, and Auschwitz were marked by the bureaucracy of death, as seen in figs. 9-12). In the collection of objects that she had to record, the wretched leftovers from the last possessions of the victims – combs, toothbrushes, shaving brushes – stand side by side with the relics of their murderers, mainly the insignia of the SS. Most of the possessions of the victims ended up as the booty of their killers. With the same obsessive efficiency with which human life was ended in the death camps, material goods were collected, sorted out, and stored away. The parsimoniousness with which every object – was neutralized into raw materials or allocated for reuse – was stands in paradoxical contrast to the lavish expenditure devoted to the extermination of human life. The frenzy of material production and human destruction seems to constitute two sides of the same perverse logic.

This apparently rational, functional efficiency was, however, permeated by a fanatical strategy of symbols. The work of recycling was carried out as a deliberate act of desecration. For instance, the parchment of the Torah scrolls was transformed into wallets, briefcases, and clothes, or even insoles; the Holy Scriptures, which according to Jewish ceremonial law, must never touch the ground, were literally trodden on. Thus material reuse became a symbolic act of negation and inversion; this form of destruction was geared to the complete obliteration of the material traces. Physical elimination was total, and its results irreversible. Symbolic destruction, however, can at least be partially reversed by restoring dignity to the desecrated objects, while at the same time preserving the traces of the heinous crime.

This is the context of Naomi Salmon's photographic archive. As mementos, they are silent witnesses to the horror, but their silence is not modified by any emotion or by any subjective gesture. Their incorruptible objectivity shuts out any empathy, and distances itself from the perspective of the eyewitness as well as from that of the later viewer. Along with all subjectivity, these photographed objects exclude time and space as they remain fixed and frozen in a permanent presence. It is this absolute objectivity that creates the impact of these pictures. They are singled out for focused and detailed perception, making it impossible to look away. The laconic repetition of the objects carves its way into the memory to depths that no dramatic representation could ever reach.

With remorseless precision, the enlarged objects confront us as elements that cannot be abstracted from or generalized, or pieced together into any narrative. Their awkwardness and isolation are in no way lessened by the fact that they are single items in a series; and the manner in which they are arranged precludes any personal identification or appropriation. Their memory power corresponds to the objective, external storage of the archive. In this respect, the minimalist sequence of pictures builds up a technically precise memory in defiance of the perpetrators' efforts to eliminate all traces. The clear outlines of the individual objects stand out against a white background, the aseptic nature of which sets the seal on the destruction of the living contexts from which these relics were taken. It denotes the *tabula rasa* left behind by the death machine. The images make no attempt to assuage the emptiness and the silence, and they avoid even the slightest hint of aestheticization. They are conceived as clinically pure documentation, presenting each object as an inaccessible *Ding an sich* ("thing in itself"). But above all, the images produce their own mnemotechnics by forcing us to confront these inconspicuous objects, to look closely and to prolong our gaze. In its detailed accuracy, each one is not only a criminological clue to counter denial and forgetfulness but also an artistic veto against the veil of pathos and the relief of escape into abstraction.

16

Beyond the Archive

The archive, as a collection and conservation point for what has gone but should not be lost, can be viewed as a reverse image of the rubbish dump, where what is past is collected and left to rot.[1] The link between archive and refuse is not purely metaphorical as both have a common boundary that can be crossed by objects traveling in both directions. What does not go into the archive will end up on the tip, and what is eventually ejected from the archive through lack of space, for instance, will also land there. But conversely, a part of what is now treasured in the archive may – as Krzysztof Pomian has suggested – once have been classified as junk. He writes: "The sequence of object, waste product, symbolic sign applies to the majority of things that go to make up the cultural heritage."[2] In order that waste products, which have by definition lost their primary function, have any chance at all of enjoying an afterlife in the archive or museum, they must be endowed with the quality of relics that have been spared the "tooth of time" (the image is vaguely reminiscent of the allegorical figure of *tempus edax*) thanks to their tough materiality. Archive and rubbish dump can also be interpreted as emblems and symptoms for cultural

---

[1] On the subject of rubbish in general, see Michael Thompson, *Rubbish Theory*, Oxford 1979; William Rathje, Gullen Murphy, *Müll. Eine archäologische Reise durch die Welt des Abfalls*, Munich 1992; Volker Grassmuck, Christian Unverzagt, *Das Müll-System. Eine metarealistische Bestandsaufnahme*, Frankfurt a.M. 1991; Horst Baier, *Schmutz. Über Abfälle in der Zivilisation Europas*, Konstanzer Universitätsreden 178, Constance 1991.

[2] Pomian, 43, (see Chapt. 2, n. 41).

memory and oblivion, and viewed from this perspective, they have become of increasing interest to artists, philosophers, and scientists over the last few decades.

Waste includes objects that are no longer of any use because they are worn out, broken, or have been replaced by newer items. The German word for waste is *Abfall*, and of course the "fall" has metaphysical connotations going back to the Garden of Eden, where at the beginning of Creation man fell and lost his unity with God. The word can be used in connection with the law, with hierarchies, with separations, and with original sin – and indeed in German it can be used synonymously with sin. In everyday use, of course, the word means the stuff that falls from our hand or from the table and lies unnoticed on the floor, or that is no longer of any use to us and hence is discarded. With its loss of practical use, an object naturally loses its function and its value; therefore, one can say that rubbish is those things in which society has lost interest and from which it has withdrawn attention. All that remains is the material of which it is composed. Art, however, which has a special regard for the concept of "uselessness," follows a different economy from that of everyday life, and thus it can focus a different eye on the waste product. When artists incorporate it into their pictures and installations, they achieve two things: they create a different economy, and they also force the viewer to transcend the external boundaries of his symbolic world of the senses and to become aware of the whole cultural system, with its mechanisms of devaluation and exclusion. Such art does not operate mimetically but structurally; it neither illustrates nor reconstructs, but it brings to light the invisible, basic structures that underlie the making and unmaking of cultural values. We now look at the work of some artists who use waste as their subject matter, primarily in the context of cultural memory or, to be more precise, of counter-memory. Through literary texts and art installations from the 1960s through to the 1990s, I try to show how in both the West and the East art uses various media to make itself into a memory of things long gone and forgotten.

THE RAGPICKERS – ON THE RELATIONSHIP BETWEEN ART AND RUBBISH

In the 19th century, rubbish had a certain value because new industrial techniques enabled some of it to be reused as raw material.

This applied especially to the manufacture of paper that reprocessed large quantities of rags. As Walter Benjamin noted, this gave rise to a new kind of roadside industry: "The ragpicker was fascinating for his time. The eyes of the first researchers into pauperism were fixed on him as if they were under a spell, silently asking the question where lay the frontiers of human misery."[3] Benjamin's view of the ragpicker was influenced especially by the writings of Baudelaire. The latter saw the *chiffonnier* as a product of the modern city, and described him in the style of a "character" from Theophrastus:

Here we have a man whose job it is to pick up the day's rubbish in the capital. He collects and catalogues everything that the great city has cast off, everything it has lost and discarded, and broken. He goes through the archives of debauchery, and the confused array of refuse. He makes a selection, and intelligent choice; like a miser hoarding treasure, he collects the garbage that will become objects of utility or pleasure when refurbished by Industrial magic.[4]

Baudelaire draws an explicit analogy between archive and rubbish, and he puts the *chiffonnier* in the category of a collector, describing him as an inverse image of the archivist who selects, collects, sorts out, arranges, and treasures his finds in the world of waste.

Baudelaire's *chiffonnier* reappears in similar form in a contemporary American novel. Here, however, he is no longer a figure of social deprivation but is the bearer of a cultural counter-memory. Leslie Marmon Silko's novel *Ceremony*, to which I have already reffered, describes the healing of a war trauma experienced by an American Indian soldier named Tayo; Old Betonie the medicine man devises a ceremony that

3 Benjamin, "Das Paris des Second Empire bei Baudelaire," in Rolf Tiedemann and Hermann Schweppenhäuser (eds.), *Gesammelte Schriften*, 1,2, Frankfurt a.M. 1978, 521.
4 Charles Baudelaire, *Artificial Paradise: On Hashish and Wine as Means of Expanding Individuality*, trans. Ellen Fox, New York 1971, 7–8. French original: "Voici un homme chargé de ramasser les débris d'une journée de la capitale. Tout ce que la grande cité a rejeté, tout ce qu'elle a perdu, tout ce qu'elle a dédaigné, *tout ce qu'elle a brisé, il le catalogue, il le collectionne.* Il compulse les archives de la débouche, le capharnaüm des rebuts. Il fait un triage, un choix intelligent; il ramasse, comme un avare un trésor, les ordures qui, remachées par la divinité de l'Industrie, deviendront des objets d'utilité ou de jouissance." Charles Baudelaire, "Du vin et du haschisch, " *Oeuvres I*, 249–250, quoted in Walter Benjamin, *The Arcades Project*, trans. Howard Eiland and Kevin McLaughlin, Cambridge, Mass. and London 1999, 349.

eventually sets the healing process in motion. On one occasion Tayo enters the old man's hut, which in traditional manner is half sunk in the earth. To Tayo's astonishment, the circular room with its open ceiling is filled to the rafters with cardboard boxes, which are piled high on top of one another. Old pieces of clothing and rags stick out of some, and in others one can see dried roots and willow branches, Woolworth's bags, with dried-up mints, and tobacco leaves wrapped in unspun wool. Other piles contain newspapers going back many years and telephone directories from large American towns. As he looks round the room, Tayo starts to feel dizzy – a reaction the medicine man had expected. "The old man smiled. His teeth were big and white. 'Take it easy,' he said, 'don't try to see everything all at once.' He laughed. 'We've been gathering these things for a long time – hundreds of years.'"[5]

Over a pile of old papers, Tayo is relieved to find the traditional instruments that the medicine man uses for his ceremonies. But right next to them, hanging one above the other, are old calendars that go back to 1939 and 1940. These last two give him a jolt.

"I remember those two," he said. "That gives me some place to start," old Betonie said, lighting up the little brown cigarette he had rolled. "All these things have stories alive in them." [. . .] He pointed at the telephone books. "I brought back the books with all the names in them. Keeping track of things." He stroked his mustache as if he were remembering things.[6]

The collecting culture of the medicine man is the exact opposite of the white American throw-away culture. The former accompanies the latter like its shadow, gathering up what is discarded and remembering what is forgotten. The instruments packed together in Old Betonie's rubbish archive are not irrelevant waste matter but the material under-pinning of actions and stories. Like the tobacco leaves wrapped in wool, these objects are wrapped in stories. What might on its own be seen as a meaningless, random piece of junk becomes a mysterious cosmos of knowledge when it is framed in a narrative and introduced into ceremonies. Because the world has been so radically changed by

5 Silko, 120, (see Chapt.10, n. 60).
6 Ibid., 121.

the whites, the traditional knowledge of the shamans no longer suffices for an effective ceremony. And so new tales must be inserted and invented and new ceremonial actions performed. A whole new cultural memory needs to be constructed in order to provide a material basis for these tales and symbolic actions, and this is the archive of rubbish.

The first novel in Paul Auster's *New York Trilogy* is entitled *City of Glass*. Among other things, the reader learns how a man named Quinn comes to play the role of a detective and shadows someone called Stillman, whom he does not know. The conduct of the latter is certainly strange, even if it is not necessarily criminal. Every day Stillman leaves his hotel and wanders through the city, sticking to one particular district. There is no obvious plan or destination behind these walks, but he meanders along slowly and never takes his eyes off the ground. From time to time he stops, picks something up, and examines it carefully. Sometimes he throws it away again, but generally it ends up in a bag that he carries with him. When this happens, he pulls a notebook out of his pocket and writes something in it, like an archaeologist on some prehistoric site, noting down the exact location of an important shard. Like Old Betonie, Stillman turns out to be in the line of Baudelaire's *chiffonnier*:

As far as Quinn could tell, the objects Stillman collected were valueless. They seemed to be no more than broken things, discarded things, stray bits of junk. Over the days that passed, Quinn noted a collapsible umbrella shorn of its material, the severed head of a rubber doll, a black glove, the bottom of a shattered light bulb, several pieces of printed matter (soggy magazines, shredded newspapers), a torn photograph, anonymous machinery parts, and sundry other clumps of flotsam he could not identify.[7]

Like Silko, Auster is not interested in the poverty of his character but in the mysterious metaphysics of rubbish. Quinn eventually gets the chance to interview Stillman, and he asks for an explanation of these strange wanderings. "You see, the world is in fragments, sir. And it's my job to put it back together again."[8] Stillman presents his metaphysical project ironically in the guise of a certain Hamlet of Denmark (H. D.) who, as is well known, had the task of setting right a time that was "out of joint." However, this project comes even closer to another

---

[7] Paul Auster, *The New York Trilogy*, London 1987, 59.
[8] Ibid., 76.

famous H. D. who figures in an English nursery rhyme and has entered
into world literature through authors such as Lewis Carroll and James
Joyce. He is Humpty Dumpty, the egg that once broken could never be
put together again. Stillman connects this fall to the original Fall in the
book of Genesis: "Man is a fallen creature – we know that from Genesis.
Humpty Dumpty is also a fallen creature. He falls from his wall, and
no one can put him back together again – neither the king, nor his
horses, nor his men. But that is what we must all now strive to do. It is
our duty as human beings: to put the egg back together again."[9]

For Stillman there is only one way to cure the ills of the world,
and that is to invent a new language that will have the same quality as
the language spoken by Adam before the Fall. Since then, language
has ceased to present a transparent image of the world, and instead
a veil has been drawn between words and objects, distorting man's
relationship with the world and leaving him with nothing but a pile
of unrelated fragments. Only a true language that can restore the
correspondence between words and things will be able to overcome
this catastrophic situation:

"My work is very simple. I have come to New York because it is the most
forlorn of places, the most abject. The brokenness is everywhere, the disarray
is universal. You have only to open your eyes to see it. The broken people,
the broken things, the broken thoughts. The whole city is a junk heap. It suits
my purpose admirably. I find the streets an endless source of material, an
inexhaustible storehouse of shattered things. Each day I go out with my bag
and collect objects that seem worthy of investigation. My samples now number
in the hundreds – from the chipped to the smashed, from the dented to the
squashed, from the pulverized to the putrid."

"What do you do with these things?"
"I give them names."
"Names?"
"I invent words that will correspond to the things."[10]

As God used words to create the world out of nothing, Stillman rein-
vents words out of rubbish. Old Betonie collected rubbish for use in a
shamanic ceremony designed to heal a war trauma. Stillman collects
rubbish in order to heal the primal trauma of the world – to reverse the
Fall of Man. This first fall deformed language and thus blocked man's

---

[9] Ibid., 82.
[10] Ibid., 78.

access to the world as it really is. And so by renaming things, Stillman hopes also to reverse the consequences of the Fall as seen in the Tower of Babel, where man was first overcome by a confusion of languages. In his postmodern novel, Auster recycles a fragment of an ancient metaphysical discourse – a single broken relic from a lost tradition of the human mind that is artistically restaged as a carnivalesque-kabbalistic showpiece of bluff, mystification, and playful profundities.

After these literary excursions, let us now turn to the fine arts. Here, too, there is a relationship between art and rubbish that has undergone various changes since rubbish began to play its part in industrial mass production. Susanne Hauser, who has made a study of this relationship, has pinpointed the different phases in art's use of rubbish.[11] The process began in the second half of the 19th century, and reached its first pinnacle in the 1920s. For this early phase, there are two quotations that are particularly revealing. The first is from a letter written by Vincent van Gogh to Anton van Rappard in 1883:

Well, today I went to visit the place where the dustmen dump the garbage, etc. Lord, how beautiful that is – [...] Tomorrow I shall get some interesting objects from this Refuse Dump – including some broken street lamps – rusted and twisted – on view – or to pose for me, if you like the expression better. [...] That collection of discarded buckets, baskets, kettles, soldiers' mess kettles, oil cans, iron wire, street lamps, stovepipes was something out of a fairy tale by Andersen. [...] Whenever you come to The Hague, I shall be greatly pleased if you will allow me to take you to this and some other spots, which, though they are commonplace in the extreme, are really an artist's paradise.[12]

The second quotation is from Kurt Schwitters, who wrote: "I could see no good reason why old tickets, bits of driftwood, cloakroom numbers, wires and parts of wheels, buttons and old junk from attics and rubbish dumps should not just as well provide material for paintings as paints produced by factories."[13]

---

[11] Susanne Hauser, "Die schönste Welt ist wie ein planlos aufgeschichteter Kehrichthaufen. Über Abfälle und Kunst," *Paragrana. Internationale Zeitschrift für Historische Anthropologie* 5 (1996), 244–263.

[12] Vincent van Gogh, *The Complete Letters of Vincent van Gogh*, Vol. 3, Greenwich, Conn. 1959, 365–366.

[13] Written on March 4, 1927, in *Kurt Schwitters, 1887–1948. Der Künstler von Merz*, Bremen 1989. Quoted from S. Hauser (see n. 11).

Van Gogh was looking forward to trophies from the rubbish dump "to view as possible models" for his paintings. Such objects had a patina, an expressive physiognomy marked by long years of use, and so they served as props that he could integrate into the settings of his pictures. Schwitters's interest in rubbish is different from this mimetic approach. He is not looking for street lamps or stovepipes, but for small items like buttons and tickets that he can integrate into his works as objects in themselves. Van Gogh used his paints to reproduce the objects, whereas Schwitters uses the objects instead of paints. His collages break the homogeneous surface of the canvas, making it seem uneven and awkward. His paintings are not paintings of things, but things as elements of paintings – an assortment, arrangement, composition of heterogeneous bits and pieces.

It is yet another big step from pictures that use rubbish for subject matter, or integrate it into the works themselves, to those artworks that put rubbish itself on display. With the *objet trouvé* and especially the *ready made*, artistic composition recedes into the background. What others have discarded and forgotten is taken up again by the artist, who sets it before the viewer and brings it – even against his will – back into memory. Arman (born in 1928 in Nice, France) began in 1959 to display filled rubbish bins at exhibitions and in museums, with the aim of producing a shock effect. He claims "that the expressive power of rubbish and unusable objects has its own value, in a very direct manner, without us trying to give them an aesthetic order, which would blur them and put them on a level with the paints of a palette."[14] For him, rubbish is no longer given aesthetic justification – his paradoxical gesture is that of monumentalizing it. His work makes us aware of how precarious is the distinction that our cultural frames draw between art and waste, between archive and rubbish.

A LITTLE MUSEUM FOR THE REMAINS OF THE WORLD – ILYA KABAKOV

Boris Groys once remarked that the Russian artist Ilya Kabakov's private rubbish collection was "the only museum of modern art in the

---

[14] Arman, quoted from S. Hauser, 256, (see n. 11).

Moscow of the 1970s and 1980s."[15] Over the last few decades, the artists of our affluent, throw-away society have become more and more interested in refuse as the hidden side of consumerism, a symbol of the economy of waste, and an ecological warning sign. These obvious associations are not, however, in the foreground of Kabakov's work. He sees rubbish as representative not of a postindustrial social system but of the system prevalent in the Soviet Union: "everything is deliberately broken, or something is wrong with it. Rubbish is a good metaphor for such a non-functioning civilization."[16] But even more fundamentally, it is a metaphor for life itself in its ephemeral state, dominated by the forces of disappearance. Transience, loss, and oblivion constitute the monotonous teleology of everything that lives. In the neo-baroque cultural frame the combination of *vanitas*, *mutabilitas*, and *memento mori* was linked to a vision of eternity. This religious contemplation encouraged people to focus sharply on the general disintegration of all things because they were convinced of a post-terrestrial eternity. For Kabakov, on the other hand, rubbish and eternity coincide: "Everything disappears, goes grey and disintegrates to find its ultimate destiny as rubbish. But for me rubbish is as everlasting as life itself. That is why I see the brightly shining poster already lying in tatters on the ground. In my eyes it becomes transformed into rubbish, and as rubbish it will exist for ever."[17]

In fact, Kabakov is speaking of two eternities: that of rubbish as the inescapable and constant oneness of decay, and that of art and the museum as another form of permanence in the "field of immortality." He does not, however, polarize the two eternities but translates them into one another's terms and weaves them together. How did Kabakov light upon rubbish as a subject for his art? He has given a very precise account of how it gradually but irresistibly became the focal point of his attention.[18] He had a studio in the attic of a large block of

---

[15] Ilya Kabakov, Boris Groys, *Die Kunst des Fliehens. Dialoge über Angst, das heilige Weiss und den sowjetischen Müll*, Munich 1991, 110. I am grateful to Schamma Schahadat for the reference to Kabakov, and to Tomás Glanc for a manuscript on Kabakov entitled *Hierarchie und Verdoppelung* (Constance 1996).

[16] Ibid., 115.

[17] Ibid., 15.

[18] Kabakov, *Söppelmannen / The Garbage Man*, The National Museum of Contemporary Art, Norway, series No. 1 (1996), 122–125. My thanks to Natalia Nitikin and Boris Groys, who gave me this book.

flats in Moscow. In order to go there, he had to make his way every day through various forms of rubbish: he passed dustbins at the gate, crossed a courtyard full of dirt and all kinds of waste, saw more bins outside the doors as he climbed the steps to the fifth floor, and would meet the caretaker as he rolled his heavy iron trash can down the stone steps – a procedure that over many years had cut grooves in the steps – and before he finally reached his studio, he would be confronted by yet another collection of waste. Thus instead of getting on with his own pictures and texts, he began to see his own garbage with different eyes and began to collect his waste papers, those last precious tokens perfumed by the scent of so many memories.

Kabakov organized these masses of personal waste in different formats, following those of archives. There are some in cardboard boxes, reminiscent of the technique of Old Betonie, the Indian medicine man in Silko's novel. These contain unsorted piles of papers, such as one might bundle together and pack in readiness for a move. Then there are chests packed with objects of all sorts that hold memories of things one would normally forget. Some objects are tied together in batches, though each item is painstakingly labeled. Generally sorting, arranging, and labeling are Kabakov's basic techniques for processing the rubbish. Perhaps the most striking example of this is the content of a duster, which he has separated into tiny grains, labeling each and every one as seen in figure 11. His so-called lifebooks are loose-leaf cardboard binders containing an accumulation of everyday useful and useless bits of paper. Each file ends with an official, clearly written list of the items within, which lends the bureaucratic orderliness of the archive to the authentic flood of papers resulting from the random contingency of everyday life. But the concept of "state memory" also evokes associations with "state control." With their certificates, invitations, drawings, prescriptions, newspaper cuttings, and other scraps of paper, the lifebooks provide a paradigmatic documentation of everyday human contact with reality, that is, with the amorphous, unwieldy, ephemeral reality of a lived life.

Kabakov is not interested in biodegradables, the offshoots of affluence, or industrial waste; all that concerns him is cultural waste that is biographically relevant and bears the traces of personal, human

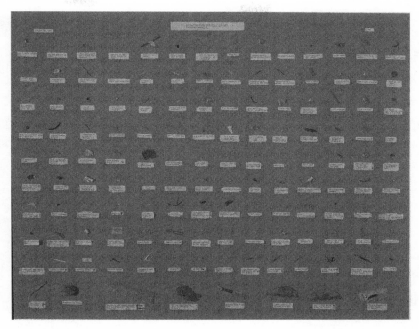

FIGURE 11. Ilya Kabakov, "Archiving the Dust" (October 12, 1985), detail from the installation "Garbage Man."

use and contact. Only this kind of rubbish intersects with the archive. The movable and indeed unfixable borderline between value and worthlessness, between cultural waste and the cultural archive, is the effect of continuous decisions and negotiations. His aim, however, is less to remove the borderline altogether, so that the whole of life can become a museum, than to focus on it and to make visible the very act of deciding between remembering and forgetting, permanence and loss. Unlike Arman's *Poubelles*, Kabakov's rubbish is not anonymous; it consists of relics from his own life that he has sorted out and preserved as memory aids and as evidence of what was. He writes: "Of course that is exactly what it is: a little museum for the remains of the world. I do not collect anything for the sake of collecting, but for visitors. And perhaps even for the government inspector, the controller who demands an account of what I have, for instance, done on this day or that. And then I can open File No. 8, and there lies the relevant documentation. It's something like a self-denunciation or perhaps even a confession."[19]

In the constant vacillation between discarding and preserving, between rubbish dump and (private) museum, there is according to Kabakov one reliable adviser: the value of an object, he says, is "dictated by a particular memory." As regards the value and importance of a paper mountain built of "paid bills, old cinema or bus tickets, reproductions received or purchased, newspapers and magazines long since read, notes concerning matters dealt with or not dealt with," he gets

a simple feeling which everyone knows who has ever busied himself looking through and sorting out his accumulated papers. It is an intense feeling about the events connected with each of these papers. Every single one gives us a jolt: it reminds us of a particular moment in our lives. To part with all these points, all these paper mementos and certifications would mean parting with one's memories. In our memories, in our recollections everything takes on the same value and importance. All these points of memory link up and form chains and connections in our minds which ultimately are what constitute our life, and the story of our life.[20]

Kabakov's description of the emotional value of otherwise worthless personal scraps of paper echoes Rousseau's *chaine des sentiments* and Antin's pulsations, both of which confirm their authentic memories. His memory work takes place, however, in a totalitarian framework. One aspect of this rubbish archive consists in collecting evidence for a later inspection of his individual life, which will have to be justified before a higher authority. The bureaucracy that already oppressed life in Gogol's Russia became an instrument of repression in the Stalin era. Under such conditions, the individual was under permanent pressure to justify his actions and to assert his individual identity. Kabakov's art accomplishes a mysterious transubstantiation of waste into archive and archive into art, as seen in figures 12 and 13. Through his work he brings about a move from the transient world into the museum that is the house of eternity. This, too, is a metaphysical project, in which self-justification and self-immortalization intersect. Behind the juridical and salvational metaphors lies the fallen man's desire for recognition

---

[19] Kabakov, Groys, 107, (see n. 15).
[20] Kabakov, *SHEK No. 8, Bauman-Bezirk, Stadt Moskau*, ed. Günter Hirt and Sascha Wonders, Leipzig 1994, 111.

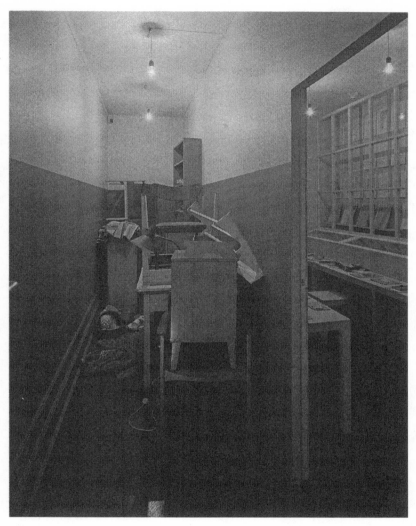

FIGURE 12. Ilya Kabakov, detail from the installation "Garbage Man," The First Room.

FIGURE 13. Ilya Kabakov, detail from the installation "Garbage Man," The Second Room.

and justification: "Indeed it is the desire, with all this junk, with all my dirty laundry, to enter culture – without being afraid of anything."[21]

Kabakov's project is not, however, solely about himself. Rubbish for him also underpins a collective Utopia, as is made clear by a text in which he describes a tour of the rubbish dump in Moscow:

The world, which I saw already with a "backward" glance, seemed to me to be a gigantic dump. I have been at few real dumps – near Moscow and in Kiev – they are sorts of smoking hills reaching to the very horizon, composed of the most diverse things. On the whole this is junk, crap, the refuse of an enormous city, but you can see, wandering around them, that the whole of it sort of majestically breathes, it breathes as though with all of its past life. This dump is full of sparks similar to stars, cultural stars you see either books of some sort, or a sea of some kind of magazines, in which there are photographs hidden, and texts and ideas, or things which were used by some people. That is, an enormous past rises up behind these crates, bottles, sacks, all forms of packages which have ever been needed by man; they haven't lost their forms, they did not become something dead when they were thrown out; they somehow howl about that life, they are a howl of the life that still resides in them.[22]

This Utopia holds out the promise that life is stronger than death and that human expression is more lasting than the powers of destruction. But Kabakov can only discover the power of life under the pressure of its negation; it gives way to a counter-memory, from which something new can emerge. From such a perspective, one can see why an artist in a totalitarian state devoted himself with such dedication to memory work with waste. The following statement once again sums up his credo: "a sensation of an enormous, cosmic nature, of actual existence, seizes you at such dumps. It is not at all a feeling of abandonment, of the death of life, but just the opposite: a feeling of a return, of the revolution of life, because as long as there still exists somewhere a memory of life, everything can be recalled to life. This memory 'remembers' everything which has lived."[23]

Both western and eastern (European) art, through literary texts and artistic installations, have discovered the importance of waste. Authors and artists have created a cultural memory with their rubbish

[21] Kabakov, Groys, 115, (see n. 15).
[22] Kabakov, *Garbage Man*, (see n. 18), 141–143.
[23] Ilya Kabakov, from "The Apology of Personalism in the 1960's," ibid., 143.

archives, their hoard of the forgotten and the rejected. In this memory art, which paradoxically remembers forgetting, *ars memorativa* and *ars oblivionalis* merge together.

THE ENCYCLOPEDIA OF THE DEAD — DANILO KIŠ

Oedipa Maas's quest for traces, as staged by Thomas Pynchon in his novel *The Crying of Lot 49*, drew our attention to the connection between cultural memory, organized channels of communication, commercial media, and new storage technology. Although recording methods — particularly of sound and image — have become increasingly true to life, and storage has become increasingly economical, it is still evident that the essentials of a human life are neither recorded nor recordable. For what is true of human consciousness and memory is also applicable on another scale to the archive: it cannot store everything; there are structural mechanisms of exclusion that cannot be circumvented. Boris Groys, who analyzes the conditions that give rise to the new, focuses in particular on what remains beyond the archive as a productive space for cultural innovation. He asks to what extent

our archives — museums, galleries, libraries, film collections, and so on — encompass everything that history can produce. This is certainly not the case; in fact, beyond this nevertheless endless archive, there is a sea of the non-historical, the everyday, the irrelevant, the maybe unimportant, the unremarkable, and everything that no-one takes any historical notice of. This is a potential reservoir for the new. For me the new is not a development dictated by time, but it is an interplay between what one already knows and has been taken into the archive, and what remains outside this archive — the inconspicuous, the unnoticed. And this realm of the non-historical, the non-archived, the everyday, cannot be erased. Every life of society and of the individual contains this unexpressed and perhaps even inexpressible dimension of what is merely there.[24]

For Groys, the inexpressible dimension of "what is merely there" remains the essential, unlosable, and inexhaustible source of art. This

---

[24] Boris Groys, Wolfgang Müller-Funk, "Über das Archiv der Werte. Kulturökonomische Spekulationen. Ein Streitgespräch," in Wolfgang Müller-Funk (ed.), *Die berechnende Vernunft*, Vienna 1993. 170–194; here, 175.

"reservoir" provides the raw material and the mechanism for artistic innovation. Art, with its norm of permanent innovation, is constantly moving along the border between the archive and what remains beyond it. Innovation entails a steady stream of entries into the archive, and yet – such are the economics of culture – the reservoir of the "profane" remains inexhaustible. In other words: a world in which everything is recorded seems inconceivable. But is it?

Highly relevant to this context is a short story by the Jewish Serbian-Hungarian author Danilo Kiš (1935–1989), who created an image of a total archive. His story is called *The Encyclopedia of the Dead.*[25] In contrast to encyclopedias of the living this one is dedicated to the forgotten and unformulated dimension of what has been. Kiš has devised an imaginary library whose dust-covered volumes are devoted exclusively to whatever has been excluded from cultural storage as being insignificant. Like Kabakov with his installations, Kiš constructs a counter-memory that contains all that is "merely there" and uncodable; therefore it cannot be recorded and so, once past, is irretrievably lost. He too directs his gaze beyond the archive and, in the paradoxical manner of a Borges, creates a negative archive of the "unarchived."

After a short introduction, elements of the fantastic become increasingly evident. After a conference, an academic is invited by her hostess to accompany her to a large library in Stockholm. It is already late evening, and the young woman finds herself entering a fantastic library that seems very like the kingdom of the dead. She needs a pass, which she shows to a silent guard, who then allows her into the underworld, where on dusty, cobweb-covered shelves she finds the encyclopedia of the dead. The aim of this project is to record in the usual format of the archive whatever remains outside the province of the conventional archive – the nameless, the inconspicuous, the insignificant, the ephemeral. Inventories, lists, registers, accounts, collections, descriptions, chronologies – all are carefully printed out and bound together in thick volumes that are very much on a par with Kabakov's lifebooks. The subtitle of this story is "A Whole Life." A life only becomes whole

[25] Danilo Kiš, *The Encyclopedia of the Dead*, trans. Michael Henry Hein, Evanston 1989. My thanks to Barbara Hahn for drawing my attention to this text.

through death, which draws a line under all the days that flow "like a river of time towards the mouth, towards death." (48) In another text, Kiš dreams of books that he would like to write, "and in which my whole past and present would be graced with articulate form."[26] The *whole* of life, however, can never be the subject of any form of representation. The very idea of such an archive is the stuff of Utopia – or of nightmares. It is not granted even virtually to the heroes of history, whose names may be recorded in the cultural memory but only at the cost of extreme foreshortening, stylization, and rigorous selectivity. But in the *Encyclopedia of the Dead*, this situation is reversed: the life of those about whom we very quickly remember nothing are here documented in full. A young woman who had tried through travel and work to overcome the loss of her father devotes a night in this library of ghosts to his life (or death) book, leafing through it, reading it, and copying things down, in so far as her cold fingers allow her to write.

The Egyptian books of the dead contained important knowledge of magic and liturgy that the dead needed to take with them on their perilous journey through the Underworld, which is why large numbers of such books were laid beside them in the grave. The "Masters of the Encyclopedia," as Kiš's archivists of the lost are known, are also engaged in a religious task: in the hour of resurrection, every dead person – with the aid of these carefully composed records – must be able to provide evidence for the uniqueness of the life he has lived. "That is why the authors of the majestic monument to diversity that is *The Encyclopedia of the Dead* stress the particular; that is why every human being is sacred to them." (51) And thus this encyclopedia monumentalizes the individuality and unmistakability of each individual life story. From this perspective of the hereafter emanates a different economy of data and a perfect form of attention that eliminate the distinction between the significant and the insignificant, and between remembering and forgetting. Because the meaning of the text of life remains open until the end, it is part of the logic of this recording program "that there is nothing insignificant in a human life, no hierarchy of events." (56) Beyond the prevailing criteria of selection there

---

[26] Kiš, *Schuhe. Gedichte und eine Betrachtung*, with drawings by Leonid Sejka, Berlin 1997.

are also no borderlines between the productive and the unproductive, between achievement and sufferance, between honor and filth:

> For *The Encyclopedia of the Dead*, history is the sum of human destinies, the totality of ephemeral happenings. That is why it records every action, every thought, every creative breath, every spot height in the survey, every shovelful of mud, every motion that cleared a brick from the ruins. (57)

The meticulous *ars memorativa* of these books of the dead is a project grounded in the fantastic. It articulates a need that cannot and indeed should not be fulfilled by any culture: memory, fame, and remembrance for *every* life. It negates the cultural as well as the psychological necessity of forgetfulness, which in this case is associated not with facilitating production but exclusively with processes of destruction. What is forgotten is as though it had never existed. The descent into anonymity and oblivion extinguishes life for a second time, and such a life has been lived in vain. The Masters of the Encyclopedia work to thwart this forgetfulness. To the daughter who with numbed fingers is copying from her father's dossier, they give proof that his "life had not been in vain, that there were still people on earth who recorded and accounted value to every life, every affliction, every human existence. (Meager consolation, but consolation nonetheless.)" (64) Readers of this story, however, are less likely to be comforted than to be prodded into awareness of the "negative mountains of data" of what has been forever lost. They will view the *Encyclopedia of the Dead* as an encyclopedia against forgetfulness, and they will take away a sense of the richness and abundance of a *whole* life as something that has not been and never can be archived.

In direct contrast to totalitarian military and civil archives, the motive for this collection of data is not mistrust, calumny, or persecution, but the biblical aspiration to have one's name written in the Book of Life. Out of this desire the Mormons, to whom Kiš refers in an epilogue, have created a major technological project. They have as it were taken the bookkeeping out of God's hands, and Kiš regards their megalomaniac scheme as a nightmare. In the granite rocks of a mountain range east of Salt Lake City they have drilled tunnels and passages to house a gigantic archive – protected by steel doors – under the best possible conditions of preservation. "Here they will preserve the names of 18 billion people, alive and dead, carefully recorded on 1,000,250 microfilms. [. . .] The aim of this massive undertaking is to record the whole of the human race on microfilm – both those who are still among the living and the rest who have already passed into the Beyond." (210) With this total memory that is permanently occupied with searching and registering, humanity – individual by individual – gives proof of its existence.

THE LIBRARY OF GRACE – THOMAS LEHR

There is a corollary to Danilo Kiš's *Encyclopedia of the Dead* – an archive that contains not the complete personal dossier of every life, but the complete works that have never gone into print. At the center of Thomas Lehr's novel *Zweiwasser or The Library of Grace* is a man with an obsessive fear of death, loss, and oblivion together with an intense desire for permanence and immortality. As a child, Zweiwasser had read a pirate story that had introduced him to the magic of letters; he experienced how these letters, although they were just black signs on a white space, carried him away to a sensually evocative harbor with all of its sounds and smells. When he learns that the author of the novel died 100 years ago, the miracle is complete:

Everything could be transformed and saved by a single person, even the gentle splashing of the ocean waves and kitchen waste carelessly thrown overboard by a cabin boy. The distance between the letters, set cleanly in the white eternity of the paper, and his own eyes seemed infinite. He was looking only as far as his own hands and yet into the very depths of time. What stood on these pages could never be destroyed.[27]

After this revelation, Zweiwasser himself yearns for immortality through authorship. What is in print is permanent and can never be removed from the world. But in order to fulfill this profound longing for immortalization through writing, he is unfortunately dependent on the support of publishing companies. And this support is denied him. Whoever he tries, back come his manuscripts accompanied by letters of rejection. To get into print he wages his own private Trojan War for ten long years, all in vain. His program for defying death by writing only bears fruit when he dies, and one of his texts is published

---

[27] Thomas Lehr, *Zweitwasser oder die Bibliothek der Gnade*, Berlin 1993, 11.

posthumously. It fills the last chapter of Lehr's book as an "epitaph" to the luckless hero. This text describes another library – a library of the "other" that counters the policies of the publishing companies and the selection criteria of the archive, and instead collects, arranges, and conserves everything that exists in written form. This Library of Grace began to advertise for items in a newspaper dated November 1997. Every work that had failed to find a publisher – so ran the advert – would be welcome. "The Library makes no distinction. Diaries, rejected encyclopedias, blurbs, theses, dreams, collected sayings, jokes, pamphlets, novels – anything that exists in written form and has been subject to humiliation will find a place here."[28]

The quantity of written material is not only to be collected, arranged, and conserved, but is also to be electronically processed with the latest methods and made available to the general public. In this manner, a "unique, absolutely value-free second brain of humankind" will emerge that is totally independent of the interests, constraints, and evaluations of the *Zeitgeist*. After a phase of development in which the institution has worked out its structure and system, and after finding solutions to critical problems relating to expansion, the imaginary Library of Grace has flourished and is now approaching its twentieth anniversary.

Love letters and poems, rejected articles and novels grievously stricken by lack of respect, volumes of poetry treated like lepers, works of scholarship, fragments, loose leaves, in some cases even isolated sentences that struck one as brilliant although incapable of continuation – all continued to be borne through the open floodgates of the Mater Libraria. The worldwide system of grace went on archiving and documenting every paper heart entrusted to it. To be accepted and distributed, to be able to move through the earth-encompassing networks and brains of one's fellow humans, to be preserved for posterity like a Pharaoh, was no longer a privilege but the everyday experience of millions.[29]

However, this dream of unlimited survival and millionfold fame cannot last. In its thirtieth year, the "Millionfold Archive of the Vanities" collapses. Zweiwasser's library meets its end on November

[28] See Günter Stocker, *Schrift, Wissen und Gedächtnis. Das Motiv der Bibliothek als Spiegel des Medienwandels im 20. Jahrhundert*, Würzburg 1997. My thanks to Günter Stocker for drawing my attention to Thomas Lehr's novel.
[29] Lehr, 354 (see n. 27).

9, 2027, just like Alexandria's library – because of a fire. But here the fire does not need to be lit from outside; the destruction is wrought by an implosion of the data network. Suddenly, on the monitors of the terminals, instead of the data that have been called up there appears the symbol of a flame that, in just a few days, completely consumes all the immaterial contents of the library. Just as mysteriously as it appeared, the Library of Grace vanishes again.

The construction of this limitless storage memory can be interpreted on various levels. First of all, it is the vision of a wounded soul, a dream of the frustrated author Zweiwasser, whose own aspirations to publication have been thwarted. But it is also a satire on the general longing for personal immortality, to be achieved through a new writing technology. With the technological leap forward in storage capacity through electronic media, everyone may hope to gain entry into the unrestricted digital library of the world-wide web. The Library of Grace, which dispenses with all information filters and selection criteria, mirrors the surging informational ocean of the Internet that offers no vantage point for a general view, let alone for any control, but on the contrary is accessible and extendable from anywhere and everywhere. The Library of Grace offers an allegorical lesson that shows how today there are two overlapping cultures: the material one of writing, which has produced a desire for the permanence of what is written and for the immortality of the writer, and the electronic culture, whose product is the desire for limitless participation, a virtual present, and total accessibility.

LAVA AND RUBBISH – DURS GRÜNBEIN

In March 1998, the *Frankfurter Allgemeine Zeitung* published an article by the poet Durs Grünbein about Los Angeles (L.A.), beginning as follows: "Los Angeles. This city is a frontal attack on memory. Its proliferating territory, which horrifies urbanologists and leaves historians stammering, is a diagram of the amnesia that is sweeping the globe at the end of the century. Little survives the last five years, the magic rotation of investments and erasures. "History is five years old," is a Californian proverb."[30]

---

[30] Durs Grünbein, "Aus der Hauptstadt des Vergessens. Aufzeichnungen aus einem Solarium," *FAZ, Bilder und Zeiten*, March 7, 1998, No. 56, 1. On Los Angeles as a

The city on the extreme western border of the United States, which once symbolized originality and the emotional drive of inexhaustible renewal, has continuously celebrated the triumph of the new and forgotten the old. This has not happened by chance, as if something had accidentally got lost along the way, but with a conscious, positive enthusiasm. Grünbein perceives L.A. as a ghost town, in the genre of the fantastic. Instead of streets and rows of houses, he sees a gigantic cemetery, with graves, mausoleums, memorial slabs: "Because it is death, a special, shortterm, insidious form of extinction that rules over everything here." On the outskirts of this necropolis rise towers of containers that hold the rotting refuse of yesterday's household goods. But the kind of deposits that might be deciphered by later generations of archaeologists are not to be found here, because the police take care that all is clean, and they bag "with white gloves whatever body parts and lucky charms might be lying around." The temporal dimension of durability, which people in this city have lost sight of, reenters dialectically in contexts such as preservatives added to foods, or toxic materials stored in the ground.

Grünbein's prose vision is enhanced by a poem entitled *Sunset Boulevard.* "Everywhere Tivoli, nowhere Rome," he writes, and "one comes here to forget, and to fantasize." Forgetful, fantastic, unhistorical Hollywood – all of these come together in an interwoven network, because as Grünbein says, it is no coincidence that the "capital of forgetfulness" is also the center of collective dreamworks, in which "Californian paradise gardeners and castles-in-the-air builders [...] earn their living with optical illusions and emotional massages."

Grünbein's text is tinged with personal bitterness and melancholy. Only someone who has not left the old world could speak in this way when he lands at LAX Airport. The clash between the United States and Europe as cultures, respectively, of forgetting and remembering has a long tradition, which has been maintained and repeated by both sides. Just how Grünbein defines his own origins and position is made clear by another text that also deals with the subject of culture, history, forgetting, and waste, although this time the structure is far more complex. This is a meditation on two extremely different mountains:

topography of forgetting see also Ruth Klüger's remarks on Orange County in *weiter leben*, 280 ff (see Chapt. 7, n. 19).

Vesuvius, overlooking Pompeii, and the rubbish dump in Dresden.[31] He establishes a connection between them in a form that can best be described in Walter Benjamin's terms as a "dialectical image." In Grünbein's imagination, Dresden's mountain of rubbish becomes the inverted mirror image of Vesuvius: whereas the latter spews out lava that buries the houses and temples of the nearby town, the houses of Dresden spit out rubbish that is loaded onto lorries and over the decades grows into a similar mountain. Once upon a time the lava flowed from the mountain into the town, but now the rubbish flows from the town to the mountain. By blending the two processes into this one dialectical image, Grünbein creates a surprising link between archive and rubbish, and between decay and conservation.

Both Pompeii and Dresden offer images of cultural memory. For the town at the foot of Vesuvius, catastrophic destruction coincided with lasting preservation. What was sealed forever in the molten lava escaped the cycle of renewal and decay, and assumed the quality of permanence. Thus violent death became the precondition for the survival of a cross section of life in this particular town, preserved as a latent memory in a place of memories that archaeologists were able to set free seventeen centuries later. For Grünbein, the catastrophic interconnection between death and memory is also an image for the memory of art, which goes off on a tangent from the economic cycle of goods and the rhythms of innovation and obsolescence, and which instead follows the "waves of burial and recovery, sedimentation and archaeological excavation. In such tides, discontinuously, flows the history of art."

Grünbein calls Dresden's mountain an "artificial Vesuvius," and the rubbish that is tipped there is "a different lava." This mountain comprises the remains of consumed life – the relics that have lost their context and hence their meaning. Like Oedipa's data bank for everything lost, like Kabakov's "breathing" rubbish dumps in Moscow and Kiev, this is a counter-memory for materialized forgetfulness, for everything rejected and ejected. But that is not all. Below the layers of refuse lies the ruinous debris of a lost city, of old Dresden, of the baroque Pompeii, which did not fall victim to a natural catastrophe

---

[31] Durs Grünbein, "Etwas wird dem Strom der Dinge entrissen," *FAZ*, May 27, 1994, No. 121, 33. I am grateful to Esther Sünderhauf for ripping this article out of the flow of things and sending it to me.

but was destroyed in World War II; this rubble of history is linked to a violent collapse and erasure of civilization. The artificial Vesuvius is a disconnected and contaminating memory of cities. "Today I know that almost every major city has its Vesuvius. Our contemporary volcanoes are the great slagheaps [...]. From time to time they launch a counter-attack, and their showers of ashes fall back on the housing estates, and they spew out poisons and filth, the groundwater becomes coloured, and the ballast materials lie upon the rooftops."

When he was a boy, Grünbein loved to explore the rubbish mountain – the foul-smelling treasure house of the lost and forgotten. The grown-up poet Grünbein is equally fascinated, however, by the counterpart of this stinking decay – the preservative lava of Vesuvius, which has given particular fragments of life a chance of survival. Both in Pompeii and in Dresden the preciousness of what has been preserved can be measured according to the mass of the irretrievable loss. As a poet, he sees the "letter" against the background of the "litter." His poetics, as he emphasizes, embrace

both the detritus of civilization and that lava in which the first moments, things and gestures, scenes and thoughts are preserved like living creatures taken by surprise. For the law of formal preservation, which for so long had a volcanic base, is changing in modern times under the pressure of mass production. Something is ripped away from the flow of things, cools down, and is sealed off from the air. Having become obsolete, it loads itself up with the very time that is always unavailable to the present from which it has departed. Once the seal is broken, sounds become artefacts, verses prove to be capsules from which fall the images of thought (*"Denkbilder"*). Those few things on which later the pickaxe alights, the brush of the excavator, the shovel of the garbage collector – this is the stuff that poems are made on. (Grünbein, 33)

Boris Groys, who viewed art from the normative perspective of innovation, took up his position on the movable border between archive and rubbish, between the meaningful and the meaningless. For Grünbein, however, who sees the new as being closely linked to the obsolete, there is a mysterious affinity between archive and rubbish, lava and detritus, that lies in the fact that both have been torn away from the present and persist in a state of latency. What has dropped out of functional circulation stands as far outside of the present as that which has been solidified through the laws of formal artistic preservation; in both states, the remnants and objects are "ripped away from the flow of things" and enter a new dimension of time. Grünbein's interweaving of Vesuvius with the rubbish mountain suggests a paradoxical interrelationship between the opposites of disintegration and solidification. For him, the time of art is not that of stable permanence but evolves in "waves of burial and recovery," and so in this image of cultural memory, remembering and forgetting are no longer mutually exclusive.

Conclusion

Arts of Memory

The arts of memory evolve on different levels. If we start with the desire to artificially enhance individual human memory capacity, we may think of Cicero, who developed cognitive strategies to discipline the brain and transform its myriad of random associations into a reliable and functional support system. But the arts of memory comprise much more than a technical aid for individual purposes. Cultural memory is also an art of memory, based on different media at the disposal of a larger group, thus enhancing the collective knowledge of its members about their past, their way of life, their values, important referents, and common orientations. This memory is a prosthetic device, an externalized and reinternalizable collective creation that is transmitted and transformed over time and reshaped by succeeding generations. While the Roman art of memory starts with an abstract spatial design on a *tabula rasa*, the art of cultural memory is unfathomable; there are always deeper layers. This also corresponds to the experience of individuals, who do not have to invent language and culture because they inherit both. Sitting upon the shoulders of giants, they and their lives are always already enveloped in the memory of those who came before and those who follow after. On a third level, the arts of memory comprise the contribution to cultural memory of artists who endow it with their unforgettable works and profit from its frameworks of immortalization. From early on, artists have both invested into and profited from cultural memory, which they have supplemented, criticized, transformed, and opposed in various ways.

395

But they are also its lucid theorists and acute observers. Today, the most conscientious and inspiring self-reflection of cultural memory resides in their artistic creations.

We have seen from all the preceding examples that the form and quality of cultural memories are determined by political and social interests, as well as by changes in the technical media. Part One of the book, devoted to functions of memory, distinguished two different realms: the inhabited "functional memory" and the uninhabited "storage memory." A functional memory arises from a partial spotlighting of the past that an individual or group may need in order to construct a meaning, to establish an identity, to find a direction for life, or to motivate an action. Such memories, which are tied to an individual or a collective carrier, are particular, perspectival, and biased: from a particular present, a section of the past is illuminated in such a way that it opens up a future horizon. Whatever memory is thus constructed is always profiled by the edges of forgetfulness. Focused, concentrated memory inevitably includes active forgetfulness – a situation perfectly captured by Francis Bacon: "When you carry the light into one corner, you darken the rest."[1] This "inhabited" memory space does not fit in with the modernist and historical concept of time that emphasizes the "separation of past and future" (J. Ritter), or the unbridgeable gulf between "the realm of experience" and "the horizon of expectation" (R. Koselleck). Alongside this historical view of time – which proceeds from the assumption that with the rise of the modern era, past and future, experiences and expectations have become more and more detached from each other – there have always been and continue to be realms of memory in which future expectations are by no means separate from images of the past, but indeed are advanced and underpinned by particular historical memories.

The possibility of writing down more than the human memory can retain led to a rupture in the balanced economy of oral memory. External storage capacity and embodied human memory were separated from one another, and since then a homeostasis between the two has become an impossibility. In societies based on the technology of script and writing, the focus is therefore not only on the preservation of memory but also on constant processes of selecting,

---

[1] Bacon, *Advancement*, I, IV, 6, (see Chapt. 8, n. 16).

distinguishing, and evaluating. Book printing and other new media have continually expanded storage capacity for the written word, and this has dramatically sharpened the discrepancy between the inhabited and uninhabited, embodied and externalized spaces of memory. How one judges this relationship is largely a matter of temperament: some see the realm of storage memory as a dark, invisible burden that threatens the clear-cut identity and vitality of a group; others see it as a reservoir of potentials, alternatives, and unused experiences that can expand our vision and relativize the present and its claims to absoluteness. The functional memory as an evenly illuminated memory space can take on the form of a thesaurus, a cultural canon, or a pantheon. As a normative and formative object of learning and interpretation, its aim is to be passed on to succeeding generations. It is also firmly established in repeatable acts of ritual commemoration, based on periodic feasts and recurrent dates in the calendar of the community. The uninhabited storage memory, on the other hand, consists in an abstract and amorphous realm, whose totality is ungraspable and whose administration is delegated to professional specialists. Archives have been organized both as functional and as storage memories: political archives contain those documents and pieces of evidence that secure the legitimizing basis of existing powers and their steering mechanisms; historical archives, on the other hand, harbor potential sources for historical knowledge and thus provide the possibility of understanding, describing, evaluating, or criticizing an historical epoch from the perspective of hindsight. However, they are not limited to pure historical knowledge. We may visualize the vast realm of storage memory as surrounding the narrow circle of inhabited functional memory, with the externalized memory building up a reservoir of not yet actualized possibilities of reconnection that constantly alter our image of what we conveniently but misleadingly abbreviate and nominalize as "the past." Depending on the demands and pressures of a given situation, one can view this store of knowledge either as a graveyard of data or as precious evidence of a different reality that can challenge the status quo of the present.

The dynamics of cultural memory evolve in a process of interaction between the active functional memory and the potential but as yet inactive storage memory. They reach into both realms, bringing them into ever new confrontations and interrelations. Cultural memory in this sense is an inclusive term, encompassing the active formation of the canon, the passive store of the material archive, and the realm of the "cultural unconscious." F. G. Jünger's term *Verwahrensvergessen* refers to this preserving power of forgetfulness itself. The unconscious is the realm in which there is no clear distinction between the concepts of remembering and forgetting. It consists not in symbols and text but in traces, remains, relics, sediments of a past time that have become illegible or yield mixed and perplexing messages. It exists materially or intellectually in a state of latency from which it may be rediscovered, reinterpreted, and imaginatively revived by a later age. It is not only through externalization but also through the permanent process of layering that memory spaces acquire a quality of "depth" that allows not only for unexpected renaissances and resurrections, but has not only given rise to the idea of a "cultural unconscious." This layered structure explains why refuse and cultural waste have acquired such importance for histography and the arts.

Part Two of the book demonstrated that the structure and consistency of cultural memory were determined largely by the materiality of its respective media. For a long time writing was regarded as a "transparent" medium that was able to keep the spirit of past articulations intact, independently of time and space. However, in the 19th and 20th centuries this transparency of writing, so prized by the humanists of the Renaissance, was challenged by the image as a more potent medium for cultural memory that, because of its density and ambivalence, has a special kinship with the unconscious. As distinct from the (more or less) continuous traditions based on texts, images were considered to produce a much more volatile, uncontrollable, affective, and in some forms more direct access to the past. In comparison with both writing and image, the human body works rather differently as a medium for recording. Although it embodies and enshrines the past in particularly affective ways, it is also notorious for modes of inaccessibility (e.g., trauma) and unreliability (such as "false" memories). Also different from writing and image as mobile media of communication, the place as a medium of memory is characterized by its unchangeable location; it is a permanent, sensual anchor for transient memories – which may with greater or lesser emphasis present the remnants of a venerated or traumatic past. If it is divested of all remnants, it is reduced to the indexical sign of the spot itself: a here without a now.

With the development of systems of recording, which codify optical and acoustic signals as well as language, the arts of memory have expanded in totally new directions. Together with written and pictorial documents, archives are now bulging with photographs, tapes, and videos, which record past realities in more mimetic ways but which are far more fragile with regard to their long-term stability. Thanks to the speed at which they can be organized and searched, the new data-carriers offer a more efficient control of information, but their material durability has been dramatically reduced. Their "expiry date" is becoming increasingly imminent, which presents the archivists with a new set of problems. In its latest metamorphosis, cultural memory has become more and more like a fully automated computer brain, which independently processes and renews its data according to specific programs. In light of this development in storage technology, anthropomorphic categories like remembering and forgetting have become less and less appropriate. The *ars* side – the technical mastery of *memoria* – may be said to be gaining its independence at the expense of the *vis* side – its uncontrollable psychic energy.

With the dawn of the digital age, not only is the unchallenged reign of the book coming to an end, but so too is that of material writing in general. Not that things are not being written and printed, for these forms of cultural practice remain irreplaceable in many domains. But in light of the now established indispensability of these new technologies, we can for the first time see the "historicity" of a previous, closed phase. This sense of historical closure clearly affects the metaphysics of writing. Based on its impressive longterm stability, writing had created in western culture the will to secular permanence, which has been called into question by the current, endless flow of digital data. The transhistorical has given way to the transitory. The ancient, central metaphor of writing as a trace, as a sign of a lost presence, as a lasting inscription at all times ready to be decoded, is gradually, almost imperceptibly being dissolved by the codes of digital writing. This revolution signals a radical structural change in the arts of memory. Material writing had been associated with experiences of depth, background, sedimentation, and stratification, which were compressed above all in the concept of a latent memory between absence and presence. Under electronic conditions such images and concepts are difficult to sustain. The dominant dimension here is the surface, below which there is nothing but technical calculations encoded in the structural script of 1 and 0.

It has been a leitmotif of this book that remembering cannot be separated from forgetting: both are necessary and indispensable operations of memory. This paradoxical yet consistent connection became especially obvious in the experiments of artists and writers who focused on rubbish as a form of counter-memory and reverse archive. The remembering of rubbish and forgetting is a plausible consequence in a culture that in the modern era has followed the doctrine of innovation with the concomitant effect of filling the refuse bin of history to overflowing. Everything that has been written tumbles "into the inevitable pit which the creation of new thought opens for all that is old," (Emerson, see Chapt. 8, n. 39) From this abyss of the rejected, the unusable, the forgotten, artists have fashioned new material archives in which they remind society of its suppressed, traumatic foundations; and in doing so they have held up their artistic mirror to the social process of remembering and forgetting.

These metamorphoses of remembering and forgetting lead to one final question: is digital writing another medium of memory, or is it a medium for forgetting? And does not digital writing extinguish the basic concept of this book – that of various arts of memory? "Whiles memory holds a seat / In this distracted globe," cries Hamlet, but today more than ever the question is: how long will memory hold a seat in our distracted globe? "We no longer live in a society," writes Harold Bloom, "in which we will be allowed to institutionalize memory."[2] Against the electronic media and their potential for distraction – as has been frequently emphasized – no memory can assert itself: "The cascades of images from the audiovisual media make [. . .] scarcely any claim to active remembrance. It is a feature of the memory policy of commercialized communications that images aim at a serialism that intensifies forgetfulness instead of judgmental remembering. Memory, which necessitates a break in the continuum of information, is becoming improbable and disturbing."[3]

---

[2] Harold Bloom, 17 (see Chapt. 13, n. 9).
[3] Schmidt, 68 (see Chapt. 8, n. 57).

I will end this survey of cultural memory and western civilization with two anthropological reflections on memory as a "break in the continuum of information." The first is by Herder, who rooted the origin of language in reflection and reflection in the faculty of memory. He regarded this faculty as equally improbable, and thus of great anthropological importance. Anticipating the stream of information on the Internet, Herder referred to an "ocean of feelings" and the "ever changing dream of images" against which humans construct their memory spaces:

Man shows evidence of reflection when the power of his soul works in such freedom that from the whole ocean of feelings, which sweeps it through all the senses, it can isolate one wave – if I may call it that – hold onto it, draw attention to it, and become conscious of the fact that it is drawing attention to it. He shows evidence of reflection when, from the ever changing dream of images that brush past his senses, he can gather himself in a waking moment and intentionally dwell on a single image, study it in the greater calm of daylight, and contemplate its specific features.[4]

For Herder, *Besonnenheit* – his name for the calm reflection that brackets thought and memory together – is the basic faculty that is "a unique characteristic and is essential to the human species," and from which has sprung language, contemplation, and culture. *Besonnenheit* produces arts and realms of memory that resist the flood of events, forming folds, hollows, layers, and thereby creating the possibility of delayed reaction, resonance, repetition, reconnection, and renewal. Remembering, which involves the capture and retention of images and signs, always involves breaking currents. With the activities of holding and separating, of paying attention, collecting and dwelling on single points, Herder has described the *active* side of remembering. If the faculty for this kind of calm reflection is indeed dwindling under the onslaught of the new media, this does not by any means seal the fate of memory. In this context, we can turn to Nietzsche, who 100 years later supplemented Herder's concept of *Besonnenheit* by describing the *passive* side of remembering – the involuntary, haunting memory: "It is a miracle: the moment, there in a flash, gone in a flash, nothing

---

4 Translated from Johann Gottfried Herder, "Abhandlung über den Ursprung der Sprache" (1772), in Ulrich Gaier (ed.), *Frühe Schriften 1764–1772*, Bibliothek deutscher Klassiker, Frankfurt a.M. 1985, 722.

before, nothing after, and yet returning as a ghost and disturbing the calm of a later moment. Continually a leaf detaches itself from the scroll of time, falls out, flutters away – and suddenly flutters back into a person's lap. Then the person says, "I remember," and envies the animal which immediately forgets."[5] That is how it is with memory: even if we neglect it, it will not leave us.

[5] Translated from Nietzsche, "Vom Nutzen und Nachteil der Historie für das Leben," in *Sämtliche Werke*, Vol. 1, 248 f.

Index